Kaleidoscope
Japan

A nation through the lens of literature

Richard Nathan is a Director and Principal of Bosquet Capital, and co-founder and Director of Red Circle Authors Limited. Prior to this he worked for Kyodo News, *Nature*, and Macmillan.

Richard Nathan

Kaleidoscope Japan

A nation through the lens of literature

Circle Editions

Published by Circle Editions an imprint of
Red Circle Authors
First edition 2024
1 3 5 7 9 10 8 6 4 2

Red Circle Authors
2nd Floor, 168 Shoreditch High Street,
London E1 6RA

www.redcircleauthors.com

Copyright ©Red Circle Authors Limited 2024

Richard Nathan has asserted his right under the Copyright, Designs and Patents Act 1988 to be identified as the author of this work.

Design by Aiko Ishida, typesetting by Danny Lyle
Set in Baskerville

ISBN: 978-1-912864-14-0 (Print)
ISBN: 978-1-912864-15-7 (eBook)

A catalogue record of this book is available from the British Library.

All rights reserved. Circle Editions is the first publisher of this work.

No part of this publication may be reproduced, stored in a retrieval system, or transmitted, in any form or by any means, electronic, mechanical, photocopying, recording or otherwise, without the prior permission of the publisher.

This book is sold subject to the condition that it shall not, by way of trade or otherwise, be lent, resold, hired out, or otherwise circulated without the publisher's prior consent in any form of binding or cover other than that in which it is published and without a similar condition including this condition being imposed on the subsequent purchaser.

Author quotations and works, including lyrics and poems, cited in this book are the property of their respective owners and translators and are used in this book as commentary and context, to highlight the works for readers, and for review, journalistic and educational purposes.

Contents

Preface	xi
Acknowledgements	xxi

Part One
Japanese Literature, Writers and Ruin

Scoping the Terrain	3
Short Story Writing	42
Rubble-Rising Prose	63
Grim Tales: Primeval Trolls and Eating Disorders	95
Literary Fallout: The Legacies of Hiroshima and Nagasaki	102

Part Two
Influencers, Dolls and Devices

The Chick-Lit of Ancient Japan	113
Ultra-Influencers: Fictional Victorians that Changed Japan	121
Doll Women and Their Literature	131
Whodunnit: Detective Fiction's Sudden Death	140
The Portable Devices Loved by Japan's Literati	162

Part Three
Robots, Runners and Riders

Tales from the Robot Nation	175
Literary Racers	205
Narratives from Off and On the Tracks	215

Part Four
Cats, Tatts and Christians

Soseki's Cat: A Quantum Leap	231
From Body Art to Literature: Zen and the Art of the Tattoo	243
Christian Stories of Japan	254

Part Five
Booze, Books and Bonking

Literary Elixir: Bars, Cocktails and the Literati	277
How to Read a Film: Kurosawa and His Books	304
Changing Nations: The Japanese Girl With a Book	311
Bonkbusters and The Land of the Rising Sun	326

A Rich and Never-ending Story

Appendix	351
Notes	358
Index	366

kaleidoscope

万華鏡

かれいどすこーぷ

百色眼鏡

錦眼鏡

カレイドスコープ

KAREIDOSUKOPU

紅毛渡り更紗眼鏡

Preface

Kaleidoscopes reached Japan only a few years after Scottish inventor David Brewster (1781-1868) received his patent in July 1817.[1] No one is completely sure how these optical devices arrived or the date the very first scope was offloaded at a Japanese port, but the most likely route is the reverse of that followed by early Japanese folding fans, *ogi*. These curios arrived in Western royal courts through the efforts of the East India Company. The British company was set up during the reign of Queen Elizabeth I (1533-1603) initially to trade in the Indian Ocean region, or what might today be termed the Indo-Pacific. Queen Elizabeth I was herself a collector of these imported must-have fashion items.

Records show that in 1819, in Japan's late Edo period (1603-1868), a mostly peaceful and prosperous time during which Japan was ruled by the Tokugawa shoguns, and was isolated from most of the world, kaleidoscopes somehow found their way to Japanese shores. While the nation was still adhering to strict rigid inherited social hierarchies, the diverse succession of changing viewpoints that kaleidoscopes can magically conjure up were already captivating some lucky Japanese consumers in Osaka, a commercial port city with a thrusting profile, similar to that of Victorian Manchester.[2] At this time Osaka, where these scopes disembarked, functioned as a national distribution and trading hub for commodities and finance, as well as intricate products such as kaleidoscopes, and already possessed an important and lively rice futures market.

Brewster named his new optical tubes by blending together three Greek words: *beautiful* (*kalos*), *a form* (*eidos*) and *to see* (*scope*) into the newly-coined word kaleidoscope to describe his device for creating and revealing beautiful, patterned forms. Before this word established itself in the Japanese language, the kaleidoscope had many different monikers. These included: *komo watari sarasa megane* (Western calico spectacles), *nishiki megane* (brocade spectacles) and *hyaku iro megane* (one hundred colour spectacles). The word kaleidoscope is used in Japanese today as a loanword, but these brilliant and enchanting devices are normally referred to in Japanese as *mangekyo*, which literally means ten thousand flowering mirrors.

Today, kaleidoscopes are not just adored in Japan but manufactured locally. They are taken home, mostly the decorative craft hand-made variety, as souvenirs by thousands of tourists visiting the country each year. They also resonate more broadly across the culture, often in decidedly unusual ways. A good example of this is how Kaleidoscope Mukashi-Kan in Azabu Juban has become a must-visit

Tokyo destination for anime and manga fans. In *Bishojo senshi sera mun* (*Sailor Moon*), one of Japan's seminal anime and manga series, lauded by a few famous feminists around the world, the eponymous protagonist, Sailor Moon, seeks out magical artifacts and curiosities, including a kaleidoscope, that transform this schoolgirl and her comrades into supercharged guardians that protect the planet. Naoko Takeuchi (b. 1967), the author of *Sailor Moon*, bought a kaleidoscope from the Tokyo shop and included it in an important scene, immediately guaranteeing a steady stream of pilgrims to the store.

In addition to quirky specialist shops, Japan has kaleidoscope museums, expensive kaleidoscope necklaces and other optical collectables, and dedicated kaleidoscope publications. Of course, stylised patterns, and their perfect or subtly developed imperfect repeats, have played and continue to play an important role in many Japanese arts including kabuki, calligraphy, haiku, kimono textile design, Zen gardens and even the performance of *kata* in karate.

Recounting history through physical objects by blending biography with the life or evolution of an object, such as a violin and the people who crafted and played it, or a house and the generations of people who dwelled within it, or a painting of a girl with pearl earrings, can be an engaging form of storytelling that generates narrative journeys with wonderful arcs and fascinating subplots. The kaleidoscope and Japan naturally lend themselves to writing of this type, but this isn't that book, though it is perhaps one that I may attempt in the future.

Rather this book is a kaleidoscope of Japan through the lens of literature. It is an assorted collection of essays, each with literature, books and creative writing at their core, written for anyone with an interest in Japanese literature, culture and publishing. These essays, edited to be read as standalones or as a collective, were initially written to help process my own exploration through the world of Japanese literature and beyond. Now, gathered here, I hope they reflect not just my own personal reading journey but show Japan as seen through the lens of some of the nation's most renowned literature as well as some of the many influences, narratives and changing phases that Japan and its authors has muddled and continues to muddle its way through.

This book isn't designed as a structured or thorough inventory-like academic survey. Nor is it an introduction to the history of Japanese literature, creative writing and publishing. Nor will it focus on Japan's portrayal in the literature of other nations, though its first part endeavours to scope out the terrain of the nation's incredible literary landscape. A kaleidoscope is not a complete picture; it is necessarily a fractured picture, an incomplete image. Counter-intuitively, incompleteness can be helpful, desirable and even additive. As Kenko Yoshida (circa 1283-1352), the 14th century Buddhist monk and leading light of Japanese aesthetics, wrote: "It is only a person of poor understanding who wishes to arrange things in complete sets." Seeking a type of freedom of method, expression or thought in limitation or incompleteness has many precedents. The reading of literature is an exploration; it's the journey that matters.

Every year around 70,000 books targeting the general reading public are released in Japan and, despite using significantly more letters than the 26 in the English alphabet and deploying a highly complex writing system, at several points in its past as well as today, Japan has had one of the world's highest literacy rates. Japan's oldest publisher, a specialist Buddhist press based in Kyoto, is more than 400 years old. The Japanese language also boasts one of the highest numbers of bloggers of any language. These facts alone demonstrate that reading and creative storytelling really do matter in Japan and that literature in all its glorious forms is a relevant and engaging way to scrutinise Japan.

Books, poems and blogs are not read just for their literary merit. The tales that their authors pen help shape perceptions, regularly generate empathy and influence national and international dialogues. Sometimes books are exploited to try to compose national narratives, but books are generally wonderful distractions and creative escapes from the everyday or the common struggles that can at times help unify us.

The languages of some European countries, English, French, Portuguese and Spanish, for instance, are spoken by more individuals and more frequently outside their home nations than within. Comparatively, the Japanese language, one of the most critical components of the country's cultural software, is still owned almost exclusively by Japanese nationals. Japan is ranked highly in terms of the number of books that have been published in Japanese language translation, but only eighth, according to UNESCO's *Index Translationum*, when it comes to the number of Japanese language books published in other languages in translation, just behind Swedish and above Danish and books written in Latin. The Nobel Prize perhaps flatters and enhances Sweden as eight of its authors, compared with two from Japan, have won the Nobel Prize in Literature and books by its authors are probably considered easier to translate. English tops the charts in this regard and the English language still dominates the world of letters. However, research shows that in other entertainment sectors, such as streamed music and audio-visual services, this type of hegemony is starting to subside, though English still remains king.[3]

In the 18th century it was the French language, not English that ruled in Europe, with French hegemony in literature in terms of prestige and much else.

French is still ranked second above German and Russian but no longer tops the translation rankings. Before French, for a millennium or so, writing in Latin was the badge of honour of educated elite Europeans. Even if similar trends were to occur again for translated book copyrights, Japan would still have a major gap to close for its rankings in these charts to reflect both its position as one of the world's largest economies and the dynamism of its literary outputs. The hierarchy of languages is persistent.

Literary canvases no matter the language they are written in allow for the type of transient fleeting moments of wonder or beauty that Japanese culture is famous for celebrating, as well as the common shards of agony that can act as a type of unifying glue, to become permanent. They can also interrogate and invert conventional thinking while providing critical, memorable and, at times, eccentric insights. However, it would appear that Japanese readers have better access to what is being written for us. They are more easily able to get delightfully lost in translation and have the potential to know more about us in terms of what we read, than we do about them.

Authors, of course, vary as much as the books they write. The writing of some Japanese authors is powered by a form of commercial cultural utilitarianism designed to please the maximum number of readers possible, while others write for intellectual elites and some simply for themselves or as a form of psychological relief. A few are ridiculously industrious with more than 500 titles to their name. Nonetheless, the vast majority of Japan's literary output has been and continues to be written for a Japanese audience no matter how small or large or where they are located.

The Japanese archipelago stretches across multiple climatic zones, from north to south a distance of more than three thousand kilometres, a similar distance from England's second city, Birmingham, to Casablanca, Morocco. This makes author location within Japan impossible to ignore, be it Arashiyama one of Kyoto's famous literary destinations, Shimokitazawa in Tokyo, the Izu Peninsula, Kafuka in Hokkaido or Wakayama in the Kansai region, especially if it changes during an author's writing career. Some regions and islands in Japan are small, others large. Switzerland, for instance, is only slightly larger than the southern island Kyushu. For some, the creators and the protagonists spawned by their imaginations, there does appear to be a type of location premium, in terms of literary impact and legacy. There can be something magically potent about place and its sense and sensibilities. That said, no matter what their motivation, or where they are penned, every book written in Japanese is in its own way a narrative of Japan written by an individual that probably shares at the very least one thing with almost all other Japanese people: a proficiency in the Japanese language.

There have, of course, been Japanese writers who have tried to explain Japan to the world, sometimes writing in English, by telling the tales of storied individuals they respect and who they consider represent Japan or the Japan that reflects their own particular point of view. One such author and classic example is the leading Christian intellectual leader and writer Kanzo Uchimura (1861-1930) with his book *Representative Men of Japan* (*Daihyouteki Nihonjin*) initially written in English before being published in Japanese, which interestingly, Johannes Hesse (1847-1916) the father of the 1946 winner of the Nobel Prize in Literature Hermann Hesse (1877-1962) translated into German from the original English. Uchimura, who penned his 1908 book about five wise sage-like Japanese men for a non-Japanese audience, writes in his introduction:

> That I may still help to make the good qualities of my country men known to the outside world – the qualities *other* than blind loyalty and bloody patriotism usually attributed to us.[4]

At times Japan seems to actively elicit decoding and even delight in the international attention it can generate. How the world sees Japan can alter Japan's image of itself or help verify the nation's existing prejudices. Superficially, Japanese people can often appear terribly sensitive about what other people will think of their behaviour, be it a neighbour, a colleague, a classmate or another nation. These are concerns that many probably share no matter their nationality. These types of comparative observations are often more a matter of calibration than anything else, but some continue to search for easily skewed comparisons to highlight perceived differences, as opposed to similarities, thereby fashioning exaggerated garments that conceal Japan's real narrative shape. Errors often arise from the supposition that all who live under a certain system of government or in a geographical area labelled with a single unifying sovereignty or communicate with a shared grammar or syntax, must be alike in character.

The prism of intellectual vanity consistently traps all of us into making fast or forced conclusions when perhaps no analysis is required and we should simply enjoy and celebrate the cultural products that elicit these phenomena in the first place, allowing opinions, if they are actually required, to wait their rightful place behind the facts. Just as sometimes it is much more productive and fun to just laugh at a joke, with liberating uncontrolled abandon, than to deconstruct one. Pursuing meaning where it may not actually exist can sometimes feel like tumbling through a mirrored maze. The question we should always ask ourselves is how evenly distributed is the particular Japan we know or are familiar with, or are being informed about and does the answer matter?

The reality of Japan is dazzlingly kaleidoscopic and the glorious patterns of the country's culture are fully reflected in the nation's storytelling. It is, of course, an exaggeration to suggest it is a simple choice between facile facsimiles and fantastic fiction. But the best Japanese authors do provide a glimpse, often a fragmented one, into the worlds behind the psychedelic haze and the cacophony of chatter surrounding contemporary Japan. Often they do this in thrillingly distinctive ways silhouetting Japan in the colour of their prose and at times with rather impressive effect.

It is this hinterland that, reflected and refracted, has led to this book. In its production, certain decision have been made concerning presentation and referential accountability. I have included the translated English language title alongside the Japanese title for most literary works discussed. In romanising Japanese words and the titles of Japanese works, a 'best efforts' approach has been adopted but it has been a challenge to achieve style consistencies and the usual editorial niceties, even though a systematic methodology has been used.

For titles written by Japanese authors and published in English first, such as the *Red Circle Minis* series, I have included the published English title first followed by the published Japanese title, if a published Japanese edition currently exists, which is not always the case. The names of Japanese individuals mentioned throughout are in the traditional English format of given name first and family name second, though this may vary case by case when pen names are used. To provide context, the year of birth of most contemporary Japanese storytellers and a limited number of other individuals has also been included for reference. A list of the Japanese-language works of fiction, excluding almost all short stories, mentioned that are available in English translation at the time of writing, including English-language translator names, is included within the appendix.

I hope the essays in this collection, which are expanded and edited versions of some of the essays published in the Red Circle online magazine, *The Circle*, as well as several new ones, provide readers with a glimpse of Japan's multi-layered and changing kaleidoscopic nature. They have been woven together into a textual

Preface xvii

tapestry with lattice-like architecture in the aim of promoting a well-read and well-rounded view of Japan, designed to conjure up new images, sensibilities and patterns that will encourage everyone to read more Japanese literature, regardless of their existing familiarity with it.

Like a kaleidoscope which is every now and then given a turn, society arranges successively in different orders elements which one would have supposed immutable, and composes a new pattern. Marcel Proust (1871-1922).[5]

Acknowledgements

In researching and writing this book I have been greatly helped by many people. My wife, Naomi Nathan, and her love of literature and her belief that reading more works of fiction would make me a better person has been the real inspirational force. Without her encouragement and support, as well as the many conversations we have had about books, Japan and the human and husband condition, this book would never have happened.

Special thanks are also due to many others for their encouragement, time, edits, insights, ideas and patience some over many years including Aiko Ishida, Iain Maloney, Hiroshi Minemura, Yoshie Moriyama, Giles Murray, Alex Pearl, Hikaru Sugiyama, Peter Tasker, and Morimasa Yoneyama.

I would also like to thank all the authors in our curated group of writers Red Circle Authors: Kazufumi Shiraishi, Randy Taguchi, Fuminori Nakamura, Mitsuyo Kakuta, Kanji Hanawa, Takuji Ichikawa, Soji Shimada and Roger Pulvers for their support and kind encouragement, and all the fascinating conversations we have had since I co-founded this boutique publisher and its various imprints.

Thanks are also due to everyone who is or has been part of the Red Circle team and continues to assist us in our mission to help brilliant Japanese literature travel even further be they a writer, translator, author, designer, editor, proofreader, typesetter, marketer, publisher, agent, rights manager, bookseller, test reader or co-founder.

Finally, I would like to thank my late parents, Rachel and Clemens, who tried their very best to encourage me in almost all of my pursuits and interests no matter how odd or bizarre they may have been considered at the time including some, such as skateboarding and motorbike riding, that I was and remain innately unsuitable for.

Part One

Japanese Literature, Writers and Ruin

Even people who seem to lack any finer feelings, will sometimes say something impressive. *Tsurezuregusa* (*Essays in Idleness*), Kenko Yoshida (circa 1283-1352).

Scoping the Terrain

Japan has a rich history of storytelling and creative writing. Its language and complex writing system with multiple syllabaries, the first of which, *kanji*, arrived from China in the early fifth century, has made it difficult for most readers outside Japan to enjoy and fully appreciate the breadth and depth of Japanese literature. Some assume that because Japanese writing is generally rendered vertically not horizontally, and the typical pagination of Japanese language books is the reverse of what they are accustomed to, that Japanese books are topsy-turvy, exotic riddles replete with elliptical paradoxes and unfathomable contradictions that turn narratives upside down. In short, that they require an off-putting degree of deciphering.[6]

It is often said that truth is stranger than fiction, so it is worth taking some time to consider exactly how unusual Japanese fiction is.

Even though Japanese authors and publishers have been massively influenced by international trends and books translated into Japanese from many countries and languages, they have focused quite understandably on their own large local market and have expressed themselves in Japanese for local consumption. Conversely, Japanese literature has been slowly and steadily influencing international literature and creative writing. This should be far from surprising given how much other elements of Japanese culture have influenced the food we eat, the games we play, the animated films we watch, how some of us sing in pubs, and even the actual words we use daily, such as emoji. Slender tendrils of Japanese culture, unbeknownst to many, have ended up in some highly diverse places.

Debates surrounding the coincidences of causality and the inevitability of publishing and literary trends, or history's exact causes, can often become confusingly circular. Whatever the precise instigators, despite the nation's authors actually being relatively under translated, more titles by Japanese authors than ever before are now available in translation in Chinese, English, Indonesian, Spanish, Russian, German, Italian, French, Thai and Korean, as well as many other languages. Haruki Murakami (b. 1949), a published translator himself, has seen his own works translated and published in some 50 languages. He and writers like

Banana Yoshimoto (b. 1964), who was first published outside Japan in Italian, have helped open the eyes of new generations of international readers to compelling storytelling that readers in Japan have been enjoying quietly for decades. Each time a Japanese author breaks through internationally it helps chip away at tenuous and entrenched views about Japanese literature and its appeal, as well as Japan itself, and opens a door for others to follow through.

In 2017, for example, the Japanese crime fiction master Keigo Higashino (b. 1958), author of *Yogisha ekkusu no kenshin* (*The Devotion of Suspect X*) and many other extremely successful titles, overtook J. K. Rowling, the author of the *Harry Potter* series, as the highest non-Chinese royalty-earning author in China.[7] It would appear that readers outside Japan, as well as inside, are actually very interested in what Japanese writers have to say. When readers gain unhindered access to their storytelling, the results can be impressive.

Japanese crime fiction, however, isn't a newly emerging genre even if some international readers and reviewers are only now discovering it for the first time. Visitors to Japan in the late 19th century were already commenting on its scope, vitality, and popularity. "The books for which there is the greatest amount of demand are those that pack the greatest amount of crime into the smallest space, and corrupt the morals of all classes," Isabella L. Bird (1831-1904) wrote in *Unbeaten Tracks in Japan: An account of travels on horseback in the interior including visits to the aborigines of Yezo and the shrines of Nikko and Ise*. The book followed Bird's trip to Japan in 1878.

In spite of the recent success of Japanese crime fiction and Japan no longer being the closed book it was in Bird's time, it can still often be an uphill task for many of the nation's talented authors to break through internationally. When compared with manga, for example, which has become tremendously successful internationally, literature lags far behind. This may be in part because images, not eloquent words and clever turns of phrase, are the form's central expressive element and images circle the globe much faster than words. This, alongside the growing importance of visual storytelling internationally, makes it far easier for international publishers to quickly grasp a title's potential appeal and quality, overcoming any perceived language or market barriers.

What brings any given Japanese author or publishing genre to international attention is often a confluence of factors, as well as a lot of hard work, raw talent, and technical skill as a wordsmith. Of course, the quality of the work—original and in translation—is also extremely important. Some, however, put international literary attention and success down to the simple serendipity of opportunity colliding with talent and good preparation. For better or worse serendipity, or what the less charitable call flukes of fate and fortune, is something that can't be easily manufactured. Formidable literary talent is nothing without a decent dash of luck. Unusual and unexpected events, even of the literary sort, can nonetheless often change the course of things.

One fascinating example of a strange confluence of author-linked events occurred in the mid-1960s, a decade when Japan and its economy was growing in international prominence, and the country was set to become the first Asian nation to host an Olympic Games in 1964. That year, the author Junichiro Tanizaki (1886-1965), whose famous works include *Shisei* (*The Tattooer*), *Sasameyuki* (*The Makioka Sisters*) and *Neko to shozo to futari no onna* (*A Cat, A Man and Two Women*) was nominated and shortlisted for the Nobel Prize in Literature.

Tanizaki's seminal essay on aesthetics and architecture, *Inei raisan* (*In Praise of Shadows*), gives a sense of his style and why he was shortlisted: "In the mansion called literature I would have the eaves deep and the walls dark, I would push back into the shadows the things that come forward too clearly, I would strip away the useless decoration." Japan was coming out from behind its post-war shadows and the world's gaze was focusing on the nation in different hues.

Tanizaki was a serious contender on the shortlist that year, so much so that the French news agency L'Agence-France-Presse (AFP) actually announced that he had won. Tanizaki didn't win. Instead, the French author Jean-Paul Sartre (1905-1980), a reluctant winner who shrugged off the accolade, was awarded the prize, which can't technically be refused. Tanizaki died in July the following year, ruling him out of contention for the prize which is only awarded to living authors.

Making the Cut

Many have speculated that Tanizaki's post-mortem ineligibility opened up opportunities for other Japanese authors to become the first to win this coveted international decoration. In fact, four years on from Tanizaki's loss, in 1968, Yasunari Kawabata (1899-1972) won, becoming only the second Asian writer to win it since Rabindranath Tagore (1861-1941) in 1913, who was himself the first non-European to win this literary prize. This helped put Kawabata, and works such as *Yukiguni* (*Snow Country*), *Nemureru bijyo* (*The House of the Sleeping Beauties*) and *Izu no odoriko* (*The Dancing Girl of Izu*) on the international literary map, as well as cement his already considerable reputation in Japan. Some, however, believe that Kawabata actually felt somewhat uncomfortable about receiving the prize and there was speculation that after Tanizaki's death it was awarded following recommendations from Japan based on seniority rather than simply writing excellence.

In the 1990s, another interesting example of publishing serendipity occurred when Japanese officials decided to hand out hundreds of copies of a newly translated novel, *Kitchin* (*Kitchen*), by Yoshimoto with the media packs to the hundreds of international journalists attending the 1993 Tokyo Group of Seven (G7) summit. The novel was quickly translated into Italian, one of the G7 nations, by Giogio Amitrano and published the same year as the summit. The novel sold more than 90,000 copies in Italy alone and sold very well in many other important international publishing markets. Yoshimoto's Zurich-based German-language publisher, Diogenes, describes *Kitchen*, which unusually for the time includes a leading transgender character, as a modern classic, ahead of its time. The publisher is justifiably effusive about Yoshimoto's ability as a writer and even though its editorial team was unaware of the serendipitous facts behind how her 1987 debut novel broke through internationally, there is no doubt the summit helped Yoshimoto to become Japan's first contemporary author to 'go global', a feat that perhaps only Murakami so far has managed to replicate.

The success of *Kitchen* in Japan probably reflects the tacit understanding that many Japanese people have of the heavy and harsh realities of life that reside beneath the veneer of society's status quo. The picture painted of contemporary Japan by Yoshimoto is not the idealised Japan that officials like to present to the world. It is thus much harder to understand the calculus behind the decision-making process that led to the officials at the Ministry of Foreign Affairs sharing this rather atypical view of Japan with summit delegates like Bill Clinton (b.1946), Francois Mitterrand (1916-1996), Helmut Kohl (1930-2017) and John Major (b. 1943).

Unsurprisingly, Yoshimoto is still much admired today and her popularity persists in Japan and Italy, and far beyond. Though her titles no longer sell in the vast quantities they did in the past, she continues to write touching and thoughtful books such as 2010's *Moshi moshi Shimokitazawa* (*Moshi-Moshi*), a deeply personal tale that highlights the central role place, be it someone's hometown or some other special location—in its case Shimokitazawa in Tokyo—or simply a room in a home or a former dwelling, can provide when trying to process bereavement or the emotional gyrations of life.

Ask any leading executive in the publishing industry and they will say that alongside serendipity, passion and people, through the infectious enthusiasm they often spawn, are the key drivers behind publishing success. This is no doubt why some of Japan's most garlanded authors have put an enormous amount of personal time and effort into establishing their reputations. Yukio

Mishima (1925-1970) was one such author, a close friend of Kawabata and another Japanese writer who was nominated multiple times for the Nobel Prize in the 1960s. He is now internationally famous for the manner of his death, but during the short period he was actively writing professionally, after the publication of his first novel—a period of just 21 years—he was highly prolific, managing to write 40 novels, 18 plays and numerous essays. Mishima even published a Japanese translation in 1954 of Lewis Carroll's (1832-1898) *Alice's Adventures in Wonderland*, a task that several other renowned Japanese authors have also felt compelled to try. In fact, Carroll's tales have been rendered in translation in Japanese more times than in any other language.

Unlike many, Mishima did not focus his efforts solely on increasing his profile in Japan and building local readership: he gave talks in English including an often cited one at The Foreign Correspondents' Club of Japan (FCCJ) in Tokyo in 1966. According to Peter Meyer (1936-2018), his once time editor and publisher and a former Chief Executive of the Penguin Group, Mishima would regularly meet publishing executives at Narita Airport, including Meyer, when they visited Japan, as well as visit them at their hotels, sometimes dressed in strange but memorable attire. Despite his Japanese adventures and successes, Meyer is probably better remembered outside Japan for publishing the incendiary book *The Satanic Verses* by Salman Rushdie, whose Japanese translator Hitoshi Igarashi (1947-1991) tragically was murdered after a fatwa was issued following the book's publication, than his more typical but still impressive Japan-related publishing.[8] Mishima's attendance at several spirited dinner parties, held in London in the 1960s by industry figures when he was passing through the city, are still the source of some wonderful publisher anecdotes and part of British publishing folklore.

Mishima was also in regular direct contact not just with his international editors and publishers but also with some of his high-profile translators who he thought sometimes took longer to translate his books than it took him to write them. Chief executives and business gurus often pose the question 'What Would Google Do?' when facing a difficult business challenge.[9] Publishers, authors, translators and creatives looking for international success might sensibly ponder the question 'What Would Mishima Do?' even if after this thought-experiment they conclude to do the opposite, it might still be a thought-provoking exercise.

The latest cohort of highly talented Japanese wordsmiths breaking through today generally take a very different, less hands-on approach, leaving much to their local publishers. They often have multiple Japanese publishers and generally avoid literary agents. Some are not overly concerned if their works are translated or not, while others prioritise English-language translation. That said, this generation are currently still rather hard to define or deconstruct; time will tell how they fare in the world of Japanese letters.

They are following in the paths of some brilliantly gifted predecessors such as the idiosyncratic and hugely gifted authors Mishima and Kobo Abe (1924-1993), members of what is termed the 'Second Generation' of major Japanese writers that appeared after the Second World War between 1948 and 1949, and Shusaku Endo (1923-1996) a member of the 'Third Generation' which emerged in the 1950s. They—and Mishima in particular—had feet in the old Japan as well as the newly emerging post-war Japan and often articulated the struggles that many faced when trying to reconcile these two very distinct worlds. Saying that these times were challenging is, of course, an understatement. These authors all had marked personalities, fascinating lived experiences, and wrote with their own unique styles, narratives that only they could have written.

Sigmund Freud (1856-1939), whose psychoanalytic methodology had arrived in Japan by 1912[10] when the first Freudian analysis of the Japanese classic *Genji monogatari* (*The Tale of Genji*) was published, would have loved to put these modern age-bridging Japanese authors on the couch. Freud would no doubt have had a field day with Mishima, probing his relationships with his mother, his father, his ambitious aristocratic grandmother who brought him up, and of course his dreams, his sexuality, and of course his seminal works such as *Sado koshaku fujin* (*Madame de Sade*), *Kamen no kokuhaku* (*Confessions of a Mask*) and *Hojyo no umi* (*The Sea of Fertility*) as well as his essay series *Fudotoku Kyoiku Koza* (*Lessons in Immorality*).

These age-bridging authors are important beacons within Japan's literary terrain and their books make for fascinating and insightful reading, as well as Freudian analysis. However, it is an open question whether they fully represent the kaleidoscopic nature of the Japanese archipelago and the eras the authors lived in, let alone Japan today. This introductory overview of Japan's literary landscape isn't the place to do a deep dive into this but *Japan on the Couch* would make for a fascinating read, even if such an analysis only focused on that generation of Japanese authors, documenting how those spirited, prodigious and highly creative individuals pollinated Japan with their prose, transferring their feeling and emotions, not onto an analyst, but to their many readers, and the consequences of such transference on Japan's post-war national psychology.

Tragically, Mishima's death by suicide has provided him with endless international notoriety that at times threatens to outweigh his literary legacy. He has acquired something of the modern-day celebrity status now sought by many, where individuals are famous for who they are, not for what they do professionally. In his life Mishima did court this kind of celebrity with eloquent brilliance so perhaps in this sense Mishima was also far ahead of his times. While the manner of his death may be bizarre, the fact of his suicide is not actually one of the things that make him so unique as a Japanese writer.

Since 1900 more than 54 Japanese authors, including some of the nation's most famous male writers, have killed themselves. This includes authors such as Ryunosuke Akutagawa (1892-1927) after whom one of Japan's most prestigious literary prizes is named. Also one of the many translators of *Alice's Adventures in Wonderland*. Osamu Dazai (1909-1948) the somewhat legendary author of the novel *Ningen shikkaku* (*No Longer Human*), which is often cited by contemporary male Japanese writers as an all-time favourite, is another, as is Kawabata, though his family dispute the facts surrounding his death. Interestingly, Dazai's death shortly after the last instalment of *No Longer Human* was published in 1948 is considered a marker. It is the turning point when the post-war period—marked by the horrific reality of defeat: social upheaval, traumatic repatriations from Manchuria, an impoverished populace, bombed out wastelands with their existential risks, and political chaos—came to an end, and the gloom that had engulfed Japan started to lift as economic and social conditions began to improve.

Tragically, within four years of Kawabata winning his Nobel Prize, both an ageing Kawabata suffering from chronic insomnia, who reportedly felt guilty for winning and had lost his lust for writing, and Mishima, who coveted the prize, had both chosen to die. There is, of course, no proof that these acts were connected, but some still like to draw a line between the confluence of events, believing that the Nobel Prize was responsible for both suicides. It has even been argued by some Japanese publishing insiders that if the prize committee had reversed their decision, choosing Mishima over his friend Kawabata, both men would have lived out their days.

Japan Unbound

One writer whose life overlapped with theirs who lived out his allotted days is Kenzaburo Oe (1935-2023). Oe studied French literature at Tokyo University in his youth and subsequently went on to win the Nobel Prize in Literature in 1994, becoming only the second Japanese author to date after Kawabata to achieve this rare status. Through his literary prize that ran between 2007 and 2014, which paid for the works of its winners to be published in French, German and English translation, Oe tried to help many different young authors manage their development by using his name and the eponymous prize to increase their international profile. One example is the so-called 'Zen Master of Noir', Fuminori Nakamura

(b. 1977), who since his debut novel *Jyu* (*The Gun*) has demonstrated an uncanny ability of challenging convention and common perspectives by allowing readers to effortlessly enter the minds of cerebral outsiders, misfits and murderers.

The generation of Japanese authors that grew up in the 1960s, when these celebrated era-traversing wordsmiths were in their writing prime and dominating the bestsellers lists, including some who are now global names like Murakami, and authors who are much less known outside Japan, are sometimes referred to by scholars as Japan's first postmodern authors. These include people like Kiyoshi Kasai (b. 1948), Kenji Nakagami (1946-1992), Masahiko Shimada (b. 1961), Soji Shimada (b. 1948), Kazufumi Shiraishi (b. 1958) and Genichiro Takahashi (b. 1951). They were all born after the Second World War, experienced the student movements of the 1960s either directly as participants or indirectly as schoolchildren, and grew up during a period when Japan was rebuilding and growing in confidence. Their formative years were a period of change and possibility when society had great momentum. Their worldview and experiences are distinct from the generation of authors that preceded them, authors like Kawabata, Tanizaki and Mishima, who witnessed devastation and national defeat directly. In contrast, they grew up in a much more optimistic period when Japan was heavily influenced by the United States with a growing mass market that included new American pulp-fiction arriving in Japan in translation. The influence of Western music, literature, film and television would also have been significant.

These principal postmodern authors were the first generation to grow up listening to the lyrics and music of the Beatles, Bob Dylan (another subsequent reluctant winner of the Nobel Prize in Literature) and the Rolling Stones, of which many of them became ardent fans. That generation also had broad access to and enjoyed foreign films as well as books, old and new.

Shiraishi, born in 1958 and thus on the cusp of this generation, and who is known for penning deeply thoughtful books about love, life and the human condition, for example, is particularly fond of *Bicycle Thieves*, a 1948 post-war neorealist Italian film directed by Vittorio De Sica (1901-1974) based on a novel by Luigi Bartolini (1892-1963). It is the story of a man searching for his stolen bicycle, alongside his plucky son, in a war-defeated, poverty-stricken Italy where bicycles were the all-important mode of transport. The film is set around the time that Ducati, now an Italian international motorbike super brand, just like Honda at its small factory in post-war Hamamatsu near the Pacific coast with its auxiliary engines, took its first tentative steps into two-wheeled transportation with the launch of a small cheap motor that could be attached to bicycles. This mass market product, like Honda's in Japan was a huge commercial hit highlighting the importance in an impoverished Italy and Japan of the bicycle and mobility. This heart-breaking film that shows how desperation and unpredictable twists of fate can change a person, had a major impact on Shiraishi and others. In fact, a young Shiraishi watched the film multiple times while seated alongside his father; father and son both went on to win the Naoki Prize, an important prize for commercial fiction, in 1987 and 2009 respectively.

The authors that have followed these post-moderns—especially after the collapse of Japan's economic bubble in the early 1990s, which turned Japan more inward-looking and led to what is often referred to as Japan's confidence-sapping 'lost decades'—have a very different set of influences and their own perspective on human existence. Many of these authors often look not to the Japanese greats of the past but to international writers who they generally read in translation for inspiration, as well as the occasional Japanese author who has been blessed by international success. For some, borders matter much less than in the past and frontiers aren't something to be feared. Takuji Ichikawa (b. 1961), author of *Ima aini yukimasu* (*Be With You*), which has sold in the millions in Japan, for instance, says he never reads novels penned by Japanese authors and looks abroad to authors such as John Irving (b. 1942) and Kurt Vonnegut (1922-2007) for inspiration.

Others say that having found publishing success they then struggle to stay on top of their ever-growing reading piles, but nonetheless keep buying books, suffering from a phenomenon that many bookworms will be familiar with, known in Japan as *tsundoku*. No matter, Japanese authors are blessed with a vast array of reading options in translation, especially when compared to what their American, Australian, British and Irish counterparts, for instance, have available to them in terms of Japanese writing.

That said, when authors reach a certain stage in their writing careers, shifting from being writers with newly won literary awards to established figures sitting on the judging panels of prizes, they often have no choice. They are compelled to make time in their busy writing schedules to read more books by contemporary Japanese authors. This is now the case for Mitsuyo Kakuta (b. 1967), Sayaka Murata (b. 1979) and Nakamura, for example, all of whom are all still very much in their writing primes but are also now judges. According to one of them, as a judge, "you have to read around five books, at the very least," and often rather quickly, a number that, of course, varies materially depending on the given prize. The time judges are given to complete their reading assignments also varies considerably on how each award they are involved with processes their long and short lists.

Some of the most memorable works penned by this new generation of contemporary writers often seem to confront the world as one finds it, with the ordinary transformed into the extraordinary, with narratives shorn of depictions of the world as it could be or one would like it to be, with well-crafted tales focused on the gritty and often quirky enormities of the everyday, framed by their empathetic kind-hearted but calamitous characters. Perhaps this could be seen as a contemporary Japanese literary version of Italian neorealism (1943-1950), the so-called Golden Age of Italian cinema which focused on the pulp-like lives and narratives of common people, as depicted in Shiraishi's beloved *Bicycle Thieves*.

These days, contemporary fiction leans towards depicting the heroics of the everyday; ordinary lives, be they those lived in Dublin, Rome, Tokyo or Osaka, can be epic. "I have experienced many little things. I write about those small experiences and revise them and reexperience them through revision," is how Oe described this phenomenon and his own works in an interview with the *Paris Review*. This outlook tends to resonate everywhere, no matter the language or cultures they are set within. Writers, often by exploiting a type of peripheral vision, through the curved lens of literature, show us that grief, loneliness, failure, injustice, absurdity, anxiety, humiliation, family dynamics and futility, are universal forces and not uniquely the sovereignty of one culture, language or nation.

The Letters of Life

Even so, the Galapagos syndrome, a term first used to describe how parts of Japanese culture and industry have developed in messy isolation, independently of international trends and globalisation, can also still be applied to a certain degree to the nation's large and diverse community of authors, publishers and readers. It is something worth bearing in mind while approaching Japan's literary terrain and this book. Japanese poetry is a good example. It developed independently, creating unique short-form writing and poetry such as tanka and haiku, centuries before X (formerly Twitter). Haiku, now a firm favourite of Do-It-Yourself (DIY) culture, is well known internationally for its elegance, sophistication and grace, which is where the similarities with the vast majority of X's posts probably end. Isolation does not preclude unusual creativity or unexpected acts of creation. In fact, isolation has often helped turn the cogs of Japanese productivity, regularly marking some Japanese individuals and Japan itself as outliers and making it a badge of the county's independent culture for some.

Hermann Hesse (1877-1962), another Nobel laureate, was enchanted by the artificial simplicity and structured brevity of Japanese verse when he encountered it during a trip to Indonesia in 1911. It changed how he saw Japan and led to a lifelong interest in and appreciation of Zen Buddhism, something that is reflected in his own writing. He is not the only individual to be touched or inspired by Japanese poetry, or other forms of powerful Japanese literary perspectives, which often put nature, not man or self, at their narrative core. Stripped-back brevity, structure and a clear theme, all of which are at the heart of Japanese textual style and poetry, are today often said to be the essential ingredients of good prose and informative writing. Hesse's interest in Japan was also fuelled by his cousin, Wilhelm Gundert (1880-1971), who lived in Japan for several decades and published translations of Zen texts in German.

The circles of literary influence and creative cross-pollination are powerful, and can seemingly miraculously overcome international barriers, as well as be somewhat eerily synchronistic. Hesse's father translated *Representative Men of Japan (Daihyouteki Nihonjin)* by the prominent Japanese Christian thinker Kanzo Uchimura (1861-1930) from English into German, introducing five Japanese men who Uchimura admired for breaking the stereotypes commonly associated internationally with Japan to the German reading world. Hesse himself subsequently became a very popular and defining author in Japan. Hesse's theme of representative searchers trying to find the individuality of the individual, has really resonated with Japanese readers, surely something with which Uchimura, a staunch humanitarian, would empathise. This turned Hesse, alongside a select group of non-Japanese authors such as Franz Kafka (1883-1924) and Fyodor Dostoevsky (1821-1881), into a highly influential author especially amongst Japan's creative artists, be they writers like Randy Taguchi (b. 1959) or manga artists. "In your distant island realm, an echo has gradually sounded out back to me, how my love has found its reciprocation there," Hesse wrote in a message to his readers in Japan in May 1955 and that echo now seems to have a permanence that reverberates through the Japanese creative arts.[11]

The seeker, like an inexperienced philosopher with unrelenting questions but not fully-fledged or satisfactory answers, asks: What and who am I? What are my measurements and fit? They crave a convenient certainty of purpose and distinct belonging, even if only a fleeting one. Perhaps Japan's lack of a deep-seated culture of raw individualism similar to that of repute in the anglosphere, and the importance the nation puts on harmony and co-operation, has amplified the appeal of this form of writing. Finding your station in life, no matter the vehicle or medium you choose, is a strong urge possessed by many. Whether Japan is actually congenitally collective or not is a moot point, if many still observe the paradigm and behave as if it is, and if more importantly the Japanese government continues to incorporate and constantly stress harmony and social cohesion in its cleverly manufactured national narrative. These forces help blend literary escape with the elusive quest for independence, purpose and individuality.

Tellingly, the name of the new Japanese era, Reiwa (officially translated as beautiful harmony) that started on 1 May 2019 following the accession of the new Emperor Naruhito (b. 1960) to the Chrysanthemum Throne, was also inspired by Japanese poetry. In this case, a collection of Japanese *waka* poems from multiple authors, known as the Manyoshu (*Collection of Ten Thousand Leaves*), Japan's oldest extant book of poetry. This ancient collection of poetic perspectives of Japan, which despite its title actually consists of around 4,500 poems, was compiled during Japan's Nara period (710-794), more than a millennium ago, when the Japanese capital was in Nara, western Japan, before it moved to Kyoto in the Heian period (794-1185) and much later to Tokyo in the Edo period (1603-1868). Arguably these days everyone, no matter their native tongue, experience ancient cursive poetry like the written verse contained in the Manyoshu, due to its age and very nature, in translation. Creating an opportunity for government-level modernising repositioning and widespread interpretation.

Rei is the first character from the word *reigetsu*, an auspicious month, used in a poem about plum blossom and an early spring breeze, and *wa,* a letter that has been used in the name of other imperial periods, means peace and tranquillity. This new imperial era name is, however, the first to have its roots within the canon of Japanese literature, as opposed to classical Chinese literature, which has historically had a major influence on Japanese writing. By breaking with tradition in this way, it punctuates Japanese history, and positions the era to come in a novel manner with poetic Japanese vernacular at its cultural core, drawing a thick and clear written cultural line between Japan and China for the new era. As we face into more man-made catastrophes and eco-disasters, we shall see if the aspiration that this new age will be a beautiful and harmonious one is auspicious and prescient or foolhardy, a demarcation that is quickly shattered by events.

The First Golden Age

Alongside poetry and verse, the significance of which is already widely acknowledged internationally, the forms of travel, diary, short story, serialised fiction, and novella writing also have long occupied an important and prestigious place in Japan's literary landscape. The diaries and writings of Court Ladies in the Heian period, including *The Tale of Genji*, an immense work with about 430 different characters and 800 poems, have been required reading for aristocratic Japanese women and social climbers for over a thousand years.

This sophisticated and aspirational pedigree, inspired in *Genji*'s case by a deftly interwoven serialised ode to classical Japan, that unfolds across 54 scrolls or chapters in the early surviving copies, as well as the fact that many Japanese schoolchildren are required to write diaries as part of their studies, perhaps helps explain the enduring appeal of these forms of writing and the extremely large number of Japanese language bloggers today. Travel writing is also an ever-popular genre that, these days, introduces Japanese readers to distant exotic locales outside the Japanese archipelago, as well as within.

The Heian period, when *Genji* was written—a slow-moving style-obsessed but peaceful time—is known as the first Golden Age of female writers, as it was dominated by pioneering female wordsmiths. These writers forged the use of the indigenous phonetic syllabary known as *kana* and catalysed early Japanese fiction in all its multitude of forms.

When they were writing, paper was a precious commodity which put constraints on the ability of many to write. How this impacted the creative process is difficult to put into perspective in our age of blogs, social media, smartphones, eBooks and mass-market paperbacks, where rules of pagination and word count limits no longer exist. But it doesn't appear to have limited the creativity for at least the individuals whose works we have access to today. The first 34 scrolls of *Genji*, for instance, written before a regular financial sponsor was found, are sporadic in length and publishing frequency, being written and released when the author had access to paper with anything from one to 26 sheets joined together forming a scroll.

Publishing, creative writing and the traditional concept of what a novel could be was in its infancy when they were writing. The role of the novel and what makes this type of writing unique even gets discussed within *The Tale of Genji*, highlighting the freshness of the format. The titular protagonist Genji explains to his adopted daughter that anything—even the mundane—can be part of such storytelling. Though he emphasises that what is written must not be simply a chronicle of events; an author needs to express "emotion so passionate that he can no longer keep it shut up in his heart."[12]

It is also worth remembering that these works of sublime Japanese aesthetics and court life were written by Heian women 300 years before Dante Alighieri's (1265-1321) *Divine Comedy*, considered the greatest work written in Italian and 400 years before Geoffrey Chaucer (1340-1400) wrote *The Canterbury Tales*, one of the great touchstones of English literature. They have, just like Chaucer, generated a mass and continued plundering and counterfeiting of their original literary ideas, structures, and narrative styles. A host of renowned Japanese authors have learned from and still lean on these gifted forebearers. In some places scholarly excavation is required to identify the faceless hidden women who contributed to the early development of the literary arts. In Japan they glitter in plain sight.

Many believe that Japan is currently experiencing a second Golden Age with a new crop of writers such as Yoshimoto, Yoko Ogawa (b. 1962), Hitomi Kanehara (b. 1983), Hiromi Kawakami (b. 1958), Mieko Kawakami (b. 1976), the aforementioned Murata and Kakuta as well as many others who are captivating contemporary Japanese readers with their art. Their works, many of which are often hard to pigeonhole, generally have a prominent feminist tone while at the same time being simultaneously both Western and Japanese in character, regularly appear outside Japan in translations, often winning awards and other accolades. However, in many markets Japanese male authors, such as Murakami and Higashino, still outsell them. There is a long and rich linage of female and feminist writing in Japan. It is not simply a new phenomenon that the current frame of increased title availability outside Japan, especially in English translation, might imply.

Refined elegance and the female gaze, however, is not the only eyeglass through which to see Japan's past or present. There are many colours in the Japanese literary palette. Violent delights, as they say, often have violent ends. Japan changed, the uncommonly peaceful Heian period when this first Golden Literary Age occurred, came to an end, and violence and expansive aggression subsequently replaced the sophisticated elegance of Heian-style. Every now and then events and the series that they fall within create a transformative cluster that varies society in ways that for earlier generations would have been considered as highly unlikely, if not totally impossible. Conflict was the new order of the day. Power shifted from the aristocracy to the military in the Kamakura period (1185-1333).

These societal shifts help generate panoplies of new and very different narrative subject matter, including tales of bloodshed and murderous skulduggery. In parallel, as literacy rates increased and broadened out in Japan, in the nation's subsequent centuries long war-torn medieval era, books started being written for the first time based on well-known oral tales. New works were also created specifically to provide narratives that priests and entertainers could introduce in the oral storytelling tradition that preceded the arrival of the Chinese textual technology, *kanji*, in the fifth century that brought written-form communication and storytelling to Japan, creating a dynamic interaction between the lively oral and the newer written traditions, integrating phonetic and ideographic writing and storytelling.

A critical work that facilitated this blending and parallel growth in the oral and written traditions is *Heike monogatari* (*The Tale of the Heike*), a collection of epic tales written between 1190 and 1221 about clan warfare between the feuding Taira (Heike) and Minamoto (Genji) clans and their epic struggle for control of the nation.

Its opening section reads: "Prosperity is sure to wane. He who boasts cannot last long. All is like a dream in a spring evening. The strong will eventually perish. All is as the dust blown before the wind." It is a tale that most Japanese children encounter in school, forcing them into something of an epic battle with medieval Japanese prose and ancient calligraphy before they re-encounter the tale or exciting extracts from it in other forms of much more accessible storytelling.

Most Japanese people know the names of those famous heroes and legendary aristocrats and samurai, even if they aren't aware of the details of this grand saga. The cognoscenti in the West regularly compare *The Tale of the Heike*'s influence to that of Homer's *Iliad*, a work often credited with the birth of traditional mythology and storytelling in the West.

The *Gikeiki* (*The Chronicle of Yoshitsune*) is another comparable important example from the same period. It tells the story of the warrior hero Yoshitsune Minamoto (1159-1189), who also features in *The Tale of the Heike*. He was a virtuous and elusive character, a type of Japanese Robin Hood gifted with the sword and the bow, as well as on occasion the fan, skilfully used to defeat sword-carrying opponents, with his own band of oddball loyal men. Minamoto is an individual who is still one of Japan's most popular classical heroic figures.

There have been many contributors to this genre of storytelling but these two works in particular are considered critical milestones in the evolution of Japanese writing, and as such are still read and retold today with the same endless re-envisaging as the Western tales of Greek and Norse gods. Some periods in history, like the ones reflected in these works, bring disorder, some resolution; other times are epochal. Many challenge us, and society, with awkward questions. A few like those mentioned above, spawn storied superhero-type characters that are destined to entertain and fascinate generations to come.

Intriguingly, both these tales were also influenced by and helped propagate the Buddhist beliefs and the emerging values of the period with narrative themes spanning, for instance, the abuse of power, the role of the monk in society, karma, impermanence and rebirth, as well as much captivating heroism. In this period of Japanese history, it was the values and attitudes produced by years of armed conflict and religion, Buddhism, and not the refined—and not so refined—pursuits, of the aristocracy that drove Japan's cultural development forwards.

Japan today is a very different nation from the periods depicted in these medieval works with their sword-carrying samurai slayers, tragic self-sacrifice, and the brutal civil wars. However, the cultural traces of these tales are ever present and can turn up in unexpected contemporary locales. *The Tale of the Heike*, for instance, was apparently a constant presence in the formative years of Murakami, who grew up in a household with two parents who both taught Japanese language and literature at schools. Despite his love for American literature, jazz and Americana, as well as his initial reluctance to embrace Japanese literature, fragments of this tale and other Japanese masterpieces, modern and old, can be observed by the keen-eyed lurking in some of his works.[13]

There are many other classic and important tales that still influence contemporary society, but it would be remiss when discussing these highly influential narrative themes that mark important cultural moments in Japanese history, not to mention another one specifically: *Ako Jiken*. Better known outside Japan as the revenge of the forty-seven *ronin*, a lionised incident that took place in the 18th century, during Japan's Edo period, a time when Japan was almost totally wrapped up in its own internal affairs. This story has also had a super-sized cultural impact. Its retelling as a doomed tale of a heroic vendetta has, alongside earlier tales of tragic heroes, helped shape honour and suicide into something emblematic of Japan and the values that some still pride, for better or worse, and continue to put weight on loyalty, endurance, sacrifice and persistence.

Escaping shame and obligations by avenging their master's death—essentially a forced suicide—does not in fact—and is not actually expected to—liberate this group of leaderless samurai, *ronin*, in this life, creating a new happy distinct future for them. It is an obligation that simply must be fulfilled. Its continued re-rendering across the Japanese arts shows that one's way of dying and its timing in Japan, in their case synchronised ritual suicide having finally avenged their master's death, as some Japanese military strategists have argued, can "validate one's entire life."[14]

For some, in Japan, even now, just as was the case for these samurai, a brand-new tomorrow doesn't begin today, or even the day after, but each day, mirroring how tenses function in the Japanese language, simply tumbles into the next, in a type of never-ending present that one can never apparently wilfully escape from. Blurring time and space together into a type of philosophical time that implies the future isn't a distinct new potential reality that one stealthily creates or escapes into from the prison of the present. It is a continuation.

Poets are often said to revel in the ambiguity of language. However, when it comes to the Japanese language an enticing opportunity is presented for every branch of wordsmithing, spanning poets and creative writers and of course translators. According to the acclaimed translator Meredith McKinney,

> Japanese tenses are wonderfully teasing about time relations, and time is a fascinatingly fluid substance in classical Japanese texts particularly. Just one more reason why it's such fun and such frustration to try to translate them.

The elusive rending of singulars and plurals in the Japanese language presents many translators with similar difficult challenges with the ambiguous.

Faith in the future, alongside a strong dose of infectious optimism, is said to be an indispensable quality for successful leadership.[15] It is probable that the lack of such faith amongst these leaderless forty-seven samurai and not only the intricacies of Japanese grammar and language and codes of conduct are at the root of their legacy-making decisions. The past can, nevertheless, haunt the present, and not everyone is willing or capable of waiting to live another day. Language reflects society and how it operates but the reverse is also true with language, its norms and use, changing how we behave and the decisions we make. Only the past and the present are demonstrable, trapping many from visualising permanent escape from duties and responsibilities. This can pull them forward treacherously with the invisible cord of momentum, forcing many to live tied existences while still facing the constant challenge of seeking what one might call life after birth. This form of entrapment, be it from societal dynamics or more insidious factors such as bullying, is a perennial theme in Japanese writing.

In spite of the massive social changes Japan has gone through, such tales and the sentiments from a disappeared past still live on in books, film, anime, manga, kabuki and even bunraku, a traditional form of puppet theatre, and resonate today. Storytelling that reflects the shadowy side of modern human nature and its unifying myths are widespread, as are stories that exploit the eternally popular narrative themes of obligation, duty, shame, fear, and compliance that often oppressively cast a long shadow over the present. Contemporary authors, such as Teru Miyamoto (b. 1947), are sensitive to this and are masters of layered timeframes and these peculiar immutable cultural forces.

Miyamoto's books, for instance, are replete with characters who are generally underdogs based in the working-class world of Japan's Kansai region (that spans Osaka, Kyoto and Kobe). They are haunted by failure and their inability to change themselves or wriggle free escaping to new futures, alongside the stark strings of fated events that drive their lives forwards. Of course, they do get to experience the rare occasional personal triumph, defying the odds, which encourages readers to keep on reading and to dream of better outcomes. Nevertheless, these are sentiments and powerful suggestions that would no doubt resonate even with the forty-seven *ronin* who trod their own fated road, wearing of course very different shoes from our modern ones, but adornments with familiar cultural pinching pressure points. Miyamoto is not alone in looking to the past for inspiration, sometimes unconsciously, and expounding such narrative tales for contemporary audiences.

Nostalgia often denotes more about the present than the past. The celebration of cowboys and their form of justice in American film, for example, is part of the narrative America tells about itself today. Britain is famous for its own particular type of period costume dramas, and Japan has *jidaigeki*, period theatricals, that often depict the lives and tales of samurai and their mesmerising sword fights, as well as tragic *47 Ronin*-type tales. Emotional and artistic alchemy probably explains why this particular tragic saga has even been reimagined as an awkward Hollywood film starring Keanu Reeves and why a reincarnated *ronin* has even found its way into a series of comics of the same name by the celebrated American graphic novelist Frank Miller set in a dystopian near future New York City. Cultural nostalgia is infectious and, when reflected in well-crafted prose can generate wonderful stories that amplifies its appeal with a strange magnetic circularity.

Enter the Shogun

The reverse side of the coin of national nostalgia can often be a strutting national pride that international film franchises such as *Top Gun*, *Mission Impossible* and *James Bond* elicit in their home audiences. Japan is no different, and even tragic heroic failure can swell the patriotic heart. Bond, that immoderate symbol of the power of a small but righteous island-nation with validating titles such as *Tomorrow Never Dies*, *Die Another Day*, and *No Time to Die*, is just as popular in Japan as elsewhere. However, Japan also has its own pride-inducing serial-storied heroes that international readers are now becoming more familiar with, mostly thanks to manga and anime. Japanese audiences enjoy tales of individuals and groups of individuals miraculously fighting back and winning against all the odds as much as the next nation, especially when it comes to narratives about sports and other team endeavours. These tales often include a group of misfits coming together, forming a group, and sometimes even finding salvation, where the collective posse is much stronger and more successful than its individual parts.

Nonetheless, Japan's temperate nostalgia ensures that the past never dies. Evidence of the past constantly pushes through into the present. Anecdotes and poetry by notable individuals, be they a shogun or a samurai from classic tales, are sometimes included in business strategy books as case studies on leadership, tools to motivate staff and make them metaphorically sing, and winning corporate strategies. Some love these samurai tales and others deplore them, a violent polarisation in taste one might say. These reactions are flip sides of the same coin, evidence of their enduring cultural relevance because no one seems to be unaware of them.

Historical fiction is still adored in Japan by the old and the young. Japan's longest-running *jidaigeki*, for example, is a 42-season series adaptation launched in the 1960s, much like Bond who was launched in cinemas in 1962 following the success of the Ian Fleming (1908-1964) books. Five different actors have played the lead role of *Mito Komon*, a larger-than-life character that protects the Japanese Edo period public from unscrupulous and corrupt villains. Unlike Bond, it is based on an actual historical figure, Mitsukuni Tokugawa (1628-1701) the grandson of the first Tokugawa Shogun, Ieyasu Tokugawa (1543-1616) the instigator of the long peaceful Edo period.

Nonetheless, Mitsukuni Tokugawa is said to have been a lusty, lazy, womanising gourmet in his youth before taking an interest in publishing, which, helped point him in other far better directions, including that of commissioning major history books, guidebooks, and travelogues. This influential feudal lord was subsequently fictionalised and reinvented within narrative tales as a wandering hero travelling the breadth of the nation in disguise, focused on eradicating evil powers and injustice from Japanese shores, helping to encourage good or better governance.

Alongside the myriad of samurai tales such as these that meld historical events into exciting fiction, local publishing formats have also played a significant role in the development of Japanese literature. Narrative scrolls, such as the ones used to write *The Tale of Genji*, are a publishing format that has had a very important role in the development of Japanese storytelling. The fusion and blurring of traditional oral storytelling and decorative cultural roll-ups are, some say, the genesis of modern Japanese graphic novels and other forms of storytelling that integrate sequences of frames, scrolling illustration and prose. Japan also boasts an array of bindings, trim marks, traditional colours and inks, and printing techniques. Tradition is what is handed down from one generation to the next. That this continues to evolve and be transmitted down no matter the ambiguities of refinement, change and adaption is due to these continuing fragments of history: still traditional, while also being modern. These and other traditional cultural ingredients and crafts when successfully combined with new contemporary conceptual approaches, no matter the era they are blended together within, is one of the secrets behind many Japanese success stories.

There is, of course, a long history of brutal authoritarian violence, but Japan's rulers and leaders have in fact actually performed a critical literary role, and not just as protagonist fodder. For over a thousand years many of Japan's emperors, alongside some shoguns, played an active role in publishing by writing poems, books and even scientific papers sometimes for influential international journals, as well as commissioning important works. This has helped root reading and writing at the core of Japanese culture, as well as help thoroughly document the nation and the immediacy of the country's progress throughout its history.

The Meiji Emperor (1852-1912) who ruled over the pivotal high-octane transitional period in Japanese history that followed the rigid rule-based Edo period and said to be the embodiment of an age with much wrenching change, for example, wrote over 100,000 *waka* poems and was known as 'the sage of poetry'. His poetry often reflected the rapid changes Japan was confronting and also the wave of new communication technologies and gadgets, such as the electric telegraph, the text messaging service of its day, trains, as well as photography and, of course, the new handheld and travelling viewing devices of his era—telescopes, in this case, not kaleidoscopes—that started arriving in Japan from abroad during his reign. Many state that the era's change was top down and forced on Japan, which may be true but it was also an overwhelming period for the privileged, and those at the very top, too, as his poetry shows.

At times, Japan's imperial literature has even stretched into science fiction with one member of the imperial family, Princess Fukuko Asaka (1941-2009), one of the Meiji Emperor's grandchildren, penning stories that helped develop the genre now known as cyberpunk using the pen name Bien Fu and other nom de plume in the 1960s. The princess's work features cyborgs and immortal imperial consorts. Having lost her title and imperial status in 1947 she reportedly empathised with Native Americans, whose position in their country she believed to be like her own in Japan, had changed after the arrival of people from afar. She was a vocal champion of their rights and the rights of others endangered with being written out of their national narratives or with cultural extinction.[16]

Literary and publishing genes have been nurtured and continue to flourish in the family. In 2017, an essay by the current emperor's daughter Princess Aiko, titled "Praying for Peace in the World", was widely praised for its literary style and content. The Princess wrote the essay for the yearbook commemorating her graduation from Gakushuin Girls' Junior High School.[17] In fact, literary and poetic writing has threaded its way into and become imbedded in courtly ceremony. Since ancient times the Imperial Court has, for instance, held an annual New Year Poetry Party. In 1964 the party's theme was paper, highlighting its precious and continuing cultural role at that time. The Showa Emperor who reigned between 1926-1989, Emperor Hirohito (1901-1989), in the 39th year of his resign, contributed the following poem:

Preparing a book
On the Nasu trees and grasses
For publication,
I touch the reality
Of how priceless paper is.[18]

It is, however, not just nobles, courtesans and royalty that have understood the importance of skilful literary composition in Japan. Many of the nation's famous warriors and warlords, no matter how savage or ruthless, practised and mastered the art of poetic calligraphy, as well as the samurai way of the sword. Sometimes the words from these unlikely scribes functioned as parting shots when facing death, ways to motivate and educate retainers, or tools to commemorate important or tragic events and anniversaries, as well as a means for legacy-making messaging. Poetic prose that has often reverberated through history, establishing a type of forceful permanence, inspiring many and also slaying opponents with words, one could say. In the Western world it is often said that the source of and inspiration of poetry and art is divine, while in Japan it is argued that it is poetry, especially in response to nature, that inspires and moves the deities.

The following defiant poem is attributed to Naganori Asano (1667-1701), the Lord of Ako, written when his demise was foretold on the day of his suicide, the very death the 47 *ronin* avenged on 15 December 1702. His tale is often referred to in Japanese as *Chushingura* (*The Treasury of Loyal Retainer*), the title of a play published in 1784:

More than cherry blossoms,
inviting a wind to take them away.
I wonder what to do
with the rest of spring.

These well-versed warriors cottoned on to poetry's consequential importance and the exceptional communicative power of short-form writing long before most, including the likes of Percy Shelley (1792-1822), the radical British romantic poet, famous for his often-quoted line, written in 1821, that "poets are the unacknowledged legislators of the world." These historical Japanese figures have set many precedents that highlight the importance of written forms of communication. Mastering poetic and other forms of written composition became an essential tool in Japan, embedding refined prose and the world of letters deep within the nation's cultural DNA.

Across Japanese history, there are many impressive examples of the writing brush being mightier than the sword. Emperors, feudal lords and many others have used short messages written in verse with sublime turns of phrase in a sophisticated form of letter writing that highlights both their author's ability to compose but also their calligraphy skills. For many in Japan, words, in written form, count, showing once again the importance literacy, despite the Japanese language's complex writing system, has played in the nation's development and why reading is such a key component to understanding the country.

The Art of Seclusion

The events that engulfed the forty-seven *ronin* took place during the Edo period when Japan was almost completely closed to Western influence, following the expulsion of Westerners and the banning of Christianity, with its dangerous imported foreign notions, in the 1630s. These decisions turned the nation inwards, creating the cultural Galapagos referred to earlier. The way that Japanese culture, including the nation's commercial publishing, flourished and developed during this time of seclusion, when Japan was run by the Tokugawa shoguns, proves that inaccessibility to the world is not always a curse to a nation and does not inevitably lead to a cultural wasteland. Nobody would describe Japan today as an amorphous nation without anything special to call its own. As Uchimura, in *Representative Men of Japan*, astutely asks his readers, "What benignant father would have his children prematurely thrown into the world that they might come under its so-called 'civilizing influences'?" Without this long period of national hibernation Japan would not be the country it is today.

Isolation protected Japan from clashing with the world and being exposed to the influence of the so-called Great Powers, creating for most in Japan an invisible cultural barrier enveloping the nation. Whether this blockade from within, this hermit kingdom status with the barbarians kept at the border really helped prepare Japan for its subsequent international debut and rise amongst the group of 'civilised' nations centuries later is an open question. Japan managed to postpone its international growth anxieties, including its search for its role and status in the wider world, through a draconian centuries-long national curfew. Restrictions that blocked freedom of movement both internationally and also to a lesser degree domestically for the people of Japan.

The option of solitude is, of course, open to all of us, not just nation-states in cultural or pandemic inspired lockdowns, and a choice that some still actually believe can empower creative output. Our horizons do seem to widen as our commitments narrow. Isolation can be a blessing, but when taken to its extremes, certainly at the level of an individual, it can also lead to odd and unhealthy states including that of, for instance, Japan's famed *hikikomori*, shut-ins, hermit-like individuals often dubbed parasites who retreat into their rooms to escape from the world. These individuals, who are numerous, appear to lack the personal strength and courage or the right opportunities to forge their own independent futures. For others, however, isolation, alongside other powerful emotional drivers such as boredom and loneliness, as well as the desire for independence, can lead to immense productivity.

For the outside world at this time, Japan was a closed book. Almost all residents were locked-in, unable to leave the nation's shores surrounded by hierarchical regulations that meant returnees from abroad potentially faced death as a punishment for international travel. This seclusion from the world's stage helped bind Japan together and create a national identity. For Japan itself the pages of a brand-new narrative started to take on highly creative new forms. The respect that the initiator of the Edo period Ieyasu Tokugawa had for publishing is thought to have been a key factor that led to the Tokugawa state lasting around 265 years. The Tokugawa sponsored the publication of books including Confucian classics and Buddhist texts and believed that encouraging the production and distribution of books was an essential part of good governance. Books became a type of operating manual for this new period, as the nation left brutal civil war behind.

Ieyasu Tokugawa famously said:

> When people forget the moral requisites of humanity, order is lost, government declines, and there is no peace. The only way to deliver those morals to the people is through books. The first step of good government is to print books for a wide audience.

It's interesting to note, too, that the Tokugawa period was one of the most stable and peaceful periods in Japanese history. The books published under his leadership and regime, however, were generally practical and educational and not just theoretical and abstract texts.[19] That is not to say, however, that there was no censorship.

Counting Culture

One illustrative example is *Jinkoki* (*The Calculation Manual*), which was first published in 1627 a little over a decade after Ieyasu Tokugawa's death, who for temporal context, died the same year as William Shakespeare (1564-1616). This how-to manual, whose title can also be loosely translated as *Eternal Truths* with a Buddhist reading of the characters used to render its name in Japanese, was written by Mitsuyoshi Yoshida (1598-1673) when commercial publishing in Japan was still in its infancy, but on a rapid upward path. It was so popular that hundreds of editions were published after its launch, some including and other excluding the solutions to the mathematical problems explained in their pages. Almost every family in Japan, whether samurai or not, are thought to have owned a copy or have had access to one, the first chapter of which is titled *The Naming of Large Numbers*. It helped arithmetic, which developed independently in Japan with the local Japanese variety known as *wasan*, flower in Edo Japan, and not just as an important foundational tool of commerce and governance but as a game-like pursuit to be enjoyed and puzzled over.

"I feel that publications such as *Jinkoki* are historic symbols captured in print, that highlight the fundamental belief held by most Japanese people, even amongst the working class and lower-rank samurai throughout history, in the importance of basic academic skills," Satoshi Saito, Chairman of Kirihara Shoten, a major Japanese textbook publisher argues. "Japanese people love learning, no matter what, and today this is reflected in widespread enthusiasm for sudoku, puzzles, quizzes, music, art, flower arrangement, and all sorts of other extra-curricular learning and activities, even wine appreciation, for example. The huge size of the informal educational market enables niche subjects and interests to thrive in Japan."

Terakoya, private primary temple schools designed to educate commonfolk in a relatively relaxed personalised manner, for example, as opposed to the samurai class, played a major role in Edo period Japan, facilitating the development of this broad-based learning infrastructure, helping generate a reading, writing and counting culture. At their peak at the end of the 18th century attendance reached 70 percent in the capital, Edo. Learning how to use an abacus, *soroban*, as well as to read and write were part of these studies. By the early 1900s, Japan had been dubbed 'the schoolmaster of Asia',[20] by international observers.

Mathematicians, alongside poets, pop up all over the place in Japan if you look out for them. The uncle of Japan's current Empress Emitera Michiko (b. 1934), Kenjiro Shoda (1902-1977) was, for instance, a professor of mathematics at Osaka University. He studied mathematics in Germany having won a scholarship, and wrote a famously difficult textbook, published in 1932, for advanced students titled *Chusho daisugaku (Abstract Algebra)*. The world's first 'compact' fully electronic calculator, the revolutionary relay-based dustproof desk-mounted Casio 14-A, was launched in 1957 in the land of the rising sum, another powerful example of Japan's ingenious and influential counting culture.

It is also worth noting that *The Calculation Manual* was published 60 years before Isaac Newton's (1643-1727) *Philosphie Naturalis Mathematica*, a cornerstone of modern science, published in 1687. Newton's book changed the Western world by spreading the "light of mathematics" on science and society, while also explaining the laws of motion and universal gravity. Japan also had key individuals, during the Newtonian age, though much less storied, spreading the light and eternal truths of mathematics. Takakazu Seki (1642-1708), a mathematician active in Japan at the same time as Newton and Gottfried Leibniz (1646-1716), a pioneering German polymath, elucidated, for instance, various types of theorem and processes, some before these celebrated Europeans, such as the concept of determinants, and the rectification of the circle. Seki and the mathematicians around him, should be much better known and far more celebrated internationally and also in Japan where many people are also still not fully aware of him and his work.

Within walking distance of the impressive museum, near Waseda University in Soseki Park in Tokyo, that commemorates Soseki Natsume (1867-1916), an important era-bridging literary author who was born in Edo and died in the renamed Tokyo and is now considered by some scholars as 'modern Japan's greatest novelist', is a small graveyard with a relatively discreet plot for this important but much-ignored mathematician. A small brown metallic plaque from the Tokyo Metropolitan Board of Education in front of his modest tombstones briefly explains who Seki was. Close to it is a grey waist-high stone plinth inscribed with geometrical markings on its top surface and vertical writing on its sides, an object that would not look out of place as a clue in a mystery novel.

To put the scale of this memorial to Seki into perspective, the area commemorating this towering mathematician, who developed an algebra based on calculations using written words not the familiar mathematical symbols we all use these days, is smaller than a dedicated area at the rear of the Natsume Soseki Memorial Museum. It is here that Natsume's famous cat, Chibi, which ironically means 'tiny', a cat that helped launch Natsume's career as a professional writer, is enshrined alongside other felines owned by the Natsumes. Despite both men leaving important written legacies and both being a real blessing to the nation in terms of Japan's cultural and intellectual development, the contrast of how they are remembered is staggering.

The Calculation Manual and other books that can also be loosely described as early educational manuals, alongside discipline pioneers such as Seki, had a major impact on Japan's trajectory. Two examples, explored in more detail in a subsequent essay, are Japan's future motorcar manufacturing and robotics industries, and the detailed manuals that are still part and parcel of the life of most employees in Japan today. Part of *Jinkoki*'s success is put down to the fact that it was very well ordered and had an easy to navigate layout, as well as a decorative binding and the fact that it contained many pictures. Of course, its content was rendered using vertical text in the cursive style, not horizontally with roman letters and Greek symbols, with notations that all students of mathematics today would find at best idiosyncratic. Its second edition was issued in a four-colour format and featured a trim mark that was hard to copy.[21] In their own ways these manuals have changed Japan and Japanese publishing by nourishing, inspiring and educating minds, as well as highlighting why it is important that sums add up.

The discipline's label, *wasan*, is of a type frequently used to distinguish the unique indigenous Japaneseness of something from the foreign. It is written with two *kanji* characters, *san* meaning arithmetic and *wa*, harmony and peace, the same character used to write the current new era name *Reiwa* and can also mean 'Japanese'. This usage is evident in the word *washo*, Japanese books, as contrasted with *yosho*, foreign or Western writing or internationally published titles. The latter can be seen in bookshops designating sections that contain books written in languages other than Japanese while the use of the former, *washo*, is generally found lurking within the jargon of publishing industry conversations, manifesting itself in meeting rooms at Japanese publishing houses and booksellers, when the international book business is under discussion.

"*Yosho* is a generic term for books imported from abroad. Books from Europe and America, or even books from China and other Asian countries, are all classified as *yosho*. The rest are Japanese books, so there is no need for a special in-store *Washo* sign," said Tsuyoshi Sonoda a member of the Yosho Books Team at Books Kinokuniya Tokyo in Shinjuku.

Waste Not, Want Not: Edo Style

Even before the Edo period, Japan was undergoing a massive urban boom. The capital Edo, was larger at around one million residents, than most, if not all, European cities at the time. Urbanisation came early to Japan and the managed unification of Japan under the Tokugawa accelerated this trend. Though, even in those days, urbanisation was actually already, as it continues to be today, an international phenomenon. The crowding together of clever people can have unexpected consequences and opportunity-rich cities still attract. Edo urbanites came up with local solutions to deal with the pressures and pleasures of their growing city, some that are now found elsewhere, such as its famed entertainment districts, and others, which are not. This includes, for example, idiosyncratic supply chains that non-meat diets and the absence of domestic animals required for meat consumption permitted. Another more familiar solution was the publication of must-have manuals, handbooks and pocket guides that ranked things like the many eating and drinking establishments of Edo, and even Sumo wrestlers and actors.

Water and its management also played a critical role in the development of the city as well as books, printing and publishing. As any city grows, so too does the problem of waste. In Europe, people focused their efforts on the development of specially designed attire such as platform shoes, *pattens*, as well as headgear, to avoid the human effluent literally washing down the street. Dirty old London had its raggers and bone pickers. Japan, however, put a practical, commercial wrapper around human waste. In Edo, piles of human excrement were sold to dealers and recycled at a profit as fertiliser to farmers feeding the growing urban throng. Edo's urban dwellers and entrepreneurs are proof without room for any doubt that the old adage that 'one man's waste is another man's treasure' is a universal and timeless truth.

The calculus of a million daily motions and their markets thus began to involve the allocation of yields and spreads reflecting the dynamics of a fluid and healthy market. The prized commercial rights to night soil, *shimogoe*, in this seller's market, impacted on how rents were calculated (gross or net of waste), and created a new form of human capital, and more besides, through treating excretions not simply as something that happens or needs to be avoided, but something of matter.[22] Edo emptied its bowels into the capital's economic waterways, one might say, contributing to a sophisticated market economy of sorts. A denial of nature, this was not.

This is a classic, but perhaps unusual, example of a business philosophy known as *sanpoyoshi*, three-way-good, for buyers, sellers and society, expounded by the era's merchants some of whom went on to create the famous international Japanese trading houses we are now all familiar with, such as Itochu. Today, this pragmatic approach to business would probably be called stakeholder capitalism and highlighted as an excellent example of Environmental, Social and Governance (ESG) investing, a voguish term coined around 2004 that some believe will not have the longevity or sustainable strategic success of Japanese *sanpoyoshi*. Still, without the publication of manuals, such as the ones to teach the populace mathematics, none of this 'do well by doing good' would, however, have been possible. Though despite what we are often led to believe, the small guy and the socially marginalised don't always in fact do that well.

Surprisingly, in 1937 the relatively unknown author Ashihei Hino (1907-1960) won the Akutagawa Prize for his novella *Fun'nyotan (A Tale of Excrement and Urine)*, a narrative about a man struggling to restore his family's wealth and well-being who becomes a private night soil contractor. In this dark, humorous tale replete with pathos, Hikotaro, the protagonist, battles against local officials and politics, as well as the complexities and momentum of the daily motions of life in Kyushu, and just as he is at last making a go of it, the rules are changed. Life seems stacked against him, and he finally snaps covering his enemies and himself with excrement, lacquering everyone with a vengeful sheen, uniting them defiled in filth under a setting sun. Japan doesn't always shine in the way one is often led to believe. Not the most appealing of subjects perhaps but a powerful metaphor of the continued depositing of rubbish on the marginalised and those on the edges of Japanese society.

Incumbents and individuals battling for recognition, as is so often the case, were outraged but according to Kiyotaka Matsuo (b. 1976), an author who often writes historical fiction and hails from the same local region where this story is set, it shouldn't actually be surprising that the judging panel unanimously supported this story. "It is well crafted and highly engaging, and for the era stylistically a pioneering example, with its stream of consciousness narrative," he explains. Sadly, he points out, not much has changed when it comes to the murky and intertwined links between politics and commercial contracts: "These days it is probably even worse than when Hino was alive."

It was the sixth time the Akutagawa Prize, an award that, unlike the Nobel Prize in Literature, publicly nominated authors are today given the opportunity to reject before the winners are announced, had been awarded. When the decision to award it to *A Tale of Excrement and Urine* was made, Hino was stuck in a very different sort of murky quagmire, on active duty as a conscripted soldier on the front lines in China. The unexpected prize helped him survive the war.

Today, Japan is praised for its cleanliness and known for its seasonal festive purification rituals, both of which are often said to be at the core of the nation's traditional culture. Tokyo has almost four times the number of public toilets per capita than London, and Japan's lavatories, considered by some including eminent authors and poets as inspirational and an important location for tranquil contemplation and spiritual repose, as well as a metaphor for society's ills, have facilitated much and many, spanning from poetry, essays, narrative fiction, documentaries, calligraphy, memorable designs and also the unmentionable.

Perhaps, it is therefore unsurprising that the combination of these Edo period phenomena, a love of mathematics, practical win–win solutions, handbook publishing, and the so-called calculus of excrement have helped generate a modern-day educational publishing sensation, the multi-million selling *unko* student workbook series: *The Poop Maths Workbook*. These are workbooks that two out of every three Japanese elementary schoolchildren allegedly own a copy of.[23] At certain ages children all over the world, not just in Japan, seem to become fixated on bodily excretions and their associated vocabularies but these sales figures show this popular book series is definitely not just a scatological publishing fluke or mishap.

That said, triangulating these trends into a credible hypothesis about Japan's selected Galapagos-like development should, however, probably be left to social anthropologists and historians to determine. Still, it would be rash to rule out coincidence here. Even though some sociologists and anthropologists continue to argue that dirt is essentially disorder, and bodily excretions produce a universal feeling of disgust, it surely really depends on your perspective and approach to classification and innate desire for organisation, as well as your skill as a publisher, in terms of creating lexical and other forms of useful creative order and insight from the world around you.[24]

All of which probably made the combination of these phenomenon and technology an inevitability in our era. A cultural mash-up that has led to the inclusion in 2010, after initially making its debut in Japan in 1997, of the pile of poo emoji, the *unko* icon, as a new digital character within Unicode, the international informational technology standard for expressing and unifying the world's writing systems and scripts. The shiny brown icon with its smiley face was added to Unicode's official documentation in 2015 and is now an emotional sheen that can be expressed and shared, for better or worse, internationally and not just Kyushu where *A Tale of Excrement and Urine* is set. This choice may seem an unusual and extreme example to illustrate a point about Japanese literary evolution and storytelling. There are, of course, many less sensational examples of delightful fragments of Japanese culture, with origins that can be traced back to the nation's Edo period, which have stealthily become part of daily lives outside Japan, as well as contemporary Japanese creative life. Nonetheless, it is a memorable and informative example.

Despite its rigid rules and regulations, Edo was not, however, an age of innocence, a benign dictatorship where citizens conditioned to submissively obey all orders simply acquiesced and did what they were told, nor was it an age of cultural abstinence. Dissent existed and labour, for example, was at times withdrawn when taxes, tariffs and prices rose too quickly. These forms of what might today be called strikes now rarely occur in Japan, but rebellion, debate and dissent were part and parcel of the age, especially as it drew to an end. Edo itself was a thriving urban sprawl with its fair share of gadabouts, rascals and chancers.

Many other forms of publishing, not just educational texts and manuals, began to flourish during the Edo period, including, for example, the illustrated adventure story format *Yomihon* and other forms of storytelling. *Gesaku*, *Kusazoshi*, *Kokkeibon*, and *Sharebon* were written for the mass market, often exploiting the colloquial language of city life in racy tales that also cleverly provided at times practical instruction on customs, travel and accommodation. These invariably conveyed popular and comic themes: stories spanning fantasy, romance, horror and other genres that readers today will be equally familiar with.

They included classics such as *Ugetsu monogatari* (*Tales of Moonlight and Rain*) with its nine monstrous chilling stories of the supernatural dreamt up by Akinari Ueda (1743-1809). On any measure, Ueda was a highly unusual man. He started life with some serious disadvantages: He was the son of an Osaka prostitute and an unknown father, with hands partly paralysed by smallpox. However, in later life he became a physician as well as an acclaimed author and poet. It is sometimes said in Japan that writers are individuals born from venerable houses who have fallen into ruin, but Ueda shows that those born into ruin can also on occasion rise and make it as writers.

A 1953 film adaption directed by one of the great pioneers of Japanese cinema Kenji Mizoguchi (1898-1956), of two stories contained in Ueda's collection of tales of dreams and disappointments that somehow manages to brilliantly balance fantasy with history, is considered one of the best Japanese films ever made. Titled *Ugetsu monogatari*, the film's spooky ghost women and haunted waters, have helped amplify the longevity of Ueda's cultural impact. Mizoguchi, himself an amazing storyteller, started making films in 1922, and directed five films in the 1950s, including *Ugetsu* which dextrously holds a stylish haunted mirror up to Japanese life, that are considered classics of the world repertory.

Racy tales of life within the licensed entertainment quarters of the time where many lived for the moment were published. The disreputable world often makes for great art and in this regard, Japan is no exception. Publications would sometimes be accompanied by colourful woodblock prints, when not banned by the authorities and censors. Authors, artists and publishers who fell foul of the authorities could be banished, exiled to remote islands and even executed. There were also lists of banned books, *Kinsho*, something sadly not unique to Japan. The Catholic Church, for example, had its own centuries long list of prohibited books, *Index Librorum Prohibitorum*, that was in place from 1559 to 1966.

For their publishers, woodblocks functioned as monetisable portable printing blocks that eventually became a new type of cultural currency. Some courted danger, like the paparazzi and scandal sheets of our age, creating prints allegedly of the leaders' courtesans and their secret lifestyles, as well as subversive parodies. Scribes also crafted limited edition censor-defying dangerous manuscripts, as opposed to prints from woodblocks that could be smashed or destroyed. All of which could get their promoters into serious trouble. It helped create a book-loving public and a vibrant reading culture with what some scholars have described as 'epic levels of book consumption' as well as the first Japanese individual, Ikku Jippensha (1765-1831), who was able to live from literary earnings alone. Japan's commercial publishing flourished in splendid Edo isolation, cut off from the 'civilising' world and its influences.

Natural Selection Nipponica

Everything runs its course and even Japan's long Edo period stagnated, and finally came to a dramatic end. International contact increased, books and products from aboard were arriving, and society faced a new series of challenges. A succession of internal and external shocks, alongside a deteriorating economy, the details of which will be discussed much later, forced Japan to change direction and plot a completely new course. The subsequent Meiji era (1868-1912) that followed the internationally secluded Edo period, was one when Japan was finally liberalising and opening up at a blistering pace to Western influence.

It was a significant time not just for Japan itself, but also for the nation's storytellers and poets, some of whom followed the emperor's example finding refuge within verse while others elected for emotional escapes by burying their heads in classical and conventional cultural pursuits. A very determined Japan, forced like a reluctant debutant coming of age to come out into 'civilised' international society, was, however, trying to demonstrate its parity and maturity as an equitable independent nation state, as well as catch up in an intense technology race economically and culturally. Remaining a shut-in hermit nation was no longer a viable option. Japan was propelled forward into the Great Game of geopolitics, empire and colonialism in its desire for 'civilised' international credentials, strategic autonomy and industrial sovereignty.

Japan rapidly adopted new technologies, including new printing and paper-making technologies the mass-communication tools of the new modern era, as well as Western-style dress and diets incorporating meat, all designed to beef-up the nation for the future, with breath-taking speed. Grabbing ideas like magpies looking here, there and everywhere, to find the tools that would help Japan find its rightful place amongst the ranks of the leading nations.

The technological and social changes also impacted on reading habits and literary tastes. With cultural barriers now removed, with barbarians and their books no longer held beyond the gates, and borders re-opened, new narratives and writing styles that Japanese readers and creative writers had never been exposed to became suddenly available in translation. New intellectual energy was unleashed by the new printing presses. Some tried to seek refuge within tradition, while many eagerly embraced change and all that was new, and others found the pace of change bewildering.

Literacy rates doubled, reaching 80 percent. *Around the World In Eighty Days* and *Twenty Thousand Leagues Under the Sea*, published in Japanese for the first time, for example, were hugely popular, and had a major impact on Japanese authors and readers, as did Sir Thomas More's (1478-1535) *Utopia*, which was published in Japanese for the first time in 1882. This book, originally written in Latin the year before the English Reformation in 1516, is a socio-political satire about a crescent-shaped island nation with 54 cities in an undisclosed location. It struck a chord with many Meiji Japan readers, resonating as it had done with English elites hundreds of years earlier, who were looking for answers and solutions to their society's ills.

Utopia isn't, like many other such fictional and non-fiction accounts and travelogues by Europeans, a patronising tale of a nation of natives that needed civilising or better forms of morality and governance. *Utopia* is a tale of an imaginary nation-state with its own unique arrangements: a collective commonwealth with no private property or monetary currency, with religious pluralism including the worship of the sun and no concept of original sin. More's Utopia is a country powered by industriousness, hard work, reason and constant gardeners, while also being a nation with a deep love of learning and one that is responsive to nature, with ordered gardens and an understanding by all its inhabitants of the importance of agriculture. The structure and rules of Utopia, the state, are outlined, alongside a discussion of the best state of a commonwealth, in More's book, by a weathered Portuguese traveller and philosopher who had lived amongst the Utopias for five years in their uniform walled but open properties, all of which possessed beautifully manicured gardens.

Raphael Hythloday, the Portuguese traveller whose name means the dispenser of nonsense and is said to be an individual comparable to Ulysses in terms of his travelled experience, explains at a series of meetings in Antwerp that in Utopia women are not allowed to marry before the age of 18 and men 22. Before betrothal men and women are presented to each other naked by chaperones for inspection and consideration. The reasoning is explained thus:

> Men of all other nations, who, if they are but to buy a horse of a small value, are so cautious that they will see every part of him, and take off both his saddle and all his other tackle, that there may be no secret ulcer hid under any of them, and that yet in the choice of a wife, on which depends the happiness or unhappiness of the rest of his life, a man should venture upon trust, and only see about a handsbreadth of the face, all the rest of the body being covered, under which may lie hid what may be contagious as well as loathsome.

Today, the word utopia, coined by More, is a loanword commonly used in Japanese, which unlike the book and its contents most Japanese will be familiar with. Due to the way it is rendered in the Japanese language the word allows for interesting wordplay as u is written as *yu*, the same sound and letter as hot water in Japanese. Hot springs, *onsen*, sometimes promote their heavenly perfect waters and resorts as *Yu-to-pi-a*. As anyone who has visited one of these rejuvenating resorts knows, they allow for mixed bathing where individuals—married or not—of all sexes and ages can mingle naked, which arguably in its own way is a utopian-type of equalising leveller.

Sadly, populist utopian aspirations can too easily collide with and slide into autocratic dystopia, another now popular term also used in Japanese as a loanword said to have been used first after More's death by a different highly influential Englishman, John Stewart Mill (1806-1873) a proponent of utilitarianism, a set of behaviours that scholars today sometimes use to frame the Japanese government and its approaches to policy-making. That is the policy-making that has followed after the nation's expansive dystopian period as the Empire of Japan and the Second World War, a problematic development phase that one might dub the nation's aggressive 'young adult' phase, as a modern international nation state, that arose in the wake of the Meiji Restoration. The creative, journalistic and storytelling allure of the two loanwords, utopia and dystopia, and the asymmetrical worlds they can conjure up remains powerful.

More's era, despite his leading role as Lord High Chancellor of England and the new phase in English history it ushered in, was also no utopia. He was, of course, beheaded by Henry VIII (1491-1547), England's well-educated king and so-called renaissance man, at the Tower of London, after uttering his famous last words, "I die the King's good servant, and God's first." The type of courageous sentiment that encouraged Japan's Edo leaders and its Bakufu, shogun-led, government to ban Christianity with its dangerous higher authority and potentially non-Japanese allegiances, a century later, in the 1600s, bringing to an end Japan's so-called Christian Century (1549-1650), but not Christianity's long-term influence on Japanese writing.

The book's initial publication reflected the tumultuous and uncertain times in England when established approaches were being either degraded or modernised depending on your point of view, including even, for instance, England's monetary base when gold coins were later mixed with other materials allowing for the creation of two 'gold' coins from one, the so-called 'great debasement', what might today be termed as a type of innovative debt management.

Some believe this currency desecration was an early form of currency manipulation and an intervention similar to that of Quantitative Easing (QE), as well as being indicative of the heady impurity of the changing times. Interestingly, the Japanese authorities in the Edo period issued alloy gold and silver oval coins, *koban*, with differing weights and gold content through repeated recoinage. Cunningly, chemical treatments were used to tint these coins, so they all glittered brightly with a golden hue, no matter the amount of gold they actually contained, providing confidence in the shogun's coinage. The over exploitation of such techniques contributed to excessive debt and inflation and the political and economic instability and disquiet of the late Edo period. In all nations inflation, its causes and consequential effects are intertwined with public opinion, national sentiment and political stability.[25]

Nonetheless, More's book, when it finally arrived in Japanese translation, just as Japan was trying to determine what type of society and nation-state it wished to become, resonated with readers. The contextual background to the book when it was written echoed many of the contemporary concerns Japanese people had who were reading it in translation for the first time in Meiji Japan. This book and others also introduced many new ideas and perspectives, generating new terminology, describing new technologies and concepts such as society, evolution, utopia and psychoanalysis to Japan, as well as new writing styles and formats.

As is so often the case in Japan, the country learnt, absorbed, adapted and then developed its own independent approaches and arrangements in a similar manner to how the nation ingested its first imported writing system from China centuries earlier. Initially, it was a struggle for Japan and Japanese people to absorb this ideographic *kanji* writing system designed for a completely different language and syntax, with its new words and concepts, and match it to their spoken language, but with additions, time, and enhancements, for example, new local syllabary such as *hiragana*, there was soon, as we have seen, no holding back Japanese written creativity. Something similar happened in Meiji Japan. It was a Cambrian moment for Japanese publishing even if the challenges it presented for the nation were, as one local author described it, like that of "a frog that tries to swallow a bull."

Writers, designers, picture-makers and poets shape culture, and culture shapes society, making storytelling and words a powerful and important tool for thought transference, especially when narratives also provide escapes from the sober realities of the times and like any good novel manage to transcend their subjects allowing people to connect with individuals and communities, they would normally have nothing in common with. This has probably always been the case in Japan, but tellingly, it took much longer for Japan's community of writers to successfully adapt and develop what they learnt from the new books they read in translation with their unusual and alien terms, than it took other parts of Japan to learn how to brew beer, distil whisky, manufacture sheet paper, use steam-powered looms and mechanise. Nonetheless, the revolutionary linage it has spawned after their arrival, despite the importance of tradition in Japan, and some major detours, has not been a moribund backward-looking one. It took time, but it has led to an extraordinary revival in Japanese creative writing and storytelling of which many are still unfortunately not fully unaware.

Old style traditional prose was replaced, literary journals and magazines were launched, modern short story writing flourished; new works (translations and local originals) were published often in instalments, and literary awards and prizes created. This started a popular tradition that is still evident today in the nation's brilliant novella writing, and the widespread commissioning and serialisation in newspapers of new creative writing. In 1894 *Takiguchi nyudo* (*The Lay Priest*), a historical romance, by Chogyu Takayama (1871-1902), known for his romantic individualism, was selected as Japan's first awarding-winning novel by the *Yomiuri Shimbun*, a new publication at this time and now one of Japan's most important national dailies, that has since its earliest days, like other Japanese newspapers, been a supportive ally of Japanese literature and authorship. Its success and serialisation helped spawn hundreds of other such prizes. Takayama, however, only wrote one novel.

More so than other newspapers the *Yomiuri Shimbun* still supports new and fine writing, as well as music and culture. Reportedly, it pays contemporary authors the best rates for serialised fiction for the morning and evening editions of its national newspapers and it also awards the annual Yomiuri Prize, founded in 1949, for fiction, translation, essays and travelogue, and poetry.

In Japan's post-war years, a very unsettling and difficult time for many when radical change was required yet again, the newspaper consciously developed a cultural counter-offensive strategy, which included launching its annual prize and other activities that it still supports that extend to music and other creative arts. This new approach focused on a cultural reconstruction designed to re-write Japan's post-war behaviours. During the Showa era's war years writing, journalism and publishing, as well as the select literary authors that became overseas correspondents, were heavily constrained through official and self-censorship. The leadership at newspapers like the *Yomiuri Shimbun* knew things had to change and Japan and its opinion leading publications must adopt new approaches.

Today, Japan boasts multiple entries in the *Guinness Book of World Records* for publishing with records that span feats such as the world's smallest printed book and the bestselling comic book series by a single author, to list just two such examples, more than 500 different domestic literary awards, as well as many international prizewinning authors, writers who have gone global, and authors who remain in the shadows, invisible to readers outside Japan. A revival that, has taken time, and according to leading Japanese commentators, European and American writers, with a few noticeable exceptions, have not paid sufficient attention to. Japan shouldn't be, and, these days, doesn't need to be, a literary afterthought.

Japanese creative writing has endured and flourished even as it has transversed several tumultuous periods in history including some violent and highly expansive times. There have, of course, also been some open and more inclusive phases of old like today's, such as the Taisho era (1912-1926), discussed later on in this collection. While being finessed by generations of storytellers, the nation's wordcraft charges ever onwards: creating new literary patterns and trends. Each time Japan faces a new catastrophic event or existential threat, be it an atomic bomb, an earthquake, an extreme economic shock, a Meiji-like forced opening, a devastating detour into warfare and military expansionism, or even an unusually long period of stability when the cogs of progress turn slowly and invisibly, society seems to suddenly be able to rapidly rearrange its components, some of which most people would have supposed unalterable, twisting and turning, and composes new patterns that are then vividly reflected in Japan's all-terrain creative storytelling. Out of crisis springs literary opportunity, and, to the delight of many readers, not all tales merely portray the nation through beguiling picture book formulaic rose-tinted spectacles.

Some of the nation's best and most-loved tales are stories of extraordinary outsiders, iconoclastic nonconformists, the silenced, the marginalised, the bullied, and other societal misfits, be they Christians practising their religion in hiding, oddball detectives, or people deemed as societal outcasts. The postmodern author Kenji Nakagami (1946-1992) is one such writer. He was the first writer born after the Second World War to win the all-important Akutagawa Prize in 1976. Despite non-conformists often being nailed back down by society, bringing those slightly out of kilter or not in line with the norm in particular back down to the mean, Japan actually has significant form in terms of the publication of atypical voices, some of whom like Nakagami even go on to win important prizes.

Unlike many renowned contemporary prizewinning Japanese authors, Nakagami, did not attend Waseda University in Tokyo or in fact any university. His work *Misaki (The Cape)*, a disturbing costal tale of complex family histories, troubled memories and hopelessness on the edges at the very bottom of Japan's social hierarchy, that reflect his own humble upbringing, won him this prestigious place in Japanese publishing history, and has encouraged many others who might otherwise not have tried to tell their stories and write. Their tales don't just provide readers with access to subcultures, they help document the quirks of the nation for historians, providing alternative studies of society, as well as fascinating entertainment.

Once we are immersed firmly between the covers, books can act as routes for creative escape and literary tools for accepting the unacceptable by perhaps reaffirming readers' acceptance of their own station in life, no matter how uncomfortable. This type of non-conformist storytelling has a long linage in Japan and the continued success of these types of books and their appeal clearly shows that Japan is not a monocultural collective blob, but a nation full of diverse and individual storytellers that regularly get published.

The struggle to conform and the pressures and challenges of life in Japan no matter the era, with the often-isolating lonely trials of trying to find one's own form of individuality and a place within society where you belong can make for some riveting storytelling. As we all know, fiction at its best can sometimes function as a much-needed reality distortion field in uncertain times, be they personal, international or national.

Japan by the Book

Since the breakthrough success of Yoshimoto and Murakami, there has been an exponentially increasing interest and awareness internationally in Japanese storytelling. This trend merits exploration concerning why this might be the case.

Astute trendsetters and culturally sensitive individuals who have left permanent cultural imprints internationally such as Hesse and David Bowie (1947-2016), who was fascinated by Japan and cited Mishima as one of his favourite authors, have picked up on the nation's importance and merits, as well as the juxtaposition that Japanese writers and Japan can provide, long before most. Rudyard Kipling (1865-1936), the first British Nobel laureate and at forty-one the youngest-ever recipient, is another good example: his writings on Japan were cited by the Nobel Prize committee when he won his prize in 1907. All of them in their own unique ways were early adopters of the delights and cultural importance of Japan. It is, however, not too late to catch up with these trailblazers.

Since the publication of Samuel P. Huntington's (1927-2008) seminal book *The Clash of Civilizations and the Remaking of World Order* in 1996, a book that with prescience predicted the world was entering a new distinct phase, we have unfortunately frequently witnessed acts of different types of terrorism, and regional conflicts, as well as a type of religious and tribal cultural collision between mostly monotheistic civilisations. As a nation of islands, Japan, even though it has its own difficult challenges and is by no means a utopia, has managed to escape what some Japanese authors, such as Kanji Hanawa (1936-2020) a former professor of French literature with a deep interest in psychology, term the "collateral damage" caused by monotheism. This has allowed Japan to retain its own culture, a culture that can often provide a stimulating alternative perspective.

Other authors like the aforementioned postmodern author Soji Shimada put it down to Japan's lucky escape from the net of colonialism. Uchimura no doubt would probably attribute this to Japan spending its development phase, its cultural adolescence, in a long-controlled isolation. Perhaps, this is simply another manifestation of the side effects of the Galapagos Syndrome and part of the overall attraction. Whatever the case, it seems to show that Western civilisation has not standardised itself fully or uniformly across the globe and is perhaps not the prerequisite for fully functioning modernisation that some have believed.

Nevertheless, this emblematic increasing fascination with Japan is not actually that new. In Jonathan Swift's (1667-1745) classic story *Gulliver's Travels*, published in 1726, Lemuel Gulliver's passage to Japan is recorded in Part III of this fictional travelogue alongside the imaginary lands of the tiny Lilliputians, the giant Brobdingnagians, and the creatures known as the Yahoos that Gulliver's adventures are now famous for. Swift thus anchored Japan and its elusive realities, including Yedo (Edo) and the duplicitous Dutch, who monopolised Western trade with Japan for long periods, alongside those of eternally inaccessible imaginary nations.

Travelling, or reading and writing about travel, can change us. Charles Darwin's (1809-1882) description of how he anticipated his own personal adventure of discovery and great passage on his vessel HMS Beagle, which ended up not just changing how he saw the world but how humanity sees itself, no doubt will resonate better with some: "I look forward to the Galapagos with more interest than any other part of the voyage... The natural history of this archipelago is very remarkable: it seems to be a little world within itself."[26]

In his case, the volcanic archipelago, he was visiting consisted of 13 major and six minor uninhabited islands, compared to Japan's archipelago of thousands of islands and over 100 active volcanoes, with their own connected creation stories—the *Kojiki*—of a land proceeded and evolved from the rising sun, a national domain that stretches thousands of kilometres from north to south. The Galapagos, with its rich ocean currents and azure shores, proved to be the perfect place, for Darwin, to observe the world and for him to develop a framework to understand our planet, his personal heritage, life itself and his place within it.

Some locations seem to have a knack for this. Geography is said to be destiny. It certainly shapes what can and cannot be successfully prioritised and preserved, the large or the small for instance, especially in nations, like Japan, prone to natural disasters and extreme weather. Japan and its writers are acutely aware of the country's terrain and of a cultural context that loves to endlessly document itself. Few would deny that Japan has its own body language and cultural landscape, even if it is not actually a single entity. It is, however, a nation one might hesitantly say that tends to write its heart out, one forged in prose and storytelling while oddly in parallel, especially by those who don't read its authors, is still often described as contradictory and inscrutable.

Some nations and speakers of given languages are famed for gestures, talking with hands, others for their slick showmanship and salesman-like styles of communication. Some countries seem to give preference to verbal and audio-visual communication skills over written content and context. What societies manage to preserve and prioritise and what they obsess about, in song or prose, verse or film, not only in terms of capturing and preserving the past, their heritage, as they try to navigate through endless cycles of change and loss, is highly indicative of the state of civic health. In this regard, Japan and by association its many writers are in rude health.

The Write Stuff

Culture is, of course, not a biologically transmitted system even if some argue, with some controversy, that through self-replicating memes it may in fact be analogous. Nonetheless, with the right map, even though these days many don't require the guidance of the past, Japanese creative writing with its sea of words, packages of prose, array of authors and genres that reflect the topography of Japan's own geographical cultural terrain, can have a similar transformative ability. Readers need to find the right entry point into the eclectic kaleidoscopic world of Japanese letters.

Entertaining false starts are common. After all, maps in Japan displayed in public locations, for instance, often reflect the immediate location the observer is looking out at for the quickest route to their desired destination, not directional geographical convention. The *kanji* character for north will not necessarily be found at the top of these maps. Rather, at times, you are just as likely to find the east located at the top commanding a central role. This form of Japanese cartography is generally two dimensional, and sadly unlike literature, has a tendency not to conjure up multi-dimensional easy-to-navigate life changing perspective even if they regularly cause amusing and memorable wild goose chases for tourists. It is not where you currently stand, it is the new perspectives from new vantage points that should matter.

Short Story Writing

Stripped back to the essentials. Compact but still complete. Intelligently and stylishly packaged with quality shining through. These are traits that have been applied to Japanese product design, art, architecture and food for generations. Interestingly, they are also the perfect terms to describe the nation's creative writing. For centuries, Japanese writers have captivated and surprised their readers, often giving them pause for thought along the way. In very many instances they have done so through elegant short-form formats.

The typical definition of a 'short story' is a piece of narrative prose that can be read in one session: shorter than a novel but as complete in terms of storytelling. It's fitting then that in Japan, a nation known to have mastered the art of the miniature, the format is flourishing with thousands being penned every year. New and established authors continue to write short stories and novellas that are adapting into new, exciting styles and formats. This type of work frequently wins literary awards. Japan has an incredible history of short-form writing that is as rich as it is diverse.

There is everything here from verse to the modern short story. Since the 10th century, Japanese readers have been captivated by tales of time-travel and shape shifting in which people are transformed into birds, for instance, and fly away from strife and turmoil. Then, of course, there are the evocative and deftly crafted poetry collections of old, such as the eighth century *Manyoshu* (*Collection of Ten Thousand Leaves*). All of which gave rise to haiku and tanka, the hugely popular Japanese-style of poetry that continues to thrive today even in a world of digital paperless publishing. Tens of thousands of people in Japan and across the world now happily publish and read tanka and haiku online.

A former Swedish Ambassador to Japan, Dr. Lars Vargo, even recommends Japanese short-form poetry as a tool for decoding Japan's intellectual DNA.[27] This may seem to some an odd or elitist way to deconstruct Japan, and one of seeing Japan only through its high-culture, but Japanese cultural undercurrents fizz with lexical-assembly and short-form writing, with poetry and author names popping up in all sorts of unexpected places.

Traditional Japanese playing card games such as *Hyakunin Isshu, One Hundred Poets, One Poem Each*, that require rapid reading skills, excellent visual awareness, sharp elbows, as well as more than a trivial knowledge of tanka poets and poems are still, for instance, popular pursuits today, especially during Japan's New Year holidays when families get together. These poetic cards function not just as cultural metaphors that encourage inter-family competition. They also provide links to Japan's long lineage of the literary arts and the importance the nation has put on wordplay, wordcraft and literary expression for generations.

The appearance of Japan's scribes is not limited to traditional family card-grabbing parlour games. *Bungo sutorei doggusu* (*Bungo Stray Dogs*), a manga about a detective agency, is a different sort of non-traditional example. In its case it features characters with supernatural powers named after famous authors including Japan's James Dean-like (1931-1955) bad boy author Osamu Dazai (1909-1948) and Ryunosuke Akutagawa (1892-1927) as well as Russian novelist Fyodor Dostoevsky (1821-1881) in its action-packed tale. The 2021 anime, *Saida no yoni kotoba ga wakiagaru* (*Words Bubble Up like Soda-Pop*), is another classic example. It features haiku and a specialist print dictionary concealed within a smartphone case as a tool for shy young people looking for love to communicate digitally using messaging and social media.

There are also works like Shion Miura's (b. 1976) 2011 book, *Fune wo amu* (*The Great Passage*), about a group of diligent and passionate individuals immersed in the intricacies of the Japanese language and its lexicography while working on a major new edition of a dictionary. *The Great Passage* has, as is so often the case with successful publications like this in Japan, morphed into a lucrative media franchise spawning popular spins-offs including a film, anime and manga. It is hard to imagine a similarly successful publishing phenomenon based around the editorial team at Oxford University Press (OUP) working on a new edition of its dictionary or other reference works such as the *Oxford Dictionary of National Biography* or the *Oxford Book of Verse*. Japan even has prime time celebrity television haiku competitions with similar formats to Britain's hugely popular television show *Strictly Come Dancing*, where celebrities learn the basics of writing haiku, as opposed to ballroom dancing, and then compete, with some improving rapidly in front of viewers' eyes, to write the best verse based on an agreed theme.

Vargo, the retired ambassador, likes to recall sitting at a dinner next to former Prime Minister Tsutomu Hata (1935-2017), who served only for 64 days. He was at a loss how to make small talk until he decided to ask Hata if he could recommend a good Japanese poet, something which Hata happily did. Hiroshi Yoshino (1926-2014) a multi-award-winning poet from Yamagata, the winner of the 23rd Yomiuri

Prize for Literature Haiku Award for his poem "Kansho ryoko" ("Sentimental Trip"), was the Prime Minister's poet of choice. Dinner conversation then flowed, encouraging Vargo to make a habit of asking the same question in similar social situations. Regularly generating comparable successful results. Many high-ranking officials and politicians in Japan are interested in literature and poetry. Short conversations about short-form writing can, it appears, open doors and encourage the superfluous and polite dignities of diplomacy to melt away.

One of Vargo's favourite Japanese poems is one by Rin Ishigaki (1920-2004), a female poet and a clerk at the Industrial Bank of Japan (Mizuho Bank) with a rebellious and cynical attitude, titled "In the stomachs of one hundred guests", that Vargo says often springs to mind, perhaps dependent on who is sat next to him and how his question is answered, at formal and large dinners:

On the table one hundred plates, in front of one hundred guests, on the plates one hundred flatfish, the subtle sound of cutlery, of the fish some bones are left a bit of the head, and the tail

(What would Her Highness say if she saw you leave too much?)

One hundred gentlemen, and ladies wipe their mouths with white napkins and speak with dignity to each other "What is it with this world?"

In one hundred stomachs lie one hundred dead fish

Long History of Blending Brevity and Beauty

Some academics including, for example, the linguistics historian Susumu Ono (1919-2008), have argued that the Japanese word *utsukushii*, beautiful, is an adjective that also expresses affection for 'diminutive objects'. The word, *utsukushii*, was used in the famous Japanese short story the "Taketori monogatari" ("Tale of the Bamboo Cutter") also known as "Princess Kaguya", which appeared in its current form between 939 and 956. This folktale is, however, probably better known today because of the 2013 Studio Ghibli animated film. When the childless bamboo cutter and his wife find a diminutive glowing child, who they subsequently find out is from the moon, within a stick of bamboo they utter the word *utsukushii* with delight. That is how their first contact is marked with a delightful extra-terrestrial child, a doorway to a host of new emotional experiences that bring them much joy, commences. The word *utsukushii* is also used in the *Manyoshu*, Japan's oldest poetry anthology as a word for love and admiration of many things, including of course the small and short.

The best-known Japanese literary allusion to the admiration of all that is small was written by one of Japan's first pioneering female authors, Shonagon Sei (circa 966-1025), who formed part of a group of Heian period (794-1158) women who could be thought of as the world's first 'Chick-Lit' authors, even though this term is now considered by some to be derogatory and dated, with negative connotations that do not apply to these important authors. In *Makura no soshi* (*The Pillow Book*) she wrote that, "All things small, no matter what it is, are beautiful." By this she meant everything including the Zen-like beauty of brevity, incompleteness and short prose. Ironically, the English translation of her book runs to more than 400 pages. It is, however, made up of short entries, anecdotes and lists, all of which are exquisitely written. In this sense, Shonagon applied the aesthetic she so admired to her own writing and many have followed her creative lead.

This all took place centuries before the term flash fiction (fiction of extreme brevity) was coined, or the appearance of X (Twitter), the dominant short-form writing of our era, which struggled unsuccessfully to restrict posts first to 140, and then 280 characters (compared to the 17 syllables allowed in traditional haiku). Unlike X, the Japanese haiku format with its eloquent economy, has managed to cross borders and languages while mostly maintaining its structure and rules and is still recognised internationally for its elegance and sophisticated wit.

As mentioned at the beginning of this essay, Japan's short-form writing isn't limited to these popular forms of poetry or to a single genre. The long tradition of short story writing in Japan is broad based and has continued mostly uninterrupted until today. The multi-nominated and award-winning authors Kazufumi Shiraishi (b. 1958), Mitsuyo Kakuta (b. 1967), Yasumi Tsuhara (1964-2022) and the madcap surrealist Yasutaka Tsutsui (b. 1934) represent a handful of the many prominent and respected recent exponents of the art, who continue to write short stories even after they have become established Japanese literary figures. Haruki Murakami (b. 1949) is another good example. As well as his many other accolades, he has won international recognition for short stories, for instance, winning the Frank O'Connor International Short Story Award in 2006.

Compact Narrative Strides

I imagined with virtual certainty that he too, like me, was a mule being pulled along by an invisible rope. I never saw him sitting at his desk, but I had a very strong sense that we were kindred spirits. I was sure he had a desk in an upstairs room, where from dawn to dusk he would sit and write short stories, just as I did. *Shinobu kawa* (*Shame in the Blood*) by Testsuo Miura (1931-2010).

In Japan, the ability to write short-form fiction is considered an essential building block in most authors' writing development and also an essential component in the literary armoury of established authors. At particular times in Japanese history the short form has played an oversized role, helping document with literary snapshots, from multiple viewpoints, a changing nation in a style and manner that allows contemporary readers to look back in time and in some cases forwards into the future. Yasunari Kawabata (1899-1972) was a prolific short story and novella writer who also actively encouraged others to follow suit. It was in fact his short stories that got him noticed after he graduated from Tokyo Imperial University. Japan's only other Nobel laureate author, Kenzaburo Oe (1935-2023), was also a fan and has penned some classics. "Fui no oshi" ("Unexpected Muteness"), a deadly tragedy set at the end of the Second World War, is a fine example.

The immediate aftermath of Japan's unconditional surrender from the Second World War which Emperor Hirohito (1901-1989) announced on 15 August 1945 was a complicated, disorientating and frightening time for all in Japan. In October 1945, immediately after the war ceased, Japan faced many unknowns and was gripped with huge new challenges. These included, for instance, unrestrained inflation with prices of products, according to the Bank of Japan, trading on the black market at 29 times higher than official prices, and a staggering 92 times higher than prices a decade earlier. Japan was cash-strapped, flattened and extremely anxious. Uncertain times make for fascinating literary settings, and often for memorable and influential short stories such as Oe's. In his tale "Unexpected Muteness", after American soldiers arrive by jeep in a small Japanese settlement just after the war has ended, they unwittingly spawn an escalating series of 'first contact' type challenges that culminate, not in joy, but in two needless deaths.

Oe's short story, published in 1958, captures the tricky disorienting times wonderfully as well as the challenges that unfiltered raw verbal and non-verbal stressed communication can elicit. Oe's tale manages to simultaneously illustrate the dangers and the power of persistent silence. "Unexpected Muteness" is a tragedy, not about something simply being lost in translation, but loss triggered by stubborn pride and a missing pair of shoes belonging to the Americans' interpreter. The irony that his role should have been to bridge understanding, not to amplify discord, is at the heart of the story. Discord that causes discomforting unease and pointless deaths, including his own.

Unlike U.S. Naval Intelligence, the U.S. Army frequently used soldiers of Japanese descent with U.S. nationality, who already spoke Japanese, as interpreters, such as the awkward and conflicted individual depicted in this unfortunate Oe tale. In these stressed and unforgiving times this could cause unintended consequences. In contrast, Naval Intelligence tended to rely more on the products, officers, of its language-training programme for its interpreters and translators, not always fully trusting Japanese Americans for these roles. The long-term repercussions of this policy spawned a cluster of highly influential Japanologists, scholars, literary translators and diplomats who have left marks and impressive footsteps in front of the many who have followed. These include, for example, Edwin O. Reischauer (1910-1990), one of the early proponents behind the Navy's Japanese language school, designed to teach linguists how to speak and read Japanese, and a future U.S. Ambassador to Japan. At Harvard University, for example, Reischauer subsequently taught John Nathan, Oe's future English language translator and the translator of many other important Japanese writers, such as Soseki Natsume (1867-1916), Kobo Abe (1924-1993) and Yukio Mishima (1925-1970). The historian Edward G. Seidensticker (1921-2007), who translated Kawabata as well as Junichiro Tanizaki (1886-1965) and Kafu Nagai (1879-1959), is another impressive example of a former student of the U.S. Navy Japanese Language School. Seidensticker also translated *Genji monogatari (The Tale of Genji)*.

The interpreter in Oe's tale is, however, very different. He is not an academically trained superstar linguist destined to play an important future role in bilateral diplomacy and research, but a self-conscious young American in Japan for the very first time, something that amplifies an already combustible situation. Despite the quality of Oe's prose, "Unexpected Muteness" is not a poetic ode to the often-depicted delights of cross-cultural communication and the cultural contortions they sometimes elicit or the art of international diplomacy. It is a compact muted statement of the bloody and uneasy times, and an excellent example of the power of Japanese short story writing with a clear narrative message.

The war years themselves were also uneasy, bloody times, creating an impossible quandary for Japanese authors and artists over whether it was their duty to support the war effort in China, the Pacific Ocean, and other locations, within their prose or to take a stand against it. Some argued it was a storm that would pass and no matter the rights and wrongs of the war, it was their duty to support the nation and individuals at the front. Some authors and potential authors, who subsequently became famous, kept quiet and tried to avoid being sent to the front by studying medicine at university.

Many liberal arts students had no choice and were conscripted. Some established authors were encouraged as members of organisations such as the Bungei

Jugo Undo, Literary Home-Front Campaign, to visit Japanese-occupied areas on the Korean Peninsula, and in Eastern and Northern China, for example, and write about their observations. These included authors well-known today and important literary critics, such as Kawabata and Hideo Kobayashi (1902-1983). Some were even hired as special correspondents for newspapers, allowing them to live overseas for the first time, generally in China, a nation, due to its long-term influence on all forms of Japanese writing, that fascinated many Japanese writers and intellectuals. Surveillance and censorship existed and being outspoken or breaking the rules could lead to an author finding themselves in jail or conscripted and sent to the front. Some, including Mishima, for instance, were subsequently consumed with guilt for not fighting, having managed to avoid being drafted. Other writers outlived the war with their reputations and consciences intact. But not all.

One such writer was Tatsuzo Ishikawa (1905-1985), winner in 1935 of the inaugural Akutagawa Prize for his novella *Sobo* (*The People*) a short narrative about a group of Japanese farmers who plan to emigrate to Brazil and their troubled escape and experiences at an immigration office in the port city of Kobe. As a result of his success he was sent by the editors of *Chuo Koron*, a prestigious monthly magazine, to China in early 1938 as a special correspondent. The determined and independent-minded young author arrived in Nanjing, China's capital at the time, just after the city was captured and devastatingly sacked by the Japanese Imperial Army.

Ishikawa was embedded within an army unit. This led to him penning a serialised short novel documenting what he observed during the so-called liberation of the city entitled *Iketeiru heitai* (*Soldiers Alive*) for the magazine. His earlier prizewinning novel was also similarly based on personal experience, in its case of finding his way to Brazil, where he had lived briefly before returning to Japan. Unsurprisingly, sections of his novella *Soldiers Alive* were censored, leading to Ishikawa's arrest and conviction on charges of 'disturbing peace and order' and breaching the Newspaper Law.

Soldiers Alive was finally published in book format in 1945 when the Newspaper Law was revoked. Censorship and limits on freedom of expression, however, continued for several years after the war ended with different sets of rules being applied within Japan by the Allied Powers to those adopted in their home nations. This, however, did not put an end to creative writing and short-form fiction for long.

Amazingly, a short story, the Akutagawa Prize, and the literary critic Kobayashi probably saved one author's life. When Ashihei Hino's (1907-1960) short tale *Fun'nyotan* (*A Tale of Excrement and Urine*) won the Akutagawa Prize in 1937, Hino, whose outspoken tendencies and union organising had already got him into serious trouble, was stationed as a conscripted soldier on the front line in China. Kobayashi, who was in China at the time the prize was announced, with the help of the Japanese military, notified Hino of this literary honour and arranged an impromptu award ceremony. Subsequently, Hino was treated as a minor celebrity and was moved to a much safer position in Central China with the military's Information Division. During the war years, Hino became well-known for his war novels, one of which sold over a million copies, about the daily lives of Japanese soldiers.

Despite criticism after the war, most of these writers were not purged, or what might be termed cancelled in today's terminology, from public life, despite being tarred directly or indirectly with Japan's propaganda output. Kobayashi, for example, continued to write from his study in his hilltop home in Kamakura surrounded by his well-kept garden, with its delightful plum blossom tree and distant views of the Pacific Ocean and their everchanging colours. He won numerous prizes for his contribution to the literary arts and has a prize for works of non-fiction named after him. Readers in Japan and internationally have benefited significantly from individuals like him and their continued post-war contribution to the world of letters. Hino, however, had a much more challenging and far less smooth post-war transition than Kobayashi and Kawabata. He killed himself in 1960 at the age of 53.

Another powerful example of a short tale depicting a similar pivotal period is "Amerikan Sukuru" ("American School"), by Nobuo Kojima (1915-2006) penned slightly earlier than Oe's tale but set a little later. This award-winning satirical short story portrays a group of Japanese teachers of English during the occupation in 1948 visiting a school on a military base in Japan. Tellingly, each teacher deals with the experience and the occupation itself very differently, again reflecting the awkward and problematic high anxiety period.

This narrative also features shoes as a motif, as well as cultural conflict between the occupiers and the occupied, and complex inter-personal group dynamics with an undertone of what might be called today institutional racism. In this case, it is a borrowed pair of ill-fitting leather shoes to be worn on the march to the American school by the tale's shy anti-hero Isa, an English teacher who hates speaking English. Isa decides to remove his uncomfortable, constricting toe-pinching shoes, going barefoot to the American school, something that a black American soldier at the base where the school is located finds odd and questions.

Cultural reaction through this type of storytelling, especially in the short form with its focused properties, can cleverly push boundaries while challenging why one set of rules apply in one location, but not elsewhere, highlighting not only inconsistencies of purpose, but hypocrisy. Short stories are also a terrific tool for quickly getting an impression of a given period in Japan's historical development, functioning collectively as a social encyclopaedia of the times. Multiple perspectives contained in one tale, or from reading several by one or many authors, can unite into a provocative whole that provides a glimpse underneath Japan's mantle, and the veneer of its polite overcoat.

One of the teachers in Kojima's tale confesses to war crimes, while another, the only woman amongst the Japanese group, a war widow who excels at English, is depicted as a goldfish in the drawings that the American children sketch of the Japanese teachers who visit them. The Americans, Kojima depicts, mostly sow tension between the Japanese teachers, or treat them with condescension, not viewing the Japanese teachers as racial or civilisational equals. In "American School", Kojima manages to generate a multi-layered short tale that pokes fun at all, not just the hypocrisy of the Allied Occupation of Japan (1945-1952) by challenging readers to question what is being reaped from the American school and the role this so-called international seat of learning should play in Japan's future.

Revealingly, "American School" was published in 1954, after the occupation had officially ended, when Japan, with its brand-new 'MacArthur' Constitution with universal suffrage, drafted in English by mostly American experts was being implemented in Japanese translation by Japan. The tale was written when the nation was back in charge of its policy-making, including how it educated its youth, designed its curriculum and trained its teachers. It makes the cultural exploration and the burden of history that lurks behind the placid modernity and superficial normality of Kojima's educational exchange, a timely reminder of the trials of a nation trying to navigate a brand-new course.

Interpersonal themes, fragmented perspectives and conflicted individuals often add largeness to short-form fiction. The Japanese cultural landscape is riddled with the signatures of Japanese authors like Kawabata, Kojima and Oe who excel at exploiting this. Compact objects, even the written narrative variety, can have a strong and mysterious pull. The importance of which shouldn't be underestimated. After all these days, even economists and central bankers study how narratives shape sentiment and societal and economic trends. Their research includes the role of so-called threat narratives, which depict how offsetting and contradictory forces contribute to both the avoidance and causing of behavioural outcomes and their knock-on influence on society and the economy, concepts at the very heart of these two important short stories from Oe and Kojima.

Akutagawa, after whom one of Japan's most sought-after prestigious literary awards is named, is another past master of the short story format. Akutagawa is best known outside Japan for his short story "Yabu no naka" ("In a Grove"), published in 1922, which cleverly employs multiple narrative viewpoints in the form of witness statements of a single crime, a rape, giving the impression that reality is never what it first seems. This story's unique multi-perspective structure and ambiguous narrative was unlike most typical translated Western stories available at the time in Japan when it was published.

Readers of "In a Grove" are left totally unsure as to the true outcome of this intriguing but compact tale, an authentic kaleidoscopic reflection perhaps of the real world in which the true nature of things cannot always be readily determined. The award-winning 1950s film *Rashomon* based on Akutagawa's story directed by Akira Kurosawa (1910-1998) introduced similar techniques to the world of cinematic storytelling. Akutagawa also wrote many others excellent short stories including, for example, "Jigokuhen" ("The Hell Screen"), "Kappa" and "Aru aho no issho" ("The Life of a Stupid Man").

Another Japanese master of the short story, from a very different genre, is the science fiction writer Shinichi Hoshi (1926-1997), who also has a literary award named after him. He wrote thousands of short stories, many of which would now be defined as flash fiction. One of his best-known short stories is "Bokko-chan", written in 1963. It is only six-pages long and a favoured text of Japanese language students looking to read their first Japanese short story in Japanese.

It is about a glamorous young female bar hostess named Bokko-chan. No one knows or suspects that she is actually a robot designed by the bar's owner. She helps enhance the bar's takings through two simple functional abilities, namely by making simple conversation offering basic replies or just repeating what she hears; and by being able to drink alcohol when offered to her by customers that frequent the bar. Drinks that can be recycled and resold. Inevitably, one of the bar patrons with suicidal thoughts falls in love with her, with dire consequences.

The Long and the Short of it: Shorts are a Western Import

Despite this rich pedigree, the modern Japanese short story is actually a foreign import. The modern format emerged in the United States, France, Germany, and Russia almost simultaneously in the 19th century, with various writers making major contributions. It is usually American writers like Nathaniel Hawthorne (1804-1864), Edgar Allan Poe (1809-1849) and Herman Melville (1819-1891) who are credited with writing some of the very first modern short stories. The new format reflected changing media consumption, as well as the growing popularity and increased access to journalism. Realistic narratives that reflected familiar sounding events and the personalities of the time became very popular.

In his 1846 essay, *The Philosophy of Composition*, Poe wrote: "a short story should be read in one sitting, anywhere from a half hour to two hours." According to Poe, who has had a major impact on many Japanese writers and is still highly respected in Japan today, "A short story is one that concentrates on a unique or single effect and in which totality of the effect is the main objective." In contemporary fiction, a short story can range from 1,000 to 20,000 words.

Many of the world's greatest authors also admired and wrote short stories. Among them, Leo Tolstoy (1828-1910), James Joyce (1882-1941) and J. D. Salinger (1919-2010) to name just a few. Famously, Dostoevsky is apocryphally cited as having said that all modern Russian literature came out of a single short story, one by Nikolai Gogol (1809-1852) "The Overcoat", a tale about a St. Petersburg clerk with a coat with a cat-fur collar.[28] This illustrates again the perceived power of and influence short-form writing can have. In recent years the publication of short stories has sadly been in relative decline in many countries, with perhaps the exception of Japan. Indeed, several journalists and commentators have written about its gradual global demise and fall from grace, even in America where it is said to have all began.[29]

While many amateur writers outside Japan use the short story format to hone their writing skills, masters of the genre in Japan are dedicated to the format and never feel compelled to graduate completely from the short to the long. Typically in Japan, short stories are also used as an important test for evaluating young writers in writing competitions held by magazines and publishers. Mishima, probably still one of Japan's most internationally recognised authors, explained the practice to Western journalists during a speech he gave in English at The Foreign Correspondents' Club in Tokyo (FCCJ) many years ago.

"It is," said Mishima, "a sort of, four round match for green boy in boxing. If he can fight four rounds, he can fight five rounds, six rounds, and more and more." in other words, if you can take the criticism and the knocks and stay on your feet you have a potential writing career ahead of you.

It is widely known that Kawabata, the great supporter of the format, who became a close and valued friend of Mishima, helped and encouraged Mishima in his early short story writing phase, something that Mishima acknowledged and was incredibly grateful for. "He was extremely kind to me, to help me, to show my short story on literary magazine called *Human*, which was very popular at the period," explained Mishima publicly to a group of Western journalists. "Because of him," he continued, "I became to have very, very small fame as short story writer, as a newcomer in literary field. But still I was out of fashion."

This, however, changed instantly with the publication of *Kamen no kokuhaku (Confessions of a Mask)* in 1949, though its overnight success did not put an end to Mishima's short story writing. Like most of Japan's best writers, he kept writing them and enjoying them as a reader too.

The Ultimate Pocket-Sized Tale

According to Donald Keene (1922-2019), one of Mishima's translators, another product of the U.S. Navy's language training programme and a highly regarded professor of Japan literature, Mishima thought that Akutagawa's "Hankachi" ("The Handkerchief"), was the ultimate Japanese short story. His choice, like the story itself, reflects the changing sensibilities of the times, Mishima's emerging political tastes and the messy adaptive development that Japan has continued to struggle through. The story, which has the following opening line: "Hasegawa Kinzo, professor in the Faculty of Law at Tokyo Imperial University, was sitting in a rattan chair on the veranda, reading Strindberg's Dramaturgy," was published in 1916 in *Chuo Koron*, the influential monthly magazine that Ishikawa wrote for when he was in China. In 1999, *Chuo Koron*, founded in 1887 and one of Japan's oldest continuously published magazines, was bought by the *Yomiuri Shimbun* newspaper group. It remains a highly influential publication and a champion of short-form writing.

"The Handkerchief" is a story touched with subtle cynicism about a Japanese professor of colonial policy married to an American woman who loves Japanese culture, and the narrative concerns itself with the struggle of modernisation. The professor is modelled on the celebrated international statesman Inazo Nitobe (1862-1933) and a criticism of his book *Bushido (Bushido: The Soul of Japan)*, now considered a classic, published in 1900 in English and subsequently in many other languages including Japanese and Spanish. Before picking up Mishima's ultimate short tale, it is, however, important to recall that Nitobe penned his book in a very different era, decades before Mishima's birth, when the world was discovering Japan and Japan its modern self, and some 16 years before Akutagawa's fascinating short tale was actually written. Many at the time felt the nation needed explaining and in those days in a distinct manner to the frameworks subsequently exploited by the authors that followed, a trend that continues today.

That said, it is hard not to admire Mishima's choice, the tale's eloquence and cunning strategic withholding of information toys with the very concept of the so-called spirit of Japaneseness. Handkerchiefs are a cut of cloth not indigenous to Japan, a loanword written in the Japanese alphabet used for imported foreign concepts and words. Still, Akutagawa manages to use one as a motif for both the spirited exceptionalism of Japan, proposed by the likes of Nitobe, and at the same time as a narrative device for pointing out the impermanence and hypocrisy of complacent long-held beliefs, including the immutable uniqueness of Japanese attitudes and behaviours such as noble endurance. Prodding and playing brilliantly with the illusion of national character, cleverly reminding readers that the soul of things is elusive and evades most.

Japan's sudden appearance on the world's stage was a shock for many inside and outside Japan. The price of internationalisation and the status it can bring is scrutiny. The rise of Japan and traces of the fears it has at times spawned, which have spanned the economic to the racial, and the perceived necessity to constantly explain the inscrutable nation of Japan, can be found in many places, some unexpected, as well as in a vast array of published works. At the turn of the century when Nitobe wrote his book, Japan's rising relevance, somewhat like that of China's today, featured in the conversations of national leaders, newspaper columns and at international summits.

In 1904, a few years after Nitobe's book was published, at an Anglo-German summit between Wilhelm II (1859-1941), the German Emperor and so-called Last Kaiser, and Britain's King Edward VII (1841-1910) in Kiel, a German port city on the Baltic Sea coast, Wilhelm reportedly, with the Russo-Japanese War (1904-1905) in mind, mentioned the "Yellow Peril," which he called "the greatest peril menacing... Christendom and European civilization." If the Russians went on giving ground, he argued, the "yellow race," would, in twenty years' time, be in Moscow and Posen.[30] He suggested that the British were committing "race treason" in their support of Japan, its ally, which some described at the time as a country of "little yellow monkeys."

The war with Russia, presented by some in Japan as a war for civilisation and the open door of free trade, was the topic of Nitobe's day. For Japan the war and the naval Battle of Tsushima, which comprehensively destroyed the Russian fleet, depicted by some as the most stunning naval event since the Battle of Trafalgar in 1805, was a quick transformational profile-raising victory that surprised and shocked many. It was also hugely damaging for Russia and its international prestige, a victory that some argue led to the subsequent up-rising against Tsar Nicholas II of Russia (1868-1918) and the first Russian Revolution of 1905, in addition to Japan gaining control of Russian territories in Korea and China.

In response to the Kaiser, King Edward, no doubt cognizant of the geopolitical climate of the age and the potential benefits for Britain from Japan's humiliation of Russia, is said to have stated that he "could not see it. The Japanese were an intelligent, brave and chivalrous nation, quite as civilised as the Europeans, from whom they only differed by the pigmentation of their skin," an observation that would have delighted Nitobe, as that was the essence of how he was trying to frame Japan in *Bushido: The Soul of Japan*.

That said, when it comes to Japan there is and often has been a considerable 'eye of the beholder' effect. These events ricocheted around the world, from Calcutta to Cairo, like a validating shot showing that opportunistic change was possible. Some found encouragement in Japan's victory over Russia while others were outraged by it. A delighted Jawaharlal Nehru (1889-1964), a long-serving future prime minister of an independent India, while a schoolboy at Harrow in England, rushed to read the news of Japan's victory over Russia when it broke and later wrote: "I mused of Indian freedom and Asiatic freedom from the thraldom of Europe."

The prominent English writer H.G. Wells (1866-1946) had his own perspective of these events. He named his "voluntary nobility" the Samurai, in his book *A Modern Utopia*, first serialised in 1904 and published in book form in 1905, the years spanning the Russo-Japanese War. The Samurai elite, in Wells's "anticipatory" tale, acted as guardians helping balance accelerated progress and stability in a kinetic society, that mirrors ours, but is actually located on another planet. A review in the international journal of science *Nature*, published in August 1905, describes Wells's tale in this way: "In the present book Mr. Wells has become still more moderate and practicable and hopeful, without in the least derogating, from his ingenuity and originality." Today, Wells is better known for works such as *The War of the Worlds* and *The Invisible Man*, which have become classics, and were both penned years before *A Modern Utopia*.

This is the lively literary and geopolitical context within which Nitobe's book should probably be read today. Akutagawa's captivating literary reaction to its author and Mishima's professional insider's view, an emotional one, also reflects how Japan continues to evolve and the freedom many authors had and have to express their views, generating three fascinating literary data points on the trend line plotting the nation's complex rise. Knotty literary nodes centred, of course, around a short story that like many of old functions as a time machine for readers making Japan's literary terrain seem even more brilliantly knottier and ripe for exploration. For those interested, an English republished translation of Mishima's favourite short, "The Handkerchief", can be found within the collection *The Beautiful and the Grotesque* published by Liveright.

Despite Japan's long literary history and its association with the art of the short story, this fact, at the time of writing, simply isn't acknowledged by sources like *The Encyclopaedia Britannica* and Wikipedia in their entries on the evolution of short stories and short-form fiction. These publications both state confidently that the short story can be traced back to the earliest development of the written word, and that the modern short story we are familiar with today evolved in the 19th century.

Russia, America, India, Egypt, Greece and Nicaragua all get a look in, but neither poor Japan, nor a single Japanese author get a mention. For long periods of time, the West and Japan were both blissfully unaware of each other's literary outputs and much more besides. Today, in many sectors the world is fully aware of what Japan has to offer and enjoys the fruits of Japan's productivity but one sector that is still sadly too often an afterthought amongst international commentators and society's many educated talking heads is Japanese literature.

Japanese Debut

Nonetheless, the modern short story arrived in Japan relatively late, in 1890, sometime after most other countries. It is generally agreed that the first written was "Maihime" ("The Dancing Girl") by Ogai Mori (1862-1922). This story, which is said to be partly autobiographical, was Mori's first published work of fiction and was initially published in the relatively new and influential magazine *Kokumin no tomo (The Nation's Friend)*. "The Dancing Girl" is the tale of a relationship between a dancer, Elise, and a Japanese exchange student in Germany who is forced to choose between love, and career and duty. Mori believed that narrative fiction should be based on personal experience, and a rapidly changing Japan, alongside their own complex personal lives, provided Mori and writers like him with much fodder for their writing.

The precocious Mori had, in fact, spent four years in Germany between 1884 and 1888, where he is likely to have come across many short stories and short story writers, and perhaps even more than a few dancers. We know he knew at least one. Mori was one of, if not the very first, modern Japanese writer to spend a significant period in the West. These pioneering authors were often totally isolated from Japan and other Japanese individuals during their time overseas and were often encouraged by those they met and studied with to convert to Christianity. They also often struck up unusual acquaintanceships and friendships. Mori was an army officer at the time and received his orders to study medicine and public hygiene in Germany in 1884. His first port of call en route was Hong Kong, which impressed him, and he visited France and England on his return journey. After his arrival back in Japan he was appointed a professor at the Army Medical College and later became Surgeon General.

1890, the year of "The Dancing Girl's" publication, was notable for other historic reasons. Japan's Meiji Constitution, the nation's first, came into force with the aim of putting Japan on par with other modern civilised nation states. Drafted locally but based on Western models, drawing heavily on Prussian traditions, it created two legislative chambers a House of Peers and a House of Representatives, the latter elected by the people. Elections were held that year in July, with 300 representatives chosen by male tax-paying subjects of age 25 or older, turning Japan into the first Asian nation with some form of national elected assembly.

This relatively short constitution, consisting of seven chapters compared to the 11 in Japan's current constitution, with the emperor at its heart as the nation's supreme leader, established a host of duties and some of the types of important basic rights that are still thought of as being essential for constitutions to have. These included: the rule of law; the right to be tried by judges; freedom of speech, writing and publication; property rights; the right to join the army or navy which the emperor had supreme control over, as well as conditional freedom of religious belief with the condition being that these beliefs are not prejudicial to peace and order, and not antagonistic to the duties of subjects, who were now considered citizens of the nation of Japan.

The Meiji Constitution evolved over time allowing universal male suffrage, but it wasn't overhauled or replaced until the 'MacArthur' Constitution some 58 years later, around the time when Kojima and Oe's short stories were set and written, giving the Meiji Constitution a shorter life span than the average constitution in Western Europe, estimated at 77 years, but a much longer life than most constitutions in other regions of the world such as Latin American. According to an analysis by the Law School at the University of Chicago, the average lifespan, calculated as a mean, of national constitutions since 1789 is 17 years, while the average when calculated as a median is astonishingly a mere eight years.

These are rather unsettling figures when you consider the importance constitutions play in the evolution of modern states and democracies and in our daily lives. Despite the deadly trajectory that Japan later found itself on, it also reinforces the importance and regional milestone of the 1890 Meiji Constitution, even if by contemporary standards it might appear deficient. It also reflects the changing socio-economic environment within which Mori wrote Japan's first modern short story, when Japan as a small and newly open economy abruptly joined the modern world and many were searching for the words and tools to express themselves and the changes they were experiencing.

The year of "The Dancing Girl's" publication was also the year of the birth of Agatha Christie (1890-1976) and the death of Vincent van Gogh (1853-1890), as well as the year when a first short novella-length version of Oscar Wilde's (1854-1900) seminal tale *The Picture of Dorian Gray* was published in the American magazine *Lippincott's Monthly Magazine*, which provides a flavour of the times and other culturally influential individuals in the so-called 'civilised' world outside Japan at the time the modern short story made its debut in Japan.

The impact of Mori's tale on both Japanese readers and writers was not insignificant, but it would be an exaggeration to say it spawned all modern Japanese literature. It might be fair, however, to say that Mori provided the world of Japanese letters with a new literary overcoat of a new cut and style that warmed, protected and nurtured, modernising Japanese authorship as it tried to find its modern feet.

Many Japanese forms of artistic expression have developed in splendid isolation and can take time to take root. In some instances, a creative impasse hinders progress, and it can take a stimulus from abroad to spawn a new initiative or creative approach, one that enhances or radically overhauls the original creative concept. Mori's short story certainly wasn't an instant hit, but gradually became recognised as an important milestone in Japanese literature, and is, in fact, still studied today by Japanese students.

Intriguingly, Mori's sister would become the maternal grandmother to Hoshi, the prolific Emmy-winning writer of flash fiction or *shoto-shoto*, short short stories, as they are known in Japan and of course "Bokko-chan". She brought him up, and probably read him some rather intriguing tales when he was child.

The modern short story tradition that Mori triggered began in a pivotal period for Japan known as the Meiji era (1868-1912) when new printing technologies were beginning to emerge against a backdrop of social change and the new constitutional freedoms, sparking the launch of a significant number of literary journals and publications. *Shincho (New Tide)*, for instance, a highly-regarded monthly still published today, was launched by the respected publisher Shinchosha in 1904.

These new magazines and journals created demand from both readers and editors for short stories and serialised novels in the same way as Western publications like *The Strand Magazine*, launched in 1891, helped popularise the format, and new genres in England. The first Sherlock Holmes short stories by Arthur Conan Doyle (1859-1930), for example, were published in *The Strand Magazine*, which also later serialised *The Hound of the Baskervilles*.

The profitability of these Japanese publications is no longer as attractive as it would have been back in the Meiji era, but most major Japanese publishers still publish literary journals today. Contemporary writers have built on this rich legacy and still receive support from Japanese publishers and readers when they write short stories. This modern foreign import has, it seems, been digested, refined and taken to interesting new creative levels.

Small is Beautiful

Following the Second World War, the prevailing ethos in the West was that 'Bigger is Better' and that everything in the United States was bigger and better than anything anywhere else. This gave rise to industry consolidation and the creation of huge multinational companies and mega scale national science and space projects. Scale is a word still loved by today's technology entrepreneurs and evangelists. Naturally, massive consolidation has also taken place in the publishing industry, with many small publishers being absorbed by large American or German groups.

Some seasoned and prescient observers of Japan in the sixties and seventies, when a defeated Japan was following in the wake of all things America, during its period of single-minded rapid industrial growth, often wondered out loud if Japan really wished to be the biggest or whether it was motivated by the shame of not being considered an equal: parity and respect not supremacy. Arguing that the answer to this would only be discovered from observing long-run behaviours once Japan had 'caught up'. Perhaps now is the time to make such judgements.

That said, when it comes to size the Japanese mentality has always been somewhat different. It took the publication of a book by an economist to highlight what most Japanese people already knew to be true, namely that big is not always better. E. F. Schumacher's book *Small Is Beautiful: A Study of Economics As If People Mattered*, was published in 1973, during the Organisation of Petroleum Exporting Countries' (OPEC) oil embargo in retaliation for the West's support of Israel in the Yom Kippur War. The period became known in Japan as the Oil-Shock. The book had a major international impact and was cited by *The Times Literary Supplement* as one of the 100 most influential books published since the war.

In the book, Shumacher argued that small cities, companies, cars, states and organisations were better for mankind and most importantly for the environment. The book is now dated and no longer required reading at business schools, where most students are focused on winner-takes-all strategies, the digital first mover advantage, and the associated network effect and benefits of being big, as well as consolidating market power through data and artificial intelligence (AI).

However, fashions and business strategies change with the ebb and flow of business cycles. Increasing concern about faceless unmanageable large multinational organisations, data privacy and bias, and environmental impact may mean the book's time could come again. As it happens, Japan is still one of the most fragmented major publishing markets where consolidation has been elusive. Its many publishers have stuck with their strategy of developing new generations of interesting authors by supporting and encouraging short story and novella writing.

The short form seems to be ideally suited to Japanese modes of perception. According to Meredith McKinney, one of the translators of Shonagon's *Pillow Book*, "There is a wonderful delicacy and amplitude to the best of short-form Japanese writing, which translators can despair of successfully conveying with the clumsy tools that Western languages offer." In modern times the short story and novella favour suggestion and a lightness of touch, she argues, expressing the essence rather spelling out the detail. Outside Japan many tend to focus on the lines where a Japanese reader would savour the negative space they create around them, and the resonance they set up, she believes.

Aficionados of the beautiful game, football, understand the tactical power of this and pundits celebrate this type of style. Players utilising empty space, not chasing the ball, the line of play, create opportunities that often shape the narrative outcomes of attacking plots. Embracing and delighting in what is not said or done, even muted silence, the gaps between the lines, and what remains vague, consciously omitted and the incomplete can be liberating for both readers and writers, but also at times shockingly deadly, as Oe shows in his tale "Unexpected Muteness".

According to Shinya Machida, a culture journalist working for the *Yomiuri Shimbun*, one of the reasons behind Japan's love of the small is that large objects and structures are much more exposed to earthquake and other climatic risks. "Appreciating small things, be they objects or the changing nature around you becomes important. Their beauty becomes enhanced by life's existential uncertainty. Smaller things can be easier to preserve," he explains. He believes the continued success of short form writing in Japan is part of this.

The 'art of the miniature' is deep rooted in Japan, and everyone can quickly cite numerous examples of Japanese objects that are small and beautiful, such as bonsai, the Sony Walkman, or netsuke, and there is also the somewhat bizarre fad of cooking tiny meals using miniature-cooking utensils. According to the *Guinness Book of World Records*, the world's smallest printed book was produced by a Japanese printer. This 'art of the miniature' spans literature, technology, product design and even scientific research.

Due to the nation's particular strength in this area of science, when *Nature*, decided to launch a new sister publication about the science of the very small, *Nature Nanotechnology*, it placed one of its editors in Tokyo to hunt-down research papers from corporate, government and university research laboratories.

Naturally, Japanese scientists and engineers aren't just focused on quantum dots and their ilk; they have even tried their hand at short stories. A number of years ago, well before ChatGPT, a group of software engineers created an algorithm designed to use AI to generate short stories. Of course, they submitted the fruits of their labour not to a scientific journal like *Nature Nanotechnology*, but to the Hoshi Awards, the science fiction short story literary award named in honour of the author of the short tragic tale, "Bokko-chan" about the robot bar waitress.

The award is consciously open to all possible authors, including computers and aliens, not to mention humans. It deliberately sets such wide criteria to help expand the concept of science fiction, making the award itself an embedded part of the genre. An AI authored short story has made the initial screening and generated significant international publicity but one hasn't yet made the shortlist. The story in question had some very stiff shortlist competition. Amusingly, its title was "Konpyuta ga shosetsu wo kaku hi" ("The Day a Computer Writes a Novel").

Weirdly, the Hoshi Awards first winner was a male human named Shinichi Endo (b. 1962), whose prizewinning story was written in the style of a scientific article, the kind that a Tokyo-based *Nature Nanotechnology* editor might be expected to find and publish. But this fictional academic article is not one from the present, but an imagined one written by advanced AI in the year 2064.

Japan has hundreds of literary awards many of which have a direct or indirect association with short-form writing. Japan even has a prize named after an idiosyncratic author of historical fiction Shugoro Yamamoto (1903-1967), who ironically refused to accept any of the many awards he won or was nominated for including the very prestigious Naoki Prize. Not believing in their merit. He, of course, penned short stories some of which, like his novels, ended up being adapted very successfully for film by high profile directors including Kurosawa, films such as *Tsubaki sanjyuro (Sanjuro)* and *Akahige (Red Beard)*, as well as the contemporary director Takashi Miike (b. 1960), who adapted his novel *Sabu* in 2002. The prize honouring Yamamoto, who had many pen names including this one that was created in honour of a pawnbroker who had supported him when he was starting out, was set up in 1987 after his death. He was no longer in a position to object.

Despite their quantity, there is, however, something rather special and appealing about the Hoshi Awards, launched in 2013 by the business-publishing group *Nikkei*, the owner of the *Financial Times*. It is open to people of all ages and even has a youth category. It challenges budding writers to imagine humanity's future and the future of our planet. As most science editors and journalists will tell you, unsuccessful experiments can generate fascinating results and insights some which are not just thought-provoking, but also pave the way to new approaches. You can be wrong, but wrong for very interesting reasons and this can extend to AIs that don't quite make the literary cut of a literary prize's shortlist. With a bit of luck, the eponymous prize will have a nurturing role with a long coat tail like Hoshi's grandmother, the sister of Japan's first author of a modern short story, encouraging new generations of wordsmiths with a love and deep appreciation of shorts to pen tales that dance off the page into the future.

Are We on the Cusp of a New Golden Age?

Some publishers outside Japan are also now picking up again on the attractiveness of the short story. In India, for example, Penguin Random House, the world's largest publisher, has announced the launch of a new digital short story imprint: *Petit*. The new imprint publishes short reads of approximately 50 pages designed for ease of reading across digital devices. In parallel, many of the world's leading newspapers have launched online sections dubbed *Long Reads* on their websites, which are longer than your typical news story, but similar in length to some short stories. Perhaps with our changing media consumption patterns the short story is about to enjoy an international revival.

Newspaper headline writers in Britain have on occasion picked up on the trend and have started acknowledging the possibilities with light-hearted headlines like: "Let's not drag this out: the short story is back" and "Short story revival cuts novels down to size," accompanied by articles about the increases in the sale of short story collections, mostly single author collections. This has been partly triggered by single publications by big names like the American actor, Tom Hanks, an individual with a growing reputation as a writer complementing his critical success as an actor, whose book, *Uncommon Type* has been something of a hit. But there does seem to be an emerging new trend.

Connoisseurs of Japanese literature know that to enjoy the best of Japanese fiction and creative writing you really can't ignore short stories. The small things in life, and expression in the miniature, can add up to something much more substantial, and great things, that make masterful impressions, are often generated by a series of small simple effects that come together, as some impressionist painters such as van Gogh have famously pointed out and brilliantly put into practice, either through design or serendipity.

In this regard literary fiction, especially of the Japanese variety, is not an exception. Perhaps, in our time-scarce world of poor and unreliable content, the short story's time to bubble up and fizz again has come. Like sushi, now considered a special treat and enjoyed by everyone, these aesthetically pleasing, small and easy-to-digest packages have been relished and developed quietly for decades in Japan. They are an excellent entry point into Japan's great and highly creative sea of letters. The time to read them in translation, or even in Japanese, has now surely arrived.

Rubble-Rising Prose

Japan is sometimes depicted as a nation awaiting its next disaster. Since time immemorial, a catalogue of natural disasters including floods, earthquakes, tsunami, mudslides, typhoons and volcanic eruptions, as well as a fair share of unnatural man-made catastrophes has affected the country.

The psychology of disaster and its management: waiting for them; mitigating them; preparing for them; and responding to them or recovering from them, is said to be embedded deep within the nation's culture. The reality of catastrophe, and its lurking dangers, has shaped Japan. In fact, the Japanese archipelago with its unforgiving geography actually makes Japan one of the most disaster-prone nations worldwide. The nation's first recorded earthquake, for example, occurred in 416.

Wikipedia has dedicated pages on the topic titled: 'List of earthquakes in Japan' and 'Natural disasters in Japan' and much more besides, including, for instance, lists of the many fires that regularly wasted the Japanese capital, Edo, between 1601 and 1855. A major fire in 1657, The Great Meireki Fire, that swept the capital a decade or so before the Great Fire of London, is a particular tragic example, lasting some three days it destroyed two thirds of the city and killed an estimated 100,000 people. Legend has it that a priest burning a cursed kimono ignited this calamity. The frequent fires were dubbed the flowers or autumn leaves of Edo, leading to the Japanese capital, one of the world's largest at the time, to be known by some as the City of Fires.

Of course, security is ephemeral no matter where you live. Every nation, like most companies, need a disaster recovery plan to mitigate and deal with rare and unexpected events. Nonetheless, culture and storytelling are also essential ingredients required by all nations wanting to thrive, as well as rise again from the proverbial rubble of a cataclysmic incident. This is something that Japan, with it seemingly endless array of calamitous events, appears to take in its stride—perhaps even manages to perfect and conquer skilfully—if stating such a thing is not considered aberrant.

This unpredictable co-existence with nature, and the longing for a peaceful existence no matter how brief, is reflected in most of Japan's creative arts in some form: through the use of constructs such as the fleeting nature of life and beauty as well as the importance placed on nature itself, and often its fragility, in Japanese literature, poetry and culture. This is sometimes termed *mono no aware*, the pathos of things, in Japanese and is a concept loved by and frequently adopted by literary critics in Japan.

A classic example of this are the essays and thoughts espoused in *Tsurezuregusa* (*Essays in Idleness*), by Kenko Yoshida (circa 1283-1352) a Japanese Buddhist monk, considered one of the definitive books on Japanese aesthetics. He famously wrote: "If man were never to fade away... but lingered on forever in the world, how things would lose their power to move us. The most precious thing in life is its uncertainty." Contemporary cultural outlooks are still often sprinkled and flavoured with traces of this consequential writer.

It's a phenomenon that international visitors to Japan in the early 1900s, including the likes of Rabindranath Tagore (1861-1941), a Bengali polymath and the first Asian winner of the Nobel Prize in Literature, and many others have often commented on or written about when comparing Japanese culture to those of the nations they had set out from. This is a trend that continues to this day. As Tagore put it in 1916, in a lecture, *The Spirit of Japan*:

> What has impressed me most in this country is the conviction that you have realised nature's secrets, not by methods of analytical knowledge, but by sympathy. You have known her language of lines and music of colours, the symmetry in her irregularities, and the cadence in her freedom of movements.

Today, these ancient and quixotic Japanese cultural sentiments are shared by many including vocal climate change activists and even some eminent international theoretical physicists, who also think of life and human existence as accidental, uncertain, and tragic. These physicists argue that nature despite its inevitabilities, and so-called constants, is fragile and has the hidden ability to generate myriad parallel histories, scenarios, dimensions, and possibilities.

At each instant in time, it is as if there is a fleeting uncertain moment of hesitation between the multiplicities of future possibilities. Instants so often beautifully reflected in the best forms of traditional Japanese art and in particular its scroll painting that often capture a bird or a fish with the freedom and uncertainty of their movements to follow left to the viewers imagination, creating undetermined observational uncertainty that make such incomplete pictures so memorable. Much like quantum mechanics, Japanese literature has its own uncertainty principle which Japanese artists, poets and writers have understood and reflected upon in their works for centuries.

Disasters Bookend Japan's Cultural Cycles

For many in Japan, disaster and change are joined at the hip with some arguing that major change has to wait until the nation is confronting or has just overcome a cataclysmic existential episode. Japan's history is, of course, not a simple progression of intermittent disasters. Nonetheless, perhaps idly enjoying the tranquillity between catastrophic events that can bookend lives, regimes and family histories is the only sensible approach: a solace-driven philosophical trade-off wrapped with the ambiguity needed to sustain short-term well-being and society's natural momentum.

Scribes such as the master short story writer Kanji Hanawa (1936-2020), whose works can be broadly categorised as situational 'nightmare' tales that explore the unrelenting pressures and challenges of life in Japan, argue that disasters and climate change have had major and often overlooked cultural as well as longitudinal political and durable economic effects on Japan and its national zeitgeist.

Unsurprisingly, this former professor of French literature, with a deep interest in human psychology and complex relationships, argues that you can't fully understand, comment on or write meaningfully about Japan without being able to read its weather patterns and taking them, alongside Japan's many other 'silent risks', into account. Be that, for example, the Isewan Typhoon (also known as Vera), one of the strongest and most intense ever that hit Japan from the sea in 1959 or some other extreme climate or seismic event or threat from afar. There have been many such tragic events each unique in terms of the event itself and the reactions provoked, but with echoes of similarity that highlight life's risks, uncertainties and fragilities.

The Isewan Typhoon alone killed 5,000 and injured almost 40,000, as well as making 1.5 million people homeless, devastating much of Nagoya. It spawned a famous and tragic television drama that the nation was glued to in the 1970s called *Akai unmei* (*Red Fate*). It is a drama about two children whose identities accidentally get swapped in an orphanage in the confusion around the time of the typhoon, changing their futures to great melodramatic effect and turning them into a peculiar type of societal collateral damage with their own parallel realities. Demonstrating to all that natural disasters are neither predictable nor rational.

Each episode of the 28-part series started with actual images of the Isewan Typhoon, accompanied by a scary opening narration, imprinting this particular disaster on the nation's collective memories and highlighting the terrible twists of fate natural disasters, hasty decisions, and extreme weather, can inflict. The year this typhoon hit Japan was around the time that limited colour television broadcasting was being launched in Japan, initially restricted to a few hours per day. By the time its tale was being re-rendered as *Red Fate*, colour television sets and broadcasting were widespread. Societies tend to call such tragedies natural disasters, but they frequently look man-made or subsequently become such.

Many of the current generation of commercially successful award-winning authors above a certain age watched the *Red Fate* series when growing up, which is how some of them learnt about this typhoon. Authors such as Mitsuyo Kakuta (b. 1967) and Takuji Ichikawa (b. 1962). Its scars and its stars left imprints.

An impressive and unusual example of the Isewan Typhoon's quirky legacy-making is the book *Heike densetsu satsujin jiken* (*Heike Legend Murder Case*), published in 1985, and subsequently adapted for television in 1987. This locked-room mystery, set in a hamlet near the port city of Kochi, involves a Ginza hostess, a fake marriage, money, an insurance claim and a series of mysterious untimely deaths, giving it all the ingredients for a really exciting potboiler.

The mystery penned by the amazingly prolific mystery writer Yasuo Uchida (1934-2018), more than two decades after the eventful typhoon, not only features his famed detective, Mitsuhiko Asami, a freelance writer who is also an investigator of legends and an aspiring detective but important historical events. Centuries earlier, members of the defeated Heike clan, a group that all Japanese children learn about in school when they study the *Heike monogatari* (*The Tale of the Heike*), had, according to Uchida's tale, fled to the settlement near Kochi where the mystery takes place. Despite this incredible and familiarising framing, Uchida still feels compelled to discuss the devasting typhoon in the book's prologue to make a point about linked events, as well as set up his murderous narrative. The prologue frames the setting for this mystery, using the Isewan Typhoon as a symbolic and accessible metaphor that all readers will be familiar with, even though the main narrative has little to do with the actual storm and the devastation it caused itself. Major climatic events and disasters in Japan have a tendency to do this, making them indelible.

In its own small way, this alone highlights the typhoon's importance and the seminal milestone that the year when this massive storm hit Japan had, at the very least for this specific popular author, as well as Hanawa who has several other such events on his list of culturally important catastrophes and, of course, *Red Fate*'s huge nationwide audience. This alongside other storytelling has given this particular typhoon and its aftermath a type of narrative permanence. It is therefore probably worth digging deeper into what else happened in 1959 as well as the work that was published in that difficult year. It is also worth considering if any stories published in the year of the super storm encouraged or reflected the nation's rise from extremes, nasty tempests or illustrate their longitudinal influence, and other aspects of society's metaphorical rubble.

The 1959 Vanguards

This typhoon occurred in the year when Switzerland rejected female suffrage in a referendum, Alaska and Hawaii were admitted as states, Singapore elected its first prime minister, Fidel Castro (1926-2016) came to power in Cuba, and the United States Navy successfully launched *Vanguard 2*, a satellite to measure cloud cover and density, one of the world's first, if not the first, weather satellite. It was a very different world from the one we live in today, technologically, economically, politically and also in terms of how news and information is disseminated, and books published.

Nonetheless, 1959 was a breakthrough year of sorts for many in Japan, and a fascinating year on the publishing front as well, with many important creatives trying to make the weather, less than a decade after the end of the Allied Occupation of Japan (1945-1952), often with narratives reflecting the immediate challenges of navigating the extreme and turbulent uncertain times, as opposed to delightful predictions of better brighter futures and sunnier days.

It was the year, for instance, when Osamu Tezuka's (1928-1989) "Zero Man", a dark tale for children was launched in *Weekly Shonen Sunday*. This manga, from a man many like to compare in terms of skill and influence with Walt Disney (1901-1966), features global destruction, climate change, murder, slavery, racial intolerance, war, political corruption, and genocide, in a highly entertaining sugar-coated format. It contains graphic detail rendered and designed for children to easily absorb and understand, preparing them for the harsh realities and tail risks, whether silent, left or right, geopolitical or climatic, of modern existence.

In this lesser-known of Tezuka's many science fiction tales, mankind battles Zero-men, technologically advanced subterranean sentient beings from the Himalayas that share some genetic traits with squirrels. These creatures are almost identical to us except for a few skewed but important traits, such as possessing large bushy tails and superior intelligence. Led by a totalitarian, human-hating dictator Grand Priest they invade Tokyo, using advanced weaponry, turning the capital into an inhumane futurist metropolis.

It is not only a tale of destructive culture clashes about those caught up trying to bridge the gaps between two opposing competing civilisations of the tailed and untailed, and the sad fact that peaceful co-existence is always a challenge, but also a storyline that highlights that there is no easy or quick solution to racial prejudice.

The manga features an erupting Mount Fuji and the climatic consequences of the misuse of technology. The Zero-men use a freezing device to prevent a potentially cataclysmic volcanic eruption but calibrate their settings incorrectly causing a new ice age, that is easier for squirrel-men to endure than humankind, a dangerous and live fictional cold war of sorts, albeit a relatively short one, once the environment reverts back to normal. Arguably, a sign of the times.

Another notorious Japanese creative Yukio Mishima (1925-1970) was active too in 1959 beavering away on new works. Mishima published *Kyoko no ie* (*Kyoko's House*) a series of unsettling connected, and some say prescient, portrait-like tales about four young men, a businessman, a boxer, an actor and a painter, each thought to reflect a different aspect of Mishima's multifaceted personality. They mirror the times and also the so-called four "rivers" of the author's life: The Flesh, Action, The Stage, and Writing.

Mishima's book didn't actually make the weather, as it was, to the author's great disappointment, not critically well received, despite Mishima spending more time on it than many of his other works. Some believe these fragmented tales foretold Mishima's dramatic subsequent death by suicide. What is unquestionable is that Mishima's narratives were a response to the awkward and culturally uncertain post-war stage that he and Japan found itself in, not the Isewan Typhoon per se, but a cold war splitting the world into opposing blocks, and a host of disorientating and disintegrating realities confronting many in Japan.

Post-war lives, not just Mishima's, were in flux. More than two million Japanese soldiers had died in battle, some three hundred thousand killed in air raids, orphaning many. Furthermore, after the war ended more than seven million soldiers were demobilised and a huge number of Japanese nationals repatriated from overseas. What resides outside and inside *Kyoko's House*, a tale set in Tokyo and New York, reflects the deep insecurities these caused, "an unscalable wall" not just the author's personal concerns. Tellingly, Mishima said that the hero of this work "is not the character but the period."[31] That said, *Kyoko's House* also subtly reveals and blends a host of idiosyncratic previously considered invisible barriers between Mishima, his work and his own stage in life, as well as the typhonic tremors that the period was still causing in the national zeitgeist. It would seem that the winds of change and uncertainty, not just from Vera, were blowing strongly through the lives of many across the Japanese archipelago.

Kyoko's House's is a poignant tale which explores beauty and decay while positioning itself as an eloquent study of the nihilism of a generation, confronting the hell of modern existence which only appears to find meaning in aestheticism, destruction and death. It is not a tale for children or the faint-hearted. This makes it, for some, oddly reminiscent of Oscar Wilde's (1854-1900) *The Picture of Dorian Gray*, Wilde's only novel, which is also said to reflect multiple aspects of Wilde's own divisive personality, as well as hedonism, and the hell of immoral individualism.

Decadence, the *maladie du style*, is said to be the cultural expression of nihilism, art the expression of exquisite contrasts and disagreements. Authorship of the type penned by Mishima and Wilde can also function as a lexical battering ram against the natural and established indelible order of things.

These parallels might not be those that some, including Mishima himself, might draw or agree with; other works by him and authors might be considered a more appropriate comparison. *The Picture of Dorian Gray* is a novel that we actually know Mishima read, as he described it in 1950 as such: "*The Picture of Dorian Gray* is the mud churned up by the footsteps of his talent. However, nobody can deny that one pair of those sloppy footprints is an angel's."[32]

This interplay between two genius wordsmiths from different eras and nations, both members of the cult of beauty and its self-appointed ambassadors, is even more ironic and fascinating given that Wilde himself wrote, in his 1889 essay *The Decay of Lying* that "The Japanese people are... simply a mode of style, an exquisite fancy of art..." Painting his own peculiar picture of Japan, while also perhaps predicting the type of cultural chicanery that has encouraged individuals such as Mishima to charge directly into cultural tempests of their own making. Wilde wrote this as a caustic response to the *Japonisme*-boom that Europe was experiencing, after Japan was opened to the world and its cultural products, such as fans and umbrellas, started arriving in Europe.

Wilde's words are arguably a not yet fully formed early example of the sentiment reflected in the ever-popular seminal 1978 book *Orientalism* by Edward W. Said (1935-2003), a key figure in post-colonial studies, who argues that the portrayal of some parts of the Eastern world in Europe exaggerate differences and fictionalise nations and people, often reflecting the observers more than the realities of the observed. Reading a text in its global context, even one about aggressive bushy-tailed climate destroying cognitive superior Asian squirrel-men or Kyoko the sorceress's house and her male guests, while not forgetting the local context or climate when they were written, is critical Said, argued. Said, who had a unique and fresh perspective, he was born in Jerusalem and later died in New York, coined with the publication of his book the now often misused term orientalism that critiques the often-skewed examples used when comparing nations, regions and people and their implied presumption of Western superiority or that of the individual expounding the examples.

Wilde's essay, which is structured as a Socratic dialogue, is also famous for coining often repeated phrases such as: "Life imitates Art far more than Art imitates Life..." and "Lying, the telling of beautiful untrue things, is the proper aim of Art." No matter the preferred colours hidden, forbidden, fictitious, primary, kaleidoscopic, calamitous, or even factual, or the direction of the cultural winds of the era, Wilde would no doubt be tickled pink if he knew that one of Japan's most notorious and fashionable authors, an eloquent poser provocateur like himself, had read his work and was writing about him, affirming both of their existences and social importance.

Writing and being written about, even pure invention, can create an immortalising permanence for individuals and events, including typhoons. That is the context of how Wilde would read Mishima's commentary and his angelic reference, if he were alive to do so, even if he thought that Mishima's wordy footprints, and his ilk, were just an exquisite fancy found within the headwinds of a certain style of the translated literary arts. Imagination and intellect are a powerful combination, whether masked or unmasked. That said, these works probably reflect each author and their delightfully peculiar art more than the years they were published in, even if bad weather is a useful metaphor worthy for each of their personal lives.

Kinokawa (The River Ki), a very different and highly-regarded layered multi-generational tale by Sawako Ariyoshi (1931-1984), was also published in 1959. Lesser known outside Japan, Ariyoshi is another important writer who, just like Mishima and many others, initially built a reputation through writing short stories. *The River Ki*, a tale about three Japanese women, depicts the traumatic rhythms and evolution of modern Japanese history, a winding narrative leading to the death of the traditional order of things, with water, a river in its case, providing the narrative backdrop, as well as the solace for three women, a mother, daughter and granddaughter, struggling to navigate these choppy unrelenting changes. It is a moving tale spanning different eras, from the turn of the 20th century through to the 1950s, told in its case through the voices of women, as opposed to the anointed male elite or their eloquent and creative antagonists. It is considered a modern classic.

> In an effort to understand post-war Japan, Hana read these magazines and found herself confused and exhausted by their unbridled attacks and wondering why the magazines sold at all. She was both amazed and displeased that Kosaku read such trash. Hana found it unforgiveable that there should be such a gulf between the intellectual level of the critical essays and the low quality of the fiction in the same magazine. Realizing the elegance and refinement which she so appreciated in literature had disappeared altogether in modern Japan. Sawako Ariyoshi, *Kinokawa (The River Ki)*.

While Japan was processing the bewildering and muddy churns of its post-war society and the aftermath of the Allied occupation, with a certain amount of help from leading authors such as these, alongside the immediate fallout from the unusually strong and devastating typhoon, the world's gaze was in contrast increasingly falling on the nation for very different reasons, Japan's so-called economic miracle. A new Japan boom was in its infancy and the world saw a very different country and context, to the one that Tezuka, Mishima and Ariyoshi depict in their works. Outside and away from Japanese shores, animosity towards Japan was rapidly changing into curiosity.

At a meeting in May that year, in Munich, West Germany, Japan was selected, for the second time, to become the first Asian nation to host an Olympic Games. These games when they occurred spurred both Japan and its Olympic and sports literature onwards and upwards. It also helped reposition post-war Japan in the eyes of the world, bringing, according to some, this problematic period to an end, allowing the nation to shed a dark mantle and slowly emerge from the shadows of war with apparent renewed confidence. In this sense, 1959 was a critical point in Japan's steady trajectory of social and cultural reconstruction, as well as an unforgettable one on the weather front.

Most notions of progress these days seem to allow for the possibility of reversals, relapses and accident, as well as watershed bookending moments. Despite some great publications and the Isewan Typhoon, 1959 was, however, not a bookending watershed year for most. It probably felt much more like a year of muddle, than a year that brought something to an end or conclusion. Nonetheless, not every year is indisputably pivotal or subsequently defined as a historical turning point, the type when a decade or generation worth of change seems to be packed together, all happening at once. Yet all years have their moments, as did 1959, and are interesting in their own right as case studies that tap a nation's temperature and climate on the relentlessly path of so-called civilised progress.

That said, this year also, like most, still had its own special eye-catching moments. Whether it was a fitting prelude for the Swinging Sixties, the tumultuous decade to come with its famous battles for freedoms, or if it really brought Japan's post-war period to conclusion, unshackling the nation from its wartime past, is an open question. Nonetheless, it is sensible to consider some of the year's other important and memorable events that may also help provide yet wider historical Japanese context to this stormy year.

They include: the marriage of Crown Prince Akihito (b. 1933), the future Heisei Emperor, to Michiko Shoda (b. 1934); the release of research in Japan indicating the cause of the dreadful Minamata Disease that killed thousands as industrial mercury; and an American supersonic fighter jet crashing into a primary school in Okinawa, which was still under direct American control, killing eleven students, six residents and injuring hundreds.

Amazingly, three quarters of all television cameras in Japan at the time were used to broadcast the imperial wedding. They were not just providing a new public visibility to this historically mysterious family and giving the nation something to celebrate but creating a new type of shared national event that ushered in the new television-age to Japan. This started a major shift from the cinema to television, and ever decreasing sizes and accessibility of screens.

This new audio-visual age allowed the storylines of television series, such as *Red Fate*, to subsequently create many more collective experiences, complementing the narratives found within the printed pages of books with moving images that could be viewed at home. The new colour broadcasting technology increased accessibility to traditional storytelling with many important works being adapted for television, launching a brand-new visual landscape with a multitude of new storylines and reimagined older ones. These made some authors even more famous as they found new audiences and readers from this increased exposure.

Much has changed and much has stayed the same since 1959 when the powerful Isewan Typhoon struck Japan. Today, that Crown Prince's son is the emperor, Okinawa is back under Japanese control but is the poorest of the nation's 47 prefectures and is still blighted with tragic incidents related to the American military. Weather forecasting, with live handheld access, has, however, been totally transformed.

Tempests are, of course, still a popular narrative device exploited by writers across the world and arguably turbulent weather, far more than fine weather, can influence, and even transform, the creative process itself:

> Leaning his body on the desk in front of him, while gazing on his own floundering manuscript, he saw the sinking of a junk through the eyes of the shipwrecked captain... But following on like a light piercing fog, his speed did not in the least slacken. On the contrary, drowning his inhibitions in the dizzy-torrents, he let those torrents come cascading to sweep him away, until at last he became their captive, and forgetting all else in the course of that flow, he let his own brush sweep on like a flood. Ryunosuke Akutagawa (1892-1927), "Gesaku zanmai" ("Absorbed In Letters").

Bullied to Oblivion

Coincidently, 1959 was also the year of the birth of the Akutagawa Prizewinning author Hitonari Tsuji, whose own life has also had its fair share of unusual twists and sweeping turns. Tsuji now resides in Paris but would have been about 17 years old when *Red Fate* was initially broadcast across Japan every Friday night, between 9:00 p.m. and 9:55 p.m. from April to October, 1976. He, like most of the so-called 'Danso Generation' born between 1951 and 1960, would have found it nigh-on impossible to avoid the series, which stared the legendary pop-idol and actress Momoe Yamaguchi. She was born in this eventful year, 1959, when the terrible intense storm made landfall.

The success of the series ensured that even after the homeless families and bereaved had moved on, indelible cultural markings remained. Tellingly, Yamaguchi an impressively determined and decisive individual as well as super-talented one, despite the success of the series, didn't herself remain in the public eye for long. She retired at the age of 21, at the height of her fame, deciding that her priorities lay elsewhere and concluding that fleeting fame, and leaving the national stage at the height of one's powers, was the best variety of celebrity. By that point she had, of course, also starred in several highly-successful film and television adaptations of books by some of Japan's most celebrated authors such as Yasunari Kawabata (1899-1972), Kenji Oe (1905-1987), Tatsuo Hori (1904-1953) and Mishima, adding to her allure and helping to sell lots of books for these authors.

But to return to Tsuji, it is perhaps no coincidence that Tsuji's prizewinning breakthrough 1996 dark tale *Kaikyo no hikari* (*The Light from the Strait*) is in its own way a disaster story with the sea and death, as well as twists of fate, at its narrative heart. It is the tale of a young mariner who ends up as a trainer and guard at a detention centre for juvenile delinquents after losing his job on a boat. The tale's eloquently crafted narrative skilfully portrays the sad and disastrous impact bullying has on both the victim and the bully when the young mariner is reacquainted with his former schoolmate, now a delinquent at the centre having stabbed someone.

Bullying is an all-too-common nightmare in Japan that the nation has curiously found almost impossible to eradicate, thereby creating opportunities for and triggering mesmerising storytelling that authors like Mieko Kawakami (b. 1976), another winner of the prestigious Akutagawa Prize, in her acclaimed novel *Hebun* (*Heaven*) have exploited. Tales that provide comfort for both readers and authors, perhaps not generating brand-new lives phoenix-like from the ashes for most, but allowing many to process potentially ruinous events, putting them on a road to recovery or at least pointing them in new directions.

Sayaka Murata (b. 1979) author of *Konbini ningen* (*Convenience Store Woman*), a massive international hit which has sold over a million copies outside Japan in translation, also a recipient of the Akutagawa Prize, experienced bullying herself at school. This led to her keeping company with imaginary friends, something that no doubt helped her on her journey to becoming an author. These days, in between writing for newspaper serials and sitting on judging panels for literary awards, she interacts with friends in the metaverse within the universes of online gaming, escaping the cacophony and stresses of life by entering a virtual environment that requires less thick skin than school classrooms and playgrounds.

Some psychologists might call much commentary on the topic and reactions to it in the classroom or outside them a fundamental attribution error: the attribution of outcomes to individual character and not sufficiently to environmental or institutional factors. The context, in other words. Others try to explain bullying away as an impossible to eradicate side-effect of the collectivist nature of Japanese society and the educational system's one-size-fits-all pedagogy that tends to blame individuals (either the bullied or the bully), as they don't follow the accepted norms or educational averages. Thus requiring them to be hammered down by a system designed to ingest all and churn out an average.

Whatever the causes, these types of recurring tragic narrative themes, as well as suicide itself, seem to relentlessly seep out of Japan's creative arts, be they triggered by man-made or naturally occurring failures of society or skewed individuality. There are a seeming infinite supply of tales of weary people under relentless pressure just like laboratory simulated earthquakes that squeeze glass beads slowly until they suddenly give. Japan has the highest suicide rate amongst the nations that are members of the Group of Seven (G7). However, the common famous association of the word suicide with Japan and Japanese authors in the international media is one, whether fair or unfair, that many in Japan resent.

Two of the most internationally renowned, and most translated, living Japanese authors, Haruki Murakami (b. 1949) and Banana Yoshimoto (b. 1964), amongst many other contemporary and historical Japanese storytellers, have featured the horror of suicide or attempted suicide in their works. Suicide features in Murakami's breakthrough 1987 novel *Noruwei no mori* (*Norwegian Wood*), a tale about loss, coming-of-age and sexuality. Toru, the book's somewhat aimless protagonist, is haunted by the suicide of his best friend Kizuki. Yoshimoto's 1994 novel *Amurita* (*Amrita*), the title of which is Sanskrit for immortality, also features a suicide connected to its protagonist. In this case, the protagonist's sister, a substance-abusing actress. Works like these help reinforce the association of the word suicide with Japan and its artists.

This is of course not a new phenomenon. There are many famous examples of suicide featuring works from the past including Soseki Natsume's (1867-1916) *Kokoro* (*Kokoro*) and *Ningen Shikkaku* (*No Longer Human*) by Osamu Dazai (1909-1948). Much older tales and plays exist that feature suicide as a plot device of last resort within tragic tales of ill-fated love, as well as self-inflicted death as a matter of honour or as final desperate acts, such as the classic *Sonezaki shinju* (*The Love Suicides at Sonezaki*), with its double suicides, by Monzaemon Chikamatsu (1653-1724), considered one of Japan's greatest playwrights. Tales of complicated and forbidden love, escape through death from a hostile world, are not unique to Japan and have a timeless and global appeal. Some like to compare this particular play to William Shakespeare's (1564-1616) *Romeo and Juliet*. Tragically, in its first year of performance in 1703, its heart-breaking popularity spawned a cluster of copycat double suicides amongst Japanese couples.

The number of such publications and author deaths by suicide in Japan has made this uncomfortable topic a matter of academic enquiry with research papers being written such as "The Portrayal of Suicide in Postmodern Japanese Literature and Popular Media Culture."[33] Its frequent portrayal, alongside bullying, and other such shocking events may make for a fateful inevitability by conditioning the population for the inescapable future struggles they are sadly all too often destined to face when digesting the consequences of these types of human catastrophes. Rehearsed emotions are easier to control than spontaneous ones, and in times of crisis and extreme stress when clear thinking aided by practiced response is required, it can be better not to be controlled only by one's emotions, no matter how authentic or raw they might be.

Nonetheless, people often cite Japan's long tradition of an 'honourable suicide' and that the act of suicide was considered in feudal times as the final statement of one's resolution and courage, as one of the main reasons for the high rate of suicide. Another common hypothesis is the lack of the Christian concept of sin: suicide being one such sin. As one of the characters in a novella, by a deeply spiritual author and Japan's most famous Catholic writer, Shusaku Endo (1923-1996), *Kiiroi hito (Yellow Man)* published in 1955 puts it: "A yellow man like me has absolutely no experience of anything so profound and extreme as the consciousness of sin you white men have. All we experience is fatigue, a deep fatigue–a weariness murky as the colour of my skin, dank, heavily submerged."

Unfortunately, the real reasons behind each such tragic event are often lost in the sands of time. However, important factors often reported to be behind these deaths include concerns over identity, the perceived need to conform, self-sacrifice for others, marginalisation, bullying, loneliness, group rejection, paranoia, depression and disconnection following major natural disasters with their haunting wild extremes, as well as, of course, economic concerns and impoverishment. It is also essential to remember, however, that death by suicide is not an exclusive domain of Japanese authors, Japanese protagonists or Japan. Ernest Hemingway (1899-1961), for instance, and many other much less famous individuals have killed themselves. International data suggests that factors that heighten suicide risk include being an older male and living in a rural area.

> Junko hadn't written about her reasons for committing suicide in her letter to her mother. Instead, she had thanked her mother for giving birth to and raising her, and apologized for throwing away the life she had received.
> Keigo Higashino, *Seijyo no kyusa*i (*Salvation of A Saint*).

Japan has a plethora of regulations and policies to prevent suicide and the rate had been falling. Something that experts have put down to the improving economy after Japan's post-economic bubble lost decades, but the rate is now sadly back on the increase, especially amongst schoolchildren.[34] A new depressing trend, however, also appears to have started to emerge: Those wounded by the ills of society, grappling with its extremes and on the nation's margins, no longer simply take it out physically on themselves, quitting through retreat or suicide. Instead they have started to lash out at others in unprovoked attacks of aggression, a phenomenon that is also not one unique to Japan. Policy fixes never seem to be sufficient. Memories of awful incidents, as well as society's recurring ills, don't disappear in a single generation, if at all. Crisis in all its myriad forms begets literary reflection and many other forms of soul-searching. These sad events morph, change and pop-up in unexpected places, and erasure or demise seem nigh impossible.

Devastation Can Spur Creative Innovation

The Isewan Typhoon—Vera—forced Japan to rethink its relief and mitigation planning, which led to many changes including the creation the following year of Japan's National Disaster Prevention Day. Now an annual event, it is held on 1 September, the anniversary of the devastating Great Kanto Earthquake of 1923, another dreadful generation-defining disaster. This type of planning has probably been more successful and thorough than the nation's suicide and bullying prevention policies. After other major natural disasters, such as the 1995 Great Hanshin-Awaji Earthquake, root and branch national and local policy rethinks have occurred, creating updated and new regulatory regimes.

A major crisis is often treated as a punctuation point in history, which does not require the appellation of an emperor's name or that of a capital city where the authority's central seat is located to define it, that marks new development cycles, an end to a trend or even generational attitudes. They often provide a different type of nomenclature that is still easily exploited and understood.

Causality can often be miss-drawn and misappropriated but it is hard to dispute the fact that catastrophe cries out for interpretation in varied and profound ways.

Literary ports in a storm are arguably a prerequisite for recovery. Intriguingly, the year the super-typhoon hit Japan, 1959, was the year chosen to found a new Japanese medium for escapist storytelling, a highly influential magazine that introduced a gust of off-balance and profound new narrative styles to Japan. It was probably the most successful and important new publication of that year.

SF Magajin (*S-F Magazine*), has since those early days helped nurture a fresh and distinct valley of new voices that brilliantly blow through much of Japanese creative writing. Initially, however, this new magazine brought on shore English-language science fiction stories in Japanese translations, but subsequently it expanded into publishing original stories by Japanese authors and awarding various prizes for the genre. *S-F Magazine*, and its publisher Hayakawa Publishing, continue to play a major role in the development of the sci-fi genre in Japan, sometimes helping nudge the genre in novel new directions.

S-F Magazine manages to provide its readers with both creative risk-free escape and solace from the unforgiving reality of risk-prone life in Japan through the depiction in its pages of alternative realities that often include post-apocalyptic worlds. Something that Isaac Asimov (1920-1992) the Russia-born American author and pioneer of the genre would have understood and welcomed.

"Individual science fiction stories," wrote Asimov, "may seem as trivial as ever to the blinder critics and philosophers of today, but the core of science fiction—its essence—has become crucial to our salvation, if we are to be saved at all."[35] Or as the Scottish author Iain (M) Banks (1954-2013), best known for his debut breakthrough novel *The Wasp Factory* alongside *The Culture*, a series of ten novels set in an interstellar post-scarcity anarchist utopian world with clashing civilisations, put it: "Ever since the Industrial Revolution, science fiction has been the most important genre there is." It has, with encouragement from magazines like this and some brilliant Japanese storytellers, without a doubt played a huge role in Japan and in a real sense 1959 was a watershed year for the genre if not the nation itself.

Many Japanese authors including some of the nation's masters who aren't genre specialists, appear to agree with the sentiments expressed by these two non-Japanese authors, and have dabbled in the genre, which has helped to bring in readers who pick up books because renowned authors' names appear on covers and not because of the science fiction genre itself. This includes the likes of Mishima, for example, who was no doubt aware of this new magazine launched in this tumultuous crunch year. It is common knowledge that Mishima admired the genre and some of its international pioneers, even if it is not possible to confirm if he had a personal subscription to *S-F Magazine* or not.

Nevertheless, less than three years after *S-F Magazine's* launch, in 1962, Mishima presented his own new take on alienation and the increasingly fraught times, publishing *Utsukushii hoshi (Beautiful Star)*. It is a weird and wonderful tale of aliens living concealed amongst us, some trying to save humankind from itself. *Beautiful Star* is set in 1961, at the height of the Cold War when the Soviet Union was testing massive hydrogen bombs with the potential to do even more damage than the bomb dropped over Hiroshima, terrifying Japan, which was almost totally reliant on the United States for its defence. It is a book that Mishima considered one of his best, a dark tale combining literary fiction and popular speculative literature and a Noh mask, with some delightful turns of phrase such as, "this is an age where war will arise from the small poem of a single individual."

Mishima's creative blend of UFOs, dislocation, love and an extra-terrestrial family living in Japan, each of whose members hail from a different planet, however, wasn't one of the critics' favourites. It only arrived in English language translation in 2022, as Mishima's English-language translator at its time of the original publication, a few years after the Isewan Typhoon, was reluctant to take on the task.

S-F Magazine has published authors such as Izumi Suzuki (1949-1986), J. G. Ballard (1930-2009), and Kurt Vonnegut (1922-2007), and its launch issue contained works by Philip K. Dick (1928-1982) and Arthur C. Clarke (1917-2008), an author who Mishima held in high esteem. 1959 was a very good year to be at the publishing vanguard; Hayakawa is now Japan's largest science fiction publisher.

Hunger and Change

Another culturally important and classic example of a high-impact extreme natural disaster, and one alongside the Isewan Typhoon that Hanawa is inclined to mention is the Great Tenmei Famine (1782-1787). When Mount Iwaki and Mount Asama erupted, disease spread and crops failed. It was a crisis that reportedly had its share of institutional mismanagement, a deadly combination that led to a fall of around 900,000 in the Japanese population. According to Hanawa, it is one of the most consequential, but least discussed calamities.

In 1780, according to the 11th Bakufu population census, Japan had a population of around 26 million compared to more than 125 million today. Consequently, the loss of nearly a million people shows proportionally how devastating this sudden extreme drop in the Japanese population in the 1780s must have been. Many factors including better planning and increased access to emergency supplies has led to Japanese life expectancy, the median age and the nation's population increasing multifold since those days, despite a constant stream of disasters.

The Tenmei Famine, which features in Hanawa's 2020 novella *The Chronicles of Lord Asunaro*, was the deadliest in early modern Japanese history. Unsurprisingly, its tragic convergence of crises had a major impact on multiple fronts, directly and indirectly, including on Japanese publishing and even on the nation's reading patterns. As we shall see, it nudged some individuals, who subsequently have become famous internationally, to make life-changing decisions they might not have otherwise made, decisions that have over time changed how the world sees Japan and Japan sees itself. As Takamori Saigo (1828-1877), one of the chief architects and rebel leaders behind the overthrow of Japan's last shogun and the Tokugawa administration in 1868 and who is now considered a quintessential hero of modern Japan, eloquently put it:

> Of opportunities there are two kinds: those that come without our seeking and those that are of our own make. What the world calls opportunity is usually the former kind. But the true opportunity comes by acting in accordance with reason, in compliance with the need of the time. When crises are at hand, opportunities must be caused by us.[36]

Looking For Answers

Naturally, all nations are compelled to respond to catastrophic events; some more often than others. These events can function as societal and institutional stress tests and the success of the responses, whether governmental or literary, often reflect the real state of a given country and a nation's character better than a so-called 'State of the Nation' speech full of hot air by any vainglorious or eloquent vote-seeking or manipulating politician. That is why some think they are important to study and understand.

Hanawa argues that weather patterns and the accumulative effects of extreme catastrophes are generally not sufficiently considered by historians, pundits or academics, in or outside Japan, when they document the past or present, despite the scarring they leave deep in national behaviour patterns, as well as within a country's literary and cultural memory.

Typically, forecasting, not just long-term weather patterns, is itself fraught with risk. Even careful thoughtful analysis can't provide a full audit of national culture and its future trajectory. Sadly, many of us can too often fall into the trap of using simplistic observational analysis to generalise and explain national temperaments. That said, pointing explicitly to weather conditions and weather reports to help read a country and its moods is also fraught with its own traps and dangers. Calamity and cliché can very easily become bedfellows. The gulf between rhetoric and obfuscating layers of reportage, and reality is often chasmic even if there is real truth in Hanawa's point. The attribution of the damp chill of the English atmosphere for the English addiction to games by Emile Boutmy (1835-1906), the French sociologist writer and founder of the illustrious Ecole Libre des Science Politiques, Sciences Po, is a classic and rather good example of this.

That said, sensitivity to the seasons and nature itself are still, most would argue, deeply intertwined with Japan and Japanese cultural appetites. Climate and weather conditions certainly do impact on livelihoods and a major famine, or a cluster of earthquakes or major storms can turn any nation, not just Japan. But cricket, with its interplay of willow on leather, is obsessively enjoyed by many across India, a nation with a very different climate and weather patterns to England. A sports-mad Frenchman, a graduate of Sciences Po to boot, is considered the father of the modern Olympic Games, and Japan's love of golf and baseball, of long-distance running, and its ever-growing entertaining canon of sports literature, can't simply be attributed to Japan's unpleasant rainy season, or can it?

Even with these types of potential analytical traps, anyone with a keen interest in Japan, even though it can be challenging, should actually look, Hanawa believes, behind the sensational news headlines and the superficial despite the fact that, as he laments in his novella *Backlight*, "News from Japan doesn't travel… It is as if Japan's winds do not travel far." The global market for attention is, of course, a highly competitive one, but the important thing is not to simply ride the easy to detect or often reported narrative winds as they blow past you. Though this is also at times sadly hard to avoid for many outside Japan when you consider the relative word count many international publications dedicate to Japan, still one of the world's largest economies, and the type of content that these small allocations of limited sentence budgets are often used for when Japan is reported on. Unfair winds can blow facts and narratives off course.

You need to look far beyond the superficial, such as the nation's quirky seasonal cherry blossom maps, or English clickbait headlines when they do appear, to decode Japan's cultural climate. Not all traits are loudly broadcast. After all, risk avoidance and unmet appetites of all varieties can often be embarrassing and, despite generally remaining concealed, can act as strong stimulants. The lenses through which any given nation looks, or is encouraged to look, at life or the outside world are not always the same ones other nations might use to frame their worldview or even know exist as observational options.[37] Japan is often observed through lenses that don't always reflect its true state as a nation of more than 125 million individuals, each with their own particular family history, appetites, and personal experience of life in Japan.

Swords, ninja, samurai and martial arts as well as *bushido*, the way of the Japanese warrior, are familiar stereotypical symbols that we all too often associate with the Land of the Rising Sun, as is its people's stoic resolve, diligence and polite resilience. Reactionary critics are quick to dismiss such platitudes as a contemporary form of orientalism and even term these portrayals of Japan in film, for instance, as the martial male gaze. Clog-wearing military men no longer walk the streets of Japan and not everyone in Japan actually has a samurai family background. But one unifying collective experience that all Japanese people living in Japan today probably have is a shared experience of national catastrophes, be it of a mega or minor variant, and the retelling of them in the nation's myriad and often brilliant forms of storytelling.

Famine-induced extreme hunger, extreme cold, and such are themes that are strikingly evident in many of Japan's oldest folktales, and ancient myths, reflecting Japan's traumatic past, and perhaps also the nation's current subconscious fears and aspirations. Japan boasts a rich heritage of tales that revolve around ravenous mountain-dwelling *Yama-Uba* (mountain crones), supernatural wives and births, grateful shape-shifting and hapless animals, handless girls, water spirits and ice demons, as well as sacrificial offerings of young girls in return for rich harvests.

In some professions and industries uncertainty is defined and calculated as a type of measurable risk. With risk explained away as the possibility that things might go wrong, a probability you can calculate, and uncertainty as simply not knowing what the future might bring. Others have said risk is simply not knowing what you are doing. This is not, however, how most ordinary people view risk or radical uncertainty, which is why the echoes and candour of uncertainty often serendipitously weave their way into the creative arts and national consciousness.

Storytelling of all kinds, no matter where or when it is penned, is generally designed as a positive psychological refuge and escape from the extremes that catastrophe can sadly expose all of us to. Such storytelling in all its media forms and formats—literary, cinematic, pictorial, animated, or poetic—can also hold up insightful looking-glasses on society, including Japan's, and its fluctuating temperatures be they *Godzilla*, *Nippon Chinbotsu (Japan Sinks)*, *The Refugees' Daughter*, *The Chronicles of Lord Asunaro*, *Tokyo Magnitude 8.0* or tales of ancient Japanese mountain trolls.

For some, crises can even be oddly auspicious.

After a typhoon, all manner of unlikely objects could be found floating in the river: tatami mats, window frames, even paintings and carved wooden objects. The children of the neighborhood would gather on the banks with long poles and nets, retrieving these treasures and setting them out to dry in the sun. They always welcomed a typhoon for the windfalls it would bring.
Teru Miyamoto, *Doro no kawa* (*Muddy River*).

Making an Impression: Printing Pleasure

One year after the start of the Tenmei Famine, Juzaburo Tsutaya (1750-1797) a future Edo period (1603-1868) publisher of woodblock prints with the Midas touch made a life-changing decision. Tsutaya decided to move from his small bookshop, which acted more as a distributor and a co-publisher than as a fully-fledged publishing house. He moved from near the gate of Edo's Yoshiwara quarters, the capital's so-called entertainment district, where he had grown up, and opened a new bookstore in Nihonbashi the commercial quarter of Edo, now known as Tokyo. This was where major established bookshops were located and, as the saying goes, the rest is history.

His decision to move in 1783, rethinking life, location and career, following a major national disaster, that no doubt had a considerable impact on other booksellers and publishers in Japan, is not an isolated one within Japan's long and rich publishing and literary history. Some call this "doing a geographical". Tsutaya developed his business into a fully-fledged publishing house in his new location, allowing him to nurture many of Japan's most famous *ukiyo-e* (woodblock) artists and authors. He had a "discerning eye for discovering new talent" as well as an amazing talent for promotion.

He started publishing Utamaro Kitagawa (1753-1806) the year of his move. Utamaro was an artist that achieved a national reputation in Japan in his own lifetime and also famously influenced some of Europe's most famous Impressionists many years later, including the likes of Vincent van Gogh (1853-1890) and Henri Matisse (1869-1954). Today the name Tsutaya, a famous eponym Japanese trend-setting retail chain run by Culture Convenience Club (CCC), adorns some of Tokyo's choicest shopping streets with a few flagship stores that some have described as the world's best designed bookshops.

Tsutaya is probably most famous for turning *Kusazoshi* books (genres of popular woodblock-printed illustrated literature) and *ukiyo-e* into fashionable, must-have items. Tsutaya has been described as one of the most important Edo period trend-setters. He also published and distributed the *Yoshiwara Saiken*, an extremely popular guidebook to the Yoshiwara licensed 'pleasure district' and, like all pioneering publishers, had a few run-ins with the censors and authorities. For him, disaster was auspicious and played a crucial part in determining the direction of his career path. This proves that we are not all destined to be boxed in by the intransigent and immutable facts of nature and geography no matter how influential they might be. We always have choices.

The Twin Shocks: Ending Cultural Hibernation

Another fascinating triggering event that occurred much later in the 1850s was when Japan was shaken once again, literally and metaphorically. This time not by extreme hunger, a powerful typhoon or volcanic eruptions, but by two major crises: The first was the arrival of Commodore Perry (1794-1858) from America with his famous black ships, four in total, two powered by steam, which forced Japan's markets open with dramatic consequences waking up the 'hermit' nation. The second was a series of major earthquakes including the Ansei Edo Earthquake of 1855, which caused a tsunami. Cumulatively these put Japan under extreme stress, both politically and economically.

One of these earthquakes killed the scholar Toko Fujita (1806-1855), who had participated in the negotiations with the Americans after Perry's arrival a few years earlier. He was also the inspiration behind the subsequent movement to overthrow the shogun and Japan's feudal system. The legendary opportunistic samurai Saigo was an admirer of his. The twist of destiny of Fujita's untimely death, when his house collapsed in 1855, perhaps allowed his large and illustrious disciple, Saigo, to create his own opportunity, helping implement national change and subsequently provoking rebellion with his famous last stand at the Battle of Shiroyama.

The confluence of these events turned Saigo with "his great booming laugh" and honesty of purpose into a heroic figure remembered today, not just for his charismatic leadership, the nobility of his final foretold failure and subsequent dignified death, something that can often turn an individual into a revered hero in Japan,[38] but also due to his poetry, which includes phrases such as:

Deeds are born in distress.
Through snow, plums are white,
Through frosts, maples are red;
If but Heaven's will be known,
Who shall seek for slothful ease!

Although one can never be sure of anything in history, this unyielding traditional warrior is the model for the so-called last samurai, in the eponymous Hollywood film starring Tom Cruise, adding to the allure and heroic mystery surrounding the mountain-like man, Saigo, with his grey beard.

The 1850s was a dramatic decade that eventually helped change Japan beyond recognition, finally bringing an end to the nation's Edo period when the country was run by shoguns, and Tsutaya's type of woodblock printing and publishing flourished in glorious isolation. It also had a series of equilibrium-shifting repercussions, some short-term and others much longer term and international, including for example a change in hairstyles, diets, the role of the samurai and dress codes, not to mention weather forecasting and the techniques used for earthquake prediction, something in which Japan now invests a huge amount of money and time.

Immediately after the earthquake—it was actually a series of quakes, including 30 or so aftershocks—publishers and newspapers started printing images of giant mythological catfish, *Namazu*, as Japanese folklore stories attributed earthquakes to the movements of these giant unhappy odd-looking subterranean catfish. This led to a mini catfish publishing-boom, probably the world's first, with hundreds of varieties of publications, some which even contained critical political undertones, being printed. Their fishy movements were considered as both a predictor of earthquake patterns, as well as protective talismans if images of them were displayed in one's home in printed form.

The catfish, a carnivore with sharp teeth and long whiskers, is a creature with complex cultural connotations. Surprisingly, the Tokyo Metropolitan Marine Experimentation Station has actually studied their fabled ability at forecasting earthquakes using observational experiments designed to verify if these creatures really display unusually active pre-earthquake movements. After a 16-year publicly funded study, they concluded that catfish might be sensitive to shifts in weak electrical fields and that the association between their movements and earthquakes was probably better than random correlation. However, the correlations measured were not material or reliable enough to be a useful tool in disaster prevention management.[39]

There is also something known in some business circles as the catfish effect. This is generally caused when a new market entrant or technology, that like these predatory fish entering new waters, forces existing weaker inhabitants facing a new existential threat to start swimming much faster, creating a ripple-effect that changes cosy market dynamics beyond recognition. The parallels are hardly precise, but a classic example of this effect is an 18-metre-high windmill erected at a similar time in 1857 in Jerusalem by Sir Moses Montefiore (1784-1885), a farsighted

Anglo-Jewish financier and philanthropist. Montefiore, like Perry, wanted to instigate change. In his case he wanted to encourage Jews living within the constricted confines of the protected walls of the Old City of Jerusalem to experience life outside those borders. Montefiore also wanted to relieve poverty and create a new environment for that community to flourish outside of the ancient city walls that restricted their potential growth.

Against the Grain

To achieve this Montefiore thought he needed to break the wheat milling monopoly, something he did by importing a windmill from Ramsgate, England. Despite some of the Arabs that ran the monopoly hiring a mystic to curse this new predatory technology from foreign climes, the windmill had catfish-like effects changing market dynamics rapidly and bringing down the price of flour. Other windmills followed, some built by the Greek Orthodox Church, and subsequently others powered by steam. In a city not blessed with strong winds there is some debate about the practical effectiveness of the Montefiore windmill. Nevertheless, his windmill has morphed into an important physical and cultural landmark. Its image features in literature, poetry and adorns Israeli banknotes, coins and stamps. The windmill operated for two decades until 1878, and the existential threat it provided to the city's millers broke open the monopoly and helped unlock the city's economy and built environment. These days, conversations have shifted from the supply and price of flour to broader property rights and prices in the ever-dynamic city of Jerusalem. Today, in Silicon Valley this type of strategic approach would be described as disruptive innovation.

Perry's sensational arrival in the waters of Tokyo within sight of the capital city's suburbs and the earthquakes a few years later, triggered a revolution that restored the Japanese Imperial Court to the centre of Japanese power and Japan opened up rapidly embracing Western science and technology. Perry himself had no inkling at the time of his first visit of the existence of an emperor in the background. The emperor at the time was Emperor Komei (1831-1867). It was his son who would replace the shogun at the head of Japan's new modernising administrative order at the age of 15 following the early death, from smallpox, of his father.

It was a tumultuous time with a confluence of high-impact, connected and disruptive events. Pre-industrial Japan decided to raise its game and swim faster. It didn't wish to end up as prey to one of the so-called Great Powers; the example of China after the Opium Wars was clear for all in Japan to see. Of course, modern practical industrial windmills, as opposed to the toy and ornamental ones Japan already had, in their case designed to pump water, soon arrived in Japan from the United States and Europe. The post-shogunate easing of regulations about the height of buildings and man-made structures also helped. These changes would later allow Japan to charge full steam ahead in new directions and into international waters.

Perry beat ambitious naval men from the other Great Powers such as Britain and Russia, creating his celebrated appointment with history. The Russian Admiral Yevfimiy Putyatin (1803-1883) visited the same year, one month after Perry, arriving in the port of Nagasaki with the British Navy watching on menacingly. If by some twist of fate it had not been the firm, blunt and highly experienced Perry that affected this pivotal change, perhaps the course of Japanese history might have flowed differently, with a new scenario that included an immediate period of semi-colonial dependence.

Much changed and there was an astonishing amount of modernising progress, but despite how it looks from today's perspective or is often portrayed, the opening of Japan and the renaissance it inspired wasn't just a single black swan-like event nor was it a smooth bloodless transfer of power. The shogunate administration didn't collapse suddenly like a cheap tent experiencing its first strong winds from afar.

The shogunate, for example, took advice from the French who were openly sympathetic to their cause. There were multiple overseas missions and even rumours of secret undertakings. The other world powers were jockeying for position and influence, foreign technical advisors were employed and there was much uncertainty, many twists and turns, and months of civil war before the shogun, who was actually a reluctant one, resigned in 1867 bringing the Bakufu Shogunate administration to an end.[40] It would, however, be an understatement to say that Perry's journey upstream into Japanese waters created only a ripple effect. It was a significant moment. Like a mythical giant catfish from the watery depths of Japan it created a major national tectonic disturbance.

This opening when it finally came was, however, actually a two-directional flow of ideas and products. Japanese products and art, for example, started being exported after initially being displayed at The International Exhibition in London in 1862, the very first major international public show that included Japanese art. It caused a sensation. Unusual and novel Japanese objects, such as umbrellas and fans, helped create huge demand in Europe not just for foldable Japanese fans but other Japanese collectibles such as the woodblock prints that Tsutaya published. This provided an essential economic and cultural boost for Japan just as it was emerging on the international stage after almost three centuries of self-imposed isolation.

The first commercial translation of a work of Japanese fiction in any European language had already been published in Austria by this time in 1847, but after Japan was rocked and shocked out of its isolation, literary and publishing connections through translations and educational exchanges increased and accelerated further during Japan's Meiji era (1868-1912) to the delight of many outside Japan. Perhaps this provides proof that globalisation has never simply meant Westernisation, but also can include popular cultural flows from other regions to America and the West.

However, this opening changed much of Japan's literary output forever and caused a subsequent reshaping of the world of Japanese letters, something that readers around the world benefit from and enjoy to this day. Tellingly, other major Japanese earthquakes, pandemics and disasters of both varieties (natural and unnatural) have elicited similar literary and publishing responses before and after the Great Tenmei Famine and the twin shocks of the 1850s. Showing that the links between climate change, demography, geopolitics, the economy and memorable storytelling are not new.

Crisis Begets Creativity: Bone Rattling Prose

After the 1923 Great Kanto Earthquake, which killed more than 100,000 people in and around Tokyo, Junichiro Tanizaki (1886-1965), who was nominated for the Nobel Prize in Literature in 1964, the year before his death, decided to move from Yokohama to Kyoto. This decision reportedly led to a more detached tone in his writing style, as well as an acute keen-eyed awareness of cultural sentiment and the nation's rapidly changing winds. His move to new waters is a classic example of a highly successful geographical. The relocation, like Tsutaya's in 1783, helped shift Tanizaki's position in the canon of Japanese publishing and many think, changed his creative output for the better. He wrote seminal books such as *Chijin no ai* (*Naomi*), *Sasameyuki* (*The Makioka Sisters*) and *Inei raisan* (*In Praise of Shadows*), after the move when his writing finally took off and his reputation flourished.

The 1923 earthquake also had a material impact on some of Japan's most important storytellers alongside Tanizaki such as Ryunosuke Akutagawa (1892-1927) and Akira Kurosawa (1910-1998), one of the world's most exalted film directors. In 1923, Akutagawa wrote *Daishin zakki* (*Ruminations on the Earthquake*) in a form of literary journalism.

Kurosawa, who was still a young boy at the time, was encouraged to walk the city after this huge earthquake (something that Akutagawa also did) with his older brother to see the death and destruction with his own eyes. The experience is reported to have had a major impact on him and influenced how he depicted death and destruction in some of the epic battle scenes in his subsequent films.

Kawabata joined Akutagawa, his friend, on one of his walks through the devastated city, which they surveyed together. An experience that left memories that he also reflected on in his subsequent work. Kurosawa was an avid reader. Books and authors including Akutagawa had a major influence on him. We know, for example, that he read "Yabu no naka" ("In a Grove") by Akutagawa as it inspired his film *Rashomon* and we can probably assume he also hungrily devoured Akutagawa's *Ruminations on the Earthquake*.

Seismic Returns: The Magical Realism of Movement

There are echoes of this in the literary response to the much more recent major earthquake on 11 March 2011, which also tragically triggered a highly destructive tsunami and the subsequent nuclear disaster in Fukushima. These linked events are now sometimes referred to by the numerical shorthand 3/11 (Japan dates go in order of year/month/day, so 11 March becomes 3/11), and the cultural responses are well documented. Seminars have even been arranged on the topic and academic books have been published such as *3.11: Disaster and Change in Japan* by Richard J. Samuels, a detailed analysis from a professor at the Massachusetts Institute of Technology (MIT) who spent around a year in Japan researching the impact. Some go as far as arguing that a border should be drawn in the canon of Japanese literature, delineating works, allowing them to fall into pre-2011 and post-earthquake literature. This is a judgement that when you look back at Japan's long history of rubble-rising prose is arguably far too early to make.

Murakami's collection of six short stories, *Kami no kodomotachi wa mina odoru (After The Quake)* was published earlier in 2000 following the 1995 Great Hanshin-Awaji Earthquake. This collection, a favourite of another important award-winning contemporary Japanese author Hiromi Kawakami (b. 1958) and many others, deftly probes the causes of a cluster of problems Japan faced at the time of its writing, not just the earthquake and its aftermath. Additionally, these types of soul-searching literary post-calamity sentiments can be traced back centuries, to works such as *Hojoki (An Account of My Hut)*, by the Buddhist monk Chomei Kamono (1155-1216) with his poetic accounts of chaos, uncertainty, the smells of famine and the disasters, which befell the Japanese capital Kyoto (earthquakes, fires, whirlwinds and famine) in his lifetime, as well as his life as a recluse living in a small hut.

In 2023, the Museum of Modern Japanese Literature in Tokyo held an exhibition titled *Writing Disaster* to commemorate the centennial anniversary of the Great Kanto Earthquake, highlighting again the importance many, not just Hanawa, put on the connections between disasters of both the natural and unnatural kind and literature and publishing. This exhibition featured handwritten manuscripts and exhibits mostly but not exclusively about the Great Kanto Earthquake of 1923, a disaster that destroyed almost all of Japan's publishing industry which was mainly concentrated in Tokyo at the time. Millions of books were burnt or destroyed. Decisive responses to the destruction helped define the future of some publishing houses such as Kodansha. The decisions and rapid actions taken by its founder Seiji Noma (1878-1938), for example, helped put the company on a new trajectory, one that would subsequently lead to it becoming Japan's largest privately owned publishing house. The centennial exhibition also featured works related to the 2011 Great East Japan Earthquake.

That said, the 2011 Great East Japan Earthquake that triggered the 3/11 triple disaster certainly brought to the surface narratives and interest in problems that had long lurked sunken deep beneath the media headlines and the typical coverage generated by the type of books often chosen for prominent and regular review. Topics such as the divide between the flourishing capital Tokyo, and rural poverty and its associated population decline. "It is not a completely new form or branch in Japanese literature," Shinya Machida, a culture journalist working for the *Yomiuri Shimbun*, who commissions fiction for serialisation in Japan's highest-circulation national newspapers, argues. "This form of writing already existed. What has happened is that the Great East Japan Earthquake spawned renewed interest and awareness in what was already there, hidden, submerged behind the scenes, ignored, out-of-sight for many." Like the mythical angry catfish of bygone ages, you might conclude.

According to experts, the response, in publishing terms, to the 3/11 cluster of linked disasters, which fused a natural disaster with a man-made one, differed from other more recent events like the Great Hanshin Earthquake. This is not down to the volume and speed of the literary responses but rather the nature of their formats, which were less journalistic or first-hand diary-like observations, even though these existed. Instead, they were far more imaginary, philosophical and poetic. They were also instantly widely available thanks to digital technology and generated a unique form of live creative reportage.

There have been many remarkable, memorable and highly imaginative responses, including *Umatachi yo soredemo hikari wa mukude* (*Horses, Horses, in the End the Light Remains Pure*) by Hideo Furukawa (b. 1966), an unusual elliptical blend of reportage, memoir and fiction that recounts the author's immediate shock of the disaster as he travels back to his childhood home. While quoting and featuring in a montage-like manner characters that have appeared in previous works by the author, Furukawa creates a layered portrait of personal and cultural dislocation that provides a strange alertness to the experience rather than the facts.

In 2022 Atsushi Sato (b. 1982) won the Akutagawa Prize for his down-to-earth novel *Arechi no kazoku* (*A Family in the Wasteland*), set in the coastal area of Miyagi Prefecture in the decade after the disaster, portraying the realities and hardships, business collapses and the wrenching family dynamics of post-disaster life. Artists working in other genres, like Hiroshima-born Fumiyo Kono (b. 1968), have also embraced these types of narrative themes, creating manga such as her two-part work *Hi no tori* (*Bird of the Sun*), which depicts the impact these linked disasters had on daily life. Another interesting example is *Shinsai-fuzokujyo* (*Disaster Prostitutes*), by Ikko Ono (b. 1966), that documents how female sex workers were back in business one week after the linked disasters struck and why this was important.

There have also been excellent books by non-Japanese writers such as Richard Lloyd-Perry's *Ghosts of the Tsunami: Death and Life in Japan's Disaster Zone*, but the one literary response that stands out in particular, amongst the dissonance of creative responses, is the simple and sparse but poignant poetic words tweeted by a high school mathematics teacher, Ryoichi Wago (b. 1968), such as: "Radiation is falling. It is a quiet night." His instant flurry of poetic tweets, laced with pathos, exploiting Japan's love and mastery of short-form writing, turned Wago into a future award-winning poet and a household name in Japan.

A nation struggling to come to terms with what had just occurred seemed to find a type of solace in his stripped back verse, which they took to their hearts. Digital technologies and the immediacy of national television neither of which existed at the time of the Isewan Typhoon, for instance, allowed for its defining narrative, not to be one published during the year, week or day the catastrophe occurred but a decade or so later as the *Red Fate* television series. The desire to respond and the need to share narratives, and the creative abilities of those doing so, have not changed, but the tools to do so have. Digital platforms made this disaster an instant collective experience, not a delayed imagined one.

Miri Yu (b. 1968), a rising literary star who grew up in Yokohama, is yet another interesting example of a Japan-based author successfully doing a geographical. She moved to Fukushima, the area most affected by the nuclear disaster, where she opened a bookshop. Her 2014 novel *JR Ueno-Eki Kouenguchi* (*Tokyo Ueno Station*) probably falls more within the canon of Japanese Olympic literature as it mostly involves the forlorn life of an unfortunate worker, Kazu, involved in the construction of the 1964 Tokyo Olympic infrastructure, but it also creatively draws on the author's experiences of the disasters, which are woven into the novel's kaleidoscopic narrative arc. The English translation by Morgan Giles won the US National Book Award for Translated Literature in 2020 putting Yu and her translator—it was Giles's first translation of a full-length work of Japanese fiction—on the international publishing map. Yu had already won several literary awards in Japan, including the Akutagawa Prize, but this international publishing milestone shows again the power and serendipity that making a post-disaster move can have.

Not all geographicals are triggered by disasters. As George Lucas, the film director and major Kurosawa fan put it: "Everybody has talent, it's just a matter of moving around until you've discovered what it is." The prose and storytelling you admire most may not always turn out to be the type you are most capable of penning compellingly yourself. Finding your long-term niche, or voice, can require a jolt, a different approach and sometimes moving around physically, as well as literally. Japan seems to provide more than its fair share of examples of this.

Murakami, for instance, famously moved to Hawaii, living there between 2005 and 2014. Several award-winning contemporary female Japanese authors now live in major European cities, as does Tsuji. After considering a move to London, the Naoki Prizewinner Kazufumi Shiraishi (b. 1958) now lives a somewhat nomadic existence in Japan having lived in many different locales including Karuizawa. Moving seems to help some writers discover the undulating and nuanced contours of existence that can eventually end up as superbly penned plots in gripping and haunting narrative fiction or memorable lyrics.

The 'move on' phenomenon is, of course, not just limited to Japanese artists. Many others have famously enjoyed the benefits or similar reinventions be it singer-songwriters like David Bowie (1947-2016) in Berlin or Emmylou Harris (b. 1947), who seems to have moved city in the United States every time she has had to confront a personal catastrophe, and in so doing, re-imagined herself as well as country music itself.

Cults, New Religions, and Bizarre Organisations

Man-made and unnatural disasters have also generated memorable literary and publishing reactions. These include the dreadful Minamata Disease, caused by industrial mercury pollution during Japan's extraordinary post-war industrial rush to rebuild the country and boost national prosperity. Michiko Ishimure (1927-2018) helped raise awareness of insidious pollution and the Minamata Disease, one of Japan's worse cases of toxic industrial pollution, and the plight of its thousands of human and animal victims through her works. The Minamata narrative and its disastrous aftermath still lives on decades later, despite its cause being identified as far back as a stormy 1959. As victims who survived grew older, the unhealthy legacies of this extreme case of heavy metal poisoning is kept in the public domain with the assistance of new poignant stories, such as *Minamata mandala*, a 2020 six-hour documentary from the acclaimed director Kazuo Hara (b. 1945).

Another example is the deadly series of coordinated attacks conducted by the Japanese religious cult, Oum Shinrikyo (Aum Supreme Truth) that shocked Japan and the world in 1995, the same year as the Great Hanshin Earthquake. Murakami tackled the morning rush hour nerve gas attacks with *Andaguraundo (Underground)* and *Yakusoku sareta basho de – Andaguraundo 2 (The Place that was Promised)* which were combined and adapted for a single English language edition *Underground: The Tokyo Gas Attack and the Japanese Psyche*. Murakami's response was the type of literary journalism that Akutagawa would have approved of. His work, which was researched, written and published in the late 1990s, focused predominantly on the victims through a series of interviews with some of the individuals caught up in the attacks. In fact, these coordinated attacks led to a flurry of highly successful Japanese novels that included cults, new religions, and bizarre organisations as part of their narratives. Important examples include *Kyodan X (Cult X)* by Fuminori Nakamura (b. 1977) published in 2014 and *Yokame no semi (The Eighth Day)* by Kakuta published in 2007 but set in 1985. Both were massive sellers in Japan and draw on the cult, with their sarin-filled plastic bags, behind the Tokyo attacks for cultural context and inspiration. Kenzaburo Oe (1935-1923) also published a book about a cult, *Chugaeri (Somersault)*, in 1999 and Murakami returned to the theme in 2009 with *1Q84*, when the first two of its three volumes were published.

A cluster of such titles suddenly arriving in translation in a given country, after an initial publishing success creates a mini trend, like the Edo period catfish, that can have unintended consequences creating distorting effects, somewhat like the crazy curved mirrors at fairgrounds, framing Japan in unexpected, exaggerated hues. Kakuta, for example, was bemused and taken aback at a series of literary events in continental Europe by the frequency of audience questions about the number and extent of cults, destructive social groups and new religions in Japan, and also why individuals in Japan seemed so isolated and lonely. These phenomena of course exist in reality, as well as within Japanese narrative fiction, but only represents a slither of Japan immense literary canon, and a slice of the many different types of lives individuals in Japan actually lead, even if most have experienced some type of national or personal calamity directly or indirectly.

Another rather different but interesting example is Randy Taguchi's (b. 1959) novel *Sakasa ni tsurusareta otoko* (*A Man Hung Upside Down*), the narrative of which draws on a personal relationship the author developed after the tragic events on the Tokyo subway system with one of the Aum perpetrators who was eventually executed for his role in the attacks. Taguchi follows a different course to Murakami, highlighting the diversity of Japanese writing and showing that the nation is not a monoculture. She frames her work from the perspective of the perpetrators, not the victims, and explores the troubling trajectories often powered by guilt, shame and fear, that led them to causing an international headline-making incident and becoming the villains of the dreadful events.

Perhaps some of these literary responses reflect something that is increasingly evident in many societies, and nowadays in Japan too: that seeing oneself as a victim in different situations can allow for one to release oneself from feeling complicity in what happens around you, even if that happens to include your role as a member of a Japanese cult or that of a bully. Slow slip events, sometimes called silent earthquakes, are after all not merely a phenomenon of geophysics.

Living on the Edge: The Art of Escape

Literature is often the sanctuary we turn to when we are compelled to confront uncertainty as well as contradictions and tragic twists of fate that lie beyond normal comprehension. That is certainly the case in regard to the two unprecedented man-made disasters that struck Japan in 1945: the atomic bombs. The literary shelter in the aftermaths of the atomic bombs that some might see as a kind of multi-generational textual escape from post-traumatic stress, has created its own international publishing genre known as 'atomic bomb literature', a genre that will be explored in more detail later in a dedicated essay, with thousands of works spanning multiple forms and formats. Tragically, age is not a barrier to horrendous experiences, first- or second-hand, and these awful events have eclipsed much historical war-related suffering inside and outside Japan, including for example the air raids that killed thousands and left millions homeless in Tokyo, as well as the prism through which the panorama of blame and responsibility are attributed.

Sadly, there will be new disasters in Japan's future, but hopefully never another nuclear one. Though Japanese storytelling doesn't overtly require any additional creative juice or major external stimuli, it will no doubt continue to receive jolts from both nature and the results of human action or inaction. Not everyone can or wants to leave the Japanese archipelago, which is riddled with volcanoes and thousands of fault lines linked to the four tectonic plates that converge on Japan. This makes other avenues of escape a compulsion and the fodder that often feeds creative writing.

Disturbances in the dynamic forces that intersect crisis and culture will ensure the country's publishing plates, genres and creative writing never become dull or institutionalised, nor evolve in a simple infinitely expanding linear trajectory, even if for given periods such as during Japan's Edo period, Galapagos-like, they may superficially appear to do so. The re-rendering of the collective and individual experiences of calamity, many believe, are one of the tragic but also magical causal ingredients that allows Japan and its people to rebuild and reimagine their collective futures once they emerge from a particularly difficult period.

Its geographical location is such that Japan will always face the risk of a new or next natural disaster, but disaster where possible must, of course, be avoided and fine-weather periods with their quiet progress enjoyed and celebrated. At times the meteorological dice seem to be weighted against Japan. However, anyone who sincerely wishes to understand Japan and its behavioural patterns, and who consciously or inadvertently ignores these important cultural responses and tailwinds, does so at their intellectual peril. Especially as anthropogenic climate change and oppressive heat storms even further into the mainstream.

Grim Tales: Primeval Trolls and Eating Disorders

Nobody can escape childhood without some exposure to monsters, demons, witches, or trolls. Be they tales about the lovable ogre Shrek, the Devil, Harry Potter, Japanese *oni* or games like *Pokémon*. *Oni*, the Japanese name for Japan's particular type of demon, including the famously ravenous mountain dwelling *Yama-Uba* (mountain crone), have had their stories reinvented and retold since storytelling began.

Oni are monsters, *yokai*, that generally have the most negative and nasty associations. Even though the actual name *oni* and the character used to render it in Japanese is a Chinese import, these legendary tales predate the arrival in Japan of Buddhism and the Chinese alphabet. The *oni* ideogram, according to Japanese encyclopaedias, is a representation of the invisible spirit of the dead, probably a corrupted use of the Japanese word for 'hidden', and an entity that in the ancient past, before Japan's Heian period (794-1184), was known as a *mono*.[41] Despite multiple versions of their tales varying by region, era, format and media, these mysterious beings always reflect our inner demons and society's deepest fears.[42]

Stories about isolated mountain dwelling *Yama-Uba* (also known as *Yamanba*), for instance, that can devour oxen, children, men and dozens of rice balls in one mouthful, and transform themselves back into their primal form (usually snakes, spiders, or badgers) have captivated and terrified people for generations. These stories can be found throughout Japan as well as in the country's art, theatre, literature and folk tales. Extreme hunger is a familiar narrative that also runs through folk tales from other cultures including the Grimm's fairy tales like *Hansel and Gretel* and the rather disturbing tale *The Juniper Tree*.[43] Alongside cannibalistic tales, famine and those who plan for its avoidance have helped shape many nations, such as Joseph, famous for his colourful cloak, in ancient Egypt and a multi-year regional famine that he helped successfully navigate.

Another example is the 'peasant Saint' Sontoku Ninomiya (1787-1856) born in the final year of Japan's devastating population-shrinking Great Tenmei Famine (1782-1787). In Edo period (1603-1868) Japan, this parentless autodidact from the coastal city of Odawara in central Japan, orphaned with his two younger brothers at age 16, was like Joseph much earlier in Egypt, a fan and early proponent of the magic-like properties of compound interest, planning, and the abacus. He famously filled and opened the storehouses to feed the starving. As a result, today his statue can often be seen outside many Japanese primary schools. Though his name and tale are much less well-known than the horde of tales about scary-looking ravenous Japanese mountain crones.

Hunger, its containment, and the decision-making and disorders it sometimes generates can leave unchallengeable legacies that can lurk in unusual places. Famine can also, of course, be released on the peasantry deliberately in horrible political acts. Cravings have also been the genesis of much memorable storytelling.

In Japan, the multiplicity of *Yama-Uba* tales show that it was no easy feat for Japan to reach the point of being able to feed the nation. Today, Japan, though still self-sufficient in rice, imports around 60 percent of its food, more than most other developed nations. Sadly, some developing nations, such as Egypt, in spite of ancient tales filled with famine management advice, still struggle to feed their populations. They can appear sensitive and overly vulnerable when it comes to food security, the terrible social impact of food price inflation, and the gyrations of international agricultural markets, and wheat harvests in particular. This is despite Egypt, for example, actually being more self-sufficient in terms of vegetables and fruit production than Japan. Keeping a nation fed, nutritious and healthy in all the forms and formats required, efficiently and at affordable prices, is a perennial problem.

Kuwazu nyobo (*The Woman Who Never Eats*) is one *Yama-Uba* story that has many variants. The narrative revolves around an old bachelor who is either too mean, too fearful of commitment, or just simply too poor to marry, and therefore tells his friends he will only marry a woman who eats nothing. As luck would have it, a beautiful woman who eats nothing does indeed come to him. In public she is young, beautiful, hardworking and gracious, but he later discovers that in private (when she is hidden and alone) she binges on food and has a huge concealed second mouth on the top of her head. Once discovered, her true terrifyingly unattractive identity as either an animal, old hag or demon, is dramatically revealed.[44]

Some versions of the *Yama-Uba* story are simpler and involve travellers being attacked and livestock being devoured whole. Others depict evil mountain crones with unkempt white hair and scarecrow-like kimonos sneaking into homes and gobbling up children. However, not all of them feature cannibalism. On occasion, they portray benign and even nurturing characters, as in the story of the *Yama-Uba* who raises *Kintaro*, the Golden Boy with super-human strength. A heroic and extremely popular character that has long been a feature of kabuki, and these days an ageless golden-child that appears in anime, manga, video games and action figure form.

Understandably, there has been much analysis over the origin and meaning of these stories, which often mirror the perspective and fears of those deconstructing them.[45] Outspoken representatives of the establishment often seem to harshly cluster marginality, deviance, seclusion and acts of condemnation together. This has allowed some to have a field day in reinterpreting and digesting the role that *Yama-Uba*, for instance, who are sometimes baited, bullied and ill-treated but are always starved of what most people crave or need to survive, play in society. While some creatives exploit her fame by trying to sate the ever hungry fascination with these societal outliers in new monetisable modern presentations.

The current longevity of the Japanese people and its rapidly ageing population are very well documented. But when resources were scarce long before urbanisation, the old, unwell and mentally ill were sometimes banished into the mountains. There is a famous legend known as *Ubasute* in which the old were carried into the mountains at a certain age and abandoned in an ancient form of euthanasia.[46] The drama and trauma of this is strikingly captured in the prizewinning novel, *Narayamabushiko (The Ballad of Narayama)* by Shichiro Fukazawa (1914-1987), which has been turned into at least two film adaptations; one of which, set in a small rural 19th century village, directed by Shohei Imamura (1926-2006) won the Palme d'Or at the Cannes Film Festival in 1983.

Today, Japan is blessed with pensions and many different types of retirement homes providing new and more imaginative options. In the mountain woods of Shizuoka in eastern Japan, for example, two retired female Tokyo social workers who worried about how their futures might evolve and who would look after them as they aged have funded their own private retirement home. Reflecting how much things have changed for some, they commissioned one of their sons, an architect, to design the perfect place for them to live out their remaining days: a down to earth hilltop location that has been described in the media as a fairy-tale village with a cluster of dwarf houses.[47] Their proactive solution is a much better one than the social dumping of the past, which for some involved your son carrying you up a mountain on his back and discarding you there in the cold, leaving you to fend for yourself.

Despite such international heart-warming headline-making examples, an estimated 25 percent of elderly Japanese women actually still live below the poverty line, and approximately one million retired individuals in Japan receive some form of state financial assistance. Old-age poverty rates are expected to increase materially.

Some see the *Yama-Uba* as a metaphor for disenfranchised and abandoned individuals on the margins of society. While others such as the award-winning author Yuya Sato (b. 1980), known for his 'strange fiction', have been inspired by these fables and the films. He says his novel *Dendera*, published in English translation in 2015, is, "the amalgamation of my own personality with the legend of *Ubasute*—leaving the elderly to die of exposure—with the snowy mountain as the backdrop."[48] Its language and message, despite being highly memorable, is by no means biblical in nature.

Sato renders his presentation into a cynical dark gory tale of abandoned aged women, determined or forced into deciding how to live and when to die, that create their own *utopia*. Not a paradise lost but a type of hilarious Japanese version of Nobel Prizewinner William Golding's (1911-1993) *Lord of the Flies* with a mountainside, instead of an island, and abandoned Japanese women all aged over 60, instead of stranded British schoolboys.

A more recent manifestation of something akin to these tales is *Aokigahara*, otherwise known as Japan's Suicide Forest. Located near Mount Fuji, this is a sad location where more than 200 hundred people are said to have gone to kill themselves.[49]

Tales about Women and Food are Generally not Happy Ones

Ancient Japanese tales about women and food are generally not happy ones and are not limited to the *Yama-Uba*, *Yamanba* and *Ubasute* stories. *Uke-Mochi-no-Kami*, the Japanese goddess of food, is a perfect example. According to legend, she spewed out game from her mouth when facing the land and fish when facing the ocean. But when welcoming her brother, the storm-god, with a specially prepared feast, he wasn't too pleased with his banquet of sisterly vomit and abruptly killed her.[50] According to the myth, her dead body subsequently produced rice, beans and millet, while her head produced an ox.

Many consider eating disorders such as bulimia and anorexia as modern culture-bound Western illnesses that wouldn't have afflicted individuals in ancient times in Japan or anywhere else. Interestingly, the word bulimia derives from the Greek word for ravenous hunger (*bous* –ox and *limos* – hunger) and is defined as "a serious eating disorder that occurs chiefly in females and is characterised by compulsive overeating usually followed by self-induced vomiting". Anorexia, on the other hand, is from the Greek words: 'negation' and 'appetite'. It was first officially defined as a medical term in 1873 by the personal physician of Queen Victoria (1819-1901), a romantic music-loving monarch, who had nine children including five daughters, and wasn't renowned for her parenting skills.[51]

These illnesses with their modern and established definitions are now on the rise both in Japan and the rest of the world. While the world has fallen in love with Japanese food, and newspapers report on Japan having the healthiest diet, anthropologists, sociologists, feminists and psychologists are starting to research eating habits in Japan.[52]

Human psyche and emotions run very deep and influence all of our eating habits. Conversely, there are studies that suggest emotional regulation and some of our thought processes are influenced by our guts and their complex ecosystems. Many languages including Japanese are replete with folklore-like phraseology about trusting one's gut. These interactions no doubt flow both ways. Some argue that a desire to remain in control or young is often the force behind these illnesses. There are also experts that believe some young girls have a deep-rooted fear that reaching maturity will lead to them becoming like their mothers, monarch or not, and that this can be avoided or postponed by not eating. Others that it is a symptom of being marginalised, narcissistic, or disenfranchised, combined with the constant media portrayal of beautiful people and the inference that the perfect body and marriage will bring happiness. The controversial American author and journalist Naomi Wolf argues:

> a culture fixated on female thinness is not an obsession about female beauty, but an obsession about female obedience. Dieting is the most potent political sedative in women's history; a quiet mad population is a tractable one.[53]

Food is and has always been a potent symbol and motif deployed in storytelling in many languages, sometimes to make a radical point or challenge the status quo, and not exclusively in Japan. Margaret Atwood's debut novel *The Edible Woman* is a particularly good example of this. A tale of a recently engaged woman who loses her will to eat and finds her world falling apart. It features a pink cake shaped as a woman and repulsion from what has been termed as modern metaphorical cannibalism. That said, protagonists of this ilk are not only portrayed as pliable victims. Stereotypes are sometimes adopted consciously or unconsciously, with roles assumed to gain advantage, positioning protagonists and clever exploiter as party to their own subjugation.

In the recent past, the Japanese expression *Yamanba* has been used to describe a certain alternative look that some young Japanese girls (known as *Gyaru* or *Kogal*) first adopted in the 1990s. The look initially involved dyed blonde hair, dark facial tans and extensive white above-eye make-up.

Gyaru Sone, whose real name is Natsuko Sone, sprang to fame and become a reasonably well-known and popular media celebrity in the early 21st century by capturing the nation's imagination with her look, attitude and appetite. Besides her look, she has also won numerous competitive eating competitions in Japan and abroad and has the dubious honour of having been crowned *Gluttonous Queen of Hawaii*. Now a mother of two she no longer eats professionally but she still has media presence and has not lost her appetite.

Monstrous Bequests

Since ancient times, *oni*, like all *yokai*, when not neglected and given sufficient religious devotion of the right sort, can allegedly be transformed into worship-worthy gods, *kami*. Modern forms of *oni* pop up everywhere. Nowadays they can be sexy and cute, and even wear short skirts, leading to some even being adulated and having their own devoted followers. But thanks to urbanisation, you're unlikely to find any *oni* if you venture into the woods or mountains at night. They can, however, be found thriving in different forms in manga, anime or digital games. The Jynx monster in the amazingly popular *Pokémon* games, for example, is said to be modelled on *Yama-Uba*. The big-headed *Yu-baba* featured in Hayao Miyazaki's (b. 1941) international blockbuster animated film *Sen to Chihiro no kamikakushi* (*Spirited Away*) is also believed to be based on *Yama-Uba*. Some primal desires, it would appear, are irresistibly inspiring.

The real demonic trolls of our time, in Japan (where online nationalists and those on the far right have their own special moniker *netto-uyoku)* as well those based overseas of all political permutations are internet trolls. From their private hidden spaces, in their real form (probably while snacking or constantly grazing to use the latest terminology), they spit their spiteful venom and vent their spleen with the rage of ogres by writing anonymously, and verbally assaulting all around them.

A much more intelligent and considered commentary on the ills of Japanese society, however, can be found within contemporary fiction. Self-destructive narratives with similar motifs and analogues of the past, of being dislocated and disenfranchised or the fear of being devoured by society's norms appear in some of Japan's best contemporary literature written by its many award-winning writers.

Nowadays, novels can be written from the perspective of the *oni*, be it a *Yama-Uba*, an attention-seeking or body conscious creature that wants to be treated like a god or goddess or some other type, who still represents society's darkest fears. They are often portrayed as lonesome disenfranchised individuals seeking meaning and companionship in frenetic urbanised Japan. These cultural responses to living on the edge shape society's perceived distortions into digestible literary shape.

Unsurprisingly, such calamitous characters can be discovered in bestselling novels written by the current cohort of brilliant Japanese female authors like Mari

Akasaka's (b. 1964) *Baibureta* (*Vibrator*) about a bulimic young alcoholic journalist, as well as *Insento worudo* (*Innocent World*) by Ami Sakurai (b. 1996) and Hitomi Kanehara's (b. 1983) award-winning *Hebi ni piasu* (*Snakes and Earrings*). Modern-day grim reading about inescapable cultural gravitational forces that, of course, include tales of all forms of hungers and their curtailment, epic tales of everyday struggles rendered in the technicoloured words of Japan's contemporary youth, not old testament prose.

Some of these contemporary 'bad girl' authors reflect their own lived experience with alienating nihilism and eating disorders in their works. Authors such as Kanehara, who was herself a troubled self-harming anorexic in her teenage years. Her third novel *Amibiku* (AMEBIC), about a young female writer with an eating disorder includes the following text in English under the title on its Japanese cover: "AMEBIC Acrobatic Me-ism Eats away the Brain, it causes imagination Catastrophe."

While mountain forests may no longer be de rigueur for today's *oni*, modern image-conscious 'creatures' can certainly be found in the kaleidoscopic urban sprawl, living on the margins of society, overeating, dressed in unconventional attire, and perhaps occasionally self-harming. Ironically, a wonderfully sating literary feast awaits those with the right sort of appetite. Some believe you are what you eat while others that you are what you read. All anyone needs to do these days is to venture out to your local bookshop or online retailer to encounter and get your fill of these mysterious creatures.

Literary Fallout: The Legacies of Hiroshima and Nagasaki

The reality of nuclear war began on 6 August 1945 and the term atomic bomb literature, *genbaku bungaku*, started being used widely from the 1960s to describe the canon of literature that the first use of nuclear weapons provoked. But the links between literature and the dropping of the atomic bombs on Japan go back much further. Arguably the first work in the canon of atomic bomb literature was written more than 50 years before the first atomic bomb was dropped over Hiroshima at 8.15 a.m. on 6 August 1945.

The Pilot of the B-29 Superfortress, Paul Tibbets (1915-2007), which flew and subsequently dropped *Little Boy*—the name given to the atomic bomb used—discovered shortly after being assigned the mission of captaining this historic flight from Tinian in the north-western Pacific, that his aircraft was nameless. In what some have described as a literary act, he named the aircraft *Enola Gay*— and had the name painted on the side of the aircraft on 5 August.

Oh, Fatal Day – Oh, Day of Sorrow

Tibbets decided that the name of his "courageous red-haired mother", who had been a source of strength throughout his life, was the right appellation for the aircraft designated to fly this momentous mission that brought about Japan's consequent surrender on 15 August. It seems an odd choice for a plane that would a day later use for the first time a weapon of mass-destruction which killed 80,000 people and injured many more, turning nuclear warfare from an abstract concept to a dreaded reality for the people of Japan.

His mother Enola Gay Tibbets (1893-1983) was reportedly not at all pleased when she learnt on national radio that her name would now forever be entangled with this fateful mission, commanded by her son, when the news of the use of this new weapon was broadcast the next day across America. Her son hadn't informed her in advance of his decision to name the aircraft after her.

Enola had herself been named after a book, and its wilful heroine, written in 1886 by Mary Young Ridenbaugh, *Enola; Or, Her Fatal Mistake*, which commences with the following poem:

Oh, fatal day – oh, day of sorrow,
It was no trouble she could borrow;
But in the future she could see
The clouds of infelicity.

Apparently, the name Enola, which spelt backwards renders the word *alone*, was coined by the author specifically for her heroine. Whether or not this 336-page novel, *Enola; Or, Her Fatal Mistake*, actually falls within the canon of atomic bomb literature is, however, questionable.

Decades later in the 1980s the British pop group Orchestral Manoeuvres in the Dark (OMD) released its celebrated anti-war song "Enola Gay", with the lyric, "Is mother proud of Little Boy today?" The single was a worldwide hit selling in the millions, becoming one of OMD's signature songs and cementing the name Enola and its destructive association in the minds of a new generation who hadn't witnessed the Second World War first hand.

Many different types of Japanese literature, storytelling and creative writing have been born on the back of these unique events, all of them adopting their narratives in myriad and often highly memorable forms. The best-known works in the genre by Japanese authors are probably *Kuroi ame* (*Black Rain*) by Masuji Ibuse (1898-1993) and the 33-volume manga *Hadashi no Gen* (*Barefoot Gen*) by Keiji Nakazawa (1939-2012), which tells the tragic tale of a six-year-old boy Gen Nakaoka and other survivors trying to cope with the aftermath of the bombing of Hiroshima. *Barefoot Gen* has been adapted for film, TV, theatre and anime, and multiple books have been written about it. Nakazawa's testimony-like work has been hugely influential in and outside Japan. Art Spiegelman, the American cartoonist famous for *Maus*, a postmodernist graphic novel based on the memories and experiences of his parents of the Holocaust with Jews represented as mice and Germans as cats and the Roma as gypsy moths, for example, is a major admirer. He wrote a preface for its 1990 English language edition.

Japanese atomic bomb writers include early survivors such as the poet Tamiki Hara (1905-1951), an English graduate with a strong interest in Russian literature, who famously described the experience of witnessing an atomic attack, "as if the skin of the world around me was peeled off in an instant." *Hiroshima noto* (*Hiroshima Notes*) by the Nobel Prizewinner Kenzaburo Oe (1935-2023), who was six years old when the atomic bombings took place, is often cited as one of his most important works. Oe, a fierce opponent of all things atomic, also edited the collection *Nantomo shirenai miraini (The Crazy Iris and Other Stories of the Atomic Aftermath)*, a collection of short stories, which includes Katsuzo Oda's moving graphic first-person account "Ningen no hai" ("Human Ashes"). This collection of powerful shorts was published on the 40th anniversary of the atomic bombing of Hiroshima and Nagasaki.

The blurred chaos of war can cannibalise and consume events, facts and memories before eventually being reborn as forceful fiction. There are now several generations of atomic bomb writers. The 'First Generation' wrote mostly witness accounts, personal records and first reactions documenting first-hand experiences. These are by and large emotive pieces that express disdain and disgust. The 'Second Generation' of writers generally tries to provide a broader perspective, and the emerging third and fourth generations an even wider, and at times highly imaginative lens to frame the memories and narratives of the past. The debate on whether the use of nuclear weapons on these two occasions over Japan was justified continues in Japan, America and beyond. This debate is nudging readers and authors to think broadly about who is responsible for these "inhuman blasts", the reasoning behind them, if they were militarily necessary or not and where responsibility actually resides, as well as focusing narrative responses on the products of the destruction they brought.

Memories and Narratives are Not History

Atomic bomb literature is not exclusively Japanese or limited to works set in Hiroshima or Nagasaki or books that directly reference the two Japanese cities that the atomic bombs were dropped over in August 1945. The genre now includes a wide range of works such as Ray Bradbury's (1920-2012) *There Will Come Soft Rains* and Kamila Shamsie's *Burnt Shadows*. Some people go as far as including some of the Godzilla films within its scope. Japanese Americans and Japanese Canadians, such as Joy Kogawa (b. 1935) in her novel *Obasan (Ushinawareta sokoku)*, have also grappled with the topic.

Some authors such as the bestselling children's book author Miyoko Matsutani (1926-2015) in her work *Futari no Ida (Two Little Girls Called Iida)* have used the date 6 August as a plot device. In this story published in 1969 about a mother and daughter returning to Hiroshima, two girls are united through time by a special abandoned magical chair in a house where the calendar is stuck frozen on 6 August.

Another interesting and unusual example is *One Love Chigusa* by Soji Shimada (b. 1948), a renowned mystery writer born in Hiroshima prefecture. While this book describes both the Hiroshima and Nagasaki bombs in its narrative, it is in fact a whodunnit in the form of a science fiction tale set in a future Beijing in which Shimada explores themes of identity, loss and love in a heartless technological world. *One Love Chigusa* was consciously published on 6 August 2020, the 75th anniversary of the Hiroshima bombing and written with a non-Japanese audience in mind. It does not, however, actually mention any *hibakusha*, the individuals affected by the atomic bombs, and is therefore something of a fringe addition to the canon of atomic bomb literature.

History is, of course, written and made by all sides. History, fiction and drama interact. Narratives and the definition of literature can also sometimes collide and diverge; being delineated very differently. How the term itself is used also varies. Despite the code name the Manhattan Project, these two deadly devices were actually designed and built at Los Alamos National Laboratory in New Mexico. In the southwestern American state with its majestic skies and scenery that have a tendency of making most who visit the laboratory sense the insignificance of their own existence. Los Alamos alongside Sandia National Laboratories, which is also based in the state of New Mexico, still play a critical role in America's nuclear and security programmes.

Today, Los Alamos, no longer an unknown top-secret location, feels much more like a university campus, especially when compared to Sandia, which has the type of security depicted in Hollywood films with identity checks, double-checking of date of birth information and the handing over of all electronic devices on entry, and no unaccompanied visits to their toilets. Sandia does many things these days including on occasion analysing literature and creating software tools for predictive security modelling and data analytics.

These laboratories use and are interested in a starkly different literary canon: scientific papers, patent databases and other datasets, not narrative fiction and diary-like accounts. Using state-of-the-art visualisation tools and artificial intelligence (AI) that blend bibliographic and biographic databases with other information sources researchers look for patterns, which may identify global security risks and unusual clusters and nodes of research activity in and outside the United States. Not just related to threats from nuclear and atomic research, but also reportedly in the past in fields such as anthrax research that can on occasion pose other types of dangerous security risks. The popular pre-print server, now known as arXiv, which plays a major role in the publication and sharing of research literature in mostly physics and mathematics, is another very different type of literature-propagating invention from Los Alamos.

It is not surprising that sets of content databases and collections of literature differ. Nevertheless, the geographical breadth and diversity of the information reflected in Sandia's visualisation tools and arXiv's ever expanding content set when observed is a contrasting and stark reminder that the ethnicity, geographic location and age of the only people to have been exposed to these weapons in an act of war, unlike contemporary research into their development, application, risks and after-effects, is extremely narrow.

Tales Recounted and Penned in the Thousands

Storytelling and narrative fiction have a long, varied, wide and immensely rich history in Japan. Before Japan's modernisation in its Meiji era (1868-1912), which led to the publication of modern Western-style novels, short stories and the prose we are familiar with today, stories were often conveyed on scrolls and fans alongside illustrations or delivered verbally by storytellers, as testaments, or in diary format.

The Japanese word for novel, *shosetsu*, used today to mean Western-style novels, initially entered the Japanese language via China in 1754 and is written using two letters or characters 'small' and 'talk', highlighting the historical importance and tradition of verbal storytelling in Japan. The word, *shosetsu*, and its use mirror the evolution of creative writing in Japan and how the nation likes to document itself. It also highlights how events instigated by those from afar can accelerate literature's evolution. Words and how they are used, alongside genres, as their usage spreads and familiarity grows, tend to change. Vocabulary also helps define and differentiate, be it the Nagasaki plutonium bomb—*Fat Man*—as opposed to the uranium bomb dropped on Hiroshima—*Little Boy*—or more prosaically emerging publishing formats that usher in new concepts and terminology. Initially, the word *shosetsu* was used for works of fiction translated from Chinese such as *Suihu zhuan* (*The Water Margin*) known in Japanese as *Suikoden*, following the success of a Japanese annotated edition of this seminal Chinese vernacular tale of legendary bandit-heroes that blends and combines ancient legends with the oral tradition in manuscript form.

Beyond the world of letters and publishing *shosetsu* was in fact used in Japanese much earlier mostly as a term of derision or for gossipy so-called street talk. The publication of *Suikoden* in Japan changed that. *Shosetsu* only started to be used in its current modern meaning in Japan's Meiji era when the arrival of new types of literary works required new terminology to define, position and refer to them within the context of the existing literary canon. In a sense, Japan's atomic literature, despite not being frivolous, reflects these earlier roots and is a return to them, with illustrated works, books combining images and prose, and accounts of *that day*—*ano hi*—delivered by *hibakusha* in their own words to schoolchildren across Japan.

Eyewitness testimonies that illustrate the power and importance of the weapon of memory are presented as even more relevant as these now ageing *hibakusha* pass away and the voices of direct witness accounts fade. Their children sometimes replace them taking on the role as narrator, often in soft small voices re-telling the tales, keeping the *hibakusha* stories alive as they talk calmly about the days that must not be forgotten. Proactively counteracting the danger posed by fading memories and the weakening moral revulsion of nuclear war that comes with the passage of time. Many Japanese schoolchildren encounter these witness accounts on trips to ground zero, for instance, during obligatory cultural pilgrimages arranged for them.

Diaries and poetry, as well as more traditional forms of fictional and non-fictional accounts and records of these catastrophic events have been penned in the thousands. The breadth and extent of the associated literature is now so broad that it has created opportunities for academics to study and write about the genre, as well as the actual historical events themselves.[54] Universities and colleges now even teach courses and modules on the genre such as 'Literature of World War II' and 'The Atomic Bomb in Japan: History, Memory and Empire', which are taught at Bowdoin College in Maine in the United States. The study and associated writings of the anti-nuclear bomb movement in and outside of Japan is also now an accepted part of the canon.

Unfathomable Atomised Lives

Understandably, not all Japanese war memories attract the same amount of interest as these atomic memories. The memories of children, for instance, living in other areas of Japan also situated far away from the battlefields overseas, who still experienced the impact of some of the dreadful and at times irresponsible decisions that adults made are often overshadowed. It is as if these events happened in a parallel world, rendering them unknown and unfathomable, with the exception being for those who experienced them directly and personally. The two atomic bombs seem to wrap a concealing mantel over them and other horrors that occurred inside and outside Japan.

> My mother's back was charred like a piece of burned wood, but when my aunt related how my grandfather's front side was paler under the cape he had worn, my father began to shake and the tears overflowed... On July 3rd in the last year of the war, my mother burned to death in an air raid shelter, and five years later my father died too. After that, I decided to make my living as a novelist. Jakucho Setouchi (1922-2021), *Basho (Places)*.

This can span those who experienced the Tokyo firebombs that incinerated up to 100,000 people. The daughter in a small Fukushima village, now a mother and old woman, whose only memory of her father is a view of the back of his head, as he marched out of their village never to return, after a family meal of special rice, *sekihan*, normally only eaten on days of celebration. The memory of being told to keep quiet when she questioned why going to war was something to celebrate. Some recall as children reading books at bedtime lit by the vast bright red night skies that the firebombs generated. Haunting dystopian landscapes, like these, tend to get burnt into collective cultural memory, even if other higher profile events and the long-term disorders they generated cast a shadow over them.

> The war began at last and soon turned into a grand-scale affair. Just before the American planes began flying through the city skies, his grandmother fell ill and died. His home burned to the ground soon after, victim of an incendiary bomb from an American plane, but this was not the only house destroyed. As he stood in the ruins of his home, there lay before him a house-less expanse of black ground as far as the eye could see. The war ended and several years passed. He was not able, however, to return to where he had once lived. One needed a good deal of money to build even a small house. Junnosuke Yoshiyuki (1924-1994) "Ajisai" ("Hydrangeas").

Moreover, being fully occupied grappling with the deadlines of everyday existence can bury memories for long periods. Memories, however, tend to resurface with age, a phenomenon many experience whether a *hibakusha*, an individual who spent time in a wartime concentration camp, a member of a migrant family fleeing their home nation as an act of survival, or survivors of other types of intense trauma. War and shared trauma affects everyone and can be passed on to future generations.

Even though nostalgia and selected amnesia can at times be dangerous bedfellows, the fusion of books, storytelling and memory, alongside the impressions of that fateful day and others in Japan, creates many vivid recollections and also unpredictable responses. The desire to forget or the urge to recount recollections often fluctuates with age before finally becoming an unavoidable duty. As was the case with, for example, Issey Miyake (1938-2020), the internationally celebrated fashion designer born in Hiroshima, known around the world for his cleverly engineered garments and permanent pleats, and a *hibakusha*.

No matter the approach adopted, the cultural climate of war and the resilience it dictates, and the direct experience of conflict tends to stick to those who live through it in their impressionable youth. The instant that drained all colour from Hiroshima, leaving a patterned charcoal-like ash city strewn with death and life changing catastrophic injuries, a blinding flash that led to the death three years later of a seven-year-old future international designer's mother, is a memory that is and should be impossible to put aside. One that survivors need to eventually start talking about even if they have concealed it publicly for a lifetime, as Miyake did until he was in his seventies and had established his international reputation, so as not to be defined by it.

Bungaku Maximus: Literature as a Nation's Conscience

President Obama described the bombing of Hiroshima in his speech there in 2016 as a day when "death fell from the sky and the world was changed." According to the multi-award-winning author Yoko Ogawa (b. 1962), "literature is the refuge we turn to when we are forced to confront contradictions that lie beyond reason."[55] And these types of narratives and the talented authors and storytellers that generate them have certainly helped stich Japan back together.

Populations with their competing tribes and social groups, under constant environmental and resource pressure, will sadly continue to generate illogical contradictions and make tragic seemly impossible choices that blindside us, making literature in all its forms and genres endlessly important.

As the generation of individuals who personally experienced 'that day' pass away, this unusual but important publishing genre may find a new freedom, creating a different literary legacy full of new contradictions and peculiarities that may very well capture the imagination of readers anew, as new ways to write these wrongs are uncovered. Hopefully, unlike the numerous literary responses, these two fateful acts will remain isolated, never to be repeated. While the memories perpetually evolve in newly written forms never being allowed to fade away.

Part Two

Influencers, Dolls and Devices

Staring in the mirror, I could feel laughter starting to well up. I was getting ahead of myself, I thought. After all, I didn't kill the guy. For all I knew, he might have committed suicide. But then it occurred to me. Since I had made off with the gun from the scene, his death was considered a murder. If the weapon that caused his death were not at the scene, it was unlikely to be deemed a suicide, which must be why the police were treating it as a homicide. *Jyu* (*The Gun*), Fuminori Nakamura.

The Chick-Lit of Ancient Japan

The amazing success of *Bridget Jones's Diary*, by Helen Fielding, published in 1996 is said to have given birth to the genre now once known dismissively as chick-lit. The literary genre is studied by academics and students and is often credited—not always correctly—with creating similar narratives in other languages and media such as *Hana yori kekkon kibi–dango (Proposal, Not Flowers)* by Mariko Hayashi (b. 1954) in Japan and the American television series, *Sex and the City*.

Hundreds of books have been published in the wake of the diary's triumph, a successful series of Bridget Jones films has been produced, and dozens of scholarly papers published including *Bridget Jones, Prince Charming, and Happily Ever Afters: Chick-Lit as an Extension of The Fairy Tale in a Postfeminist Society*. But is this really the first time in literary history that women have written stories from their perspectives and been genre pioneers?

As Bridget might write in her diary, *it strikes me as pretty ridiculous: is it any wonder girls have no confidence? This is as old as that Japanese Pillow thing/and Genji...Durr!* And she would be right. The first golden age of female writers was in ancient Japan, in the Heian period (794-1185), a very long time ago.

This was a creative and peaceful period in Japanese history. So much so that its name reflects this. The character *hei* means flat and *an* safety, creating the word 'peaceful'. The imperial court in Kyoto was at its height. Buddhism and the creative arts of the time including poetry, literature, calligraphy, music and art, all flourished. Aristocrats, nobles, and ladies-in-waiting were expected to be literate and capable verse writers. Attraction, appeal and desire came through poetry and beautiful calligraphy, skills that the thirty-something Bridget Jones clearly lacks and never deploys in her pursuit of love and marriage. As Heian high society was polygamous, their timely deployment was critical.

The Tale of Genji, written by the noblewoman Shikibu Murasaki (circa 978-1014) was written in chapter instalments which were handed out to the ladies at court, who eagerly waited for the next episode on Genji's promiscuous liaisons, lovers and troubles. Similarly, *Bridget Jones's Diary* started as a column in the British newspaper

The Independent in 1995, instantly striking a chord with readers, and was published weekly on Wednesdays for three years. Initially, however, before a financial sponsor emerged, Genji's readers had to wait for its author to precure precious sheets of paper before her next instalments could be released. This unpredictable frequency of publication no doubt enhanced the tale's allure.

The Tale of Genji is often referred to as the world's first novel. *Makura no soshi* (*The Pillow Book*), however, written by a contemporary, Shonagon Sei (circa 966-1025), is probably closer to diary format and is filled with sharp and caustic writing, notes, observations and musings. Some have described Sei as one of the world's first feminists. Her style of written miscellany and observation is still popular today and is a style that our contemporary internet world with its multitude of dedicated bloggers would certainly understand, but when Sei was writing it was a delightfully new form of textual expression that was all her own, *sui generis*.

Blaise Pascale (1623-1632), the French mathematician, author and philosopher, with his *Pensées, Thoughts*, perhaps comes closest to *The Pillow Book* style in the West, according to Meredith McKinney, *The Pillow Book*'s English translator. But how different they are. She says that "it feels like she could do with an elegant flick of the wrist what he had to labour and chew his pen over."

Sei's compelling hodgepodge and the irrepressible force of her marked personality make her, says McKinney, "one of the great early woman writers not just of Japan but of the world" and no doubt a writer that it is easy to imagine Bridget and her creator Fielding enjoying. It is a form of writing, still popular in Japan today, that when it is done well provides a delightfully kaleidoscopic image of the writer themselves. According to McKinney, journal writing, such as the fictional *Bridget Jones Diary*, is what comes closest to it in format, but "it has a much lighter touch than the ponderous introspective entries in most people's journals." Despite many attempts in English and other languages, McKinney likes to point out, "it's actually very difficult to do it well."

Japanese diaries and journals sometimes crop up in highly unusual places and can often be eloquent private self-portraits of extreme stress, and personal ruin, as well as moving and harrowing insightful ones when read by unintended others that capture complex times, contemporary and wartime, not just those of ancient Japan. They can also be just boring records of everyday existence and weather patterns. At times diaries provide their authors with someone to confide in, much needed companionship, and for some source materials for future writing projects.

Diaries can also help established and re-establish reputations. Diaries kept during the Pacific War, for instance, but published afterwards, have sometimes allowed individuals to purposely reposition themselves. By pointing to anti-militaristic thoughts expressed in their diaries, for instance, they could show themselves as being in line with the post-war rejection of Japan's military past as a strategic and tragic folly.

Donald Keene (1922-2019), who was a U.S. Naval Intelligence operative before he became one of the most renowned scholars of Japanese literature, specialised in translating the diaries of Japanese soldiers killed in action during the war, looking for clues to help America in its campaign against Japan from the patchwork of information found within these handwritten journals. He describes the experience as follows:

> As I read the diaries of men who were suffering such hardships, it was impossible not to be moved. By contrast, the letters of the American sailors I had to censor once a week revealed no ideals, and certainly no suffering, but only their reiterated desire to return to their former lives. Throughout the war this contrast haunted me – the consecration of the Japanese to their cause and the total indifference of most Americans to anything except returning home. Although I did not in the least accept the ideas of the Japanese militarists, I could not help feel admiration for the ordinary Japanese soldier, and in the end I came to believe that the Japanese really deserved to win the war.[56]

Diaries are of course what you make them, giving their authors, and those who read them unbeknownst to their authors, much poetic licence. The excitement of discovery, especially of hidden decoded thoughts, can be intoxicating. Another important diary-like example from the Heian period, but written slightly earlier, is *Kagero nikki*, an autobiographic work, considered by some scholars as one of the first autobiographies written by a woman. It covers a 20-year period (circa 954-974) in another noblewoman's life, known simply as the Mother of Michitsuna Fujiwara, a work generally referred to as either *The Gossamer Years* or *The Mayfly Diary* in English.

It is a mixture of memoir and forthright, often sarcastic diary-like day-to-day entries from a neglected secondary wife of an aristocrat, Kaneie Fujiwara (circa 929-990). In it she goes on an emotional journey that includes jealously, marriage crises and much disappointment, searching for meaning and purpose in life. Feelings that Bridget would know ever too well. It provides a self-portrait of a poem-writing young woman, a mother of one, navigating Heian aristocratic society, who looks for solace in religious rituals and even considers becoming a nun. Something that in Bridget's case would seem unthinkable.

Rewriting and reimagining these early works for contemporary Japanese readers recurs every generation, ensuring their narratives and formats remain seductive and compelling. The diary format and serialised fiction both remain highly popular in Japan and are still being exploited by Japan's best and most creative writers. Remarkably, *The Tale of Genji* has, since its very origin, been required reading for Japanese aristocratic women. For a thousand years *The Tale of Genji* was mostly inaccessible to the general Japanese public. According to scholars, for a very long time "it remained an aristocratic text, its manuscripts the property of aristocrats and aristocrats its principal interpreters."[57]

Nonetheless, from the 17th century onwards it became more widely available after an edition was printed using movable type, a technology which first arrived in Japan in 1593, and subsequently in woodblock printed editions. Due to its restricted availability, the refinement it portrays and its association with the highest and most sophisticated levels of Japanese society, it became an aspirational read for emerging upwardly mobile Japanese families in Japan's Edo period (1603-1868) and their daughters, as well as, and perhaps somewhat surprisingly, an important tool in women's education. Home teachers, often women, used the text to teach girls reading and as part of their overall education.

According to the Japan expert and former editor of *The New York Review of Books*, Ian Buruma, *The Tale of Genji*, which is replete with rather promiscuous characters, is a novel all "about the art of seduction."[58] This has led, at times, to concerns being raised about the appropriateness of its content. In 1880s Japan, for instance, many worried that its lusty and emotional content might damage the morals of Meiji era (1868-1912) young women. This was not, however, the first time the tale's morality was questioned. At certain points in Japanese history exponents of Buddhism argued that fictional tales such as these violated the precept forbidding the propagation of falsehoods. This, however, didn't put off future generations of Japanese women and writers from reading *Genji* and learning from it.

Hisako Yoshizawa (1918-2019) is one such interesting example. She is more famous for writing and publishing lifestyle books and broadcasting on how to live a good and refined life. But at the end of the Second World War during nightly air raids, wearing her silk nightgown and a steel helmet, Yoshizawa, reportedly, liked to read *The Tale of Genji* to while away the noisy dangerous nights.

The tale's attraction, like *Bridget Jones's Diary*, has sparked significant academic interest too. Its deconstruction in 1912, in what is believed to be the first Freudian analysis of a Japanese work within a series of papers published in the Japanese literary journal *Enigma*, is a shining example. Impressively, its publication occurred one year before an English translation from the original German of Sigmund Freud's (1856-1939) seminal book *The Interpretation of Dreams* was available.[59] All this has helped make this 11th century tale by a Japanese noblewoman an international publishing sensation, with translations, spin-offs and adaptations for manga, anime, film and theatre. It out-franchised Bridget, who has so far only spawned three feature films, as well as being, alongside the ingenious miscellany *The Pillow Book*, and the *Mayfly Diary*, a highly influential literary and cultural linchpin.

Furthermore, there has been a long tradition of one of Japan's leading authors from each generation updating and publishing a new version of this "seductive novel" about the Japanese prince Hikaru Genji, literarily Shining Genji, who was uncommonly handsome, charming and intelligent. This multi-generational trend has helped keep the rather long and esoteric tale, which in its original version consists of 54 scrolls or chapters (around a million words) fresh, and relevant to contemporary readers while helping to expand its readership.

Mitsuyo Kakuta (b. 1967), author of the award-winning and million-plus-selling novel *Yokame no semi* (*The Eighth Day*) about a regular office worker in love with a married man who suddenly snaps after an unwanted abortion, is one such author. When Kakuta started work on her three-volume edition, the final volume of which was published in 2020, she says, she knew she had a "heavy" task ahead of her, but she didn't fully anticipate the amount of work and time that would be required. It took her more than three years to polish off her Genji. She says, perhaps naively, that she expected (due to the large number of books on *The Tale* and existing modern 'translations' by some of Japan's most famous authors) that her task would be like sketching "a vast scene" while looking out at a beautiful well-documented expanse in front of one's eyes and the "mountain stretching far beyond."

She didn't expect to have to decode and decipher ancient Japanese prose, nor the amount of reading that would be involved. Indeed, the idea of "sketching" out the narrative, as she had hoped, turned out to be a "ridiculous" and naïve concept. The essence of *The Tale of Genji* was in a sense hidden from view, with its myriad scenes and 430 characters veiled behind a curtain that just left "impressions" making it hard to judge "what was important and what was not." The only way to "rip through this curtain" was to delve into the original prose itself. The process, according to Kakuta, was "painstaking," more like "trudging through a muddy rice field" and then climbing, ascending and then descending a series of distant mountains on an absurdly ambitious herculean quest to create a series of publications that would inspire and light up this Japanese classic for a new generation. This is something that, according to the reviewers, she has done with aplomb.

It is apparent from the original version that the tools for seduction in Japan's Heian period were the sophisticated deployment of art, poetry, calligraphy and style. Unsurprisingly, it took Kakuta considerable time to decide on the right style and rhythm required to make the novel readable, accessible and compelling for today's readers who are more familiar with digital dating, and its core tool—swiping—than ancient methods of courtship. One of the other challenges Kakuta faced was a troublesome computer and a disappearing file, something that almost brought her to tears as publication deadlines approached. Kakuta decided that the pesky file must have been deleted by Shikibu Murasaki, with a spiritual smite, as she disapproved of the adaptation of the sections lost. That was the attitude, Kakuta says, she adopted when she started writing those sections again from scratch and is something she hopes she will be able to laugh about one day.

Many articles and reviews have been written about Kakuta's new adaptation including articles that compare and contrast sections of Kakuta's 'translation' and her choice of words to those made by previous generations of authors like Junichiro Tanizaki (1886-1965), Fumiko Enchi (1905-1986) and Jakucho Setouchi (1922-2021), that latter of whom Kakuta was encouraged to meet before starting her writing journey. These articles compare how each author decided to render the exact same text in the style and words of the Japanese of their respective eras. This all helps make the publication of a new edition by a highly regarded author, like Kakuta, a major media event in Japan.

Kakuta believes that the world of Genji behind its curtain is not so different to the one we live in today. If you have everything you want within your grasp, but nothing flows the way you wish or think it should, you are left with the question of how to live out one's limited days. "That is the same today, as one thousand years ago," Kakuta argues.

That said, the first modern 'translation edition' of *The Tale of Genji* is said to have been published by the feminist poet and author Akiko Yosano (1878-1942) in 1912. She, like Kakuta, also had document management problems. According to a report in *Fujin Sekai* published in October 1923, thousands of pages of Yosano's original handwritten manuscripts were destroyed during the Great Kanto Earthquake that hit the capital that year, presumably including her original drafts of the first modern translation of *The Tale of Genji*, teaching the author a precious lesson about manuscript management and the importance of keeping handwritten papers related to seminal works stored safely underground. Impressively, this issue of *Fujin Sekai*, which reports about Yosano and her burnt paperwork, was published the month after the earthquake hit Tokyo on 1 September, a devastating earthquake that alongside the fires it caused destroyed most of the homes in Tokyo and Yokohama and the publishing industry infrastructure located there. It killed tens of thousands.

One of the first proper English translations was produced by Arthur Waley (1889-1966), a British translator of Chinese and Japanese literature, who interestingly never visited Asia, in the 1920s. Also, like Yosano, a fascinating character, Waley is said to have often got lost walking home or to the homes of his relatives from their synagogue in London on important Jewish festivals, when he attended, immersed in his thoughts and in the world of letters he created so brilliantly through translation; literally lost in translation. Since then there have been many others turning this massive work into a highly influential must-read classic for Japan's literati and anyone in Japan who wishes to appear well-read and well-educated. In an unusual twist, Waley's edition has been translated back into Japanese by two sisters and published for contemporary readers in four volumes with striking covers, the first of which was published in 2017. There is also an endless debate about whether the original *The Tale of Genji* had a single female author or multiple authors. When you consider what the tale has spawned in the wake of its publication it does make you wonder if the elusive answer to this question matters?

Yoko Ogawa (b. 1962) is another example of a contemporary author who has comfortably mastered these types of classical Japanese genres. Her beautifully crafted novel *Hakase no aishita sushiki* (*The Housekeeper and the Professor*), which was even reviewed in *The American Journal of Mathematics* (57(5)) and the international journal of science *Nature*, instantly brought her international attention and recognition. However, her short haunting story, *Ninshin karenda* (*Pregnancy Diary*), replete with sisterly angst, published in English translation in the *New Yorker*, is probably a better contemporary example of a brilliant modern rendition of the dairy format. The current cohort of trailblazing Japanese female writers who are regularly winning Japan's major literary prizes are rightfully gaining recognition outside Japan in a way that was impossible a thousand years ago for Murasaki and Sei.

New twists on the diary genre from both female and male authors continue to emerge such as *Yamada-San nikki* (*The Yamada Diary*) by Masato Takeno (b. 1966), in its case not a traditional diary but a tale about a frustrated schoolboy preparing for his university entrance exams who purchases a video game called *The Yamada Diary* which the schoolboy subsequently becomes obsessively addicted to, seductively blurring routine reality with the virtual, losing himself within the intricacies of game. This digital diary oddly reflects his mundane present monotonous existence, not an exciting, distinct shining new reality. Nevertheless, his digital diary still provides escape from his everyday through restricted fantasy. Until, that is, he hits his mother and the game comes to an abrupt end.

The launch of the film *Bridget Jones's Baby* in 2016, the third film in the series, more than a decade after the last film *Bridget Jones: The Edge of Reason*, has provided academics and commentators the perfect opportunity to review the development of contemporary popular women's fiction and its international impact. Regional varieties have been spawned across the globe in India, Italy, and Russia as well as many other countries, appealing to young women with their own income, living alone or with friends, with dreams of independence and an exciting urban lifestyle. When the genre's popularity in Japan was called into question by *The New York Times*, one reader wrote to the editor of the newspaper from Japan in disgust stating that, "Japan is the world capital of chick-lit" and "novels by women for women in Japan are no imitation—they are the real thing, a lively and varied genre."[60]

The latest Bridget Jones film was launched internationally, which created challenges for the subtitle translators of a very different type to those Kakuta confronted. Bridget's racy coarse language and pet words such as "fuckwits", and "bugger" as well as passages such as, "Actually, last night my married lover appeared wearing suspenders and a darling little Angora crop-top, told me he was gay/a sex addict/a narcotic addict/a commitment phobic and beat me up with a dildo," are extremely hard to translate, and often incomprehensible even to some first language English speakers.

Analysing the genre and how these expressions are interpreted or ignored in different languages and cultures has created a field day for feminist cross-cultural studies. Explanations abound. Hiroko Furukawa, a professor at Tohoku Gakuin University, for example, has written several papers on the topic deconstructing the "striking gap" between Bridget in the original English and Japanese translation, something that fans of Genji often do when they compare their favoured translation to newly published versions.[61]

Bridget writes in her diary at one point that her mother said, "Apparently he had the most terrible time with his wife. Japanese. Very cruel race," something Bridget repeats. Therefore, it seems unlikely that the self-obsessed but ever optimistic fictional Bridget would be interested in how she is being translated into Japanese or make the effort to pick up a diary or book written by one of her many talented contemporaries in Japan, despite working for a period for a London-based publishing company. Probably because Bridget, now a British cultural icon, spent most of her working day at the publisher obsessing about her love life or lack of it and her boss, a devious, charming womaniser with a shining career, and not international literature.

This is a great pity because if she made the effort, as many more readers around the world are starting to do, she would be surprised and delighted by what she'd read in the oodles of books, diaries and essays of Japanese writers and bloggers following in the long wake of the first golden age of women writers of the Heian period, a time with its own type of vigorous and unreliable menfolk. She might even find the cultural differences titillating. The differences might in fact help her understand herself and her bizarre predicaments better and she would love the similarities, especially discovering that existential angst and grappling with fateful decisions on how to live out one's life is so universal, international and timeless.

Ultra-Influencers: Fictional Victorians that Changed Japan

Lasting influence, the power or capacity of causing an effect indirectly or directly in others, is a powerful and elusive trait that some individuals possess in abundance. Coupled with charisma, it's something most of us can only dream of possessing. This elusive power is thought to make one immortal as its effects ripple through time and space, and the one essential quality for possessing it, according to experts, is authenticity.

Influence can, however, also be delusional, manufactured, imagined or even brilliantly conjured up through the pages of a book or on the screens of our phones. In our social media age, with its enslaving metrics of perhaps illusionary and superficial import, the words 'influence' and 'influencer' are now mostly used as terms for shaping audience attitudes. This is usually done through public perceptions of personality, conduct, character and style, often of the most excruciating attention-grabbing type. In an age replete with incredibly short attention spans, this is something that comedians, models and actors and actresses with millions of followers strive and struggle to achieve, or simply maintain.

The media in Japan, like elsewhere, now obsessively tracks those who are commanding the rankings and can be deemed, for example, the top 10 and top 20 Japanese influencers. The art of concealment and modesty seem like qualities from a bygone age. The urge to standout, however, is not a new one. Tenshin Okakura (1863-1913), a philosopher and art critic, writes about it in his sublime 1906 essay, *Cha no hon* (*The Book of Tea*), explaining why according to his Zen rules for life and art such urges should be avoided:

> Hide yourself under a bushel quickly, for if your real usefulness were known to the world you would soon be knocked down to the highest bidder by the public auctioneer. Why do men and women like to advertise themselves so much? Is it not but an instinct derived from the days of slavery?

The destructive power of digital auctioneers in our age and the curse that the relentless cycle for attention getting can spawn is ever too real and well documented.

Whether these moments of fame and influence will be fleeting, lasting only one or two software evolutions and upgrades, is anyone's guess. There are, however, precedents: two enduring fictional characters with strongly marked personalities that arrived on Japan's shores from Britain in the space of two years—1894 and 1895—in the pages of books, and subsequently in every form of new media upgrade that has followed in the wake of the printed page.

They have shaped Japanese audiences and their attitudes across many aspects of life and art including how to dress, how to think, and observe the world around them. Their influence continues to this day. Their arrival in Japan in translation was at a time when the Land of the Rising Sun was opening up to the West, modernising, and expanding its ambitions during the First Sino-Japanese War (1894-1895). A period when Japan forced open Korea's markets, and as a result, China had to initially recognise Korea's independence. Korea had been an important 'client state' of China's at that time. Japan also drove China to cede control of Taiwan and other territories. These historical events that still impact the geopolitics of our times link both of our fictional characters in terms of their Japanese debuts in the Japanese language.

However, their actual inceptions were, in fact, more than two decades apart, in 1865 and 1887 respectively. On the surface, both are inquisitively independent and determined individuals, but here the similarities end. They are actually poles apart; one being a violin playing middle-aged man with a close male friend and the other a pinafore-wearing seven-year-old girl, whose most important acquaintance is a talking rabbit. Nonetheless, they have both left an enormous creative and cultural legacy, spawning thousands of imitations and adaptations, and have undoubtedly shaped the attitudes of many in Japan, from the rich and famous to the ordinary man on the street. All this on a scale that even today's influencers would find inconceivable.

Sherlock Holmes arrived first in 1894. The translation of *The Man with the Twisted Lip* by Sir Arthur Conan Doyle (1859-1930) was published in the January issue of *Nihonjin*. The seven-year-old girl named Alice arrived one year later with the first Japanese translation of *Alice's Adventures in Wonderland* by Lewis Carroll (1832-1898). Their mantras, however, were about purpose and curiosity, not rank and self-promotion.

Eccentric and Virtuous

Alice's debut was in a Japanese magazine, *Shonen sekai* (*A Boy's World*), in serial form in 1895, and followed by a second appearance in 1899 in another magazine *Shojo sekai* (*Girl's World*). That said, neither of these translations of Alice were faithful to

Carroll's original prose published in 1865 in English by Macmillan, but *The Man with the Twisted Lip*, despite being an abridged version, was more faithful to the original, which was first published in English in 1894.

According to Japan's National Diet Library, the first full and complete translation, in book format, in which the whole story of the original Alice was translated faithfully, was published in 1910 with a protagonist called Ai-chan (*chan* being a diminutive term of endearment mostly used for girls). This edition, translated by Eikan Maruyama (1885-1956) and published by Naigai Shuppan Kyokai, also contains copies of John Tenniel's (1820-1914) celebrated original illustrations depicting Alice in her knee-length puffed sleeve dress and her pinafore and practical ankle-strap shoes, which arguably have been as influential as the story itself in Japan. Holmes fans had to wait until 1955 for the full-Sherlock, when all of the Holmes stories were finally translated into Japanese by Ken Nobuhara (1892-1977).

The Creative Fog of Translating Personality

The arrival of Carroll's Alice in Japan in 1895 spawned thousands of translations and adaptions, with more translations into Japanese than any other language. Not all nations and regions have, however, greeted Alice so warmly. The depiction of animals, whether an extinct dodo with a cane, a mythical griffin, a Jabberwocky, or an actual living creature, with psychological depth and attitude can be threatening for some. In 1931, *Alice's Adventures in Wonderland* was banned in Hunan province in China, as the authorities apparently objected to animals and humans being portrayed as equals and speaking a common language.

Nonetheless, the difficulty of rendering the Alice books into the Japanese language and the freedom of the early translations has helped inspire many in Japan to try to create the perfect translation or a brilliant creative adaptation or homage to either or both of the Alice books. This enticing rabbit hole of a challenge has compelled many of Japan's most renowned and important authors like Ryunosuke Akutagawa (1892-1927) and Yukio Mishima (1925-1970) to take the leap. If one wishes to speculate on the reasons for this, and why Mishima had a crack at it himself, one needs to be careful as such supposition can easily lead to one vanishing into a consequential rabbit hole of conjecture.

Following rabbits, tumbling into enticing challenges, or unbeknownst being conditioned by societal or peer group trends, the acts of others even, for instance, and magical penship or clicking on an inviting link can be curiously consequential, as Mishima highlights in his 1963 novel, *Gogo no eiko* (*The Sailor Who Fell from Grace with the Sea*):

> It was a trap – a rabbit trap. The grown-ups expected the captive animal's rage and the familiar odours of his lair to transform themselves into the resignation and tolerance of a creature who has confined himself. A hideously subtle trap: the rabbit, ensnared, was no longer a rabbit.

Although, all translation is said to be mistranslation; language can confuse even when spoken or shared in written form between first-language users. Sometimes intriguingly that is exactly what it is designed to do. Translation often involves interpretation, but all translations, like all forms of writing, are by their nature a skilful succession of choices and careful, and at times, playful editing. Translation does not and should not necessitate omission or wholesale rewriting or brand-new authorship.

Straddling the line that balances authorship and readership is the art of translation itself, a fact that Alice and her innumerable and occasionally curious Japanese translations mirror so finely. It is not each word selected or rendered but what sits under them and between their gaps and the lines of the page where meaning often resides and is forged. In this regard, language is not simply an instrument for communication. It is also a type of mental space, a cultural operating system, a wonderland one might say, within which creative homage—fan fiction, clandestine satire, parody as well as propaganda, new ways of thinking and adaptation—can flourish in the wake of an exceedingly good translation.

Sherlock Holmes has also seen countless creative adaptations. Despite probably not actually being the first fictional foreign detective to arrive on Japan's shores, he continues to inspire, be reimagined, reinvented and rewritten. Indeed, many, including the Japan Sherlock Holmes Club,[62] regard him to be the most famous Englishman in Japan.

The detective's popularity is, of course, not limited just to Japan. Holmes, according to the *Guinness Book of World Records* has been depicted in film and television more often than any other literary human, ahead of William Shakespeare's (1564-1616) Hamlet, who is ranked at number two. Holmes is only pipped at the post by one other literary character: Dracula, who first appeared in 1897 in the pages of a book by the Irish author Bram Stoker (1847-1912).

There is, however, something seemingly special about this consulting sleuth's presence in Japan. Surveys of school libraries in Japan of the top five books read or requested often include a Sherlock Holmes title in some form. Booksellers and librarians, who often came across Holmes for the first time in primary school in various adaptations including comic book form, cite his endearing, super-intelligent and honourable personality as the reasons why he is still one of Japan's favourite literary characters. Authors like the mystery writer Soji Shimada (b. 1948) also point out that another important factor in his popularity is the quality of the stories and the writing. Interestingly, the Naoki Prizewinner Kazufumi Shiraishi's (b. 1958) favourite book when he was a child was also a book by Conan Doyle but one that doesn't feature his famous detective: *The Lost World*. Books featuring Holmes in all his myriad Japanese forms have sold in the tens of millions.

Nonetheless, many of the world's most influential books, which boast international reach, impact and influence amongst decision-makers, opinion leaders and world leaders, are often books that haven't actually been read, and this may also apply in Japan to both *Alice Adventures in Wonderland* and *Sherlock Holmes*.

The Japanese literary critic and writer, Sadao Yasunari (1885-1924), for instance, adapted *The Man with the Twisted Lip* in 1912 in his work *Kasuga doro* (*The Stone Lantern*), after coming across the famed English detective in *The Jewish Lamp*, a 1907 adaptation by Maurice Leblanc (1864-1941) in which Holmes, the gentleman detective, confronts Leblanc's gentleman thief Arsene Lupin. Others such as the popular contemporary mystery and crime writer Mizuki Tsujimura (b. 1980), for instance, first encountered Sherlock Holmes as a child, but only really "met" the detective in the 2010-2017 BBC series *Sherlock* starring Benedict Cumberbatch, which inspired her to read the full editions in translation for the first time.[63]

In this regard she is now in very good company as some of Japan's most influential authors such as Junichiro Tanizaki (1886-1965) and Akutagawa have read and analysed Conan Doyle's prose and adapted him or filleted him as only a highly skilled fan can do. This type of creative blurring and "fan fiction" has been accentuated by multiple film adaptations. This also applies to Alice, who many in Japan have come across through the 1951 animated musical Disney adaptation and not the actual Alice books, *Alice's Adventures in Wonderland* and *Through the Looking Glass, and What Alice Found There*.

Curiouser and Curiouser

Initially, the Holmes tales were read as entertainment and grew in popularity as more were translated into Japanese, but not everyone fully understood the science of deduction. Nonetheless, the detective had a strange type of duality of being the protagonist of popular mass-market novels and also a tool for education, sometimes for Japan's elite. Some early translations were annotated, and Conan Doyle's text was also used to teach English in a textbook-like way, in a similar fashion to how a certain type of English schoolboy might study Lucretius (99BCE-55BCE), the Roman poet and philosopher, and his poem "On The Nature of Things", and commit to memory such lines as "to none is life given in freehold; to all on lease" and "some nations increase, others diminish, and in a short space the generations of living creatures are changed and like runners pass on the torch of life."

Japan's police force and its aspiring detectives probably first read about Holmes in the pages of their professional journals and newspapers as opposed to the original English versions or faithful translations. He was introduced in the early 1900s as a role model and educational device for training Japan's law enforcers on how real detectives should go about their work with professional competence, using a combination of logic and scientific reasoning. However, not all readers have stuck to these derivative forms. Some in Japan haven't only been interested in seeing Holmes through the eyes of his many interpreters but to observe him as he was originally conceived, a sentiment that Holmes himself would no doubt have approved of. Such individuals have famously included aristocrats like Count Nobuaki Makino (1861-1946), Prime Minister Shigeru Yoshida (1878-1967), and a Vice Minister of Finance, Kohki Naganuma (1906-1977). They each decided that reading the original English editions was, shall we say, elementary. They and others believe you can learn and deduce a trick or two, in their case about how to modernise and safeguard Japan, from a direct relationship with this British supersleuth and the clues in the English prose that describes his methods. Many others who, like Tsujimura, came across Holmes for the first time in adapted Japanese language digests in their primary school libraries, have been inspired to study English so that they can enjoy the original tales first-hand. Some have gone on to become life-long fans, graduating from Japanese children's editions to full editions in Japanese, and then to the full-Sherlock in English.

Tweedledee and Tweedledum: Logic, Nonsense and Values

Alice and Sherlock arrived in Japan in the mid-1890s when America became the world's largest economy. It was a disorienting time when many people in Japan were struggling to find a modern and appropriate way to live, dress and behave, a time when the cultural values of modernity were not yet cemented, and cultural appropriation was fashionable. These two fictional characters arrived in Japan almost two decades after the emperor had cut off his topknot. It had been barely a decade since the empress had started wearing Western-style clothing in 1886.

Even though Western hairstyles were becoming increasingly common in Japan, dress codes were still in flux and many weren't sure how to dress themselves, let alone their children and young girls who were starting to go to school in increasing numbers. Lines sometimes blurred: Modern, wealthy kimono-wearing men sometimes wore Western-style hats, carried Western-style umbrellas and those who could afford them liked to show off their pocket watches.

Much was changing. Japan was in the early phase of developing a nationwide railway system after the first railway line between Tokyo and Yokohama had been opened in 1872. The nation was urbanising and modernising rapidly, and there were also huge changes being made to the way the nation educated its youth. The torch of modernity had come to illuminate Japan and the nation was hardly diminishing it was in an astonishingly expansive mode.

In 1890 only 31 percent of girls, for example, completed primary-level education but this rose to 72 percent by 1900, the year when school uniforms for secondary school female students were introduced. In 1920, 10 years after the first full translation of *Alice's Adventures in Wonderland* by Maruyama (with Tenniel's famous images of Alice wearing her knee-length puffed sleeve dress and her pinafore and practical ankle-strap shoes), St. Agnes's in Kyoto is said to have become the first Japanese educational institute to introduce the distinctive sailor-style uniform for schoolgirls that Japan is now so famous for. Some say this uniform is based on or at least reminiscent of Alice's practical style of attire portrayed in Tenniel's illustrations, even if these very first uniforms were actually modelled on a British Navy uniform.

Translating these two quirky characters into Japanese with their unusual dialogues and narratives, which can at times be delightfully nonsensical even for first language English readers, wasn't easy, but the protagonists had a major impact on Meiji-era Japan (1868-1912) with these two fictional characters holding up sensational mirrors on apparent Western ways.

Despite the tumult, Sherlock was considered the personification of essential Western values, a virtuous individual, and an excellent role model. Alice was thought to represent the ideal way a polite young girl should dress, behave and explore her environment while making sense of an emerging world that could at times be highly perplexing and nonsensical.

Managing the Impossible

So much was changing in Japan that things that had seemed improbable, impossible or even unimaginable in the past must have started to feel like everyday occurrences. Changing the natural order of things that had developed over centuries must have been disorientating. Some thought control had been lost to Moriarty-like dark forces. Japan had in a sense been socially conditioned by the long-armed but peaceful Edo period (1603-1868) with its rigid inherited hierarchies and shogun-run state apparatus. These cultural and state institutions were in decay or at least in flux and Japan now found itself on the cusp of a feverish new era.

The Meiji Emperor (1852-1912), the figurehead of these new times, had announced that he and his family would begin eating beef and mutton. This was something that until then had been taboo and not part of Japanese establishment protocol. Western cookbooks and etiquette books were being published. New sports such as rugby, baseball and tennis were being played. Japan was shifting from a country focused inwards to an international power marked first by the First Sino-Japanese War (1894-1895) and then the Russo-Japanese War (1904-1905). In both Japan emerged the victor but it was the defeat of the great European superpower—the first time an Asian nation defeated a European one in modern times—that marked Japan's emergence on the world stage. It also helped fuel the first Russian revolution in 1905 and weakened Russia's tyrannical monarchy, leading to their eventual overthrow in 1917.

Some believe that this period, with its struggles and the challenge of fusing long-held traditions with modernity and conflicting imported new concepts, has shaped and conditioned contemporary Japanese attitudes, inclinations and psychology more than any other period in Japanese history. More so than even Japan's post-war occupation by Allied Forces. Learning, coping with, and dreaming about the extraordinary kaleidoscopic adventure of modern life was for most ordinary Japanese people somewhat like Alice's own adventures in Wonderland: It had become an essential life-skill.

Alice and Sherlock who both in their own ways pursue order and understanding, provided a lesson on how to deal with the impossible. Alice, like Japan, is full of allusions to mathematics and puzzle-like problem solving, spanning proof by contradiction and the confirmation of reality through the possibilities and impossibilities of logic and imagination. Perhaps this goes some way in explaining the popularity of these two inquiring individuals. Sherlock famously says, "when you have eliminated the impossible, whatever remains, however improbable, must be the truth"[64] and Alice also has an interesting dialogue on the topic:

> Alice laughed: "There's no use trying," she said; "one can't believe impossible things."
>
> "I daresay you haven't had much practice," said the Queen. "When I was younger, I always did it for half an hour a day. Why, sometimes I've believed as many as six impossible things before breakfast."

These two slightly eccentric and righteous individuals arrived in Japan during this pivotal period of profound political and cultural change and have had a major influence. In this sense, Japan has acquired the rights to these two individuals not on a licence or lease but on a freehold basis for perpetuity. They are both now integral parts of Japanese culture even if the meaning and narratives of both Alice and Sherlock have morphed and been reshaped into different unique local forms and formats. Today, Alice is adored by many including Yayoi Kusama (b. 1929), probably Japan's most famous contemporary artist, known for her polka dot installations and the self-proclaimed High Priestess of Polka Dots, who is these days also a very influential individual in her own right. Kusama references Alice in her work and identifies with her personally. She has created illustrations, joining many other celebrated Alice illustrators such as Salvador Dali (1904-1989) and Peter Blake (b. 1932) who have also taken up this creative challenge, for a special edition of *Alice's Adventures in Wonderland*. Kusama's edition has been described by critics as the perfect pairing.

Japan now even has *Sherlock Bones (Tantei shadokku)*, a manga about a crime-solving dog who can talk using a pipe belonging to his teenage owner's grandfather, an English edition of which was published in 2013. In 2018, following the success in Japan of the BBC's series *Sherlock*, *Miss Sherlock* was released as a television series, an irreverent adaptation featuring a cello-playing high-heel wearing female detective, alongside her companion, a female doctor named Wato Tachibana, or as she is often referred to, Wato-San.

Despite all the references to and versions of him in Japan, according to the Japan Sherlock Holmes Club, there are actually only six references to Japan in the canon of Sherlock Holmes. Japanese cabinet (*The Adventures of the Gloria Scott*), Japanese armour (*The Adventures of the Greek Interpreter*), baritsu (*The Adventures of the Empty House*), the Emperor Shomu and his association with the temple Shoso-in near Nara (*The Adventures of the Illustrious Client*) and the Japanese vase (*The Adventures of the Three Gables*).

Mirror Memory: Victorian Fiction through the Looking Glass

Alice, who some still argue embodies the perfect young girl of the Meiji era, has shape-shifted effortlessly into a symbol of contemporary female freedom and adventure. She can seemingly be reinvented again and again in manga, anime and film for each new generation. An excellent example of this is the 1980 *Alice* adaptation by Katsuhiro Otomo (b. 1954), best known for his 1988 post-apocalyptic animation

Akira. His superb adaptation has helped to encourage many of Japan's most creative artists to plunge down a similar creative passage of adaptation and interpretation for manga readers. Otomo's version contains a Mao-suited white rabbit and clever use of illustration size and graphic panels to depict the shrinking or enlarging proportions of the worlds Alice descends into as she leaves our physical reality.

But where did Sherlock Holmes disappear to between his apparent death after his fall at Reichenbach Falls in *The Final Problem* and his dramatic reappearance three years later at 221B Baker Street, with a flask in his hand, in *The Adventure of the Empty House*? Japan of course, according to *Sharokku Homuzu tai Ito Hirobumi (Sherlock Holmes: A Scandal in Japan)* by Keisuke Matsuoka (b. 1968), an adventure, a sleuth's guide to Japan, that involves the Japanese Prime Minister Hirobumi Ito (1841-1909) and the English detective trying to acclimatise to 19th century Japan in a very special case, published in Japanese in 2017 and in English in 2019.

British Immortals?

It is not just Japan that has taken these two very British characters to heart, but Japan's peculiar enthusiasm for pastiche and adaptations has helped ensure that their cultural influence has evolved and been reincarnated in new creative forms that are now finding their way out of Japan and into international markets in a creative virtuous circle. This is a creative testament to the power of independent-mindedness and human irrepressibility.

The reasons for this, like the number of adaptations they have inspired, are myriad but perhaps it is best to leave the final word to another British author who also penned a tale about a rabbit, her debut tale, and had the foresight to know how to safeguard where she lived for future generations. The area protected in question was the Lake District, and she ensured an important physical as well as literary legacy. Her name was Beatrix Potter (1866-1943): "I hold that a strongly marked personality can influence descendants for generations."[65]

Doll Women and Their Literature

Images of human-like dolls or doll-like humans are widely associated with Japan. The most famous of all must be the geisha, which have captivated people for centuries in all their forms: human, doll, literary, animated, drawn, painted and computer generated. Dolls and their modern equivalents, figurines or figures, are everywhere in Japan. Reporters and television journalists love covering the latest models, evolutions and uses when they write about the sophisticated, the geeky or dark sides of modern Japan.

Dolls go back to ancient times in almost all cultures and not unexpectedly feature in many different genres of Japanese literature, especially ghost and horror stories. Dolls from the Heian period (794-1185) were used to protect, bring good health and happiness, and purify at all stages of human life, from creation to birth, and onwards. Sometimes they would be displayed and at other times given as offerings at shrines.

The Japanese doll festival, *hinamatsuri*, was originally all about purification, something that has historically been and still is important in Japanese culture. This can manifest as leaving heaps of salt in buildings and homes to ward off pollution and protect the pure, or sumo wrestlers throwing salt before their bouts. Protecting sacred things, habits and places from defilement, be they ritual, secular, spiritual or cultural, are considered by some as elemental acts. According to Tenshin Okakura (1863-1913), a philosopher and art critic, many of what he terms the so-called "mental peculiarities of the Japanese" owe their origins to "the love of purity and its complementary hatred of defilement."[66] The extent of how these immutable peculiarities extend to dolls and their associated festival in contemporary Japan and whether they have become a representation of women besmirched with modern cultural dirt, as some argue, or are simply a cultural product to be enjoyed is for others to debate, determine and write about.

That said, the doll festival now takes place on *Momo no Sekku* (Girls' Day) on 3 March before spring every year, in a celebration of femininity. Dolls start appearing before the day itself and should be put away and not be displayed immediately afterwards otherwise, according to myth, all the girls in the family will miss the elusive chance of getting married. "I imagine it has been passed down as a type of etiquette, mother to daughter over generations, designed to train girls to be tidy, and capable of managing their responsibilities in a timely manner, and thus one day be a *good wife*," explains Aiko Ishida, a Tokyo based book cover designer.

In ancient times, dolls made out of paper, representing each doll-maker's imperfections, impurities and flaws, were cast away in rivers as an act of protective purification. The festival today is more about the collection, admiration and display of dolls often on platforms covered in red cloth. The festival is also associated with and linked to Japan's first novel *The Tale of Genji*, written over a thousand years ago. Not all Japanese dolls, however, are about purification, cultural order and the status quo, and femininity. The nation has many varieties including, for example, its own form of voodoo dolls, *wara ningyo*, used to curse.

Puppets, dolls and their motifs are embedded in many components of Japanese culture, traditional and pop, which explains why Japan is sometimes called 'The Land of The Dolls'. *Bunraku*, founded in Osaka in 1684, a traditional form of puppet theatre that historically competed with *kabuki* is one famous example; *Hello Kitty* is probably the ultimate doll representative of *kawaii*-culture. More than 60 million Licca-chan dolls, Japan's answer to Barbie, have been sold since this 22-centimetre-high fashion doll with her mixed Japanese and French parentage, Japanese designer mother Orie and French musician father Pierre, made her debut in Japan in 1967. Licca-chan has an extensive back story as well as many siblings, and of course favourite books: *A Little Princess* by Frances Hodgson Burnett (1849-1924) and *Anne of Green Gables* by L.M. Montgomery (1874-1942). Her preferred fictional cat is a blue one from the future called Doraemon, not Hello Kitty.

Anime and manga have their own doll cultures of cosplay and figures. Smart dolls and emoji are available for the technology obsessed. The hobbyist movement make their own; the craft movement have origami dolls. Lonely men have, as is often reported, synthetic life-sized dolls.

> "There's meaning in living alongside a doll you care for. Owning a love doll is entirely different from dating a woman. A barbarian like you who only sees them as tools for sexual gratification probably can't understand, but what we're dealing with is a highly evolved form of love." That was Ozu's take. Tomihiko Morimi (b. 1979), *Yojohan shinwa taikei (The Tatami Galaxy)*.

Doll motifs and narratives started appearing in the works of many leading Japanese writers in the Meiji era (1868-1912) at the time of Japan's frenzied modernisation. For many this was a period of economic and cultural shock. A similar revolution in fiction writing was also taking place and the number of novels in translation available in Japan increased rapidly. The invention of new expressions and words were sometimes required to translate these books. Not just new scientific, technical and medical terms, but also new words and expressions to reflect concepts such as the Western ideal of 'romantic love' and the Western concept of a novel in Japanese.

Arrested Development

As the country was encouraged to embrace all things Western in its race to catch up and take its place as an "equal amongst the leading Western powers", societal rules changed. Homosexual male sex was banned for the first time in 1872 (for a period of eight years), for example, and relationships between men and women, as well as romantic expectations, changed. Traditional roles and responsibilities were questioned; society, which now had a brand-new Japanese word to define and describe it, *shakai*, was in flux. New institutions were founded, hairstyles changed with topknots abandoned, and new forms of architecture and technology arrived.

Some academics think that it was during this period, which some of them argue caused sexual repression, that Japanese men first started to focus their attention on inanimate objects that reminded them of tradition and the good old days with their less complex relationships.[67] It is, of course, discomforting for most people to be confronted with seemingly contradictory viewpoints, negating long-held beliefs. The challenges change can present sometimes strengthen strongly held established views or simply lead to those beliefs being hidden from plain sight.

> Not forgotten, the dolls
> Their faces until now
> Long concealed away in boxes.
>
> Buson Yosa (1716-1784)

Not all change is a temporary blip that should be ignored or rejected. At times you need to change your mind, cut your losses and alter your approach, accepting the so-called lessons in loss, though change is never an easy avenue for all to follow. Clinging to the past and subverting reality, using literature or inanimate objects as a form of escape for instance, whether consciously or not, is perhaps an unusual example of what might today be termed by psychologists as the perils of belief perseverance. Attachments, wanted or of the undesirable type, to people, the past, fashions, places (towns, buildings or schools) or even dolls can still paint unforgettable pictures of society, as well as institutional change. This is particularly true when words are moulded into distinctive narrative prose that reflect or react to new or imported invasive cultural trends.

Periods of backward-looking reverie, in all their creative forms, are typical during times of rapid socio-economic change, mirrors of the moment. Following directly in the wake of these manic and frenetic periods of change in Japan, 'doll-love' novels started to appear that featured dolls and also the aesthetic of 'human-dolls', far removed from the famous freedom-loving dolly-birds of London's Swinging Sixties. These works, some penned by Japan's finest authors, were and continue to be dark, satirical, and occasionally macabre, but are more often than not rendered in a style designed to provoke.

One of the very first such novels is said to be the short story *Hitodenashi no koi (Love of a Brute)*, by Ranpo Edogawa (1894-1965), which includes a sex scene with a doll.[68] The highly-influential Edogawa pioneered modern mystery writing in Japan and a prize named after him has been awarded to mystery writers since 1955. Several of his works feature doll-like people and human-like dolls. This particular story is a tale of a man who is incapable of love, as most of us know it.

Junichiro Tanizaki's (1886-1965) novel *Tade ku mushi (Some Prefer Nettles)*, first published in a newspaper serialisation and then in 1929 in book format, where the protagonist Kaname falls in love with a *bunraku* puppet, Koharu, from the Edo period (1603-1868), after his marriage to an assertive Westernised wife starts falling apart, is another important and illustrative example. It is said to be autobiographical, one of his best works, and a good example of the so-called Madonna-Harlot dichotomy sometimes deployed by Tanikazi, reflecting skewed female stereotypes.

Other slightly later notable examples include narratives of a man falling for a shop window mannequin and a wealthy young man with a significant inheritance in love with a beautiful actress (with opinions) who after he kills, he tries to keep and love in an unnatural doll-like state. *Moenai ningyo (An Unburnable Doll)*, by Tadashi Iijima (1902-1996), a very different type of tale is another interesting example, with tiny echoes of some acclaimed proto-feminist Western narratives. Within which a young, betrothed women defiantly throws a doll she has received from her probable future husband into a fire, rebuffing a gift that she believes objectifies her, turning her into an article of innocence, in an act of brazen repulsion from societal gender roles, refusing to be defined by society.

The Nobel Prizewinner Yasunari Kawabata's (1899-1972) novella *Nemureru bijo (House of the Sleeping Beauties)*, published in 1961, featuring drugged young women who become doll-like partners that old men can sleep next to, is yet another often cited and a highly significant example. Ian Buruma in *A Japanese Mirror: Heroes and*

Villains of Japanese Culture includes this title within his category of *The Human Work of Art*. Kawabata writes:

> Were not the longing of the sad old men for the unfinished dream, the regret for days lost without ever being had, concealed in the secret of this house? Eguchi had thought before that girls who did not awaken were ageless freedom for old men. Asleep and unspeaking, they spoke as the old men wished.

According to Mariko Kaga (b. 1943), an actress famous for playing femme fatale characters in Japanese films, when she was about 15 in the late 1950s she often met up with Kawabata, generally for breakfast but he also came to plays she performed in. This would have been a few years prior to the publication of *House of the Sleeping Beauties* in 1961. Kaga also met the writer Yukio Mishima (1925-1970), Kawabata's friend during this period. Like the visitors to the house in Kawabata's novella there was no physical component to their relationship. But the relationship did develop, with Kaga starring in the 1965 film adaptation of Kawabata's novel *Utsukushisa to kanashimi to (Beauty and Sadness)*, originally published in 1964. In it Kawabata observes reflectively, "I suppose even a woman's hatred is a kind of love."

House of the Sleeping Beauties has been influential in and outside Japan despite some arguing that it has an element of unhealthiness to it. It is credited, for example, with being one of the inspirations behind the 2011 Australian film *Sleeping Beauty*, written and directed by Julia Leigh. This "erotic film" won critical acclaim and was shown at many different film festivals including Cannes and Stockholm where the Kawabata connection was discussed. A key plot device in the film is a sedated young woman, like in Kawabata's novel. The film also features a *Go* player in an apparent reference to the author.

In one of the contemporary writer Ira Ishida's (b. 1960) short stories, depicting marginalised youth, in his collection of pacey 1997 urban mysteries *Ikebukuro Uesuto Geto Paku (Ikebukuro West Gate Park)*, there is a tale of an anaesthetist that drugs young girls to the point of death in prearranged transactions with them. So, as you can see, this narrative of the compelling attractive aesthetic of lifeless doll-like women is still very much alive and well in Japan. These works are perhaps the embodiment of how society can at times see Japanese women with the male gaze laid bare, so to speak, next to naked sleeping women.

This is, of course, not a narrative theme exclusive to Japan as the international popularity of Disney's 1959 *Sleeping Beauty* clearly indicates. The origins of the original fairy tale that this version is based on are open to debate, but one author credited as the source of many of its versions is the Italian Giambattista Basile

(1566-1632) with his short, twisted tale "Sun, Moon, and Talia". His plot includes several of the darker elements contained in some of Japan's doll-love novels such as adultery, jealousy, death and sex with a comatose beauty. This latter horrific trope of rape leads, in Basile's version, to the birth of two children while the victim remains unconscious. No matter the actual provenance, each such tale is frozen in an immutable state for eternity within its own particular narrative structure for us to enjoy or be revolted by.

Walking, Talking, Living Dolls

Bizarrely and somewhat disturbingly, the cult of doll-worship extends beyond the printed page and into the real world. Around 2010 there was a trend among young Japanese girls to look like living dolls. It was a phenomenon widely reported by the likes of *The New York Times*.[69] Articles highlighted the staggering amounts some young girls were willing to invest to look like a traditional French porcelain doll or a Barbie. Other pieces drew the reader's attention to the ways in which visitors to the famous doll museum in Yokohama are dressed.

Digital media and celebrity culture is making people much more image conscious than in the past while allowing niche groups of people with obscure and unusual shared interests to connect. Nevertheless, there is still generally a major drive to be seen as authentic in many countries. In contrast, some people in Japan are striving to look as synthetically artificial and doll-like as possible.

Doll-making, and doll-culture like literature changes and evolves. Modern ball-jointed dolls (BJD) were pioneered in Germany in the 1930s by the German artist and surrealist photographer, Hanns Bellmer (1902-1975) spawning a new development lineage leading to the BJD hobbyist movement in Japan today, which tens of thousands of people are now part of, and Asian ball-jointed dolls (ABJD). These dolls have been influenced significantly by traditional Japanese dolls.

These types of contemporary dolls often inspired by anime look realistic and come in different sizes. They are sought after and collectable. The owners customise them, dress them, and even assign them personalities. The Super Dollfie (SD), is an example of a particularly sought after brand, which even has a secondary market for dolls that have been pre-customised and clothed.

The prevalence of dolls in Japan has fostered all types of interpretation, analysis and hypotheses. Doll metaphors have been commonly used to describe Japan since the 19th and 20th centuries, a period when Japanese dolls were already very popular in Europe and America. These days it is an association often drenched in cliché that is regularly dismissed as a modern manifestation of orientalism. Nonetheless, unflatteringly, perplexed Western commentators can still on occasion compare some of the female television announcers and personalities on Japanese television to mascots, elevator girls in stores and hotels to dolls, and female staff working at Japanese department stores, who line up wearing white gloves and bow gracefully when the doors to their stores are opened each morning, to humanoids.

There is a long history and pedigree of these types of comments and observations. Before the Second World War Japanese dolls were often referred to as 'Jappy', 'Jappie', the 'Jap doll', or 'a little Jap' and children's books, songs and advertisements often used similar language or stereotypes of Japanese people being doll-like, sleeping on the floor and frequently bathing.[70]

The definition of a doll differs from country to country and person to person. The Japanese word for doll, *ningyo*, is made up of two characters: 'person/human' and 'form/shape'. Everyone seems to have a view or opinion on Japanese dolls from the elegant to the sordid. Psychologists, anthropologists and Japan experts: all you need to do is ask and they will interpret doll culture for you with intellectual rigour. Perhaps this is the very essence of their popularity in that you can project whatever you want onto them: you can admire them, display them, play with them, mimic them, or study them for an academic thesis.

> But were the dolls of that night really a dream? Were they an illusion that I had created in my subconscious mind because I so urgently wanted to see the dolls once more? Still now I am at a loss to know whether or not it were true. But in the depths of that night, I saw my elderly father gazing on those dolls. Of this alone, I am sure. Even if it were but a dream, I doubt that I would have any regrets about it, as, in any case, I saw before me my father.
> Ryunosuke Akutagawa (1892-1927), "Hina" ("The Dolls").

Modern and contemporary authors like their predecessors from the past are finding dolls a rich backdrop and an easy to exploit motif for creative writing. Unsurprisingly, they also have their own modern perspectives, unique ways of dressing them up, creating their own spin and interpretations, while developing their own narratives. Fuminori Nakamura's (b. 1977) gripping murder mystery *Kyonen no natsu, kimi to wakare* (*Last Winter, We Parted*), for example, involves a group of people all connected through a craftsman of full-sized silicon sex dolls. This work deftly places Nakamura in a literary lineage flattering both those who came before, such as Edogawa and other established writers, as well as acclaimed contemporary narratives, for readers alert enough to notice.

Other fascinating similar examples include: *Echizen takeningyo* (*Bamboo Dolls of Echizen*) by Tsutomu Minakami (1919-2004), Kanji Hanawa's (1936-2020) short story "Kise kae namida ningyo" ("Dress-up Crying Doll"), and Hiroka Yamashita's (b. 1994) award-wining 2015 novel *Doru* (*Doll*). This last one is the tale of a seven-year-old boy who, having found a discarded doll on the street, becomes entranced with dolls leading him on a journey to purchasing a sex doll. Takako Takahashi's (1932-2013) novella about a woman who enjoys the pleasure of her young male doll every night, *Ningyo ai* (*Doll Love*), is a less frequent but equally absorbing example of another novel, alongside Yamashita's, featuring dolls written by a woman.

> Obsessively burning impressions into my eyes, I looked at the doll's body bit by bit. Oddly her breasts, rear and legs, instinctively sexual, and other similar areas of her body, didn't evoke any such emotions or arouse me. Also, as originally she was unfunctioning, she appeared assembled strong armed together. Well that is how I felt. She was supposedly now complete, in her perfect form, but it seemed to me she would continue to grow, mature, and change, not an imperfect doll, it was as if I was looking at a living creature. Hiroka Yamashita, *Doru* (*Doll*).

Humans, no matter their provenance, tend to project onto non-human beings—pets, treasured toys—features and characteristics generally attributed to us. That said, traditionally in Japan, inanimate, man-made objects including dolls and needles are thought to have a form of spirituality, even souls. This, surprisingly, gives rise to 'funerals', *kanshasai*, last-right appreciation ceremonies for dolls, and *hari kuyo* for broken needles, which are conducted at temples and shrines. They take place on special days and have been conducted for centuries. Dolls are brought, prayers made, and financial offerings of around 3,000 yen given, before the dolls are discarded. The number of dolls being brought to the Meiji Shrine in Tokyo, located near Harajuku, which is famous for youth fashion and culture, increases every year. These events put an encouraging ritualistic blanket around letting go of treasured objects allowing some to make the emotional leap required to tidy up their closets, and not to endlessly hold on to objects just in case they feel the urge to touch, hold, or gaze on them once more.

The spiritual boundaries between people and treasured objects is not as clear-cut in Japan as in the West. People sometimes connect at a deep level with inanimate human-shapes (*ningyo*) like traditional dolls, robots, *bunraku* puppets or even a beloved word processor. Nakamura, for example, can't bear the thought of throwing out his old-style word processor that now resides hidden in the back of a closet surrounded by a mass of other stuff.

Many Japanese people have a special respect for non-human objects that have helped them, he explains, this admiration can, he says, border on love at times. Nakamura didn't attribute the writing device that propelled his career forward so successfully with a personality or give it a name. He can't even recall which brand or model his device is, but it is the machine he hammered away at when he started writing before turning professional, when he still had a series of part-time jobs. A funeral isn't planned for it yet, but Nakamura explains, if he feels that way about an out-of-date unusable writing device, it probably isn't surprising that treasured dolls, with their human-like forms, play such an important and emotive role in Japanese culture and make for delightfully exploitable plot devices.

Some observers go as far as stating that the array of dolls and statues in Japan is a form of cult-like pagan idolatry. That Japan today is how most societies might still be if Judeo-Christian values hadn't gained momentum with its important narrative of Abraham, a man with an idol-making father who smashed his father's idols while his father was away, thereby creating a new relationship with humankind's maker. Destroying prior perspectives and belief systems, a tale, also important in the Islamic world, that is retold pervasively.

Without over analysing things, and spoiling the fun, we should safely conclude at least two important things: firstly, dolls are an integral part of Japanese culture and will remain so. Secondly, fortunately, Japanese authors will continue to write unusual, compelling and highly-readable books about them for many years to come, generating fresh new perspectives.

Whodunnit: Detective Fiction's Sudden Death

Crime fiction has a very long history in Japan and early Western visitors at the end the 19th century, including the famous Victorian travel writer Isabella Bird (1831-1904), commented with fascination and some disgust on the large number of crime fiction titles on sale in Japan in the 1870s.[71] The genre's development in Japan has, like any good detective story, faced some unexpected twists and turns, as well as the odd decoy and unforeseen disruption including when, for instance, the Japanese government deemed some books unpatriotic or "un-Japanese" in the lead-up to and during the Second World War.

The genre's messy evolutionarily development, like that of Japanese publishing itself, has mirrored Japan's. Major changes occurred in the Meiji era (1868-1912) and the aftermath of the Second World War (1939-1945). Both were caused and catalysed, one could argue, by American military men with advanced weaponry, and from sustained outside pressure, *gaiatsu*, leaped upon opportunistically from within.

The first was triggered by Commodore Perry's (1794-1858) arrival on Japanese shores with his now infamous black ships that helped wrench Japan open in 1853 with dramatic consequences leading to the subsequent Meiji Restoration. Perry's momentous entrance led to new international treaties, often dubbed the 'Unequal Treaties',[72] as well as the subsequent unlocking of Japan and its markets to the world. The Christian intellectual leader and writer Kanzo Uchimura (1861-1930) eloquently describes the changes it triggered in his book *Representative Men of Japan* (*Daihyouteki Nihonjin*) as follows:

> I think the Japanese Revolution of 1868 signifies a point in the world's history when the two races of mankind representing the two distinct forms of civilization were brought to *honourable* intercourse one with the other, when the Prospective West was given check in its anarchic progress, and the Retrospective East was waken from its stagnant slumber. From that time on there were to be neither Occidents nor Orients, but all to be one in humanity and righteousness. Before Japan awoke, one part of the world turned its back to the other.

For many, however, the arrival of the Americans felt like a Sword of Damocles hanging over Japan's head, a consequential constant threat with the potential to cause severe economic uncertainty and cultural impoverishment, leaving the nation and its honour in peril.

In more recent times this type of dramatic abrupt policy reform, an unexpected shift in geopolitics, and economic opening, leading to nations turning towards each other was called *perestroika* and *glasnost* in the Soviet Union. The terms are generally translated into English as 'reconstruction' and 'openness'. Not all turns in geopolitics and openings last. In this case, these 1980s changes led to an untidy dissolution of the Soviet Union, not a Meiji-like reformation with a mostly ordered rejuvenation, generating a vibrant repositioning. That said, Japan's Meiji Restoration also involved many hard choices, some made at a brisk pace including the giving up of sovereignty, and a huge amount of disorientating change.

This spanned much including, for example, the plumbing behind the Japanese economy, as well as Japanese literature and publishing. Japan's hundreds of feudal clan lords handed over lands, authority and their domains. Currency union alongside a coordinated national interest rate policy, for instance, was also suddenly required. Convertible notes issued by around 200 clans (local governmental domains) as well as magistrates and the shogunate authorities were replaced with a new currency, the yen. The yen was subsequently adopted as the basic unit of monetary reform in 1871, replacing all clan notes, after which a newly-created central bank, the Bank of Japan, based on Belgium's after an unsuccessful experiment with a system based on the American model, was given exclusive authority to issue banknotes and coins in Japan. The Bank of Japan spawned a new structure linking together banks across the nation.

The first yen banknote issued by the Bank of Japan was a light blue coloured ten-yen note, issued in 1885, called the *daikoku-satsu*, as it contains an eponymous image of one of the *Shichi Fukujin*, the seven lucky gods of fortune, the deity of fortune, commerce and prosperity. Wearing a cap and carrying a bulky sack over one of his shoulders, making this particular rendering of the friendly faced deity *Daikokuten*, with his podgy moustachioed atypical Japanese face, look somewhat like Santa Claus, who also incidentally made his first appearance in print in Japan, putting him into circulation in his case within the minds not the wallets of Japanese children, in the Meiji era. Other banknotes, thanks to the help of an Italian painter, engraver and lithographer, Edoardo Chiossone (1833-1898), used images of individuals such as the mythical Empress Jingu and Michizane Sugawara (845-903) an important Heian period (794-1185) poet and politician, for example. The image Chiossone created for the one-yen banknote depicts a somewhat European-looking

Empress Jingu, wearing heavy ornate necklaces in an oval on the righthand side of the banknote. These new notes changed the size, look, control, and nature of paper money in Japan.

The transformation was extremely broad-based and distinct from how the Soviet Union changed, hesitantly and some might say chaotically transitioning after the end of the Cold War and the fall of the Berlin Wall. Japan's early transformation also differed markedly from how the European Union (EU) has emerged. The EU has evolved over decades through a series of at times controversial and contested treaties in a long, grinding process developing its own type of protective strategic sovereignty and a new unifying currency to go with it, one that not all its 27 members, have, as of writing, decided to join.

Despite the nature of the new international treaties, which bestowed significant rights on non-Japanese, not just to enter Japan but on their behaviour and activities once they had, as well as the establishment of treaty ports (what might be termed free ports today with low tariffs) Japan still controlled its cultural sovereignty. It escaped fully-fledged occupation, as well as colonisation, even though some argue that the treatise created a form of quasi-colonialism. Japan still had power over its destiny, for better or worse. China, of course, also had similar treaties imposed on it and its ports in Shanghai, Ningpo, and Guangzhou. A decade earlier in 1840 various North Island Māori tribes signed the *Treaty of Waitangi* with Great Britain, thereby allowing Great Britain to annex New Zealand and appoint a governor giving its subjects full rights in that country, an outcome that Japan managed to evade. That said, compromise sometimes gives a false sense of stability and can poison what initially seems like a peaceful outcome. This can sometimes lead to unfortunate long-term consequences.

A literary occupation of Japan was also avoided, despite entrepreneurial non-Japanese individuals launching books and publications in Japan. The nation was free to publish books and books in translation, as it desired, unlike during the preceding Edo period (1603-1868) and during the immediate post-Second World War period, when permission was required. International content and pioneering locals functioned as a type of supercharging fertiliser, enriching Japan's publishing sector and pushing it into a state of creative hyper-drive. Making this turn of the wheel in Japanese history a dynamic and revolutionary one for the Japanese world of letters: a sign that the once-insular country was truly opening up.

This helped transform detective fiction and the broader genre of crime fiction in Meiji Japan as waves of new books were published in translation, magazines and newspapers were launched and new types of narratives penned. It was a type of inflection point for Japanese publishing, as well as the nation at large, with an explosion of new and diverse unrestricted narrative and educational textual outputs. Much changed in Japan including, of course, the nation's indigenous "corrupting" crime fiction, the word used by Bird to describe Japan's criminal publishing creations.

It is hard to draw parallels but the sudden 1972 visit to China by then-President Richard Nixon (1913-1994), a former Navy commander, is one worth highlighting. It was a dramatic entrance that took the world by surprise and led to massive generational international change, and so might also be considered one such watershed event. It certainly shocked Japan, considered the closet American ally in the region at the time, who were given no advanced warning of Nixon's visit. China's period of isolation before its 1970s 'opening' was, however, decades long, not centuries long, despite what some call China's "century of humiliation" at the hands of foreigners between 1839 and 1949. Additionally, when China finally acceded to the World Trade Organization (WTO) much later in 2001, under the umbrella of being a market economy with Chinese characteristics, the balance of its position within the network of rules that govern international commerce, and on which side any inequality of these associated treaties reside is perhaps less clear, and still a topic for much debate. Healing the scars of history requires the co-operation of losers as well as winners and is generally not a linear progression.

China was allowed to prohibit much, setting rules for foreign companies operating in its sovereign domain, including, for example, foreign ownership of publishing and media companies, as well as regulating (censuring) the books imported, translated and published. As we all know, cultivating and regulating culture are not synonymous. Confusing the two can lead to unreliable narrators, warped national narratives and at times false solutions that have a tendency to suddenly unravel. Just like in a good detective novel when a plodding sleuth is drawn to a seemingly efficient solution that subsequently is shown to have been a resource-sapping dangerous red herring.

The approach adopted has forced China's talented creative provocateurs to focus their talents on a limited number of genres, such as science fiction, to provide different perspectives and alternative commentary by penning, satirical techno-totalitarian dystopian worlds, often with multiple timeframes cleverly woven into their narrative structures reflecting China's present and its potential problematic trajectory. These tales can function as a type of cipher blanketed with irony depicting the struggles that some young and open-minded individuals face battling against what might be termed by some as the illusionary progress. The march from Maoism to markets and a "socialist democracy with Chinese characteristics" is, of course, still a work in progress. In contrast, initially at least, Japan's Meiji creatives had no such limitations imposed on them helping generate unapologetic creative ferment, and a healthy cultural marketplace of ideas.

Despite the 'Unequal Treaties', Uchimura heaps praise on Perry for his approach and describes Japan's escape from other possible scenarios in his book as thus:

> I consider Matthew Calbraith Perry of the United States Navy to be one of the greatest friends of humanity the world has ever seen. In his diaries we read that he bombarded the shores of Japan with doxologies, and not with ordnance.[73] His mission was a delicate one of waking up a hermit nation without doing injury to its dignity, yet keeping its native pride at bay.

And boy did this "honourable intercourse" wake-up the nation. It turned Japan into an archipelago of excited enthusiasts looking here, there and everywhere, snatching ideas to find the best devices to help it on its pathway to modernisation, to rise and find its rightful place amongst the ranks of leading nations, as a modern great power with Japanese characteristics. Even if Uchimura's optimism about the nature of mankind and the innate human condition underestimated the type of entropy that has plagued almost all national development cycles in terms of the seemly inescapable trend towards disunity, pride, confrontation, and far too often bloody and murderous outcomes.

When nations or a community are threatened from the outside or afar through external forces or perceived dangers—real or imagined—intimidation can often foster instant solidarity and rapid change from within. For centuries Japan's authorities and ruling elites had protected their status and the nation's through isolation and a formal rigid social hierarchy. This was no longer a viable sustainable option.

In stark contrast to external threats, when a community feels endangered by threats or changes from within that may rock its harmony and structures through those who are malevolent, unconventional, considered religious zealots, non-conformist, or those deemed simply as obscene, these individuals are often punished or ostracised (labelled as deviants) allowing rules, hierarchies and social structures to be reaffirmed for the many. Crime fiction invariably features rule breakers, villains, the virtuous and innocent, and they can from a safe seat depict potential scenarios, imagined case studies, with probable and fathomable uncomfortable outcomes for those considering rebellion. They can, of course, also provide momentary escape from the suffering that the challenging side-effects of change can produce.

Intriguingly, there is even some academic research that indicates that this type of storytelling with its 'scary play' can have benefits spanning the development of emotional skills and coping strategies for real-world situations through fictional 'play-fighting' type simulations for the law-abiding.

One such study shows that horror fans and morbidly curious individuals who engaged in frightening fictional experiences, for instance, were a more psychologically resilient demographic during the Covid-19 pandemic and better than expected at handling anxiety and fear.[74] Highlighting some of the unusual cognitive benefits reading can have and why reading fiction, supplementing our daily diets of non-fictional textual content, is so important.

Meiji Japan was engulfed with both external threats and a blistering rate of internal change, something that transformed its literary landscape beyond recognition, and powered its crime fiction and murder mysteries onwards. As anyone who has picked up a potboiler when sick in bed knows, dabbling in fictional death can speed up convalescence (real or pseudo, individual or national) by creating a narrative of recuperation each time a murderer is caught by a rational modern detective, no matter the literary merits of the work itself.

Criminal Exposure

It took time and occurred mostly after the arrival of highly-influential Western-style detective fiction in Japan in translation, but by 1889, the year Japan adopted its first concrete written constitution, known as the Meiji Constitution, Japan's first official modern detective story, *Tantei shosetsu*, was published. This was *Muzan (Cold Blood)* by Ruiko Kuroiwa (1862-1913). The interplay between Kuroiwa's important local work as opposed to a translation, and the canon of detective fiction, in parallel with the evolution of the Japanese novel has, many believe, significantly shaped and influenced the long-term trajectory of modern Japanese storytelling.[75]

Kuroiwa, a newspaper journalist, initially joined others in translating European books, such as Jules Verne's (1828-1905) *Le voyage dans la lune*, before penning *Cold Blood*. He also translated *The Time Machine*, by H.G. Wells (1866-1946) and the mystery *A Women in Grey*, by Alice Muriel Williamson (1858-1993) under the title *Yurei to (Ghost Tower)*.

His new original work, *Cold Blood*, features two detectives: one who digs out the facts following the discovery of a male dead body in a river in Tsukiji Tokyo. A detective who relies on modern scientific methods, of the type portrayed in the translations of Western detective novels. The other one relies on instinct and experience. In this sense, the work's sleuthing duality bridges two narrative styles, as well as two distinct Japans: the old and the newly emerging modern one. Having found three strands of hair in the victim's hand and subsequently determining, with the help of a microscope, that they may have a major international incident, involving China, on their hands, it is of course the detective that deploys the modern forensic tools of deduction that solves the mystery.

Hugo Gernsback (1884-1967), after whom the prestigious Hugo Awards are named and to whom the coining of the term science fiction is generally attributed, would have approved as it meets many of his criterion for successful writing. He defined this as "a Scientific Detective Story is one in which the method of crime is solved, or the criminal traced, by the aid of scientific apparatus or with the help of scientific knowledge possessed by the detective or his co-workers." *Cold Blood* also avoids many of the pitfalls he advises writers to try to avoid including, "don't fall into the misapprehension that, because your story has plenty of science in it, a plot is therefore unnecessary. The science improves the plot—not vice-versa."[76]

Kuroiwa reportedly translated and adapted around 100 novels from French and English into Japanese. His translations, like his detective story, unleashed creative and cultural waves that changed Japanese storylines for the better. Kuroiwa's influence has, for instance, reportedly reached as far as Hayao Miyazaki (b. 1941), the internationally acclaimed Japanese animator, co-founder of Studio Ghibli, and contemporary storyteller, who read *A Women in Grey* as a schoolboy with great interest. The translation he read apparently influenced Miyazaki's animated film, *Rupan Sansei: Kariosutoro no shiro* (*Lupin the Third: The Castle of Cagliostro*), released in 1979, the first animation co-written and directed by him.[77] The protagonist Lupin the Third in this animation is the grandson of the fictional gentleman thief and master of disguise Arsene Lupin, a character created by the French author Maurice Leblanc (1864-1941) in 1905. Interestingly, an eponymous bar, Lupin, in Ginza frequented by authors such as Osamu Dazai (1909-1948) and Ango Sakaguchi (1909-1955) in the past has now become a tourist destination for literature, anime and manga fans.

Cold Blood and Kuroiwa encouraged the development of numerous new inventive channels for Japanese crime fiction and storytelling to flow into, including *Shinseinen* (*New Youth*), a magazine launched a few decades later in 1920, packed full of short stories targeting the new generation of 'urban modern men'. *New Youth* quickly became an outlet and publishing platform for both reality-bending science fiction stories and detective stories. To manage the inflow, the editor of the magazine and others working around him reportedly grouped stories by Japanese authors into two broad categories: the first *Honkaku* (classical or orthodox) and the second *Henkaku* (irregular) stories.[78] Science fiction fell into the latter category and over time the broader publishing genre *Tentei Shosetsu, Detective Books*, as well as the term *honkaku* were better defined and differentiated after much debate, subsequently coming into wide use.

That said, the actual genesis of this outcome, just like the type of writing these two terms try to pigeonhole, is somewhat mysterious and hard to pin down. Interestingly, the term science fiction was also coined in the English reading world about this time by Gernsback, founder of the American magazine *Amazing Stories*, launched in 1926.

1926 was also a genesis year in Japan for a very different type of informational medium and publishing venture, but also a highly transformational one with long-term repercussions. It was the year that Japan's broadcaster, Tokyo Broadcasting Station, the precursor to NHK, launched its radio English lessons service, *Kiso-Eigo*, and the broadcaster's associated textbooks. Literally millions of individuals in Japan have learnt English through these broadcasts and their linked books since they started initially in radio format.

New Youth's editorial decisions and processes were no doubt primarily designed as a workflow tool for practical editorial purposes, but the new methodologies adopted by it and others helped establish a new creative fork in the messy development of the taxonomies of Japanese crime fiction. *Honkaku* was subsequently and continues today to be used as a term to describe tales about complex and unfathomable murders, often involving locked rooms with dead bodies in them, which require puzzle-solving skills to determine who committed the crime.

It was, however, Taro Hirai (1894-1965), an economics graduate writing under the pen name Ranpo Edogawa, a playful name chosen as a homage to Edgar Allan Poe (1809-1849). When this pen name is written in the traditional Japanese order, 'Edogawa Ranpo', and read rapidly in that sequence it sounds to the Japanese ear as being reminiscent: *edoga waran po*. Edogawa was the key creative force behind the genre's ensuing development in Japan, even if the genesis of modern detective fiction is generally attributed to Kuroiwa and *Cold Blood*. Edogawa popularised detective fiction by combining Holmes-like scientific method with oodles of Japanese cultural sentiment, injecting subtle nostalgia into the genre through the inclusion of the suspense-type narratives that had been popular in Japan's Edo period, before Perry's tipping-point arrival. His influence, alongside Poe and Sir Arthur Conan Doyle (1859-1930) live on. Interestingly, the version of *A Women in Grey* that the Oscar-winning animator and storyteller Miyazaki actually read, that had such an impact on him in his youth, was in fact an adaptation by Edogawa of Kuroiwa's turn-of-the-century translation. This shows again how creative storytelling and literary pollination often work in mysterious ways.

The Kaleidoscope Turns

The second pivotal period occurred after the Second World War with change this time caused by national defeat and the occupation led by General Douglas MacArthur (1880-1964). This second pivot point in the arc of Japanese history, is a fascinating one when traced back to Japan's Meiji opening, which first brought modern detective novels and their fictionalised murders and scientific solutions to Japan. Another new starting point was created, on this occasion with an army, not a navy man, rebooting Japan onto a new national trajectory.

After a war full of brutal savagery and atrocities, Japan was now a conquered nation under occupation for the first time.[79] It led to root and branch changes in rules and regulations with a spiral of new rubrics that even affected publishing and specific genres in different ways, as well as the nation itself. It was the beginning of a new Japan, one without the Japanese military playing a central role though the military were still in charge. During the American occupation of Japan (1945-1952) all publications, for example, were reviewed by MacArthur's team at GHQ (General Headquarters) and at one point they even considered banning the use of *kanji*, something that had been proposed by educational reformists in the Meiji era too.

Tellingly, MacArthur, the Supreme Commander for the Allied Powers (SCAP), recommended *The Long Winter*, the sixth book in Laura Ingalls Wilder's series for publication. It was published in 1949, under the title *Nagai fuyu* by Kosumoporitan-sha (Cosmopolitan Publishing) translated by Aya Ishida (1908-1988). *Nagai fuyu* is generally cited as the first translated book to be granted permission for publication by SCAP.[80] During the war itself, the publication, distribution and reading of books in English were prohibited in Japan alongside speaking English and more than a thousand books were banned or censored. *The Long Winter* is not, however, a work of crime fiction. It is a tale of survival and resilience against the odds, a tale of how the Ingalls family in the *Little House* series survive being snowed in with limited food supplies during a long eight-month winter. *The Long Winter* was apparently chosen to aid "democratization" and to "buoy the morale of a defeated and starving people."

One of the stated strategic goals of the occupation was "to build a future for the people of Japan based upon considerations of realism and justice" and "to infuse into the hearts and minds of the Japanese people principles of liberty and right heretofore unknown to them."[81] Learning about America and its values was part of this. GHQ actively encouraged the book's distribution to public, and school libraries across Japan. German translations were published in a similar effort.

Laura Ingalls Wilder wrote a special message, dated 8 July 1948, to the children of Japan, which appeared in the book. It ran as follows:

things of real value do not change with the passing of years nor in going from one country to another. These I am sure you have. It is always best to be honest and truthful, to make the most of what we have, to be happy with simple pleasures, to be cheerful in adversity and have courage in danger.

The book was very popular even though the series was actually originally written during the Great Depression with its first title published in 1932. Echoes of Wilder's message and her book can be found in many unexpected Japanese places. One of Japan's all-time bestselling books *Madogiwa no Totto-chan* (*Totto-Chan: The Little Girl at the Window*), written by Tetsuko Kuroyanagi (b. 1933) now a Japanese media celebrity and UNICEF Goodwill Ambassador, published in the 1980s, is one such example. It is also a tale of a young girl, an unusual education and the importance of values. In its case those experienced by Kuroyanagi at an unusual ideal elementary school in Tokyo during wartime. A tough period for many Japanese schoolchildren, even for the most resilient and privileged which this is not a book about, with shortages of food and constant aerial bombardments. The book has sold more than 5.8 million copies in Japan and has been translated into more than 16 languages including many local Indian languages, a country, like China and Japan, where the book has been popular. The Japanese government has promoted it and also encouraged its use in schools embracing its themes, of the value of learning with fun, freedom, positive thinking, and love, showing how much Japan and its place in the world has changed.

Obscene Regulation

After Japan signed the *San Francisco Treaty of Peace with Japan* in 1951, full sovereignty returned to Japan. The Allied Occupation of Japan (1945-1952) came to an end on 28 April 1952, the eve of the emperor's birthday. Japan had another new constitution, originally drafted in English, that it was putting into place in translation after a proposal by Japanese officials that the nation's existing Meiji Constitution be amended, was rejected. The new 'MacArthur' Constitution, with its famous clause renouncing war "as a sovereign right of a nation," was being implemented just as nations around the world were adopting the Universal Declaration of Human Rights (UDHR), which some 48 countries voted in favour of. Japan's new constitution drafted mostly by American experts was also influenced by the New Deal, a series of important reforms in the United States enacted by President Franklin D. Roosevelt (1882-1954), whose wife Eleanor (1884-1962) helped draft the UDHR.

Amazingly, the text of the UN Declaration has been translated into more languages than the works of any contemporary Japanese author.

Legal responsibility for the new constitution and the power over new rules and regulations transferred back to Japanese control. This included the regulation of the press, publishers and the media. During the occupation various controls existed including GHQ, for instance, determining which foreign books could or could not be published. Despite this, Japan's new constitution, drawn up by GHQ and ratified in 1947, prohibited all forms of censorship and guaranteed academic freedom and freedom of expression. Times were still, however, very tough for many.

> It was the summer of 1947, and the citizens of Tokyo already crushed with grief and shock over the loss of the war, were further debilitated by the languid weather. The city was ravaged. Seedy-looking shacks had sprung up on the messy sites of bombed-out buildings. Makeshift shops overflowed with colourful black-market merchandises, but most people were still living from hand to mouth. Akimitsu Takagi (1920-1995), *Shisei satsujin jiken (The Tattoo Murder Case)*.

This was a material change to the regulations that had governed publishing in Japan, which had seen very limited development since major changes to these laws were implemented in a flurry of new regulations in Japan's Meiji era, when newspaper and magazine publishing started to flourish, initially unbound by most forms of regulation. The post-war, liberal Western-influenced atmosphere had a major impact on Japan, even on its publishing. This encouraged the setting up of thousands of new publishing houses and new waves of books arriving in Japan in Japanese translation, often for the first time. It was a second explosion of creativity and entrepreneurial activity in the publishing sector, similar to that of the Meiji era, providing Japan's creative kaleidoscope of storytelling with a new and exciting sharp turn. Publications and publishers sprung up everywhere. One industry insider compared it to bamboo after rain.

This had profound effects on intellectual life and the nation's institutions. The new freedoms facilitated much debate with the open exchange of content and ideas, sometimes the predictable and at times the unpredictable. This spanned the sexual, the moral, the emergence of individual's labelled decadents and deplorables, and the purity and identity of the nation itself. Purity and purification rituals can be a somewhat peculiar cultural force in Japan, that can range from the purification of steps leading up to sacred waterfalls through the burning of bales of fire to cleansing ceremonies that involve water, beans or salt, as well as other purification agents and ritual regimes dating back to prehistoric days. At this time the worry was not just about desecration through the Americanisation of Japan, but anxiety that even stretched, for some, to the DNA of "mixed-blood children" and their implication for the nation's future.[82]

In June 1950, a new self-regulation body was established. This became known as the *Shuppanbutsu Fuki Iinkai* (Publishing Morals Committee). It was established shortly after the publication in spring of the same year, of *Lady Chatterley's Lover* in Japanese translation for the first time. The book by D. H. Lawrence (1885-1930), his last, which was first published in 1928, was translated into Japanese by Sei Ito (1905-1969) and published by Oyama Publishing. Japan was determined to manage and contain the flourishing threats to the nation's norms and morals, a potential new blend of cultural pollution, and decide how to deal with the new types of deviants appearing on the printed page that might end up endangering the country's development.

The publication of *Lady Chatterley's Lover,* with its narrative of forbidden desire, tested these new laws and a trial took place on the grounds of the content of *Lady Chatterley's Lover* being obscene. The trial went all the way to Japan's supreme court, setting a legal precedent that lasted for decades. The Supreme Court decision, in this first post-war obscenity trial, defined obscenity as anything "unnecessarily sexually stimulating, (which) damages the normal sexual sense of shame of ordinary people, or is against good sexual moral principles."

According to Kristen Cather in *The Art of Censorship in Postwar Japan*, "The Chatterley trial staged a very public struggle to define literary, cultural, and legal identity, engaging a far-reaching debate over the relationship of domestic Japanese and imported Western traditions." The Japanese Supreme Court concluded that parts of the book, consisting of about 80 pages, were obscene and banned those sections from publication and fined the translator and publisher in a landmark decision that concluded that the sex in *Lady Chatterley's Lover* was not normal, and was against good sexual moral principles.

Despite Japan's long history of erotic publishing of woodblock prints including *shunga* in the Edo period, erotic guidebooks and tales of man-eating demon women, this imported fictional prose about Lady Chatterley, an aristocratic woman married to an emotionally and physically crippled man, and the day-to-day life of her English gamekeeper, that in addition to their intimate adulterous relationship includes 'peripheral' passages on pheasant raising and managing a shooting estate, was deemed obscene. Thus the whole book, which would act as a vector for spreading unhelpful poisonous corrupting foreign principles and sexual practices, was banned.

A subsequent trial relating to an abridged translation by Tatsuhiko Shibusawa (1928-1987) of a version of *Histoire de Juliette* by the Marquis de Sade (1740-1814) also led to a successful conviction. Interestingly, Shibusawa, was a relative of Eiichi Shibusawa (1840-1931) one of Japan's most influential early industrialists, the so-called father of Japanese capitalism. He helped found around 500 companies, including the first Western-style paper mill in Japan in 1875, an often overlooked important component in Japan's overall development, as well as the Imperial Hotel in Tokyo of which he was the first chairman. Western-style paper, which was initially imported, played a hugely significant role in Japan's modernisation, not just in the printing of modern-style banknotes and ownership certificates, but also in mass-communication allowing mass production and the projection of influence and power through all printed media formats. Fittingly, an image with a three-dimensional hologram, apparently a world first, of this industrialist Shibusawa, not his obscene younger relative, now adorns a Japanese banknote.[83]

How countries regulate their content can be culturally indicative. Oppression of culture and language often seem to go hand in hand. The lengthy nine-year trial dragged in several famous Japanese authors as witnesses including the likes of Shusaku Endo (1923-1996), Shohei Ooka (1909-1988) and the Nobel Prizewinner Kenzaburo Oe (1935-2023) helping increase the younger Shibusawa's public profile. For some Japanese critics, even today, pornography and the publication of materials that are on the periphery of falling within scope of Japan's official definition of the obscene is seen as a subversive tool through which to resist the puritan authorities and assert a type of provocative cultural national independence.

> "...Those police! What a race apart they are, with their narrow little imaginations. To them, Lady Chatterley, the Marquis de Sade, they are nothing more than pornography; they don't know what pornography is, that's what I say." A sort of grandeur entered her speech, as she continued. Masako Togawa (1931-2016), *Ryojin nikki (The Lady Killer)*.

Some artists such as the controversial photographer Nobuyoshi Araki (b. 1940) have managed to make an artistic career out of bending bondage, eroticism, exploitation, and art into critically acclaimed works while somehow mostly avoiding run-ins with the law. Career-spanning persistency of purpose seems to provide individuals like Araki with the perfect alibi differentiating them as artists, as opposed to seedy perverted criminal pornographers. Turning his works, such as *Tattooed Fuck*, that many countries might consider exploitative pornography, into desirable commodities and him into an artist feted by pop stars and luxury brands. Others decide to simply take refuge in the insubordination and rule-breaking displayed within crime fiction, which despite Japan's very low homicide rate, is at least as abundant and popular today as in the time of Bird's visit to Japan in the 1870s.

That said, *Lady Chatterley's Lover* was not just controversial in Japan. It was banned in the United Kingdom until Penguin books won a landmark obscenity trial in 1960, allowing its full publication in English. This decision had a profound cultural and social impact in Britain. In contrast, it was only in 1996 that the full book was finally published in Japanese, which allowed newspapers in Britain and America to report with glee on this publishing breakthrough with such headlines as "Japanese to see more of 'Lady Chatterley'" and "'Chatterley' to bare all in Japan".

> The phrase 'sordid quotidian' refers, of course, to the nature of my work as a reporter for a third-rate weekly magazine. This is not to say I started out in this calling. When I joined the company it was a publisher of decent books. There was an extremely limited market for such books, however, and most were returned to us. The company changed course. By turning out a magazine carrying salacious articles and exposes, its employees were able, though just barely, to make a living wage. Junnosuke Yoshiyuki (1924-1994) "Fui no Dekigoto" ("Something Unexpected").

Surprisingly, it took 51 years from Japan's first post-war obscenity trial for the first manga obscenity trial to take place. The erotic adult 144-page comic book, *Misshitsu* (*Honey Room*), written and illustrated by Yuji Suwa, using the pen name Beauty Hair, achieved this questionable historic honour in 2002. The case, which initially took place at the Tokyo District Court, was concluded after an appeal at the High Court and final escalation to the Supreme Court in 2007. The author and the manga's publisher were both found guilty of violating article 175 of the Japanese Criminal Code, which relates to pornography.[84] Besides being the first trial of an obscene manga, of which there have been many since, this was the first obscenity trial in at least two decades in Japan.

The similarities and differences with the translation of Lawrence's *Lady Chatterley's Lover* are noteworthy. Both depict anal sex, one with extreme graphics and the other through written prose. The female protagonist of *Honey Room*, however, was a prostitute with a sadistic client, and not an upper-class lady who gets involved with an employee. In their defence, Japan's colourful erotic publishing history was unsuccessfully cited as an accepted precedent. The defence team used the fact that *shunga*, erotic woodblock prints, were not only published in Japan's Edo period but were also reproduced and circulated in contemporary Japan. Nonetheless, at all three levels of court, the defendants were found guilty due to the detail and realism of what was portrayed and the fact that graphic novels due to their very nature have the potential to be more obscene than simple prose.

It was a precedent setting series of trials defining the limits on what manga publishers can legally publish. Experts expect similar trials in the future to set similar parameters for anime, and digital publishing on mobile phones and the internet. These decisions, however, have not held back gruesome crimes and extreme violence, and unsavoury characters, being depicted in Japanese storytelling, leaving murky genre boundaries for commentators, scholars and authors to construct, deconstruct and creatively fuse to meet their unquenchable professional desires.

Lexical Extinction

New post-war regulations that impacted on publishing, however, weren't just limited to censorship of the obscene. In 1946, the detective fiction sub-genre, *tantei shosetsu*, was hit by a rather unexpected title-killing obstacle and in this case not by the courts. New regulations governing the use of the Japanese language in print were introduced by the *Kokugo Shingikai* (The Japanese Language Council). These new regulations and the standards they set for official documents forced the Japan's publishing industry to rethink how it referred to and labelled detective fiction in Japanese. This untimely intervention happened just as the pioneers of the genre, including Edogawa, author of 150 short stories and novels, were trying hard to revive and promote it. Hoping to transform this type of fiction from a neglected one, dominated by translations, into a distinctive and thriving national tradition.

The new standards included the creation of an official list of 1,850 *kanji* characters, known then as *toyo kanji*, that were deemed appropriate for daily use in, for example, national newspapers and schoolbooks, leaving some publishing phraseology in-scope and others out-of-scope for official and general use. Unfortunately, one of the two *kanji* characters, *tei*, used to write the word *tantei*, detective, wasn't included on the list so new ways of writing the term using another Japanese syllabary or a completely new term was required.[85]

Japan ingested and co-opted *kanji* ideograms after their arrival from China in the early fifth century, allowing, despite the Japanese language being grammatically distinct and the syntax of both languages having nothing much in common, this foreign script to be used as Japan's first form of written communication. Additionally, one should also not forget two other major Chinese contributions, the invention of paper and printing that have also been cornerstones for publishing and creative outputs in Japan and other nations. Today, textual design, labelling, printing and packaging are essential ingredients in our lives and most businesses, but they also propagate biases and cloak provenance. On occasion this is by design and it is therefore sometimes essential to connect with our 'inner detective' to unmask the true nature of things and the facts behind societal noise, positioning and marketing.

The development of language and creative ability are, according to psychologists, so entangled they may be to all intents and purposes the same thing. It is hard to imagine today any society or nation without the ability to write and document itself, but humans actually managed to spend some 45,000 years conversing before scribbling, until the emergence independently of writing in different geographical locations such as China, Egypt, Mesopotamia and Mesoamerica. It is also hard to conceive of a world without books.

Initially, this foreign Chinese imported lettering was complemented and enhanced with new local syllabary, encouraging this first written form of communication in Japan, as well as the new words ideas, and concepts imported alongside it to flourish. *Kanji* is, of course, much more than a series of letters that capture speech allowing it to be written down. Each ideographic letter provides deeper meaning, adding their own characteristics to phonetic notation. It is one of the most fascinating examples of the stealth-like power of migration. In its case the non-biological variety.

Subsequently, during the first phase of the Cold War, this Chinese cultural import was regulated, putting limits on how these ideograms, numbered in their thousands, should be used and engaged with, through these new standards introduced after the Second World War. This readjustment created a major new challenge for Japanese detective fiction, but not a unique problem, in terms of an imported cultural or commercial product reaching a sudden local impasse. Japan has a wonderful knack for and a long history of importing things and after a period of often awkward isolated ingestion and regulation, sometimes involving odd and fascinating detours, generating refinements, as well as brand-new linages leading to brilliant new concepts, approaches and outcomes that are then re-exported with considerable commercial success.

Fine Young Carnivores: Holy Cow!

There are many fascinating examples of this but a classic one is beef. Japan is now proud of its internationally famous cattle breeds, *wagyu*, and their tasty fatty flavoured varieties such as Kobe beef, which are now exulted and consumed with delight around the world at considerable expense. Cows, just like *kanji*, paper, kaleidoscopes, movable type, motorcars, trains, photocopiers and modern detective stories, are not, however, indigenous to Japan.

These four-legged creatures that Japan is now renowned for, descended from as few as 80 animals originally from an area located in the proximity of Turkey and Iran initially arrived from Korea. For long periods eating them in Japan, alongside other meats, was actually considered impure and taboo. In spite of this, cows were never culled or banished. At times, such as during Japan's Edo period, beef and other meat was eaten occasionally for medicinal reasons due to its perceived nutritious nature, often in miso-marinated formats.

However, it was only in the Meiji era that consumption became common, though early adopter trendy carnivores were considered as risk-taking off-menu hipsters. This emerging dining trend was picked up by the author and journalist Robun Kanagaki (1829-1894), ironically a son of a fishmonger, who exploited the eating of the holy cow in a satirical illustrated book published in 1871, *Aguranabe* (*The Beef Eater*), a book that portrays trendy experimental urban free-spirited individuals, who were proud to walk on the wild side and munch on meat. Today, the situation has changed dramatically with Japanese people eating more meat than fish every year.

Kanagaki is known for many things including being the author of two of the first modern books, guides and recipes, published in Japan on Western-style cooking, as well as his tale of a murderous she-devil, *Takahashi oden yasha monogatari*, about the last Japanese women to be beheaded, after a trial that lasted more than two years, in 1879. She was accused of killing her lover and the suspected poisoning of her husband. The trial and the events surrounding this real crime helped encourage a so-called *dokufu*, female-poisoners, publishing frenzy and the narrative of over-sexed femme fatale criminality, echoes of which still remain within Japanese storytelling.[86]

Thanks to Kanagaki and the encouragement of others, in the subsequent Showa era (1926-1989) beef demand increased sufficiently, leading to the sumptuous new expensive cuts and enhanced produce that Japan is now renowned for, including Omi, Matsusaka and Kobe beef. This highly successful infusion with a type of beefed-up nativism, with storied beer-drinking cattle that are played classical music in their sheds, makes it easy to forget that cows, like many other Japanese export success stories, were in fact introduced and are not actually native to Japan.

The question authors, editors and publishers faced after the Second World War was how to plot a new path, for another relatively recently introduced new species: Japanese detective novels and modern crime fiction. Some nations would appear to be better at sticking to the script than others. In contrast to Japan, Korea simply jettisoned *kanji* after gaining its independence from Japan. This helped increase national literacy, by adopting its own previously invented phonetic-like easy-to-use replacement, *hangul*, as its official syllabic alphabet. In 1949, the People's Republic of China decided to water down its indigenous highly influential ancient lettering (removing some of the subtle idiosyncrasies of scripted communication) through a process of simplification of how each of its numerous letters is rendered. Mao Zedong (1893-1976) also briefly considered adopting a romanised replacement, an approach MacArthur's team had considered for Japan, but a committee ended up creating a new official roman-letter, latinised, transcription of Chinese, *pinyin*, similar to Japan's *romaji*, to be used as a tool for learning the newly simplified characters.

Taiwan, on the other hand, has stuck with tradition, keeping classical Chinese *kanji* ideograms in their original complex forms. Modern Vietnam, for instance, has chosen, after using a complex composite script including *kanji*, to adopt a Latin-like alphabet developed and introduced by Portuguese missionaries, initially for use in churches in Vietnam. All these approaches in their own distinct ways have spurred local cultural development, increased literacy rates and helped create a unifying glue-like sense of national identity through how words and sentences are rendered on the page, with or without sticking to embedded classical Chinese characteristics. Arguably, a great lexical leap backwards for China.

The differing approaches adopted no doubt reflect the politics and economics of their times, as well as the searches for national independence when these decisions were taken, and other broader power dynamics and cultural trends. Scripts, fonts and calligraphy, how we write, are, of course, a presentational, as well as a communication tool if they include ideograms or not.

> The penmanship showed uprightness; the characters were written clearly with no abbreviations. Imanishi stared at the words. This was the writing of the unfortunate Miki Ken'ichi. No matter how he tried, Imanishi could not connect the style of these characters with the man's brutally beaten body.
> Seicho Matsumoto (1909-1992), *Suna no utsuwa* (*Inspector Imanishi Investigates*).

Contemporary Japanese authors have a multi-dimensional lexical palette to choose from when they render their tales in written Japanese. It is not just a choice of fonts and their sizes, or words and how to order them but syllabary and how they are mixed, as well as the ideograms themselves. Advertising copywriters on top of their game, for example, often exploit unexpected mixes of *katakana* with *hiragana* and *kanji* in their headlines to grab attention and give their copy memorable rhythm. Writing the name of a city, for instance, using *romaji*, in traditional *kanji* or in phonetic *katakana* creates subtle differences in both presentation and meaning. Many writers render the location name and word Fukushima in *katakana* when they are writing about the linked disasters of the 2011 earthquake, tsunami and Fukushima nuclear accident and not the two ideograms that make up its *kanji* name, *Blessed Island*, that are used in other contexts.

This gives authors and book cover designers, alongside copywriters, a multitude of creative options to play and tease readers with, and translators endless headaches. For some authors ideograms and the choice of *kanji* are critical, while others focus more on a verbal style of narrative lettering capturing differences in male and female voices, demographics, and regional language, and others prefer *Yamato Kotoba*, the so-called native language and words of Japan, used before the arrival of *kanji* and pseudo-Chinese and its imported loanwords. Cleverly allowing these writers to insert shards of traditional verbal storytelling and ancient simple poetic voices into their composite narrative terrains. For some, plot is all that counts and their interest in the quirks of language only extend to the extent required to deliver the all-important plot to their readers.

This modern Japanese alphabet soup no doubt reflects that the stretched Japanese archipelago is close enough in proximity to the continent to have been heavily influenced by Chinese cultural trends and literature, but far enough away, with an awkward geographical structure, that makes it a very hard place to invade and dominate, both physically and culturally. Unsurprisingly, the new post-war Japanese reforms triggered a fierce debate amongst authors, publishers and the literati about the best way to render the name of the ever-popular publishing genre of detective fiction into written post-war compliant Japanese. This eventually led to the creation of a new broader term to describe Japanese detective fiction, *suiri shosetsu* (reasoning or deduction books) written using Chinese characters.

Nevertheless, some author groups continued to use the word *tantei* in the names of their organisation and writer collectives until at least the mid-1960s. The demise of the Japanese detective novel was thus somewhat like a Hollywood thriller, when you can't quite tell if the protagonist has or hasn't actually been finally killed off before bowing to the inevitable. The new term, however, actually expanded the genre and its narrative scope so that it could also in theory encompass horror, mysteries, thrillers and more, and importantly could be written using two *kanji* characters included on the official list.

The term, *suiri shosetsu*, is generally believed to have been coined or proposed by Takataro Kigi (1897-1969) who in addition to writing books within the genre was a full-time clinical doctor and brain physiology expert.[87] As a dedicated investigator rather than a lauded instigator of the genre, he thought that detective fiction should be positioned as a literary genre and not as something completely different, or as a niche, distinct, standalone local Japanese genre as some advocated. *Suiri shosetsu* books are also now known as mystery, *misuteri* (written using *katakana*) books and the authors that write them as mystery writers.

According to Koichi Nakamura, a retired Tokyo-based publishing executive and an avid mystery reader and a fan of Seicho Matsumoto, quoted earlier, in particular "the health and vibrancy of a given nation's crime fiction reflects the state and maturity of its democracy." He believes that Japan, alongside Britain and the United States, has one of the most dynamic and creative markets for crime fiction and mysteries in all their myriad forms.

Since the Second World War, many new labels, genres and formats have emerged in Japan and continue to do so. Some have stuck, such as *suiri shosetsu*, but there is often considerable debate regarding the definitions, taxonomies and classifications of genre and sub-genre. With some stressing the importance of links to the past and the established canon of works, while others wishing to create breaks with the past, and some who still wonder if the genre, in the case of *suiri shosetsu*, should be classified as literary fiction at all. The evolution and rigour of the debate surrounding the nomenclature and definitions of the genre, as well as the volume and the number of types of authorship in Japan would seem to confirm, if one takes Koichi Nakamura's assertion as a given not a hypothesis, Japan's enthusiasm for democracy, its likely continuation and the overall strength of the nation's civil society.

Written Japanese and the rules governing it have also continued to change due to increased flexibility regarding *kanji* use, for example, in first names, as well as from the impact of technological developments. The invention of the Japanese word processor in the late 1970s and the more recent rapid development of mobile and smart phones alongside social media have transformed how most Japanese people write. Ironically, as is often the case with these types of intense debates once the new label was established the *kanji* character *tei* fell back into scope for use within official documents and newspapers.

The post-war regulations imposed on the publishing industry and its terminology, as well as local debates about the various competing schools of Japanese mystery writing, often get lost in translation outside Japan or seem somewhat futile or unfathomable to younger generations less familiar with post-war changes and Japan's publishing history, despite the excitement that the debates can sometimes generate. New sub-genres have emerged often after publishing successes or breakthroughs such as the publication of *Senseijyutsu satsujin jiken* (*The Tokyo Zodiac Murders*) by Soji Shimada (b. 1948) in 1981, which helped renew interest in and rebrand whodunnits and locked-room mysteries in Japan through the subsequent creation of a new sub-genre known as *shin-honkaku* mysteries, neoclassical mysteries.

All of this helped turn Shimada into a household name in Japan, leading to some dubbing him as the post-modern Japanese master of the whodunnit.

"At that time, social realism in the style of authors like Seicho Matsumoto dominated the Japanese literary scene, and *honkaku* mysteries based on logic and deduction, weren't held in high regard, falling outside the interests of the critics," says Shimada. "Mystery writers were looked on with scorn and disdain by Japan's literary circles, and authors of so-called *jun-bungaku*, pure literature," he points out. "It was a type of village mentality, with insular rules governing tastes, not the quality of what was being written, and books just weren't appraised or reviewed." As they like to say in the current crop of self-help books, lean into the problem, and that is what some authors, such as Shimada, have cleverly done generating new publishing labels directly associated to their style of writing. Facing the problem creating opportunities, as opposed to suffering from or becoming the hapless victim of the consequences of change.

On Shimada's lean-in list was to scope out his genre, differentiating and defining it on his terms. Shimada wrote a manifesto, *Sengen*, in 1989 on the scope of the new sub-genre he represented and published schema mapping out the definitions of the various crime fiction and mystery publishing classifications and sub-genres. A schema, like some of his brilliant and delightfully unfathomable plots, that is slightly beyond the deductive skills of some, such as the author of this book. That said, his schema is not entirely without merit and has been well received by the specialists whose province it resides within and is designed for, a type of literary physiology that the brain-mapper Kigi might have admired. Shimada continues to enthusiastically promote and encourage the *shin-honkaku* genre in Japan and abroad even if its wave of popularity has now peeked in Japan having probably reached its summit at the turn of the century. Outside Japan, Shimada has taken a particular interest in up-and-coming Chinese practitioners of the genre, just as China is embracing crime books by Japanese authors that make it past its censors.

Even though this has helped create an aura of mystery around the genre itself and its tightly knit practitioners, who often tend to see themselves as members of a distinct and exclusive order, these debates have probably actually had limited real public impact in Japan. There is, however, probably one exception to this, the clever exploitation of terminology, using these myriad taxonomies as a cloaking smokescreen, to market and promote books and authors to readers with an appetite for all things mysterious. The slicing and dicing of the canon and schools of Japanese crime fiction seem to continue endlessly with titles now positioned as 'Whodunnit', 'Howdunnit' and even 'Whydunnit', as Japanese authors pen new works with narratives that span the full range of creative plot options.

These range from classical, complex and unfathomable puzzle-like murders to socially conscious commentaries on society's ills and deepest darkest fears, delighting Japanese readers and giving them much to choose from. Authors such as Tetsuya Honda (b. 1969), whose atmospheric beautifully crafted books have sold in the millions, manage to fuse procedural tales with the everyday nitty-gritty of those living on the margins of Tokyo and oddball detectives with marked personalities reflecting competing elements of contemporary Japan, alongside the nation's pulsating capital.

According to Teruya Makino, the Editor-in-Chief of Asahi Bunko, a publishing imprint linked to one of Japan's most important national newspapers, police procedurals, more so than dark crime fiction, are currently in-style. They allow their readers, often men who generally work for large Japanese organisations, to read about internal processes and procedures in different settings and institutions. Showcasing relationships with colleagues and how bureaucracy always seems to manage to hamper, getting in the way of talented individuals focused on results. Perhaps mirroring some of the challenges in and frustrations of their own workplaces, Makino explains.

That said, evidence of the past and past masters constantly pushes through into the present. A kaleidoscopic rush of crime fiction-induced thrills, in many new incarnations, awaits daring readers. As for the curious case of the sudden disappearance of *Tantei shosetsu*, detective books, a death foretold, in the Land of the Rising Sun, it was the government whodunnit!

The Portable Devices Loved by Japan's Literati

Treasured by emperors and clutched by royalty as status symbols, these multi-functional devices initially evolved from wooden sticks used for note taking and record keeping. Subsequently, the arrival of paper helped transform this early form of 'cool-tech'. The devices, known in Japan as *ogi*, were a transformative technology in their own right, and provided much more than portable sophistication. Over time, upgrades and enhancements turned the *ogi* into highly fashionable handheld canvases that displayed art and poetry, short-form writing, as well as delightful and entertaining prose, allowing their proud owners to project sophistication, taste and wealth at a flick of the wrist, at home or on the go. Japan's literati loved them. The Japanese folding fan was the must-have magical product, the 'it device' of its age.

Broadly, there are two types of traditional Japanese fan: fixed fans, called *uchiwa*, and folding fans, *ogi*. The origins of fixed rigid fans, which are still popular in Japan today, go far back to antiquity. The Egyptian pharaohs and Chinese emperors used them to symbolise majesty and authority, as well as to keep cool. Beautiful examples were, for instance, found in Tutankhamun's tomb. However, the foldable fan, according to most experts and connoisseurs, is a Japanese invention, a typical recreation and repurposing of imported know-how from China that was opportunistically re-exported with lasting global repercussions.[88]

In pre-modern Japan, in the Asuka (552-710) and Nara (710-784) periods, the nation's aristocrats, bureaucrats and rulers used portable narrow strips of wood, called *mokkan*, as notebooks.[89] The folding fan is thought to have developed from these and was then upgraded with a brand-new precious display technology, thanks to paper, after its arrival in Japan (also from China). Tens of thousands of *mokkan* have been discovered to the delight of archaeologists and scholars of ancient texts, some describing crown princes, other emperors, and some religious texts.

However, many of these sticks actually had much more mundane roles functioning like the metadata tags of our age, labelling and documenting items, creating records of ownership, formalising tax rates and recording regulations. *Mokkan* were used in other countries too, such as Korea and China. Nevertheless, carrying around bundles of small-inscribed wooden sticks was not ideal even in pre-modern Japan. This burden of bureaucracy was too much even for Japan's bureaucrats of old.

Rivets were attached at their base binding the strips together into expandable, fan-like, readable and portable collections. At some point, these developed into foldable wooden fans. Evidence of their use can in fact be traced back further still. A folding cypress fan inscribed with the date 877 made from wooden strips was discovered in 1959 inside an arm of a Buddhist statue at one of Japan's oldest temples in Kyoto. This ancient fan is decorated with pictures and inscribed with text as well as a date. Archaeologists have also found fan-shaped wooden strips in Japan dating back to as early as 747.[90] The arrival in Japan of paper-making techniques in 610, which was initially a highly coveted technology before paper was commoditised, predates these fans.

Legend has it that in the reign of Emperor Tenchi (626-672), Japan's 38th emperor, the discovery of a dead bat with burnt wings inspired a Japanese craftsman to make a prototype that was in fact the world's first functioning folding fan.[91] Still it is hard to pinpoint exactly when these early wooden folding fans, known as *hiogi*, were developed and then upgraded into the beautiful folding paper fans Japan is now famous for. Fans in Japan have many names, the folding variety, are sometimes actually referred to as *kawahoriogi*, bat-fans, due to their resemblance to the open wings of a bat, as well as *hiogi* (wooden fans often made of cypress), *kamiogi* (paper or silk fans) or the generic *ogi* and *sensu* (folding fan), while fixed fans that pre-date folding fans are known as *uchiwa* (fixed or round fans).

The Unfolding of a Handheld Narrative: Literature Fans

In 988, Chinese historical records show, two types of folding fans, 20 wooden and two made of paper, were presented to the Chinese emperor by a Japanese Zen monk, which later led the Chinese poet Su Dongpo (1036-1101) to document in a poem his surprise that "the barbarian Japanese produced such a complicated folding fan." Despite this 'poetic' and somewhat backhanded compliment, references to fans in the canon of Japanese literature (in poems, dictionaries and manuscripts) can be found in some of Japan's oldest and most important literary works long before the birth of this famous Chinese poet, and the start of China's Song Dynasty (960-1279).

Fans appear in Japan's oldest poetry anthology, *Manyoshu* (*The Collection of Ten Thousand Leaves*), a collection of thousands of poems compiled in 759 that provided the inspiration for the name of Japan's current imperial age, Reiwa, that started on 1 May 2019. Interestingly, this collection was compiled during Japan's Nara period (710-794) when Japan's capital was located in Nara, and the era from which many of the ancient *mokkan* found so far date. Most now believe this is when the first *hiogi* were made.

Fans also appear in early Japanese dictionaries and folding paper fans feature in Japan's oldest novel *Genji monogatari* (*The Tale of Genji*) and in a famous scene in *Heike monogatari* (*The Tale of the Heike*), an epic account, considered a milestone in Japanese publishing, of the battles between two feuding Japanese clans.

In *The Tale of the Heike* the warrior Yoichi Nasuno (circa 1169-1232) riding his horse shoots a fan off a pole on a swaying ship with a single shot from his bow and arrow. This collection of tales written between 1190 and 1221 is considered a pivotal milestone in the development of Japanese publishing and storytelling as they facilitated the parallel growth in both the oral and written traditions of narrative communication. Another example of a heroic literary fan appears in the tales of Yoshitsune Minamoto (1159-1189) an archetypal Japanese tragic hero and an elusive Robin Hood-like fugitive. In this legend, Yoshitsune a relative pipsqueak famously downs a warrior monk known as Benkei, a mountain of a man like Little John, with his fan, having put his sword aside. In a demonstration of agility and brains over brawn, that turns Benkei into a loyal companion.[92]

Nonetheless, experts believe that the first Japanese paper folding fan was probably created in the middle to late eighth century close to the start of Japan's Heian period (794-1185) when the Japanese capital had moved to what has now become Kyoto. This was a peaceful slow-moving period when Japanese literary arts and culture flourished, creating the first golden age of female creative writing in Japan, and perhaps arguably in the world. Style and its perfection dominated culture. *Kisha*, for instance, the shooting of arrows at a target while riding a horse was considered a performing art not a militaristic pursuit or simply training for battle. The appreciation of beauty in nature and in art has since those early days been a fundamental component, perhaps even the core cultural motif, within Japanese culture. It still affects how the nation sees, understands and tells tales about itself.

Richard Storry (1913-1982), a distinguished British historian of Japan, once observed that "the love of beauty is never utterly crowded out by utilitarian and commercial considerations. Its expression may be in miniature, like a single fresh flower in a Tokyo taxicab, but it is rarely, if ever, absent." In Japan one can thus expect the unexpected in miniature, small gardens at airports, for instance, that delight and provide islands of nature and aesthetic calm in unusual frenetic modern locations, or an isolated single rose displayed in a busy hotel lift. "Irrepressible vitality and an instinctive love of beauty form the basic constituents of the Japanese character and are among its most admirable traits," according to Storry.

The roots of much of these cultural sentiments can be traced back to the refined elegance of Heian style, a sophisticated age when most Japanese aristocrats lived extravagant lives. The Heian period was also a time in which fans clearly played their part. As fan fashions developed in Kyoto, they quickly became part of aristocratic dress codes, with wooden fans becoming part of winter collections, and paper fans the summer wardrobes of Japanese noblemen and women.

Miniature Portable Museums

Fans also became increasingly decorative, so much so that they have been described as miniature portable museums. These handheld galleries were offered as gifts and presented as tributes to foreign rulers and emperors, as well as Japanese warlords, which in itself generated demand and interest both in Japan and across Asia. Alongside Japanese screens and swords, fans became must-have Japanese products in countries like China, as well as in Japan, and further afield.

In fact, Japanese fans have played an important role at famous festivals such as the Gion Matsuri (Gion Festival) in Kyoto since it started in 869, and fans were even used as communication tools by Japan's warlords on the field of battle. Fans have and are still used as ritual offerings to the gods and tools to summon them. They have at times become substitutes for swords. They regularly appear, sometimes discreetly and at times overtly, at important milestones in the lives of most Japanese people when, for example, celebrating turning three, five, seven and 60 or getting married.

Fans, Commercial Art and Storytelling

Scholars cite fans as one of the first examples of commerce and art becoming entwined in Japan, thereby generating increased production and employment, while spawning creativity, new skills and techniques as well as international trade. As a result, fans became widely available in Japan allowing many, regardless of their status, to buy and collect commercial art that often-included palm-sized portable prose and poetry, probably for the very first time.

Perhaps unsurprisingly given their genesis, fans started depicting stripped-down scenes from famous literary works in digestible formats. Sometimes they had cryptically shortened poems encouraging admirers to guess the origins and if successful show-off their knowledge of literature when a fan was opened, and the prose revealed. Japan's rich world of storytelling has a long history of combing art, illustrations and narrative prose, and the development of paper folding fans gave the creative arts new impetus, creating new demand and delighting Japanese literati as well as the general public.

Designs developed to include, for instance, watermarks, tassels and carved ribs and fans were made for men and women of all ages and for all the seasons. By the time of Japan's Edo period (1603-1868) there was a fully-fledged highly creative fan-making boom and an innovative industry to support it. In fact, almost all of Japan's established artists jumped on the fan painting and making bandwagon. "The Edo period is probably the historical period that I find the most interesting," says Satoshi Saito, Chairman of Kirihara Shoten, a major Japanese schoolbook publisher. "It was peaceful and mostly relaxed, rich in culture, and industrial and economic development thrived in its own unique ways."

Fans, despite their perishable nature, became a precious creative platform that couldn't be ignored by struggling or even established artists. They were easy to monetise, became the mass-market canvas of choice creating a platform for artists to distribute and sell their creativity, a phenomenon that ended up as an inescapable trend that even many of France's famous impressionist painters would eventually feel compelled to follow years later.

The Pursuit of the Cool: Posing with Fans

Despite fans becoming fashion items and the must-have accessories of Japan's affluent mass-market, they still remain important ceremonial items at official events and as part of formal, if no longer everyday attire. In Japan, their use and roles have and continue to be widespread, creative and dramatic. Fans still symbolise prosperity, but much more besides. They feature at weddings, at tea ceremonies, in traditional games such as, *tousenkyo* in Japanese theatre, in *rakugo*, traditional Japanese comedy, as a prop used by comedians, as well as at important national events including, for instance, the official events that surrounded the new emperor's enthronement during which all female members of the imperial family clutched specially designed folding Japanese fans. This fondness for fans, their power to make a dramatic point or enhance gestures, and the benefit of posing with them, especially the handheld folding variety is not just limited to Japan and its elite.

Queen Elizabeth I (1533-1603) is perhaps one of the best-known early adopters of fan-power. She enjoyed clutching and collecting folding fans and had a collection of 27 by the end of her life. Fans arrived late in her reign as gifts from afar brought by individuals like Sir Francis Drake (1563-1596), the first Englishman to circumnavigate the world. Queen Elizabeth I employed these fans when power dressing for some of her many portraits that were designed to project her status and authority.

A portrait painted in 1592 by Marcus Gheeraerts the Younger (1561-1636), which hangs in the National Gallery in London, is one such example. In it Queen Elizabeth I can be seen standing on a globe of the world with her feet on Oxfordshire, while holding a Japanese-style folding fan in her right hand. This is, in fact, one of the oldest European paintings featuring a folding fan. The image is an important one because it clearly shows that folding fans and the perceived benefit and importance of posing with them had reached the royal courts of Europe.

The route that the Queen's fan would have actually taken to end up in this portrait is unclear. It may well have been through Portuguese sailors who first made contact with Japan in 1543 or through China and the Silk Road, the vast network of trade routes that linked Asia to Europe, or it may have been assembled from imported parts in England. British trade with Asia really only took off following the establishment of the East India Company in 1600, which helped spread trade and British influence three years before the Queen's death. The East India Company is known to have imported lots of fans mostly from China during this period.[93]

The Queen's 1592 folding fan portrait was painted before this and long before the permanent Dutch trading post in Nagasaki opened in 1641. This trading post known as Dejima (Exit Island) was actually an artificial island created especially to house foreigners at a safe and controlled distance from the Japanese mainland. It was, of course, shaped like a fan. Their presence allowed a small group of Japanese men known as *rangakusha*, scholars of Dutch learning, to gain exposure to and try to discover and study the scientific and medical knowledge that resided outside Japan in Europe. Traces of their influence remain. Some Japanese medical terminology, for example, still uses Dutch loanwords to describe medical products used for wound care.

Fan Fever: An International Boom

Nonetheless, Japan was isolated from much of the world between 1603-1868, during the nation's Edo period. Despite this, Japan's fan makers, artists and designers had a large domestic market with sophisticated local tastes. They flourished in creative isolation from most external influences honing their skills and developing new decorative styles.

However, nine years after Commodore Perry (1794-1858) and his famous black ships forced Japan's markets open again in 1853 with dramatic consequences, the nation's artists and their fans were more than ready for their international debut. Japanese products and art were initially shown at the International Exhibition in London in 1862, one of the very first major international public shows that included Japanese art. This was followed by a series of highly influential events in Paris, which had historically been a major centre for fan making, including the Exposition Universelle (World Fair).

People flocked to the shows and were fascinated by the exotic objects from Japan. At one exhibition in Paris a hundred different folding fans were exhibited in the Japanese pavilion showcasing fans from different periods and schools. By 1872, a French art critic had invented a new label helping define and brand the growing obsession with Japan and the Japanese arts: *Japonisme*.[94] This would later prompt Oscar Wilde (1854-1900) to caustically and famously write in response to what he saw as aesthetic fancy inspired by French intellectuals and artists: "The whole of Japan is a pure invention. There is no such country, there are no such people."[95]

Despite Wilde's pronouncements, *Japonisme* even reached the likes of Albert Einstein (1879-1955). A photograph on display at the Einstein Museum in the Swiss capital Bern shows a young Albert Einstein and his sister Maja (Maria) holding an oriental Japanese-style umbrella. At the height of *Japonisme* in the 1880-90s all things Japanese were popular including fans, kimonos and umbrellas. This boom also reportedly extended to and influenced a young artist based in Barcelona, now hugely popular in Japan, Joan Miro (1893-1983).

Art in Life: Enjoyed Anywhere by Anyone

The fan itself was certainly not a new device, but France at least was ready for a new wave of designs that, from their perspective, rethought what a handheld fan could be. France's connoisseurs, artists, intellectuals and posers had seen nothing like the fans from Japan before.

These events—like international trade shows of today where new products are revealed to gasps of excitement—turned the Japanese folding fan into a global sensation. Their price points helped. The fact that they were probably the lowest cost Japanese items one could attain also made them exceptionally attractive to Western eyes. These highly desirable multi-purpose handheld devices, these pocket-sized miniature galleries of *Japonisme* were both cutting-edge and cool, while being very affordable.

It seems hard to imagine today, but this had wide-reaching impact. The iconography from Japanese art and fans started being incorporated into European art and design. They would eventually famously influence the likes of Vincent van Gogh (1853-1890) and Henri Matisse (1869-1954). At the fourth Impressionist exhibition in Paris in 1879, Edgar Degas (1834-1917) reportedly wanted to include a room devoted entirely to fans painted by him, Camille Pissarro (1830-1903) and other impressionists. This didn't in fact happen, but 21 fans by him and Pissarro and others were exhibited.

One French art critic dubbed it *"une epidémie d'éventails"* (a fan epidemic). In a similar manner to Japan's Edo period artists, many of the French impressionists found that painted fans were one of the easiest forms of commercial art from which to earn a living.

From Fanology to Emoji: Are We now all Fans of Japan?

From today's perspective of instantaneous global product launches it may seem odd that it took so long for the Japanese folding fan to make the transition from the aristocracy to the affluent in Japan and subsequently to consumers around the world.

Perhaps the delayed international release is one of the factors behind the success. But whatever the reason, when they finally arrived in Europe, fans from Japan started selling in the millions. A new culture emerged that included its own special messaging, dubbed 'fanology', the emoji of the Victorian age. Curiously, the ubiquitous emoji of our digital age, unlike fanology, is another Japanese reinvention. They emerged on Japanese mobile phones in 1997, thanks this time to Shigetaka Kurita (b. 1972), before they arrived on phones and devices around the world. The word emoji, despite sounding similar to emoticon (emotional icon), is in fact Japanese, from *e* 'picture' and *moji* 'character, letter' often referred to as pictograms.

Victorian fan salesmen, including the French master fan maker Jean-Pierre Duvelleroy (1802-1889), produced fanology guides to show women how to send out messages at a discreet distance using their fans to indicate 'follow me', 'I love you' or 'I am engaged.'[96] Publishers also got in on the act and books about Japanese fans also started appearing in English such as Charlotte Salwet's 1894 book, *Fans of Japan*, which included colour images and illustrations. Interestingly, this book credits Japan as the nation that invented the folding fan with its 'bamboo frame'. Many books have followed, somewhat breezily, in its wake.

A New Industry and a New High for Fans

It is only when an industry and an ecosystem, to use modern business terminology, develop around a product that its real importance and status is firmly established. In this regard, folding fans are no exception. Kyoto already had a specialist periodic fan market in 1490. In Edo, long before European women were being shown how to use folding fans as communication devices, folding fan venders would employ handsome young men to sell fans door-to-door and specialist shops were opened. Remarkably, some shops first opened in Kyoto in the 17th century are still in business today. The majority of trends are fickle, but fans in Japan have shown persistence and true staying power.

Europe also had its own fan industry long before the arrival of *Japonisme* and direct Japanese imports. In 1670, just over a hundred years after Queen Elizabeth I posed for her famous Ditchley portrait, broadcasting her power and wealth, a group of fan-making businesses in London petitioned the nation's parliament to introduce regulations to protect the London market from outside competition. This led to the granting of a royal charter by Queen Anne (1665-1714) and the foundation of a specialist fan livery company in 1709, the Worshipful Company of Fan Makers. This probably marked the height of fan making in England and as in Japan's Edo period, English fans of the period also reflected life. Designs included everything from religious and classical subjects to cartoons and British satire and humour.

Foldable Cool: a Lasting Motif

Long before the Japanese government had a modern branding strategy and its *Cool Japan* programme for promoting Japan as a cultural superpower, Japanese folding fans were cooling and charming the world. Perhaps it is not surprising that Japan is now still at times referred to as the country or land of fans.[97] Many associate the words fan and Japan in the same breath. The words regularly appear in popular culture, journalism, lyrics and imagery, making the fan one of the many cultural motifs and emblems that seem to personify, for better or worse, the Land of the Rising Sun.

In the 1950s, for instance, the signature song of the Broadway musical *Can-Can*, which was a major hit in London and New York, contained the following lyric:

> 'Twill be so easy for you.
> If a lady in Iran can,
> If a shady African can,
> If a Jap with a slap of her fan can,
> Baby, you can can-can too.

The musical is about showgirls in Montmartre's dance-clubs in Paris in the 1890s, a period when *Japonisme* was already peaking.

Many headline and caption writers have and still make similar painful knee-jerk cultural associations, but perhaps a more appropriate and politically correct example of a lyric with this word association is the song "(I'll Never Be) Your Maggie May" by the American singer-songwriter Suzanne Vega:

> be like those ladies in Japan
> rather paint myself a face
> conjure up some grace
> or be the eyes behind a fan

This, as well as a Japanese fan being the favoured accessory of the likes of the designer Karl Lagerfeld (1933-2019), has no doubt helped put fans high up on the shopping lists of the millions of tourists who now visit Japan every year. This portable device is still an object of desire today. Like their creative predecessors from the Edo period, today's Japanese fan-sellers have developed new marketing techniques that are right for the times. YouTube videos now provide instructions on how to use a fan properly and English language manga-style instructional sheets are available for children.

A Visible Hand with a Folding Future?

Fashions, just like reading habits, change. Japan's literati have moved on to reading on new devices and most of these are no longer made in Japan. Short-form creative writing is, however, still extremely popular in all its myriad formats. Displaying and creating hands-on exciting imagery that can be easily shared with a click or swipe of the finger, as opposed to a flick of the wrist, is as important as ever.

Initially it was cell phones and now it is a generation of smartphones that have led the charge. Storytelling, in Japan at least, has again been part of this. Following the long tradition of writing on and for handheld devices, it is perhaps not surprising that the world's first cell phone novel, *keitai shosetsu*, *Ayu no monogatari* (*Deep Love*), published in 2003 was Japanese. Written by a 30-year-old Japanese man, it's a gritty tragic young-adult novel about a 17-year-old girl, drug addiction, AIDS, prostitution and the relentless search for funds required for heart surgery.

Following its success, authors and publishers jumped on this trend quickly and by 2007 half of the top ten best-selling fiction titles in Japan originated as *keitai shosetsu*. This publishing boom is, however, now over. Nevertheless, new portable devices are already in development designed to exploit the next generation of wireless technologies and engineers are experimenting with folding screens with some success.

A new generation of portable canvases, infinity chambers that echo with creativity, exploiting fan-like designs that blend and display exciting new content may be just around the corner. It may seem fantastic, but could this be a chance for Japan and its creative storytellers and designers to become international trendsetters once again? Now that would really generate an opportunity for the fans of Japan, putting *Japonisme* back on the page and between the covers of international creativity.

Part Three

Robots, Runners and Riders

In the Artificial Intelligence (AI) circuitry of the *Stand-in Android*, the functionality for becoming aware, either through self-discovery or by learning from others, that he or she was an android was disabled. For instance, even if Yutori was to say to Hayato now, "You are, in fact a *Stand-in Companion*," he would be incapable of understanding Yutori's words. For this reason, there was no way she could convey to him that there remained, in his life span, only a little more than eight years. *Stand-In Companion,* by Kazufumi Shiraishi.

Tales from the Robot Nation

Japan is renowned for embracing robot technology and automation in the workplace and has enjoyed a long love affair with dolls and robots of all kinds, whether factory-bound, practical, impractical, imagined, drawn or animated. Japan has always valued efficiency, craftsmanship, diligence and hard work whether it is conducted by man, machine or even a madcap science fiction writer creating uncomfortable and bizarre alternative realities.

Even though Japan lacked the technology and resources to shield its people from military defeat and occupation, Japan has come to rely on robots time after time to protect its economy from impending doom. This was the case, for instance, when the value of the yen rose dramatically after the 1985 Plaza Accord, and when other nations followed its modernisation programme and caught up. Robots provided assistance after Japan's massive economic bubble burst in the early nineties and when the tsunami hit in 2011 causing the nuclear disaster in Fukushima.

Since the end of the Second World War, robots have consistently been coming to the rescue of Japan in the nation's creative media, most notably in books, manga, anime and film. They are also expected to do so once again as Japan's population ages and shrinks, only in this event these new robots will take the form of carebots such as *Robobear,* an experimental nursing care robot.

As a nation, Japan apparently has no qualms about its readiness to embrace robot technology. Some OECD measures indicate that Japan has more industrial robots than most countries, and more Artificial Intelligence (AI) patents than any other.[98] According to the International Federation of Robotics, just under half of new industrial robots are supplied by Japanese firms.

The government has even written a strategy that articulates the steps it intends to take towards becoming a 'Robotics Superpower'.[99] Japan's nation building narrative is a distinctive one. Despite what we are often told, history would appear to confirm the adage that seemingly unconnected random events and how a nation deals with them can become part of a nation's story and thus its identity. It is not arguably all simply a matter of strategic national planning, even if government officials wilfully try to convince us that it is all down to their work and long-term planning.

Japan's quest to build a 'Robot Kingdom' can be traced back to the 17th century and its fascination with mechanical toys. The journey has been fraught at times, and involved considerable hardships, many twists and turns, some brutal dead ends and some very poor decision-making by the nation's leaders. But Japan's robot story mirrors the nation's history and spans industrial, literary and popular culture. Fascinatingly, whether planned or not, it involves some of Japan's most creative individuals: founders of global companies, brilliant authors, animators, toy designers, and engineers.

Following the Japanese Brick Road to the Robot City

Japan's 'official post-war narrative' framed around technology and science, has been consciously woven into Japan's cultural zeitgeist. But has the journey so far been as planned and run as smoothly as some would have us believe?

While many attribute the first steps on this journey to the 17th century mechanical Japanese toys known as *karakuri ningyo*, they were by no means the world's very first of their kind. Many examples of early automata existed in ancient Greece, China and other countries, as well as the legendary automata and robot created by Leonardo da Vinci (1452-1519). There is, nonetheless, something special about *karakuri ningyo* and their impact. Intricately designed, these beautifully clothed Japanese automata were unique. The literal meaning of their name is 'trick dolls'. Though this is a little misleading since they were never seen as a threat or a hoax as they were designed to entertain, not to deceive, and the name also implies a mechanical doll.

Very different in form from the typical wooden or metallic automata or robots we are all accustomed to seeing, *karakuri ningyo* were created to resemble *noh* actors, traditional Japanese entertainers, that still today perform an ancient form of musical drama. They wear masks, beautiful kimonos, and express themselves not through facial movements, but intricate and slightly exaggerated movements. *Karakuri ningyo* can be grouped broadly into three usage categories. Those designed for family home-entertainment, those found in puppet theatres and those used at public religious events and festivals. The home-entertainment variety climbed stairs, served tea, and did traditional ink brush calligraphy. They were the home-entertainment systems of their age. They are said to have initially been invented in Osaka, where Japan's first famous *bunraku* puppet theatres were first located. They were essentially an ingenious fusion of Western watch-movement technologies and Japanese doll-making techniques.

Their popularity was increased significantly by the publication of *Karakuri Books* in 1730 and 1796. The 1796 book, *Karakuri zui*, sometimes described as Japan's first mechanical engineering textbook, provided detailed diagrams and descriptions of how to make the automata. The influence of these books, like the automata themselves, has had long-term and significant impact on Japan, its industry, and even the wider world. These engineering manuals were published more than a century after books such as *Jinkoki* (*The Calculation Manual*), by Mitsuyoshi Yoshida (1598-1672), which was first published in 1627, publications that encouraged and fostered the development of Japanese mathematics, *wasan*. They helped turn Japan into a nation infatuated with problem and puzzle solving, while at the same time encouraging reading and publishing innovation.

To such an extent that during this period mathematical problems and their solutions, mostly extremely complex geometrical theorems, were left on tables as offerings at shrines in a practice known as *sangaku*.[100] Notoriety and rewards awaited congregants and visitors that brought proofs and solutions with their prayers. Perhaps they found a unique form of enlightenment by connecting them with the soul of mathematics.

One of the most fascinating *karakuri ningyo* has to be *the yumi-hiki doji*, an archer with a quiver and arrows that is programmed to fire at a target. It takes each arrow out of its quiver, looks at the target and takes aim before firing, but is programmed so that one of its four arrows misses, thereby projecting an aura of un-robot-like fallibility and a heightened sense of delight when the next arrow does hit the target. Incomplete tasks and acts have their own mesmerising appeal and importance. This particular popular *karakuri ningyo* model was created by the brilliant engineer Hisashige Tanaka (1799-1881) founder of a firm called Shibaura Seisakujyo (Shibaura Engineering Works), which subsequently became the global concern we know today as Toshiba.

Another Japanese multinational with *karakuri ningyo* roots is Toyota. Its founder Sakichi Toyoda (1867-1930) started out designing looms, the first of which, a wooden handloom, he patented in 1891. He and his son Kiichiro (1894-1952) improved and developed loom technology considerably allowing many Japanese firms to accelerate their implementation of automation, while switching from imported looms to superior local ones, made by Toyoda.

Unlike Britain, where resistance to industrialisation of textile manufacturing and the associated job losses in the 18th century gave rise to the Luddite movement, there seems to have been no similar high-profile resistance with its own moniker to technology-driven change in Japan. The Type G Automated Loom would become Japan's first power loom. Designed by Kiichiro, it incorporated mechanisms and design concepts directly from *karakuri ningyo*, drawing on the concepts outlined in the 18th century books.

The descendants of the power looms and steam engines that facilitated the Industrial Revolution surround us today. Japan's car factories are filled with the world's most successful robots: assemblers, painters, welders and testers. We can trace an extraordinary transformation linage from mechanical dolls to looms by a company that would ultimately become the world's largest manufacturer of cars, renowned not just for its extremely reliable vehicles, but the robotic arms and the automation equipment used to produce them.

The Turk and its Long-term International Repercussions

In 1770, the Hungarian Wolfgang von Kempelen (1734-1804) created the Turk, also known as the Mechanical Turk, a chess-playing automaton designed to look magical and very unfamiliar. It was in actual fact a deception. Tickets were sold to people who wanted to play against this seated, exotic life-size wooden man-like individual with a turban. It was designed to make opponents uncomfortable and to always win. The machine moved the chess pieces using a mechanical arm, making all kinds of machine-like sounds in the process. Despite this, a master chess player was in fact hidden within.

Many people played against the Turk or saw it in action including Benjamin Franklin (1706-1790) and Napoleon Bonaparte (1769-1821). Almost all lost. Its secret and winning formula, however, was kept hidden for almost a century. In the same way as *karakuri ningyo* has had long-term and unexpected influences, so too has the Turk. The English inventor of the power loom Edmund Cartwright (1743-1823), which he patented in 1785, 111 years before Toyoda's, became convinced having seen the Turk, that if a chess-playing machine could be developed so could a similar weaving machine.

Similarly, Charles Babbage (1791-1871), inventor of the mechanical computer (his Difference Engine), was also reportedly amazed and impressed by the Turk when it came to London when he was a small boy. The Turk has even left its mark on Amazon, one of the most innovative technology champions and automation-focused companies of our generation. In 2005, Amazon launched a new marketplace service, the Amazon Mechanical Turk, to crowdsource human help in an automated manner to assist with mostly technology projects.

During the Turk's almost one-hundred-year period of mass deception, new sciences and trends in automation began to find their way into both Western and Japanese literature of the time. Many feared the progress of science and technology. This concern didn't just mirror the Luddites' anger over job losses; it was a deep-rooted mistrust of technology-driven change itself.

In Europe, much was changing on several fronts. Following ground-breaking research by Luigi Galvarni (1737-1798), knowledge of bioelectricity, then known as galvanism, was spreading. Michael Faraday (1791-1867) was publishing research on electromagnetic induction. The slave trade was banned in the United Kingdom in 1807. The first commercially successful steam-powered locomotive was created between 1812 and 1813 by John Blenkinsop (1783-1831). In the literary world, Mary Shelley (1797-1851) published her novella *Frankenstein* in 1818. This was the period of revolutions, both industrial and political, thanks to the French Revolution (1789-1799).

By contrast, Japan at this time was still enjoying a relatively tranquil period, its Edo period (1603-1868), and had cut itself off from almost all Western influences. The Japanese lived in blissful ignorance of Luddites, steam engines and Victor Frankenstein as well as growing international angst over the seismic changes taking place in Western society. Though this is in fact when, one year after Shelley's tale was published, the first kaleidoscope is said to have arrived on Japanese shores. This was a period when *karakuri ningyo* flourished by providing entertainment for the masses at home, in theatres and at major religious festivals.

Despite this isolation, Japan was still able to advance. In 1804, for instance, Seishu Hanaoka (1760-1835) performed the world's first operation, a partial mastectomy, using a general anaesthetic. His methods never reached the West, nor the attention of writers like Mary Shelley. It would take another century before the details of this medical milestone became widely known outside Japan with the publication in 1966 of *Hanaoka seishu no tsuma* (*The Doctor's Wife*) by Sawako Ariyoshi (1931-1984). Ariyoshi was a pioneering Christian writer, and her book was based entirely on Hanaoka's life. The novel was later made into a film in 1967 and subsequently published in English in 1978. Despite this, an American dentist and surgeon at the Massachusetts General Hospital in Boston are often credited as the first to have achieved modern surgical aesthesia, using ether, in 1846.

Western literature has long been fascinated with technology. When it came to America, the likes of Edgar Allan Poe (1809-1849), who invented the device of the amiable detective sidekick that complements and distracts as well as narrates curious cases, were fascinated by the Turk. His personal physician even ended up buying it. In fact, Poe wrote two pieces linked to the Turk: *Maelzel's Chess Player: Exposing the Fraud* (1836), and *Von Kempelen and his Discovery* (1849). The first covers the period after its owner Von Kempelen died and the machine's new owner Malzel brought it to the United States in 1826. The second tells the tale of a German alchemist turning lead into gold.

Unsurprisingly, this unusual Turk also sparked the curiosity of David Brewster (1781-1868) a pioneer in the field of optics who invented a cluster of curiosities, including of course the kaleidoscope. His *Letters on Natural Magic; Addressed to Sir Walter Scott, Bart*, and "Letter XI" in particular 'Mechanical automata of the ancients', which contains 10 detailed illustrations, are also often cited as one of the critical sources behind the final debunking of the Turk's trickery. Brewster's letters were published in the early 1830s before Poe's pieces. These stories, just like Brewster's scope, of course, eventually found their way to Japan.

Poe himself had a major direct literary impact on Japan when his works started to appear in Japanese translation from around 1887, after the Edo period with its closed borders had ended. Poe's use of science and logic, alongside works by Sir Arthur Conan Doyle (1859-1930), to solve mysteries like the Turk, helped spawn a new approach to Japanese storytelling. Many important Japanese authors fell under their spell. Authors like Taro Hirai (1894-1965) who created his pen name Ranpo Edogawa as an homage to Poe, and Osamu Tezuka (1928-1989), the creator of Japan's best known fictional robot Tetsuwan Atomu (Astro Boy).

Everything would change during Japan's Meiji era (1868-1912) when Japan opened up to the West and entered a revolutionary-like period of intense rapid development and modernisation that spanned everything from sport, transport, books and fashion, to science and technology. It was very different from the Edo period when Japan was wrapped in an isolating blanket that protected it from international cultural and technological trends. Science fiction also arrived in Japan for the first time and traditional comforts, such as *karakuri ningyo* quickly fell out of fashion. Many were sadly discarded or simply forgotten in much the same way as old toys in the Hollywood animation *Toy Story*.

The Meiji transformation gave rise to a degree of social angst as new unfamiliar concepts and words found their way into Japanese vocabulary. Words like *shosetsu* meaning Western-style novels, and the word *shakai* meaning society, for example. One of Japan's most respected authors Soseki Natsume (1867-1916), who himself would subsequently become a milestone in the evolution of robotics in Japan, reportedly described the mood of the period eloquently: "Japan was running a race with Western history: only by reaching the Western nation's advanced stage of development could Japan regain cultural autonomy and control of its destiny."[101]

For some, these changes destroyed the familiar and rigid social etiquette and hierarchy of Japanese society, making expectations society had of them uncertain.

This extended to the realms of trust, romance and relationships, which provoked some distinctly bizarre and disturbing novels and short stories. Doll motifs and narratives built around Doll-Love themes, for instance, started appearing in the works of leading Japanese writers. Fictional asymmetrical love apparently reminded some of tradition, quiet contemplation, as well as innocence, and perhaps even the entertaining comfort of *karakuri ningyo*. Surprisingly, this all mostly took place before the word 'robot' had even seen the light of day, but it is trend that has continued.[102]

The New Label 'Robot' Triggers a Literary Response

The play *R.U.R. (Rossum's Universal Robots)* by Karel Čapek (1890-1938), written in 1920 and first performed in Prague in 1921, had a major impact in Japan in the twenties and thirties after its arrival in translation in 1924. This was on the cusp of a new period in Japanese history known as the Showa era (1926-1989), corresponding to the reign of Emperor Hirohito (1901-1989). The industrialisation was gaining pace and the relentless development of new technologies continued to generate creative angst, as well as broader concerns amongst the general population.

A recent huge natural disaster didn't help either. In 1923, a devastating earthquake that some saw as divine punishment for the new 'extravagant' and 'immoral' lifestyles and the jettisoning of traditions, wiped out much of Tokyo killing more than 100,000 people and requiring 200,000 buildings to be rebuilt. It was by all accounts the largest urban disaster of its time. It was widely believed that it would take Tokyo decades to be returned to its former state. But in actual fact, the city was rebuilt and modernised quickly, ushering in a new era. Nevertheless, it was an extraordinarily difficult and stressful period for many and formed the basis and setting for a number of Japanese works of fiction.

At this time, science fiction was also an emerging literary genre. It may not have been properly named or defined as one, but its popularity was certainly undeniable. This was given a significant boost on the world stage by the launch in America of the first science fiction magazine *Amazing Stories* in 1926. Its publisher, Hugo Gernsback (1884-1967) is generally credited with the first use of the term science fiction. Japanese magazines would follow in its footsteps and play a critical role in the genre's development. This time round, the nation was becoming even more exposed to the West and was actively participating on the world stage. At the 1928 Olympic Games, for instance (the second Japan participated in), Japan won its first gold medals. Having defeated Russia in the Russo-Japanese War (1904-1905), Japan was growing ever more confident, despite the war leaving Japan close to bankruptcy.

The play *R.U.R.* not only coined but also popularised the word 'robot', which came from the Czech word *robota*, meaning 'work' as in 'forced labour' or 'servitude' in Old Slavic. *R.U.R* triggered a flurry of robot stories in Japan sometimes described by scholars as "early Showa robot literature."[103] *Jinzo ningen (Artificial Human)*, written in 1928 by Hatsunosuke Hirabayashi (1892-1932) is often cited as a classic example of this genre. It is about a *moga* (modern girl), a married scientist, an artificial human and scientific fraud.

Stories about *jinzo ningen*, a catch-all term that can mean robot as well as artificial or man-made quasi-human, were generally published in magazines and were popular. At least one magazine devoted a special issue to these artificial creatures that often looked just like us but were synthetic or androids with mechanical insides. *Robboto to beddo no juryo (The Robot and the Weight of The Bed)*, by Sanjugo Naoki (1891-1934), who the Naoki Prize—one of Japan's most prestigious commercial fiction awards—is named after, is another important example from this period.

Naoki's story, written in 1931, is about a dying man's plan to leave a robot as a 'companion' for his wife after he has departed this world. It is set in the future when Japan has electrically controlled cars (not dissimilar to the electric and autonomous vehicles being developed today) designed and engineered to automatically avoid accidents. This story, however, is about a robot designed to ensure a wife remains faithful to her husband after his death in an ominous form of forced companionship.

Other stories from this period feature enhanced or modified humans as well as robots and dolls. Robots at this time were not considered by these Japanese authors as merely tools or slaves to serve humans; they were also seen and presented as potential threats to human and biological life.

The Four Temperaments: Do Robots Fit the Matrix?

Some researchers outside Japan have tried to deconstruct robot literature and have attempted to shed light on why and when they appear in our collective imaginations and the creative minds of authors. Such research hasn't relied on high-speed statistical analysis, ChatGPT and other AI-like pattern recognition algorithms. Instead, its authors have generally resorted to good old-fashioned methodologies: trips to the library, reading and research. Their conclusions are that there are apparently four main robot-types: tools (slaves), superiors (masters), companions (doers) and equals (enhancers).

According to the research, tools and superiors tend to appear during periods of massive technological change. Slave-type robots, tools, represent the fears of the average person, while the superior-master robots reflect the arrogance, hubris and the perceived superiority of the leaders during these periods of uncomfortable technological transition that can polarise society.

Robots that act as companions or are our equals, however, apparently tend to appear during periods of significant social change or unrest as opposed to change driven by new technology cycles. They are socialised robots that authors and readers find appealing when rules, roles and the long-established social dynamics of society, as well as demographics, change significantly as is the case today in Japan's new so-called Post-Max world of a shrinking population and economy.[104] Designed to function safely alongside people these robot hands complement our lives as 'doer-companions' or as 'equals with special abilities' and strengths. They are expected to be more trustworthy and reliable than most humans, during these periods of intense social change, and perhaps even more reliable in love.

How does this all square up when technological and social change happen at the same time, as in Japan's Meiji and Showa eras or perhaps even the period we currently seem to be facing into? If you are unfortunate enough to reach maturity in one of these traumatic periods in history, will you become enslaved or liberated by your artificial companion? Do character and personality matter for both us and the robots?

These four robot types seem oddly reminiscent of the Four Temperaments, the famous proto-psychological theory that goes back to the time of Hippocrates in ancient Greece. These four temperaments were a very early type of Myers-Briggs analysis (16-types) ever popular with Human Resources (HR) departments for sorting their company's talent. These personality types have been updated and adapted many times since the ancient Greeks used them by various impressive individuals including famously by the psychologist Alfred Adler (1870-1937). He employed taxonomies, like many other individuals striving to bring order to our complex world, creating the following four labels: avoiding, ruling, getting, and the socially useful to group and describe individuals. Perhaps human personalities and imagined robots are not so dissimilar after all.

The amazing success of a Japanese self-help book, *Kirawareru yuki* (*The Courage to be Disliked*) by the Japanese philosopher Ichiro Kishimi (b. 1959) and Fumitake Koga (b. 1973), which has sold in the millions, perhaps also helps corroborate these observations. Based on Adler's theories, the book shows readers how to free themselves from their innate temperaments that they were created with and find real happiness by breaking free of type. It struck a chord, becoming a publishing phenomenon in Japan, leading to its publication in translation in America, Taiwan and China. *Marie Claire* describes it as "almost spookily relevant in this age of digital one upmanship and increasing anxiety. A real game-changer." Books, such as a recent one by Hiroshi Ogura (b. 1965), about and based on Adler's theories continue to be published in Japanese.

This no doubt reflects the universal desire to live and not to just exist, a longing that some fictional robots also seem to share, even if they are yet to discover the attractions of this publishing genre, and the tools that many think they require to nudge themselves into new directions and mental states. *The Courage to be Disliked* is, however, just one example of a multitude of such self-help and self-improvement books published in Japan every year. Creative writing, as well as these types of self-help manuals, which encourage readers to lean in, embrace the change, live more harmoniously, or come to terms with themselves or the fact that someone has moved the cheese or natto, still, it would appear, have an important role to play in Japan and internationally.

That said, if you ask a contemporary Japanese author to share their thoughts about the relationships between robots, types, writing and Japan their initial reaction is often one seeking qualification, not of function or personality type, but of engineered form. Industrial, artificial human, mechanical, humanoid, synthetic, adult or child or cyborg: not all robots are created equally and semantics matter. AI instils foreboding, but robots with familiar names, from the future or the past, discreetly powered by AI and other technologies don't.

Socially Useful Robots, even Nuclear-powered Ones, Sell

Japan's most popular fictional and literary robots are socialised and generally socially useful. However, all four types have featured regularly in Japanese fiction. But the ones people seem to remember and talk about most are companions or equals that get things sorted for their human companions or social equals with special complementary talents and enhancing strengths, not the evil fear-inducing superior types.

Since the Second World War, these socially useful robots have probably left the broadest cultural imprint on modern Japan. The nation's singular most popular robot among those of a certain age is Tetsuwan Atomu (Mighty Atom), better known outside Japan by his English name, Astro Boy. He was created by Tezuka in 1951, as a companion for his fictional inventor, Dr. Tenma, to replace his son who was killed in a traffic accident on Route 66 with an autonomous vehicle (AV).

Tezuka, who was born in 1928, the year Hirabayashi's *Jinzo Ningen* (*Artificial Human*), was published, had a major cultural impact on Japan, one that is probably on par with the likes of Walt Disney in America. He was a very well-read medical student when he dreamt up *Astro Boy* and had already read *R.U.R.* and works by Japan's early fantasy and science fiction writers Edogawa and Juza Uno (1897-1949), the so-called father of science fiction in Japan. One of Edogawa's stories, *Panorama-to kidan (Strange Tale of Panorama Island)* published in 1926, about a fantastical utopia, apparently led to Tezuka's creation of *Robot Land* in the *Astro Boy* series.

The early 1950s was tough. Many Japanese children had been orphaned or killed and a new society was emerging. There was a widely held belief in Japan, (including, allegedly, that of the emperor himself), that Japan had lost the war due to overconfidence, an over-reliance on training and the samurai spirit and an insufficient understanding of science and technology. Arguably, most key outcomes are often actually the product of the compounding of chance rather than deep structural or cultural forces, alongside poor judgement. Nonetheless, the national goal became wealth without military power. Resulting in Japan becoming infinitely more benign in terms of its relationships with its neighbours and the world.

Since then, Japan as a nation has invested significantly less on defence than other countries relative to the size of its economy. In the United Kingdom in the early 1950s, for example, nine percent of national income was allocated to defence. Such spending has fallen significantly, dropping to below three percent in 1995 for the first time. NATO has a more recent standard for its members of two percent of GDP, that the United Kingdom now aspires to exceed, reaching three percent again by 2030, as it works through its other investment priorities. Japan in comparison, since the 1970s has spent around one percent of GDP on national defence and since 1945 has not been contaminated or distracted by international warmongering. However, Japan's defence spending is now expected to rise substantially.

As a result, all things technological were embraced and encouraged, eventually generating stunning material progress, which also developed into a new manufactured national narrative. Some might consider this as a pivot to techno-nationalism, perhaps. *Astro Boy* reflected this new impetus. He was, after all, a scientific creation, and not a magical one. Nor was he a character with superhuman strengths from outer space. He was the product of painstaking research, engineering and planning. He was a showcase for everything good about technology, a product that highlighted the importance of engineering.

Astro Boy was given an atomic-powered nuclear reactor as a heart, a symbolic precursor perhaps to Japan's adoption of nuclear power. Tezuka's book showed that atomic energy could be a force for good, as well as destruction, and could power Japan's technology-centred future. Some argue that as post-war Japan was forced to close down its industrial military complex and encouraged to focus its creative energies and skills, as well as storytelling, elsewhere, far away from warfare, that it was probably inevitable that battling robots would start popping up here and there in the realms of fiction. Individual publishing successes, as we all know, tend to create trends.

Japan's non-military, nuclear research programme started in the fifties and Japan's first commercial nuclear plant, Tokai-1, imported from the United Kingdom, began operating in Ibaraki Prefecture in July 1966. This was two years after Japan's neighbour China acquired atomic weapons. At this time, *Astro Boy* was still being published weekly. Eventually, the number of plants increased to around 50, supplying almost a third of Japan's power until the 2011 earthquake and tsunami, that killed some 18,000 people, caused the nuclear disaster in Fukushima. After which they were switched off and have only very slowly been reconnected to the national grid.

Steady relentless incremental change can take place in Japan without much reaction from the general population. It is only when the nation is hit by a disaster or shock of some kind that visible wide-scale comment or resistance seems to occur, such as the backlash against nuclear power since the Fukushima disaster. This can on occasion force a major change in direction.

Astro Boy was published weekly in comic book form until 1968 but has been remade again and again in anime and film format. Set in a future when robots and humans coexist, Astro Boy protects, helps, and saves Japan from evil human-hating robots. He is governed by more rules (ten) than the now famous and often cited Three Laws for Robotics published in the 1942 story "Runaround" by the American science fiction author, Isaac Asimov (1920-1992).[105] Astro Boy's rules are more restrictive. He can't go abroad or change his appearance without permission; robots have to call their maker father; they can never change their gender; they are forbidden to assemble robots out of discarded robot parts; they must not damage human homes or tools. Most importantly, they must serve mankind. The mass market success of *Astro Boy* generated awareness and a widespread comfortable familiarity of happy coexistence between humankind and humanoid robots.

Every decade or so in Japan a major new robot character arrives on the scene. After Astro Boy it was *Doraemon* in 1969, a blue robot cat from the future who lives with a young boy called Nobita and his family. He is Nobita's companion and helper sent by his great-great grandson to secure a better future for the family. *Doraemon* has now become a global phenomenon and is even broadcast in Hindi. Though he is the companion-type, it is debatable whether or not he is socially useful. The sentiment of wishing to have had better forbearers in 1960s Japan and elsewhere is of course very understandable.

Another example is a very different kind of robot from 1974, *Ganbare!! Robokon*. The term *kon* translates as 'guts', and the character is a spirited young robot, but one prone to error and mistakes. He attends a robot school where he is taught the necessary skills to participate in human society, hoping one day to be able to graduate into happy and successful co-existence.

The Frankenstein Complex

The publication 200 years ago *of Frankenstein; or The Modern Prometheus* by Shelley is a noteworthy moment in the world of literature. Shelley wrote "I bid my hideous progeny go forth and prosper" and prosper it has as one of the world's most fertile fictional narratives and is considered the first science fiction novel. Its first print run was only about 500 copies, but since then it has been reborn in more than 170 films, thousands of newspaper articles, and a cluster of new books published in 2018, on the two hundredth anniversary of its publication, explaining its ongoing significance. These include such titles as: *Frankenstein: How a Monster Became an Icon*, and *The Science and Enduring Allure of Mary Shelley's Creation*. There is even the term, created by Asimov, *The Frankenstein Complex*, which is sometimes used to mean irrational anti-scientific behaviour or fears about the dangers posed when a scientist or human inventor starts taking on the role of a god-like creator.

The scenario of man creating a robot, and the robot killing man, led Asimov to propose his Three Laws of Robotics as a potential safeguard. Journalists, and even King Charles III on occasion, have added the word Frankenstein to new technologies or products that they don't approve of: Frankenstein Food or FrankenFoods, for instance, for gene edited and modified crops. Some have even gone as far as suggesting that a new Hippocratic oath is required for the world's engineers and scientists. This all occurred before the world's media started obsessing about AI and a possible associated extinction event.

Japanese observers and engineers have noted, often proudly, that the nation's love affair with robots is open and easy simply because Japan does not have a Frankenstein Complex. For some it, alongside other reported so-called facts, has become a universal grammar to explain Japan's uniqueness. There is a multiplicity of reasons cited for this, both cultural and religious, but perhaps the most convincing argument is simply that Japan's development and angst cycles have been out of sync with the West. It was isolated from the negative side effects of the industrial revolution. This said, a further and much simpler explanation could be that Shelley's book was not published in Japanese until 1948 when Shinjinsha published

Masaki Yamamoto's (1899-1960) translation, *Kyojin no fukushu Furankenshutain* (*The Giant's Revenge: Frankenstein*). Other translations followed.

According to Yuri Aono, a well-respected Tokyo-based science journalist, there is hesitancy in Japan towards different types of new technologies, such as genetically modified (GM) crops, but this isn't labelled with the menacing name Frankenstein. Often concerns arise around new technologies that are associated with biological or bodily absorption such as foods and the HPV vaccine, for instance, to prevent cervical cancer.

Japan's Frankenstein exposure came late in film format and toys, many of which were made in Japan after the Second World War for export to the United States for Halloween. When Japan was already embracing all things technological, not in Japan's early pre-war Showa era when the robot literature of that time did present robots as potential threats to human and biological life.

Today, Japan is often depicted as an analogue nation in a rapidly digitising world, with many Japanese individuals still trying to resist all things digital. Even if in other aspects of their lives they have fully embraced a huge amount of technological change such as automatic gears in cars over manual gear sticks, for instance, and other much more recent impressive driver auto-assistance tools. There is still resistance, especially when it comes to the digital collection of personal data by the government and the provision of some associated digital services. This type of industrial information automation, robo-advisors, dynamically responsive forms, and nameless robo-customer service chatbots, isn't welcomed with much enthusiasm, even if there aren't Luddite-like, smartphone-smashing, aggressive responses. This lack of enthusiasm is the case in particular, when tax and regulation or customer complaints are potentially involved and of course journalists in Japan, just like in other nations, write articles about the risks of rampant uncontrollable monstrous AI.

Japan's industrial revolution when it came also had its own negative environmental and social side effects, but Victor Frankenstein or his monster weren't part of their narratives. Even so, Shelley's book and its nameless monster seem to take on a new meaning for each generation. The book is about ambition, hubris, and uncontrolled science, but also the importance of taking responsibility for what we create and the consequences of our actions such as parental rejection or other forms of creator misuse. Such duties and obligations known in Japanese as *giri* and *on* resonate within Japanese society, so it's hardly surprising that 'Frankenstein-type narratives' have not been totally ignored by Japanese authors, although they are not typically brushed with the same familiar labelling or Hollywood narrative frameworks.

Japan's Issues and Complexes: The Perfect Narrative?

Even if Japan doesn't technically have a Frankenstein Complex it has its own monsters and demons, generating folkloric totem. Ancient ones from folklore including shape-shifting animals, time-travelling spirits, and creatures that have inspired, and at times sought refuge in Japan's thriving creative industries, including the gaming and publishing industries. But Japan also has its new post-war monsters, *kaiju*, such as Godzilla, with very up-to-date narratives.

Few nations have managed to successfully and deliberately isolate themselves for hundreds of years from the rest of the world, as Japan did during its Edo period. If this period of self-isolation has benefited Japan or not is perhaps open to discussion, but what isn't is the effort and determination as well as the compliance that must have been required to achieve this. This may go some way in explaining why Japanese leaders have been reluctant to openly follow other countries and import cheap foreign labour. The idea of coexisting with homegrown robots programmed to do what's asked of them, following etiquette instructional manuals precisely, will certainly appeal to most Japanese households, and will no doubt seem to some a more attractive proposition than resorting to mass immigration, even if under the surface migration is actually stealthily on the increase in Japan too.

Japan's economic downturns and financial crises are often given names that imply external, unpredictable, and uncontrollable causes: The Nixon Shock (1971), The Oil Shock (1973) and more recently The Lehman Shock (2008) to name just a handful. Japan's most recent geopolitical complex, something the nation has not had to face for a very long time, concerns China's return to greatness and the shift from having the type of neighbour complex, when it felt superior to most of the nations surrounding it, to one bordering on inferiority. Japan's elite is very aware and puts considerable importance on the nation's place and rank in the world and takes great pains to constantly evaluate where Japan sits within the global hierarchy and rankings.

The implications of all this still remain very unclear. However, Japan's longest-serving premier Shinzo Abe (1954-2022), and one of the nation's most consequential since the post-war Allied occupation, called this threat an existential one comparable to when foreign gunboats started appearing on Japanese shores in the mid-19th century culminating with the arrival of the famous American black ships that forced Japanese markets open, and the nation to open up and rapidly change course.[106]

That said, as in most countries, the average Japanese person thinks and acts locally, ignoring global power games until they affect them directly. They have enough to contend with, struggling to coexist with nature's power in the form of earthquakes, storms and volcanoes. Terms such as asymmetric alliance theory and trilateral alliances, as well as the emerging Quad and its Quadrilateral Security Dialogue mean very little. In this respect, of course, technology provides essential assistance and comforting protection. That is its point.

Japan's media's constant use and creation of new terms, such as the Lolita Complex and Peter Pan Syndrome, to name just two, move the fear of technology down the increasingly long list of things Japan has to worry about. But imagined and real shocks, not to mention monsters, do still raise their ugly head, often from the sea, or from overseas.

Godzilla, the monster Japan is perhaps best known for, came from a cave at the bottom of the Pacific Ocean in 1954 and appeared on Japanese screens to wreak destruction on Japan. This prehistoric dinosaur, awoken and transformed by atomic fallout from American nuclear testing, represented a plethora of Japanese fears. The film may well have been cathartic for some, allowing them to see Japanese crisis management and planning in action acting as a cinematic type of scare-play. Nightmares and dangers in caricature like this usually bare limited resemblance to the threats worth worrying about in reality. Laughing at them and being entertained is perhaps cleansing.

The original film was launched just two years after the occupation of Japan ended in 1952. Japan was now able to take direct control of rebuilding its economy and infrastructure. It was also the year in which a Japanese tuna fishing boat was contaminated by nuclear fallout from American nuclear testing near the Marshall Islands. The 16th Godzilla film released in 1984 is one of the most popular. It returned to the original theme of nuclear weapons. According to Teruyoshi Nakano, who was responsible for the film's special effects, this was because "they were forgetting how painful it had been. Everyone in Japan knew how scary nuclear weapons were when the original film was made, but it wasn't like that in the 1980s…We decided to remind all those people out here who had forgotten."[107]

Literature, poetry and film do help us understand deep cultural attitudes and to some extent, the mood of a nation. However, societies including Japan, are much more complex and fragmented than the national media channels will have us believe. To simplify and exaggerate is an old journalistic technique that works brilliantly in our social media age. It also works very effectively when applied to Japan: making great headlines, amplifying differences and projecting Japan's image of oddness. Japan's so-called unique lack of robophobia is a case in point. Polluting the zeitgeist with refuse-like commentary so that whole is less reliable, something we all should be careful of being part of.

The Inflection Point: Authors Become Robots and Robots Become Authors

In 2016, a group of researchers at a Japanese university decided to build an android based on a dead celebrity. Not because they felt they might be infringing the intellectual property rights of a living celebrity, but simply because they wanted to commemorate an important anniversary. The celebrity in question was the author Natsume and the anniversary was the centenary of his death. To make him realistic they scanned the novelist's death mask using 3-D imaging and recorded the voice of his grandson to develop synthetic speech designed to resemble the author's voice as closely as possible.[108]

Natsume, one of Japan's most revered authors, well known for his novels *Wagahai wa neko de aru* (*I am a Cat*) and *Botchan* as well as spending a very unhappy two years in the United Kingdom, can now give lectures on Japanese literary history and recite extracts from his novels written over a hundred years ago. His importance is reflected in the fact that he has even been featured on 1,000-yen banknotes. Besides promoting sales of his books and perhaps generating royalties for his grandson, he will, according to his engineers, contribute to research into human robot co-existence. What Natsume, who suffered from awful culture shock while in London finding the experience fuzzy, awkward and rootless causing him to develop a type of social paranoia, would make of his new reanimated state and contemporary students at Nishogakusha University is anyone's guess.

Japanese researchers and engineers are also working on new technologies to cure a problem that has existed for generations: writer's block. A group of software engineers have created an AI powered algorithm designed to write (perhaps generate is a better word to use here) short stories thereby relieving authors who have run out of good ideas, generating new works on behalf of dead authors, or just creating AI authored content for us to enjoy. They aren't the only ones doing this. Google, OpenAI and others outside Japan, are also working on programs that generate poetry, passable prose and provide the much-needed technical writing support that many require. It has taken a long journey to reach this point, a journey that can be traced back to 17th century mechanical dolls but this inflection point has not yet become what some now refer to as the point of technological singularity, when artificial super-intelligence leads to runaway technological growth, changing our society beyond recognition. But change is coming.

Four of the world's six largest industrial robot makers are Japanese. With high levels of employment, an ageing and shrinking workforce, fracturing international supply chains, and automation, robot research will continue to increase in Japan, with limited resistance. Indeed, many welcome the march of the Japanese robots as the solution to Japan's economic and demographic problems. Automation, after all, is potentially cheaper and lower risk than outsourced or imported Chinese or Vietnamese labour. For this reason alone, the march of the Japanese robot writers will persist.

Is Japan's Robot Culture Unique?

Robots, like dolls, are everywhere in Japan. There are robot hotels and robot restaurants and robots regularly feature in all of Japan's creative industries. Robots, like Honda's ASIMO, named in honour of the author Asimov, though no longer being developed, are and have been used as a tools for international diplomacy. It is a narrative that is easy to report, and one many wish you to see or read making the whole subject something of a self-fulfilling prophecy. It's even a field of academic study and a topic of graduation theses and PhDs. There are plenty of learned books out there like *Robo Sapiens Japanicus* by Jennifer Robertson, and papers like *The Buddha in the Robot: A Robot Engineer's Thoughts on Science and Religion*, by Masahiro Mori (b. 1927).

Animism, the ancient religious belief that all objects have a spirit, is deep rooted in Japanese culture and is often cited as a unique reason for Japan's acceptance of robot co-existence. Perhaps, it is harder to project and amplify the dangers of a god-like superior scientist, over-stepping the mark, playing creator, in a society, which is not monotheistic. Biblical tales of the smashing of idols and the dangers of idol worship differ significantly to Japanese cultural customs and religious practices. A society where man-made tools that have served craftsmen and women well, are treated with the kind of respect or reverence one might have for an exceptionally good work colleague or a benevolent ancestor.

Nonetheless, in a country with, as alluded to earlier, an official government paper titled *Japan as a Robotics Superpower* and a Ministry of Foreign Affairs which publishes its Japan Brand Program in English on its website, the depth and uniqueness of Japan's love of robots is probably still a conjecture worth reflecting on in more detail. Some argue that fads come and go, and that Japan is much more ambivalent towards robots and technology than we are often led to believe. When technology fails to do what it is designed for—to protect and serve—people start to express what they really think and only then their opinions can be clearly observed and surveyed. It's also argued that foreigners, especially Americans, aren't actually so robophobic despite the success of Arnold Schwarzenegger's film, *The Terminator*, which casts robots in a villainous role, and the many other forms of sentient murderous robots adored by Hollywood.

Frederick L. Schodt, who translated *Astro Boy* into English, discusses in his book, *Inside The Robot Kingdom*, the attitudes of some of Japan's most eminent robotics engineers towards technology and robots. The book gives us a broad cultural analysis in which he argues that it is Japan's flexible 'anything-that-works-goes' attitude to religion and its practical approach to making small improvements, combined with a long history of embracing tools that will defend against external disasters and enemies, that has as much to do with Japan's readiness to embrace robotics than anything else.

The physicist Michio Kaku (b. 1947) explains this practical attitude well: "Before someone builds 'a super-bad' robot someone has to build 'a mildly-bad' robot and before that a 'not-so-bad' robot." Technology is advancing and impressive, but we are still at an early evolutionary stage of robot and AI design. 'Super-bad' robots still generally seem like a horizon event for most people in Japan.

Major Japanese cities have had to be rebuilt multiple times due to man-made and natural disasters that insurers in the West would call 'acts of God'. When Japan has had to respond to such events, it seems to just get on with it without much fuss. In between periods of massive change or intense rebuilding a natural momentum tends to return, and in these quiet spells people do many things as well as tinker, build and write. In fact, this now includes restoring *karakuri ningyo*, as interest in them has started to return, something that would not have been possible without the books published in the 1700s that document their creation.

Nonetheless, to really understand Japan's attitude to robots, technology and science, one would be well advised to steer clear of most engineers, bureaucrats and politicians or perhaps also geeks. Instead take a look at some of the country's brilliant contemporary literature and robot tales. It is a very good and enlightening place to start.

> From near-vegetarians to avid meat eaters, from wearers of swords to carriers of Walkmans, from rigid federalists to eager believers of democracy, from arrogant militarists to self-flagellating pacifists, probably no society in the world has undergone so many dramatic, radical changes in so short a time, with so little hesitation and introspection.

Schodt's words are true but there is, of course, introspection, not perhaps of the public type familiar in many nations. Japan tends to write itself out, not shout itself out. Japanese authors continue to imagine alternative worlds and document this change. They retell very personal stories and recount clever and original strategies for coping with modern life or even future lives. They continue to do what they have always done so well: educate, provoke and entertain. Robots and computers may have mastered statistical prediction, pattern recognition and more, but are still no good at providing most of the other types of deep insights we seem to crave be it satirical or uplifting. Introspection exists, if you know where to look, and it can often be found lurking in genre fiction in narratives designed for escape.

The Uncanny Valley

The Uncanny Valley isn't a work of fiction, science fiction or an article about how curious, weird and unknowable Japan is. Neither is it an odd tourist destination in Japan. It is, in fact, a 1970 scientific hypothesis about robots put forward by Mori, one of Japan's best-known engineers working in the field. The theory can be applied to imagined literary robots, Japanese *bunkaku* puppets, and even monsters like zombies and Frankenstein's creation.

Mori's theory, presented when he was a professor at Tokyo Institute of Technology (TIT), *Bukimi no tani*, is that there comes a point where a robot's human-like attributes become less appealing to humans. Human-like traits displayed by robots can be endearing and socially acceptable up to a point. But once a robot becomes uncannily human-like, it is likely to elicit feelings of revulsion in us. According to the theory, our responses fall within a predictable psychological spectrum that can be measured and represented graphically on a curve. The sudden repulsive response to some humanoid robots is The Uncanny Valley. The Uncanny Valley is where robot designers dread their robots will end up.

This is something that robot engineers may have only figured out and formalised in a scientific hypothesis in the 1970s, but Western authors have had an inkling that this may have been the case for at least two hundred years, since Shelley published *Frankenstein* in 1818. Arguably, in Japan the repulsive response has been known for longer.

The designers of the 17th century mechanical Japanese toys, *karakuri ningyo*, would have instinctively known this. They designed their devices to resemble *noh* actors who express themselves through intricate and subtle movements. Scientists have found in studies of the brain, using MRI brain scanning, that 'perceptual mismatch' between 'appearance and motion' in very human-like androids cause considerable unease. It is these behavioural mismatches between how things move and look that *noh* actors and *karakuri ningyo* designers have exploited so cleverly for hundreds of years. The uncanny valley has come to occupy an important place in the study of human-robot interactions. It is now even possible to plot on a chart, degrees of empathy and aversion to human-likeness, *shinwakan*, and compare the human emotional response to various types of robots ranging from industrial robots to their eerily lifelike counterparts.

In the US, Boston Dynamics has been developing military robots that are more animal-like than human, and these have been met with a nervous foreboding from the general public. Japan, of course, is better known for its cute social robots that are widely publicised, and its industrial robots, some of which are decorated with smiles and are not often on public display or operate in restricted areas in factories.

Famed for its 'robot-embrace' and love of all things technological, Japan certainly superficially doesn't appear to show the slightest hint of robophobia. Nevertheless, there isn't yet a theme park in Japan where you can hug and play with either uncanny or adorable robots depending on your preferences.

Today, Japan is one of the world's leading developers of advanced robotics. Japan's robot engineers may be world-class, but so too are Japan's robot-obsessed authors who, like the nation's industrial robots, have been beavering away mostly unseen for years. For generations, the best literary authors have been describing imagined creatures that sometimes mirror us or at times are slightly physically or emotionally out of kilter. This often depends on the emotional responses their narratives are designed to elicit from their readers.

A contemporary and revered author who has used robots as a plot device and rarely writes about anything that would normally be classified as science fiction is Kazufumi Shiraishi (b.1958), who followed in his father's footsteps and won the Naoki Prize in 2009. Shiraishi's *Stand-in Companion* is a touching story about finding meaning and balance in a society in which advanced technology and major demographic problems limiting reproductive rights are very evident. Naoki would no doubt have understood some of the sentiments expressed in Shiraishi's tale even if the companion in his robot narrative from the 1930s was designed for control not comfort.

Another notable contemporary example is *One Love Chigusa* by Soji Shimada (b. 1948), the so-called Japanese master of the post-modern whodunnit, who is a household name in Japan. Shimada's novella, also an unusual type of narrative for him, is a love story and a homage to Tezuka, set in a future Beijing with love and empathy portrayed as bug-like unnecessary social side effects. The emotional needs and empathy sought out by a young man, looking for companionship and love, struggling to find his place in the high-pressure technology engulfed Chinese capital.

Japan's robot tales are many, brilliantly varied, and penned by a broad array of authors. In fact, it's no exaggeration to say that many of Japan's best-known authors have at some time written short stories or books about robots. A common narrative theme that seems to appear in many of them, but not all, is one that features highly unusual 'companion-robots'. These stories, as discussed earlier, tend to say more about the state of society and human relationships at the time of writing than Japanese attitudes towards technology and automata.

It is not a genre that's simply confined to the writers of science fiction, manga and anime. Even though there are many excellent examples of these, such as the extremely influential 1989 cyberpunk manga, *Kokaku kidotai* (*The Ghost in the Shell*) by Masamune Shiro (b. 1961), that has subsequently morphed into an international media franchise. Delve into this world and one can discover everything from cyberpunks, post-humans, cyborgs and blue robot cats to nuclear-powered robots, aquatic humans, and hybrid sex and housekeeping robots. An incredible literary 'theme park' featuring extraordinary robots exists. The price of a book is always going to be much more affordable than a ticket to one of Japan's many theme parks, or a meal at a trendy Tokyo robot restaurant, or even a flight to Japan.

Post-war Robot Literature Reflects a Rapidly Changing Japan

Even though Japan is an excellent example of how economic growth can transform a nation, actually building harmonious societies out of material abundance is never smooth or a linear act. Following defeat in the Second World War, Japan went through a period of introspection, figuring out its place in the world and what it meant to be a modern democratic nation. It did this during its occupation by Allied Forces, and then throughout the Cold War years. As the blinkeredness and brutality of the Second World War, with its staggering number of deaths, gave way to the Cold War and then globalism, so too did Japan's economy start to reflect global trends and challenges. All of which provided a rich narrative backdrop for Japan's finest writers of science fiction and robot literature to deliver some much-needed escapist introspection and emotional solace.

Kobo Abe (1924-1993) was one such writer. Dubbed 'The Kafka of Japan', his best-known work of science fiction, *Daiyon kanhyoki* (*Inter Ice Age 4*), published at the height of the Cold War in 1959, a vanguard year on many fronts in Japan, is arguably one of the best ever written by a Japanese author. It tells the story of a submerged world in the near future in which the polar ice caps have melted, leading to the creation (through genetic engineering) of an 'aquatic human' capable of breathing underwater. In terms of its scale and sheer imagination, its impact on the science fiction genre in Japan was significant. Nevertheless, Abe is best known for his social commentary novel, *Suna no onna* (*The Woman in the Dunes*), a jarringly dry novel about the futility and repetitiveness of modern Japanese existence.

Abe was himself no stranger to the world of science and science fiction. In the 1950s he had studied medicine at the University of Tokyo before becoming a writer and writing a series of enlightening stories about robots, mostly dealing with the theme of alienation and marginalisation within Japanese society. Somewhat of a renaissance man, he also has a few inventions and even a patent to his name, including a prizewinning device to change tyres. He was also active in the field of linguistics research. He is a fascinating individual, born in Tokyo and brought up in Manchuria with family records that place his and his family heritage in Hokkaido. He is still a hugely influential author. Contemporary Japanese storytellers such as the manga artist Mari Yamazaki (b. 1967) known for her works *Terumae romae* (*Thermae Rome*) and *Orinpia kyukurosu* (*Olympia Kyklos*) and the film director and screenwriter Yuka Eda (b. 1994) admire both his use of language and perspective and cite him as a continuing powerful creative influence. They are not alone.

Kenichiro Mogi (b. 1962), a Tokyo based neuroscientist and broadcaster, describes Abe as a "genius" with a different audience, writing at a completely different level to those drawn to robot tales such as *Astro Boy*, which are so often attributed to Japan's enduring love of robots. What you need to ask yourself, he says, is whether, today, popular tales are and have been sufficient for a general audience to make them comfortably familiar with humanoid robots, even if much grimmer tales that they may not be aware of have been penned by the likes of Abe and others.

The war and Allied occupation cast a shadow over post-war Japan. So-called progress came at a social cost, as the benefits of the centralised planning and reforms took time to filter through to the men and women on the street. It continued to be a very difficult period creating a tremendous sense of dehumanisation for many. Abe's robot narrative, *R62 go no hatsumei* (*The Invention of R62*), written in 1953, reflects this national mood. It tells the tale of an engineer, which would resonate with British Luddites, who loses his job after new technologies from an American firm are introduced at his workplace. Desperate about his predicament, he decides to kill himself. But before doing so, he is persuaded to enter into a financial arrangement with a university researcher who is trying to develop robots capable of replacing workers and making Japanese industry more efficient through automation. As a last act he agrees to have his brain replaced with a controllable artificial one by the researcher. The procedure is successful, but the consequences are unexpected and painful, especially for the engineer's former employer.

Abe's other robot stories from the period including *Eijyu undo* (*Perpetual Motion*), have similar themes echoing the painful times. Abe's heroes generally inhabit modern cities, but their actual locations are cleverly obscured with the masterful details of reality leaving readers guessing, projecting their preferential perspectives on where they are set.

By the 1960s, Japan's so-called economic miracle was starting to increase the country's prosperity markedly. This was the decade in which the economy started to grow at 10 percent annually and Japan overtook West Germany as the world's second largest economy. A consumer society was emerging, and the national narrative was changing from one of suffering and enduring. Inevitably, new robot narratives were coming to the fore. One particularly interesting example was *Bokko-chan*, written in 1963 by Shinichi Hoshi (1926-1997), one of Japan's best-known science fiction authors, who has an important literary award named after him. *Bokko-chan* was published the year before the first Tokyo Olympics, when Ian Fleming's (1908-1964) novel *You Only Live Twice* brings James Bond to Japan.

Bokko-chan is about a glamorous young female bar hostess, a type of Bond girl, with limited dialogue. Like all Bond girls, she too has an interesting sounding name: Bokko-chan. What nobody knows, of course, is that she is in fact a robot designed by the bar's owner. Bokko-chan helps increase the bar's takings with her important functional abilities. Firstly, she does this by making simple conversation and providing basic replies without expressing anything remotely like an opinion, often just repeating what she hears. Secondly, she utilises her ability to drink copious amounts of alcohol, especially when offered to her by visitors that frequent the bar, where Bokko-chan sits at a dimly lit counter, drinks that can be recycled. Inevitably, one of the bar's customers falls in love with this woman of few words, which has terrible consequences not just for him, but for the others drinking at the bar. Unrequited love and the mixing of drinks make for a dangerous cocktail of consequences.

During the 1960s, Abe was very active. Aside from writing books that were social commentaries of the times, he also had a theatre troupe, which performed internationally including in New York. He wrote plays and wrote for television and radio, often with avant-garde themes. He also didn't forget how useful robots could be as a narrative device. In the sixties he wrote a script for a television programme entitled *Anata ga mo hitori* (*One More Like You*).

One More Like You reflects the contrast of the previous decade when he wrote *The Invention of R62* and *Perpetual Motion*. Austerity was now over, and consumerism was gaining momentum. Set 50 years in the future, a wealthy woman decides to order a robot that is an identical copy of herself to conduct all the chores she doesn't want to do. She eventually discovers too late in the day that, in real life, you can't have your cake and eat it, especially when it comes to technology.

Robot Companions: New Modern Relationships

By 1965, almost half of Japan's urban population was between the ages of 15 and 34 and the number of men exceeded that of women in most major cities. Much was changing and it wasn't all sex, drugs and rock and roll. The 1960s was a decade of political and social revolutions across large swathes of the globe. It was also a decade of major protests and social unrest, including the civil rights movement in the United States and student protests in many countries, including Japan.

Japan was a rapidly Westernising nation, and many similar issues were coming to the surface in Japan. City-based youth with new values and attitudes wanted to express themselves and make themselves heard by the establishment. Against this backdrop, Japan's robot literature wasn't entirely confined to the world of male authors. There were stories written by women too, though fewer in number. One example is the 1961 story by Yumiko Kurahashi (1935-2005) *Gosei bijo* (*Artificial Beauty*). Kurahashi was a controversial author and like Abe had an avant-garde bent, who often challenged gender and relationship norms. *Artificial Beauty* is set in the distant future when robots are sophisticated, genetically engineered, synthetic beings. The protagonist, Michiko, decides with her husband to buy a top-of-the-range beautiful robot-housemaid at a department store, as it is the trendy thing to do. They name her Eriko. Initially, Michiko is delighted with her new accessory. She makes sure Eriko has lovely clothes and knows how to do her make-up perfectly. Alarmingly, this is something people are now doing in Japan with their Super Dollfie (SD) dolls.

Inevitably and sadly Michiko's husband and Eriko start spending more time together; he even starts using her as his secretary. This makes Michiko incredibly jealous. She hires a private investigator to find out what is going on, and then decides to kill Eriko only to discover that Eriko is not actually a robot at all, but a human. Conversely, her husband is not just emotionally robotic at times, but actually a robot, one of the privileged artificial men that secretly control society, a fact that is finally proven after Eriko's death when he overcharges himself and self-destructs. The story no doubt reflected how repressed and angry many Japanese women may have felt at the time and the underlying gender inequality issues that were coming to the surface.

In the 1970s, the women's liberation movement started to make its presence felt in several countries. Britain's first national women's liberation demonstration, for example, took place in March 1971 in London. Women carried placards demanding equal pay, free contraceptives and abortions on demand, and held up such items of oppression as aprons, stockings and shopping bags. Japan had its own movement, *uman ribu*, which made many similar demands alongside local ones. Japanese women, however, got their movement going a year before British women, and held their first demonstration in October 1970.

Many of these Japanese women demonstrating were reportedly furious over the way the Japanese student protest movement between 1967 and 1969, which had caused riots and deaths, had treated female students. Not only had female students been denied an equal role, but some women had been forced into having abortions following 'experimenting' with 'free love' with radical male students.

Women's Lib, the Pill and Unexpected Robotic Consequences

Like American and British women, Japanese women also campaigned for abortion rights and access to the contraceptive pill but it wasn't until 1966, six years after its approval in the United States, that a high-dose pill was approved in Japan. Even then, it was restricted to those with medical conditions and Japanese women were reliant in most instances on male doctors for prescriptions. In contrast, birth control was made legal in the United States for all, irrespective of marital status, in 1972, and a low-dose contraceptive pill became available in 1980.

Not all Japanese men were comfortable with *uman ribu*. What might the long-term repercussions be for men, and how might their lives change? Some men who harboured such concerns would label women who were part of the movement as 'unattractive' and 'hysterical'. This was the perfect background for the brilliant madcap surrealist and famed science fiction author, Yasutaka Tsutsui (b. 1934), who has an uncanny prescience.

The timing of some of his stories is also interesting as their publication came hard on the heels of an important international conference on women held in Mexico City in 1975. The first United Nations World Conference on Women, which coincided with the International Women's Year, was designed to remind the international community that discrimination against women continued to be a persistent problem in much of the world. Tsutsui's stories were written to remind readers of something altogether different.

The first story, *Narushishizumu (Narcissism)*, starts by listing Asimov's famous Three Laws of Robotics: a robot may not harm humanity, or, by inaction, allow humanity to come to harm; a robot must obey orders given to it by human beings except where such orders would conflict with the First Law; a robot must protect its own existence as long as such protection does not conflict with the First or Second Law.

Narcissism is the tale of a man who buys a second-hand hybrid robot that combines the functionality of a sex robot with a housekeeper robot. Tsutsui creates a world in which male demand for female androids is so great that men who crave real women are few and far between, making such men highly desirable. Nevertheless, our protagonist ultimately succumbs to market trends when the second-hand android market begins to take off. Interestingly, in this future world there are no robots designed for women's needs or desires, and all the regulators and manufacturers are men. For servicing men, however, almost every type of robot you could possibly imagine has been developed.

This might not seem like a very credible future scenario, particularly when you take into account the growth of the women's liberation movement at the time. But then again, one can consider the ridiculously long approval process for the low-dose contraceptive pill in Japan, which took decades to be approved in 1999, despite its approval in the United Sates much earlier. In fact, Japan was one of the very last countries within the United Nations to grant approval. Viagra, with a different target customer base, on the other hand, took just six months.

In the story, our protagonist eventually buys his android who looks 'utterly incredible' and non-robot like. However, she is not what the new owner expected or had hoped for, since she wants to be treated as a humanoid, not as an order-obeying robot, and wants to be called Mari. In short, she is too lifelike, and too much like a real woman. She even wants to be told that she is loved and is beautiful.

The owner phones the salesman the next day from his office to complain that he has been sold a "narcissistic robot." The reader is left wondering if Mari is in fact a "jilted woman" pretending to be an android, and looking for a stable, long-term relationship. But unlike Kurahashi's story from the sixties, this tale finally reveals that Mari is not human. The reader comes to understand the relevance of Asimov's Three Laws of Robotics, and why Mari has been looking for a new 'owner'.

The second 1970s Tsutsui story, *Sadizumu (Sadism)*, takes a different tack altogether. The tale revolves around a female television celebrity, and a regular in the gossip columns who visits a manufacturer of sex robots to make a very angry complaint. Her lawyer has 'discovered' that the factory is making and selling an advanced android that looks just like her, thereby infringing her intellectual property (IP) rights. In this bizarre story that explores themes of vanity and identity, the manager finally decides on taking a high-risk strategy and introduces the actress to R5-13M 1095, the model in question, in order to let the consequences dictate the solution.

As they wait for R5-13M 1095 to arrive, a discussion ensues. The celebrity wants to know why demand for androids is increasing and is furious when the manager suggests that it might be because women have become too domineering and demanding. He also suggests that men have become sick of having to deal with the stress created by both their emotional and material needs.

Interestingly, Japanese fertility rates have fallen, as Tsutsui seemed to predict in the 1970s. According to surveys, one third of Japanese men between the ages of 16 and 19 have lost interest in physical relationships, with many saying they now prefer virtual girlfriends, as you don't need to marry them. A company called Gatebox has even launched a virtual wife service.

In the story our celebrity eventually gets to meet her doppelganger who is identical in appearance to the actress but our protagonist is shocked by the android's aggressive and hysterical attitude, and complete lack of class. She isn't very self-aware. Instead, she becomes convinced that she now has to licence her IP to the company to allow them to make a model that is closer to her 'real' self, reflecting what would today be called her truth. Inevitably, the story ends up with a twisted and tragic case of mistaken identity. It utilises the type of logic that philosophers would call, and Tsutsui is a master of, *reductio ad absurdum*, to make its point and is also a reminder that we are sometimes lucky that all great minds don't think alike.

Did Japan's Post-war Robot Literature Predict the Nation's Future?

Following trends and attitudes to their extremes and pushing narratives firmly to their logical conclusions, no matter how uncomfortable or awkward, or the type of robotic shape adopted, is something that the best Japanese authors seem to do brilliantly and very entertainingly. Luckily, they are still writing new narratives and aren't yet using their imaginations and computers to print three-dimensional robots, as opposed to tales about them. There can, however, be little doubt that science fiction can influence future events by encouraging them to happen more quickly or by ensuring that certain scenarios stay within the pages of books. Naturally, only the best stories that resonate with the times or strike a national chord create a legacy.

Given that the Japanese government had its written strategy published in 2015 that articulates the steps the nation will take to achieve its ultimate goal—Japan as a Robotics Superpower—it is interesting to look back at robot stories published in the post-war period. One might expect 50 years or more to be long enough for some narrative fiction to have become a reality, especially as authors often set their stories 50 years in the future. Conversely, reading today's robot stories may give us an inkling into what life might be like living in a robot superpower 50 years from now.

Today Japan does actually boast robot restaurants and cafes, as predicted. While there are no fully functioning blue robot cats currently on the market, you can buy a robot dog. The AIBO has been developed by Sony and is now in its second generation. While human brains haven't yet been replaced with robot brains to create industrial robots, most Japanese factories and warehouses are now heavily automated and use robots, and electronic devices are starting to be embedded into human brains. These include robots like Toyota's Kirobo, which looks somewhat like Japan's favourite fictional robot, Astro Boy, and the Japanese space drone Int-ball (JEM Internal Ball Camera), have been sent into space.

Hayabusa-1 a robotic Japanese autonomous spacecraft has even visited a near-Earth asteroid and brought back samples. This droid, sometimes depicted with a square-like golden face, captured the nation's imagination with its amazing journey. It was given the honorific *kun*, a diminutive term of endearment often used for boys and sometimes girls when growing up differentiating them from, *san*, (Mr, Mrs or Ms) and *chan*, generally but not exclusively used for young girls. Using *kun* in this way seemingly gives it a personality. On its return *Hayabusa-kun*, having sent his samples ahead in a special capsule, faced certain destruction on re-entry. This led, according to the journalist Aono, to primary schoolchildren, who had been following the extensive media coverage of *Hayabusa-kun*'s seven-year voyage, calling out for the droid not to be forced to die, becoming a victim of humankind's quest for new scientific knowledge.

After burning up on re-entry, a cluster of Japanese feature films and an anime were made about this small spacecraft's epic quest to land on an asteroid called Itokawa, take off again, and bring back the first asteroid dust samples to planet Earth. *Hayabusa-2*, a next generation space droid, was launched in 2014, designed to bring back a larger sample size of rock from a different asteroid. The way Hayabusa's narrative was framed, as a small tragic hero on a journey against the odds, probably reflects more Japan's love of these sorts of tales, a genre of tales of tragic heroic underdogs known as *Hoganbiiki*, than something deep and meaningful about technology and its adoption itself. To become a hero, a villain is required and in this case like many *Hoganbiiki* tales the villain is society and its thirst for progress and knowledge.

In fact, as we have seen, many of the world's largest industrial robot makers are Japanese. Lifelike androids and sex dolls are now more realistic than ever before. In terms of everyday, practical use, robots have been designed to vacuum, cut the grass and do the laundry, to varying degrees of success. Companion robots are also becoming increasingly popular for accompanying and entertaining both the young and the elderly. Our newspapers are strewn with headlines about new forms of automated mobility and machine learning. Is this eerily prescient or just good storytelling?

Robots provide authors with a brilliantly rich vein of inventive literary avenues to explore, ranging from the comic and absurd to the downright menacing and tragic. They can be used to question many of the fundamental issues in our lives: our attitudes to gender, beauty, our bodies, our parents, as well as the boundaries of society itself, be it in Japan or elsewhere. They can provoke and satirically help reimagine the future. Robot literature at its very best, no matter its provenance, can even help us understand ourselves better whether the tales are penned by an author who resides in a nation that loves robots, fears them or is ambivalent, or even one generated by an AI. Now that really is uncanny.

Literary Racers

Some nations have running in their blood. Japan is known for its discipline, long hours and endurance, as well as its respect for hard work. Long-distance running and marathons, and the discipline they engender, are therefore perfectly at home in Japan. Before jogging and marathons became trendy in the West, and long before Phil Knight famously visited Japan in 1962, which led to him founding the firm that went on to become Nike, Japanese runners had been enthusiastically pounding the streets in long-distance races, since at least 1917.[109] Running in all its myriad manifestations is a pursuit that Japanese authors have not ignored, some have in fact embraced and co-opted it as part of their writing routines.

Japan has internationally famous runners and famous people that run marathons, and others who just prefer to write, watch or read about running from a comfortable distance. It has its very own rather wacky races. Over the last decade or so, the number of people taking part and officially completing marathons in Japan has more than doubled, and more than 50 marathons take place every year. These include famous and important ones like the Tokyo Marathon, but also lesser-known ones including the Kaga Night Marathon, the Nagoya Women's Marathon, where all finishers get a Tiffany necklace, as well as Sweet Marathons where hundreds of different kinds of bite-size sweets are served at 'aid-stations' along the route.

Not all of Japan's races are the standard modern marathon length. Initially, the length of a marathon varied, as does the use of the Japanese word *marason*. It only became fixed and standardised at 26.2 miles at the London Olympics in 1908, when the race started from Windsor Castle. As most know, the word marathon derives from the name of the location of a famous battle between the Greeks and Persians from where the messenger-runner Pheidippides (530-490 BCE) ran to Athens to inform officials of the news that the Greeks had been victorious. Nonetheless, the word is now part of international vocabularies, and has many different meanings and usages.

The Tokyo Marathon is indicative of why some have called Japan the world's 'most running-obsessed country'.[110] It is one of the world's six major marathons and the only one of this group to be held in Asia. Besides being tough to run, it's one of the hardest races to participate in as more than 300,000 people apply for the right to stand on the starting line in its annual ballot for tickets. Only about 10 percent or 30,000, win the right to do so each year. For marathon enthusiasts who dream of completing 'the six-majors' (Boston, London, Berlin, Chicago, New York and Tokyo), just getting a ticket to run in Tokyo feels like winning.

Perhaps Japan's best-known person that runs is the author Haruki Murakami (b. 1949), who *The New Yorker* dubbed 'The Running Novelist', after his book, *Hashiru kotoni tsuite katarutokini bokuno katarukoto* (*What I Talk about When I Talk about Running*), was published in English in 2008.[111] However, long-distance running is not confined to Japanese men of a certain age. It is popular amongst women. People of all ages run, even 80-year-olds. Japan's most famous marathon runner (b. 1987), is known as the 'Citizen Runner' as he is an amateur with a full-time job as a local bureaucrat for Saitama Prefecture. In 2018, he made it into the *Guinness Book of World Records* for running 76 marathons with finish times of under 2 hours 20 minutes, becoming the world's most consistent high-speed marathon man.

You only need to take a walk along the banks of Sumida River in central Tokyo on a Sunday afternoon or stroll out in the direction of the five-kilometre path next to the moat snaking around the Imperial Palace on a Tokyo lunch time weekday to have this national obsession confirmed. This obsession is widespread and is not limited to a few high-flying authors like Murakami or frontrunners working in a given genre. Many working in the Japanese publishing industry run, including authors and editors of all ages.

Flying-Feet & Relays: Winds that Run through Japanese Fiction

Long-distance running is an activity that has long been part of Japanese culture. *Hikyaku*, flying-feet, runners, who acted as message carriers, played a critical role, akin to the American pony express, in Japan for centuries. They acted as an ancient courier service on some of the main routes connecting important Japanese cities in the days long before telephones, telegrams, faxes, email and messaging. Horses were also used, but on some routes runners were faster. *Hikyaku* would carry official letters and documents, but there were also independent networks of messengers open for hire.

During Japan's Edo period (1603-1868) runners would run to stations and checkpoints where messages were passed on to the next runner in a type of relay race. This was before the arrival of new technologies in Japan's subsequent Meiji era (1868-1912), when Japan pivoted and sprung open to the world, modernising, after more than two hundred years of self-imposed confinement, changing many professions and how some messages, for example, were delivered. The arrival of Japan's first telecommunication line in 1869, and both contributed massively to Japan's development and transformation and put an end to the need for these types of long-distance fleet-footed runners. In the decades to come, and by around 1913, the proportion of Japanese people living in cities had more than doubled, making Japan no longer a rural economy based mostly around agriculture requiring nationwide running messengers. However, Japan's fascination with running and runners and sending each other messages including in a manner that allows individuals to show off their talent for both calligraphy and composition didn't end.

In 1917, the *Yomiuri Shimbun*, a major Japanese newspaper, sponsored a race along a 508 km route over a period of three days, with runners handing over a *tasuki* (sash cloth) rather than a baton at each station to the next runner. Ever since, these *ekiden* races have been hugely popular in Japan and have become culturally important signposts that for many signals a new year with fresh challenges and objectives is underway. The best known of them, which started in 1920, is the Hakone Ekiden, a two-day race with 20 teams of 10 male university students who run from Tokyo to Hakone, close to the foot of Mt. Fuji where a historically important checkpoint on the route to Tokyo was located, and back. The 135-mile race is broadcast nationally on 2 and 3 January each year and watched by about a third of the population.

Unsurprisingly, with this level of interest in the race there have been numerous books and short stories written about runners, running, and the *ekiden*. Shion Miura (b. 1976) is a good example of one of Japan's contemporary writers who has taken up the *ekiden* challenge. She is probably best known outside Japan for her novel *Fune wo amu* (*The Great Passage*), which won the commercially important Japan Booksellers' Award, *Honya Taisho*, in 2012. *The Great Passage* is about a group of passionate and somewhat obsessive publishers working on the marathon task of completing a new dictionary. Her 2006 novel, *Kazega tsuyoku fuiteiru* (*The Wind Blows Hard*), however, is about a similarly dedicated and determined university student in his final year, trying to fulfil his dream of taking part in the Hakone Ekiden.

First, he needs to find 10 people to join his team. Then they need to train and qualify. It is a classic tale of a group of misfits coming together as a team, growing mentally and physically, and somehow making it from the fringes to the all-important races where they run alongside some of the most famous university teams in Japan. The book has two parts: the race to the starting line and the Hakone Ekiden itself. In the same way as *Tokyo Olympiad*, the acclaimed documentary film made for the 1964 Tokyo Olympics by Kon Ichikawa (1915-2008), depicts the 1964 Olympic marathon in an almost poetic manner mentioning the runners' professions and other details alongside images of them competing, Shion uses each stage of the actual race to describe not just the race and the terrain, but explore each runner's background and personal issues, turning the race and it challenges into a metaphor for contemporary Japanese existence.

The huge media exposure means that teams, coaches and individual runners can capture the nation's imagination turning them into media celebrities. There are many gripping narratives and stories around this annual event: some turn people into legends, and others create content for novels. Susumu Hara (b. 1967) is one such lionised individual. He took over as the coach for the Aoyama Gakuin University team in 2003. Six years later, in 2009, his team qualified for the first time in 33 years for the *Ekiden* and then they went on to win for an unprecedented record four consecutive years 2015, 2016, 2017 and 2018, and then again in 2020 and 2022.

Atsuko Asano (b. 1954) is a prolific author of young adult sports related narratives, often about young men and their relationships, such as the one between the pitcher and catcher in her hugely successful prizewinning book series *Batteri (Battery)*. Running is, of course, a compelling sports narrative that she, like a meaningful number of other Japanese authors, find impossible to ignore. As a graduate of Aoyama Gakuin University, with two sons and a daughter, her interest in this particular race and more broadly running is probably unsurprising. She published the first of three books about runners in 2010, *Ranna (The Runner)*, the year after Aoyama qualified for the Hakone Ekiden. She went on to publish *Supaikusu (Spikes)*, in 2013 and *Ren (Lane)*, in 2016. Asano is also a notable member of the Japanese Communist Party (JCP), which has hundreds of thousands of members in Japan, a newspaper, *Akahata Shimbun*, as well as almost two dozen members sitting in the national parliament. She has said she wants to believe in the "brilliance of teenagers" and as a middle-aged woman wants to depict in her narratives adolescent boys that are "upright" and "independent" and "strong-willed" who break society's perceived barriers and strictures in a way she couldn't when she was a teenager.

Another illustrative and important Japanese novel about running, written by another of one of Japan's many talented contemporary female writers is *Isshun no kaze ni nare (Become the Wind in a Moment)*, by Takako Sato (b. 1962). This tale is about sprinters not marathon runners. That said, just like long-distance runners, Japan now has many top-class sprinters that win international medals in, for example, the 4 x 100 metre relay. Sato's book won the Japan Booksellers' Award in 2006, an award chosen not by a judging panel made up of established authors but staff working in bookshops across Japan, highlighting the theme's perennial popularity. There are also books with running in their titles such as *Yama o hashiru onna (Woman Running in the Mountains)* by Yuko Tsushima (1947-2016), which aren't actually about running, but the lonely marathon-like challenge for some of existence in Japan, especially for those alienated and living unconventional lives on the edges of society. In this book's case, a single mother in the 1970s.

These are just a few examples of books and authors that use running as an analogue for life or are about running races. The cultural impact of the *ekiden* and running as a sport and how their associated nifty narratives intertwine with the lives of many writers and readers in Japan, should not be underestimated.

Marathon Monks and Marathon Running Authors

You only need to see images of Japan's famous 'marathon monks' who have been trying since at least 1885 to reach enlightenment by completing a thousand 'marathons' in a thousand days to understand the narrative appeal of long-distance running in Japan. Only some 46 monks have achieved this extraordinary feat of extreme spiritual and physical endurance.

The stories of these *Running Buddhas,* who have worshiped at Mount Hiei, northeast of Kyoto, for 1,300 years, have captivated the world, not just Japan. In 2013, when Yusai Sakai (1926-2013), a monk who had completed the *Sennichi Kaihogyo* twice—only the third monk ever to do so—died, international newspapers such as the London-based *Telegraph* ran obituaries on him.[112] *Sennichi Kaihogyo* is a seven-year journey that these ascetic monks believe allows one to reach enlightenment in this life without having to wait to be reborn. The practice, a type of punishing moving meditation, involves circulating the mountains around their temple in a meditative state, making offerings and reciting prayers at temples on route. There is also a 100-day practice as well as the mammoth 1,000-day practice.

The 'Running Novelist', Murakami, likes to compare writing to running a marathon. He has run at least one a year, health and pandemic permitting, for the last 30 years and has run the New York Marathon on at least three occasions. For him, running and writing seem interdependent. "Marathon running is not a sport for everyone, just as being a novelist isn't a job for everyone," Murakami says. "Nobody ever recommended or even suggested that I be a novelist—in fact, some tried to stop me. I simply had the idea to be one, and that's what I did. People become runners because they're meant to."[113]

For many authors, not just Murakami, writing and running require a similar discipline and attitude. Mitsuyo Kakuta (b. 1967) is another example of a well-known Japanese author who runs marathons. She started running marathons when she turned 40 and now runs two or three a year. Takuji Ichikawa (b. 1962) is another example of a Japanese author who runs and sometimes writes about running. He ran the 800-metres competitively when he was a university student and is on record as saying that running is an important part of his creative process. He thinks the experience of running and writing is comparable.

As you get into your stride when a race commences your legs, he says, seem to take over, almost moving automatically and you enter a new different mental space. When you write your fingers pound the keyboard without much thought required, moving on their own, sometimes you need to remind yourself to breath and catch your breath as the storyline's route unwinds in front of you and your fingers go where they go. Once you are in the concentrated flow of writing, you fall into a state dominated by the rhythms of your narrative, he explains.

Not all writers, however, are sporty, and some prefer other completely different types of sports to running, such as the crime writer Keigo Higashino (b. 1958), whose books keep on hitting the bullseye in terms of sales and bestseller lists. His preferred recreational sport is archery, not of the traditional Japanese martial sort known as *kyudo*, but Western-style archery seen around the world at Olympic Games since 1900, a sport that he got involved with at university.

Olympic Narratives

When Japan hosted the Olympic Games for the first time in 1964 in Tokyo, it made sure that it was the first Olympics to broadcast the entire marathon live. The Tokyo Olympics created tremendous excitement and many new narratives about Japan, as well as all sorts of stories and myths in the country. The world came to Japan for the very first time. The flagship event, the men's marathon, was certainly a key highlight that many were waiting for.

Kokichi Tsuburaya (1940-1968) was the local marathon favourite. He ran a strong race entering the stadium in second position, in the very last athletics event of the Olympics, with the nation's eyes fixed on him and a potential silver medal in the offing. Sadly, he was overtaken on the final lap by Britain's Basil Heatley (1933-2019), who somehow managed to find enough residual energy for a final sprint, and Tsuburaya finished third, something he never got over. Instead of being a proud winner of a bronze medal he became the man who lost his silver medal on the last lap with all of Japan watching. He killed himself less than four years later. His body was found with his bronze medal in his hand along with two suicide notes.

Shizo Kanakuri (1891-1983), who founded the Hakone Ekiden, holds one of the oddest Olympic marathon records. Kanakuri, a founding figure in Japanese marathon history, competed in the 1912 Stockholm Olympics. Unexpected weather made it a particularly tough marathon, with many runners forced to drop out. Kanakuri, who had arrived in Stockholm after an arduous trip including the Trans-Siberian Railway, lost consciousness during the race. A local family was kind enough to take care of him and he quietly returned to Japan unnoticed without informing the officials. He was thus technically classified as a 'lost' runner. In 1967, a television crew invited him back suggesting he might like to consider finishing the marathon, which he did with an official time of 54 years, 8 months, 6 days, 5 hours, 32 minutes and 20.3 seconds. "It was a long trip," he remarked. "Along the way, I got married, had six children and 10 grandchildren."

The first women's marathon at an Olympics took place in 1984, at the Los Angeles Olympics. Since then, Japanese women have participated and performed well, often better than the men. In 2000, at the Sydney Olympics Naoko Takahashi (b. 1972) set a new Olympic record for the marathon and become the first Japanese woman to win, not just a gold for the marathon, but for an Olympic track and field event. Four years later at the birthplace of the Olympics, in Greece in 2004, Mizuki Noguchi (b. 1978) won the marathon, bringing home gold for Japan yet again. All of which has helped amplify interested in and a growing love for this sport across Japan.

The current marathon running craze, may eventually die down. For many the COVID pandemic has changed priorities at least for the short term. Some have had the experience of running masked marathons, not a yet to be invented flamboyant fancy dress quirky Japanese-style marathon, but races designed to protected runners from viral infection. Unexpected future scenarios are possible, and new popular sports may emerge. Japan's first Olympic novel, *Orinpusu no kajitsu* (*The Fruits of Olympus*) by Hidemitsu Tanaka (1913-1949), published in 1940, for example, was about participants in a different endurance sport, rowing. This is something that the surrealist and science fiction author Yasutaka Tsutsui (b. 1934) explored in his 1971 short story, "Hashiru otoko" ("Running Man"). Tsutsui, who has a strange foresight for envisaging things that subsequently actually happen, and like others has been unable to dismiss Japan's obsession with marathon running as a useful plot device, subtly pokes fun at the Olympics and much else in this story, showing why some call him the cynical bard of modern Japan.

In this short story, set in the future, restaurants are automated and run by robots, marriages are arranged by computer-matching that analyses both physical and personality compatibility, and nobody is interested in long-distance running or the Olympics at all. Most have completely forgotten about them. Some don't even know what the word Olympics means, and nobody or almost nobody runs.

Olympics still take place in this imagined world, but most people are lazy and uninterested in sports or competition, and many die young. Nobody really knows why someone would bother running a marathon. Nevertheless, one man decides to join the Olympic marathon, a race with only two other competitors, which takes him most of his life to complete.

He drops out halfway after meeting a woman and decides to start a family. But after his wife Yoko ends up in a nursing home, he decides to complete the race. Once he does, he actually wins, but he isn't treated to applause or a glorious medal ceremony, as nobody knows or cares. Unlike the case with the real Olympic runner Kanakuri who finally completed his marathon four years before Tsutsui wrote this short story, there were no television crews either, just a couple of officials working for the Olympic Organizing Committee Final Accounts Office waiting at the finish line.

The Running Shoe Becomes the Narrative

Phil Knight, who was a runner in his University of Oregon days, famously visited Japan in 1962, having just graduated from the Stanford Graduate School of Business. As an accountant he was desperately keen to become an entrepreneur, and on visiting Japan, he found precisely what he was looking for, an amazingly well-made running shoe manufactured in Kobe and sold using the Tiger brand by a firm called Onitsuka.

Knight persuaded the owner to give him the sales and distribution rights for North America. When Knight returned from his graduation trip, he set up Blue Ribbon Sports, which subsequently became Nike. The rest, as they say, is history, which has been documented in his book *Shoe Dog*.

Today, Nike is the global market leader for sportswear and shoes. This was achieved with help from some people Knight headhunted from Onitsuka. When it comes to sports shoes and sportswear, today Nike has the largest market share in both the United States and Japan, and Knight is now one of the richest men in America. Onitsuka still makes excellent shoes under the ASICS name, but in terms of sales, sits in joint third place behind Nike and Adidas with another Japanese brand, Mizuno. All of which reads a little like the story of Japan's decline during what economists have called Japan's lost decades since her economic bubble burst at the beginning of the nineties. Shoes, as plot motifs, alongside running, have featured in many memorable narratives by Japanese authors, spanning short stories by the nation's Nobel Prize winners to full-length novels bridging different genre, and the urge to mirror the Nike narrative within Japanese fiction has for at least one Japanese author been irresistible.

Jun Ikeido (b. 1963), a former banker turned management consultant then author, is known for business-themed novels, some of which depict Japanese businesses fighting back against impossible odds. His bestselling novel *Shitamachi rokketto* (*Downtown Rocket*), for example, tells the story of a small maker of engines in Tokyo who develops a highly sought-after patent forcing the firm to decide if they should licence the patent to a major firm or build their own rocket. The book won Ikeido the prestigious Naoki Prize in 2011.

Again, following the narrative theme of the economic slump of the 1990s and Japan's slow return to form, Ikeido followed up his bestselling *Downtown Rocket* with his novel *Rikuo* (*Land King*) in 2016. This is an entertaining work of corporate fiction about a small Japanese company named Kohaze-ya that manufactures traditional Japanese socks known as *tabi*, taking on the American based global sporting goods market leader, Atlantis. It is the story of a two-year tenacious marathon-like struggle to develop the best running shoe from scratch. Koichi Miyazawa, the fourth generation President of Kohaze-ya, stakes the firm's future on this new shoe. The story bears similarities to *Kinky Boots*, the 2005 British film and Broadway show, about a fourth-generation man trying to save his family-run shoe factory from closure by making high-heel boots for drag queens.

In *Land King*, Miyazawa recruits people to help him, including a 'shoemeister' from Atlantis, who is tired of the American giants' relentless focus on profits, and a marathon runner, Hiroto Mogi, who was previously sponsored by Atlantis. Atlantis is obstructive, but with the help of ultra-light new material and a patented processing technology the Japanese underdog fights back. Agility, engineering and brains beat American brawn and scale in a highly readable tale that fortunately only presents a veneer of high-minded business analysis.

Another interesting, but very different, example of a story featuring running shoes, about a former runner turned running shoe salesman is Murakami's short story "Kino" from his collection *Onna no inai otokotachi* (*Men Without Women*). This story, which in typical Murakami fashion features the unifying symbols of a jazz bar, a cat and two snakes, can be read in English translation in *The New Yorker*.[114]

Meditations on Movement

Many entertaining, eloquent and intelligent things have been written or said about marathons, running and reading. The American author George Saunders (b. 1958) describes reading as "a form of prayer, a guided meditation that briefly makes us believe we're someone else, disrupting the delusion that we're permanent and at the centre of the universe."

"Reading is an exercise," says the British author and Children's Laureate Malorie Blackman (b. 1962), "that involves walking in someone else's shoes for a while." Even if that happens to be the shoes of a shoemeister. A good book, unlike long-distance running, is never about endurance, even if it has a departure and an arrival or is about a race.

Emil Zatopek (1922-2000), known as the 'Czech Locomotive', who was the first man to win the triple, at the Helsinki Olympics in 1952—the 5,000 metres, 10,000 metres and the marathon, which he won in a time of 2 hours 23 minutes 4 seconds—famously said "if you want to run, run a mile. If you want to experience a different life, run a marathon." There are other options. If you don't like running, pick up a book by one of Japan's current cohort of award-winning authors and you will be assured to experience a different life, one that may still leave you breathless.

Narratives from Off and On the Tracks

During most weekdays more people pass through Shinjuku station, Tokyo's busiest, than live in Paris. The figures are staggering. Of the 50 busiest stations in the world, 26 are located in Tokyo, and 45 in Japan. But it isn't just the *Guinness Book of World Records* that loves writing about Japan's stations and rail network. Japanese trains and stations feature in many of the 70,000 new books published in Japan every year, as well as in thousands of newspaper articles and online posts.

Most journeys in Japan involve reading and writing. More than 80 percent of people commute to work by train and commuting time, according to a survey by the NHK Culture Research Institute, is now on average 1 hour 19 minutes per day, and rising. Stations and trains, the backbone of modern Japan, are also brilliant narrative devices.

Shinjuku station, the world's busiest used by 3.5 million people every day, is actually a city-like hub collective of five different interconnected stations, with 51 platforms and 12 lines running through it. This Tokyo station has almost as many exits as London Underground (Europe's largest) has stations. Shinjuku is not just linked physically through subterranean walkways to famous bookshops like Kinokuniya, but like other important Tokyo stations (including Tokyo, Ueno and Ikebukuro) it is linked to books written by some of Japan's most famous and interesting authors.

All Aboard the Japanese Literary Express

Nine years after London Underground started operating the world's first underground train service, the Tokyo-Yokohama line, Japan's first passenger rail line, opened for service in 1872. Reportedly, some of the first passengers took off their shoes and left them on the platform before boarding the trains.[115] The cultural changes that trains brought about were enormous. Some modern nations including Japan are said to have been built on railways, leading to them being depicted as metallic rivers of modernity, transport and transformation.

Japan's first railway was brought to Japan through the efforts of a Scottish merchant and entrepreneur, Thomas B. Glover (1836-1911), who arranged for track to be laid in Nagasaki in 1865. Japan's first steam train dubbed the Iron Duke was demonstrated using this track. Despite it never actually being used for commercial or passenger services Glover's Nagasaki track is considered a critical milestone in Japan's modernisation, and its location is marked with a memorial stone.

The one-fourth scale Norris Works steam locomotive that Commodore Perry (1794-1858) brought to Japan as a gift during his second visit to the country in 1854, following his initial dramatic arrival with his black ships, that ran on a mile-circumference track and the awe it inspired, as well as one demonstrated by a Russian envoy a year earlier, are also often noted by railway historians and enthusiasts as interesting landmarks.[116] In addition to showing their transportational forces, and what could be achieved through the power of steam, these mechanical creatures also spawned some memorable images of kimono-wearing men astride small carriages riding the model steam railway with their so-called "lilliputian locomotive, car, and tender."[117]

The arrival of train technology and the new Tokyo-Yokohama line took place during the period known as Japan's Meiji era (1868-1912) when the country was in flux following the resignation of the shogun. Japan was finally unlocking itself to the world after hundreds of years of inaccessibility and searching for a new and suitable gage to drive its society forwards. Trains, however, may have had a bigger impact on Japanese society than anything else at this time. Trains and urbanisation played a critical part in Japan's rapid modernisation programme. It was the age of cities and trains. So much so that the nation has been firmly committed to rail transport ever since.

Aside from new influences from foreign literature arriving in translation, Japanese authors responded to the arrival of this new mode of travel and the new professions and jobs that it threw up in its wake. Penning tales spanning rites of passage narratives, stories for children and adult romances, as well as, of course, murder mysteries.

These days Japan has surpassed Uncle Sam in terms of the type of railway diplomacy it was the recipient of in the past, with Japan inspired, funded and engineered tracks and rolling stock now found in places like New Delhi, Buenos Aires, the United Kingdom and Indonesia. Azuma, a lauded modern Japanese train built by Hitachi, for instance, now speeds from London to Edinburgh in Scotland and back, a feat that would astound Glover, the Nagasaki-based Scottish merchant. Trains and travel continue to feature in some of Japan best storytelling that is itself now travelling further afield, crossing historical frontiers and superficial cultural barriers.

Poetic Pilgrimage

Even so, the subject of travel had already established itself as a popular literary genre long before the arrival of the railways. *Tokaidochu hizakurige (Shank's Mare)*, for instance, a timeless comic novel written by Ikku Jippensha (1765-1831), follows two amiable scoundrels on a madcap road trip adventure along the Tokaido, the great highway leading from Edo (present-day Tokyo) to Kyoto. Matsuo Basho's (1644-1694) *Oku no hosomichi (Narrow Road to the Interior)*, a travel diary published in 1702, covering a five-month 2,500-kilometre trek through Honshu, Japan's main island is considered a classic.

The Narrow Road to the Interior is a poetic narrative that is said to reflect the soul of Japan itself, highlighting the importance of and opportunity for finding truth and clarity through nature, as well as cleverly highlighting the risks, dangers and joy of travel. It, and other such works and travel journals, have induced a fascination with the presence of the natural world, blended with tales of Japanese travel.

For many, however, Basho is more immediately associated with a poem about a different type of motion all together, a frog breaking the silence of meditation with a leap into an old pond, that is considered Japan's most famous poem. For them it makes Basho Japan's best and most consequential poet. Rendering his short poem with an elegance and beauty that does it the justice that reflects its importance in any language, is a challenge that many talented translators simply can't resist, which has allowed his simple poem to travel in a multitude of linguistic forms internationally.

Naturally, rail transport made travel much more accessible and commonplace and created a host of new locations for authors to write about or use for chance mood-breaking life-changing encounters. These books, as well as the quality and extent of Japan's rail network, have helped imprint stations and trains on the Japanese national psyche.

Popular children's books across the globe often feature trains, stations and travel by train. While the English have their *Railway Children* by E. Nesbit (1858-1924), Japan has *Gingatetsudo no yoru (Night On the Milky Way Train)* by Kenji Miyazawa (1896-1933). This is probably one of Japan's favourite children's books and was written by a man who also wrote a very popular and well-known poem, "Ame ni mo makezu" ("Strong in the Rain"). It has a similar iconic resonance as Rudyard Kipling's (1865-1936) poem "If", a traditional favourite of many English teachers in Britain. This gives Miyazawa, despite his rather short life, a very special place within the canon of Japanese literature and the hearts of many.

Miyazawa's deft ability to combine spiritual and religious sensibilities with responsiveness to nature and displacement still draws many to his works. Both the book and the poem have worked their way into Japan's cultural zeitgeist. *Night On the Milky Way Train* is a much-loved classic, studied and read by children at schools across Japan. The book has been adapted for anime and the stage. Miyazawa wrote the first draft of his book after the death of his little sister Toshi in 1922, the year before the Kanto earthquake that killed more than 100,000 people. Bereavement was in the air. *Night On the Milky Way Train*, which Miyazaki spent seven years writing, was published after his death, and deals with such universal themes as the challenges of growing up, friendship and loss.

It is a magical story about a young boy, Giovanni, with a special green ticket that allows him to travel on a train through the heavens, getting on and off at various fantastic locations with his only friend Campanella. Giovanni meets other young children on his adventure who, sadly, like Campanella, are *en route* to the next world. Giovanni, however, is in a privileged position with his special green ticket, which allows him to return home with newly found purpose and a new attitude for living a fulfilling and happy life.

Night On the Milky Way Train is a story that has captivated countless readers. And many have translated it including Roger Pulvers, whose serialisation in 1983 in *The Mainichi Daily News* was one of the very first in English. This book in particular has delighted each generation growing up and continues to provide essential comfort to anyone when dealing with personal tragedy. It has also contributed to Japan's national obsession with trains, stations, and the romance of train travel itself.

Urbanisation and Mobilisation

Trains proved to be the great game-changer in Japan, creating far-reaching 'networks of modernity' that affected people from different classes, regions and professions. The Japanese world was shrunk by distance-destroying technology. Many cities, especially Tokyo, changed, physically, culturally and socially following the arrival of the trains and subsequently trams.[118] People moved to Tokyo with great expectations for their future. By the same token, it became harder for local elites to remain local and elite. It was also game changing in a very different way for Tokyo's tens of thousands of rickshaw drivers and the nation's *hikyaku*, flying-feet long-distance runners who acted as message carriers.

Technological transformations can lead to knotty cultural ones with fascinating literary consequences. Literacy rates were rising, fresh narratives were penned and a new generation of authors and readers who lived modern urban lives emerged. One such author was Soseki Natsume (1867-1916) whose works appeared in print in the early 1900s. Many of his books include descriptions of long-distance train journeys and urban stations, as well as odd but interesting encounters with people from different walks of life.

Natsume's novel *Botchan*, published in 1906, beautifully illustrates the impact that trains and increased mobility had on Japanese society. In this story that's still popular to this day, a Tokyo-raised and spoilt young man named Botchan arrives in Matsuyama in Shikoku, a fishing village in the smallest of Japan's four main islands, as a teacher. Like many inexperienced teachers arriving from afar, with their own views and values of how things should be, he clashes with both staff and students. He gives the locals slightly ridiculous but entertaining nicknames like Red Shirt, Squash, Madonna and Porcupine, and tries to defiantly fight the local system. While his antics and endeavours leave their mark, he only stays a couple of months before returning to Tokyo to get on with his life, having given the reader a very entertaining detour.

Unlike Matsuyama, Tokyo was the place to be in the 1920s. The population of urban Tokyo increased by 30 percent reaching 5.4 million in 1930 and then went on to increase by a further 36 percent in the next decade. In Tokyo, trains and urbanisation also created suburbs and an 'inner-city' with new entertainment districts with their own sub-cultures and personalities. Here writers would discover and write about delinquents and marginalised youth. Indeed, many still write about these youngsters on the fringes of society today proving that the sordid and beautiful are not mutually exclusive.

Junichiro Tanizaki (1886-1965), for example, wrote about suburban Tokyo at night in his novels, such as *Chijin no ai* (*Naomi*) as did Yasunari Kawabata (1899-1972), who went on to win the Nobel Prize in Literature in 1968. Other notable authors from this period of burgeoning railways include Shusei Tokuda (1871-1943) and Toson Shimazaki (1872-1943) as well as the tanka poet Takuboku Ishikawa (1886-1912) who penned many poems about trains and stations. "At the Station", translated by Roger Pulvers, is a good example of one of these: "I slip into the crowd/Just to hear the accent/of my faraway hometown." This angry young man, of the Japanese literary scene of the period, who died age 26, has since those days been turned into a national treasure.

He famously said, "what I demand from literature is criticism." Another example of his poetry reflecting this non-conformist's strained relationship with his father, a Buddhist priest, translated and titled by Pulvers as "Fathers and Sons" is: "Why is the air so thick between them?/Apart in spirit when facing each other/Close in absolute silence." Poetry like Ishikawa's and some types of narrative fiction are more poignant in terms of their ability to capture the essence of a given time, and as Aristotle (circa 384BCE-322BCE) famously put it, "a higher thing than history, for poetry tends to express the universal, history the particular."

Kawabata describes the inhabitants and shifting sub-culture of Asakusa, which is now more famous as a tourist destination, in *Asakusa kurenaidan* (*The Scarlet Gang of Asakusa*). After being serialised in a Tokyo newspaper from 1929 it was published as a book, three years after Asakusa's station opened. Of course, urbanisation impacted on places within easy reach from the capital. *Izu no odoriko* (*The Dancing Girl of Izu*), also by Kawabata and published in 1926, demonstrates this rather well. It is a novella about a 19-year-old Tokyo student who travels by train from Tokyo to the Izu Peninsula where he meets a troupe of dancers and encounters one young dancer that takes his fancy. Its depiction of young unrequited love is so well known in Japan that for well over 30 years a train that runs from both Tokyo and Ikebukuro to Izu has carried the name *Odoriko*, The Dancer.

Other train operators with conveniently located scenic tourist spots on their routes, perfect for short stays of one night or more, have followed suit by dreaming up similar names for their trains. *RomanceCar* being one of them. *The Dancing Girl of Izu* is still influential in contemporary literary circles and regularly appears in new works such as *Monkey Man*, a creative adaption of the Chinese 16th century classic *Journey to the West* (*The Monkey King*), by Takuji Ichikawa (b. 1962), where it features as a dog-eared treasured book that accompanies the protagonist, Yuri, on her quest for freedom and escape from dark conspiratorial forces. Another earlier fascinating pastiche-like example of its influence is the *Noha sojushi* (*The Brainwave Controller*), by Ikujiro Ran (1913-1944). This science fiction reimagination of Kawabata's novella includes twist of fate and garbled transmissions that lead to uncontrolled consequences for the young girl and her visiting admirer.

The literary associations with railways aren't all rosy by any stretch of the imagination. The railways had their fair share of dark periods too. Growth comes with chaos, not order. Riots, for instance, would occasionally flare up when fares were increased. There are many books that depict scenes in which trains play a role in wartime by mobilising troops, for example. As the novelty of trains dissipated and rail transport become part of the regular fabric of modern Japanese society, their employment as plot devices also evolved, often in very interesting and creative ways, never disappearing completely, but by becoming part of the overriding structure of the novel, and not the main focus of the story. Perhaps with the exception of some detective fiction and murder mysteries.

Station to Station

An excellent contemporary example is Haruki Murakami's (b. 1949) short story "The Town of Cats", published in English translation in *The New Yorker* in 2011.[119] Train travel plays an important narrative role in this thought-provoking story on multiple levels. The story starts and ends with stations: Koenji and Chikura. It is the tale of a young man by the name of Tengo who is trying to understand himself and his relationship with his father, a man who spent his adult life with the thankless task of collecting subscription licence fees for Japan's semi-governmental television network, NHK, and who is now living in a sanatorium near Chikura by the sea. The trip to see his father is one that Tengo is not looking forward to but feels compelled to make.

On the train Tengo reads a book by a German author about another young man who is also on a train journey. Unlike Tengo, this young man has no particular destination in mind, and oddly finds himself in a town that has been vacated and is now occupied by cats. Tengo eventually reads part of this fantastical novel to his father and despite hardly speaking to each other it helps them reach some kind of understanding. It is a touching story, beautifully crafted, with travel, trains and stations, wheels within wheels, subtly embedded into its narrative structure. A tale of emotional voids being filled consciously or through simple momentum, as well as the entropy of ageing.

Murakami reportedly had his own complex relationship with his father. Journeys, whether by trains or other means, and joint activities that don't require much actual personal expression, such as fishing, can sometimes encourage resolution. While for others parental dynamics can remain immutable points on a line, impossible to bridge, as one of Yukio Mishima's (1925-1970) characters in *Gogo no eiko* (*The Sailor Who Fell From Grace With The Sea*) puts it:

> There is no such thing as a good father because the role itself is bad. Strict fathers, soft fathers, nice moderate fathers – one's as bad as another. They stand in the way of progress while they try to burden us with their inferiority complexes, and their unrealized aspirations, and their resentments, and their ideals, and the weaknesses they've never told anyone about, and their sins, and their sweeter-than-honey dreams, and the maxims they've never had the courage to live by – they'd like to unload that silly crap on us, all of it!

Stations and railway journeys do not just provide a vehicle to frame a story. Many contemporary authors have followed in Kawabata's footsteps and used large city-like stations or areas around them as settings. Many have also taken a similar path and focused on sub-cultures, for which some railway stations are famous.

A good example of this genre is Ira Ishida's (b. 1960) collection *Ikebukuro Uesuto Geto Paku* (*Ikebukuro West Gate Park*), or *IWGP* as it has become known. *IWGP* is about marginalised youth, and the adventures of 20-year-old Makoto, his friends and a local gang leader, all of whom hang out at the park near Ikebukuro Station, Tokyo's third busiest. It is an area with an edgy reputation, girly bars and a small Chinatown. The prizewinning *IWPG* was Ishida's debut work. Not only did it establish him as a writer, but it went on to become a popular manga and television series with Makoto playing an urban crime-solving youth.

Another excellent example can be found in the writing of the Akutagawa Prizewinning author, Miri Yu (b. 1968). Her 2014 novel *JR Ueno-Eki Koenguchi* (*Tokyo Ueno Station*) now probably falls within Japan's corpus of so-called Olympic literature and uses the Olympics and Ueno station for social commentary. It tells the tale of Kazu, a man who moves to Tokyo from Fukushima to support his family at the time of the 1964 Tokyo Olympics. Thirty-seven years after his Olympic-timed arrival at one of Japan's busiest stations, Kazu finds himself back there once again. This time living in a homeless camp in a park near the station's entrance "used and discarded" a decade after the Japanese economic bubble collapsed. His story mirrors in a kaleidoscopic arc, the missed opportunities, and the lows that the failing economy had brought about.

At the other end of the spectrum, Mikie Ando's (b. 1953) *Yumeminoeki ishitsubutsugakari* (*Yumemino Station Lost and Found*), is a young adult novel that exudes hope and inspiration. This tale revolves around a lonely young girl who feels lost, having changed schools, and finds herself in a station's lost and found office where the attendant starts reading her stories that have been found in a notebook. She returns daily to listen to a different tale each time until she decides to set off on her own journey, to find her own purpose, and to create her own narrative.

Stations in Japan are part of the daily fabric of the lives of many, reflecting their own particular circumstances. Despite some stations being shared daily by millions of people of all ages, including those famously packed commuter trains, the experience of passing through them can still often be unique, isolating and at times lonesome. Nonetheless, life's rich tapestry can be found in the world of railways. Stations can be magical nodes, life-affirming and life-transforming places. Places where unusual sub-cultures and economies take root. They can also provide detours, or in the worst scenarios, be miserable dead ends reflecting the different sides of the nation's moods.

Stations and some iconic ones, those steeped in history such as Tokyo Station, alongside their tracks and trains, have influenced Japanese art, as well as literature, spawning the so-called genre of railway art. Within Tokyo Station itself, a small world-class gallery with exposed red brickwork often exhibits painted visual narratives of modernity, rail travel and Japan. It would be hard to find or imagine a similar dedicated art zone, a destination in itself, within most central stations in major international capital cities.

Trainspotting and Timetables

The rail network, as well as the individuals that use it, can also provide a fascinating narrative. For some it is something of a fanatical obsession. "Just as Japan's trains are in a league of their own," writes *The Washington Post*, "so too are its trainspotters."

For a mountainous island nation plagued by earthquakes, Japan's railway network is remarkably large with slightly less than 30,000 kilometres of track. For comparison, this is about 60 percent of the size of Germany's network, yet more than three times the number of passengers ride on Japan's network each year. That's an amazing three billion trips, triple the number of books distributed each year in Japan, for example.

There are quite literally tens of thousands of people in Japan who are obsessed with the network: its sophistication, the different jingles at its stations, its timetables, its punctuality and cleanliness, the multitude of *bento* lunch boxes on sale and, of course, the countless varieties of trains themselves, including Japan's famous bullet train, launched in 1964, ten days before the start of the Tokyo Olympics. The bullet train now comes in many different editions with different speeds and designs, including a special Hello Kitty pink model on the Osaka-Hakata route.

It is probably much harder to spot someone who hates trains in Japan than it is to find a trainspotter. In fact the trainspotters, like the trains themselves, have been classified into different types with their own monikers like *eki-tetsu* (station geeks) and *sharyo-tetsu* (train-design/carriage geeks) to name just a couple.

Closed spaces, punctual trains and complex timetables are dream ingredients for authors of locked-room detective fiction, in which murders are committed in seemly impossible to fathom circumstances. The genre has been very successfully revived in Japan by writers like Soji Shimada (b. 1948), of *Senseijyutsu satsujin jiken* (*The Tokyo Zodiac Murders*) fame.

Murders on the Oriental Kyuko (Express)

Let's not forget that tragedy can also befall the railways. Two Japanese prime ministers have been assassinated at Tokyo Station: Takashi Hara (1856-1921) and Osachi Hamaguchi (1870-1931) who died from infected unhealed wounds nine months after he was shot. More recently, the Tokyo subway was attacked in 1995 by a religious cult using the nerve agent sarin, killing 13 people. Fascinating books have been written about this tragic event by Randy Taguchi (b. 1959) in *Sakasa ni tsurusareta otoko* (*A Man Hung Upside Down*), and Haruki Murakami's (b. 1949) *Andaguraundo* (*Underground*).

Unsurprisingly, legends about the railways abound. Tokyo Station, which survived the huge Tokyo earthquake in 1923, but didn't escape the firebombing of Tokyo at the end of the Second World War, is rumoured to have a secret hidden network of tunnels and platforms. In the 1965 James Bond film *You Only Live Twice*, 007 comes to Japan and the head of the Japanese secret service Tanaka travels on a private underground train from his own secure and secret platform, which helped fuel rumours over this secret network. Another urban legend is known as *Teke teke* and concerns a woman or schoolgirl who fell on a train line and was cut in half, and who at night makes a teke teke noise as she pulls herself along by her elbows.

> A train station also holds the sediment of countless farewells. The damp residue of grief that all train stations share might well come from a burden of tears they have all absorbed. Jakucho Setouchi (1922-2021), *Basho* (*Places*).

The world's most famous railway mystery has to be Agatha Christie's (1890-1976) novel *Murder on the Orient Express* published in 1934. The book and films have been very popular in Japan to the extent that there is now even an Agatha Christie Award for unpublished Japanese authors. In 2015 the book was adapted for a two-part television special, with a stellar Japanese cast, part one faithful to the original but set in Japan in 1933 and part two with a new original story. Interestingly, Ogai Mori (1862-1922) who wrote Japan's first modern short story, *Maihime* (*The Dancing Girl*), in 1890 after studying in Germany, is reportedly the first Japanese person known to have actually travelled on the Orient Express, which began operating in 1833.

Train timetables have also featured in Japanese mysteries as alibis that are hard to refute. Something that few other countries whose trains are much less reliable could ever pull-off. The first Japanese railway murder mystery novel that used the timetable as an alibi is said to have been *Funatomike no sangeki* (*The Tragedy of the Funatomi*), by Yu

Aoi (1909-1975) published in 1936, two years after the publication of Christie's novel. The book is about the murder of a mother and daughter from Osaka.

However, it is Kyotaro Nishimura (1930-2022) who is in this regard Japan's answer to Agatha Christie. His 1978 debut novel, *Buru torein tokkyu satsujin jiken* (*Blue Train Express Murder Case*), was set on a train, as was his highly successful 1986 novel, *Shindai tokkyu satsujin jiken* (*Murder on the Limited Express Sleeper*). These cemented his reputation as an author of whodunnits and travel-related mysteries. He has gone on to write more than 550 novels which have sold around 200 million copies in print. According to the *Guinness Book of World Records*, Christie, who holds the world record, has sold a staggering two billion copies. Nishimura's fictional detective Totsugawa is one of Japan's most popular, and a two-hour mystery show broadcast on national television, based on his books, is the longest running series of its kind in Japan.

That said, *Ten to sen* (*Points and Lines*), by Seicho Matsumoto (1909-1992), published in 1958, is sometimes cited as one of the best Japanese railway mysteries ever written. It is a classic whodunnit set in post-war Japan, which makes interesting reading in itself. *Points and Lines* also relies on timetables and maps to break a cast-iron alibi and solve a double-murder that looks like a double-suicide of two lovers. It is quite literally a tale told from the tracks as it was written in a room at Tokyo Station Hotel. It has inspired countless fans, and is the favourite of many, including the American author James Kendley, who writes horror stories set in Japan.

Many Japanese authors such as Shimada have carried on this tradition brilliantly. Shimada, who has earned the moniker as Japan's 'God of Mystery', for example, has penned several books featuring trains and murders that have been successfully adapted for television in Japan. Another high-profile book blending murder and trains is Kotaro Isaka's (b. 1971) *Maria bitoru*, translated into English as *Bullet Train* and turned into a film starring Brad Pitt in 2022. A recent and interesting upshot of all this train mystery activity is a mini-boom in the launch of new luxury sleeper trains. Needless to say, these trains, which look like super-luxury boutique hotels on wheels, are crime free. Some have impressive names, that might make good titles for future novels, such as *Towairaito ekusupuresu* (*Twilight Express*), *Nanatsuboshi* (*Seven Stars*) and *Shiki-shima* (*Four Seasons Island*). They all boast murderously expensive ticket prices.

A Digital Hoax or True Love?

Regrettably, train whodunnits aren't as popular or common as they once were. But *Densha otoko* (*Train Man*), by Hitori Nakano, a pseudonym, is a more recent novel that has certainly given the genre a shot in the arm and demonstrated that trains and train travel can still provide a compelling narrative, one that hasn't run out of steam and probably never will.

The book is an unfolding love story involving a young man, a geek with limited social skills who can't talk to girls. He manages to inadvertently change the course of his life by stopping a drunk man from harassing a young woman (known as Miss Hermes) on a train. She thanks him and asks for his address, and a relationship begins to blossom, a relationship that our protagonist shares online with his followers up until the point that a sexual encounter is likely to occur. The story takes the form of a stream of digital posts over a period of 57 days and has a very authentic feel to it, though whether or not this is a true story isn't at all clear. Nevertheless, the book published in 2004 has led to a number of spin-offs including a film, a television drama and manga, not to mention a flurry of similarly themed books. Drunk men, and their avoidance, are also still a feature of late-night Japanese train travel.

Yesterday's revolution in railway networks has today been superseded by digital networks. Gone are the days of reading newspapers and manga only in print. Tablets and smartphones are now ubiquitous but interestingly, you still do see people reading print format books. One way or another, reading continues unabated. According to the Research Institute for Publications, sales of digital manga in Japan surpassed print editions for the first time in 2017. Digital manga sales rose 17 percent on the previous year, while sales of physical print format manga fell by roughly 14 percent. A new point on the line towards media digitisation had, it seemed, been reached.

Reading habits have in fact been changing and still are over the last decade or so rather significantly. Initially, it was cell phones and now it is the next generation smartphones that have led the charge. In 2003, the world's first cell phone novel, or *keitai shosetsu*, titled *Ayu no monogatari* (*Deep Love*) was released in Japan. Like *Train Man*, it was also subsequently published in print, manga and made into a film after finding initial success on the small screens of mostly young women commuting to work. In traditional book format it sold more than 2.5 million copies.

Keitai shosetsu are sent out by text message or email as part of a subscription in small chapter instalments, each consisting of about 70–100 words. Japan has a long and rich history of fiction in short-form and serialisation, making it the perfect environment for this. Reading a confessional slightly over-the-top love story on a tiny phone screen on a packed commuter train provides many with an entertaining few moments of escape as they ride the train on their way to or from work. In 2007, half of the top ten best-selling fiction titles in Japan originated as *ketai shosetsu*, but this publishing boom is now over and technological advances have encouraged the spread of streaming and video-based escape as well as audio alongside the purely textual.

Tales from the Network: To be Continued...

Nonetheless, billions of train journeys still take place and almost all passengers carry reading devices of some form. Narratives from off and on the tracks are destined to continue and start new publishing trends, both local and international that are currently hard to gage or predict. Stations, trains and tracks have provided a versatile and rich channel for Japan's creative writers and have managed to convey so many facets of Japanese society along the way.

We are often encouraged to view our draining daily commutes as punctuation in a larger tale. Books and authors, especially of the Japanese variety, can help ensure that our daily transportational encounters aren't simply pesky wayward commas and unruly wanton syntax, but the type of punctuation that confronts us, making us pause momentarily, creating diversity expectancy and golden distraction. For the curious looking for authentic moments, it's best to look past nebulous headlines, and micro blogging and social media content, and turn to literature.

These days Japan's literary locomotion, with its endless destinations, has reached as far as the likes of the Delhi Metro. Where the growing population of enthusiasts for tales penned by Japan's authors, now enjoy reading books in translation, often about different, unusual Asian magical labyrinth-like worlds, while travelling through another growing transformational network, also grounded on Japanese creative industrialism. The Delhi Metro, a modern mass rapid transit system hailed as a symbol of and role model for Indo-Japanese cooperation and diplomacy, alongside several other Japan-supported metro-developments in other major Asian cities, is creating new excuses for many to pick up tales as they speed towards new or daily destinations.

Locomotion is a force that pulls and pushes in many directions. Showing that liberating modernity and distance-destroying cultural devices, physical and emotional, now come in many varied formats. There are few breaks on this literary train. Novels, like stations and trains, take people to places they've never been before, switching our emotional gears and perspectives. Some may well have magical moments and mystery about them but what matters most, however, is getting onboard and in the case of books, turning to or clicking on the first page. Japanese magical mystery tours await the ticketed-willing, wherever they reside, no matter on which side of the tracks or the nature of their gauge.

Part Four

Cats, Tatts and Christians

Xavier took the southern passage to Japan. There weren't any Western controlled colonies yet, so he must have only encountered stubborn hostility. Japan was the first place he was welcomed, and invited to dinner. This hospitality continued across the entire country. Xavier may have feared that Christianity would ruin the nation, as he wrote to a clergyman friend saying he should not come and that it was better if he stayed far away, since Japan had the worst weather, and its inhabitants displayed perverse attitudes, like no other country. *Backlight*, Kanji Hanawa.

Soseki's Cat: A Quantum Leap

The mysterious and magical effect of cats is widely celebrated. Cats entertain, evoke stress-reducing emotional responses, bring good luck, constantly and often counter-intuitively amuse, and cats—of a certain variety—can even cause paradigm shifts.

Schrödinger's cat, which changed quantum physics, is probably the best example of the paradigm-shifting nature of cats, but it is certainly not the only one. Devised in 1935 to mock and critique the scientific wisdom of the time, the Nobel Prizewinning physicist Erwin Schrödinger (1887-1961) dreamt up his fictional feline as a paradoxical thought experiment. His cat is both alive and dead until a box is opened, and its narrative structure, designed to point out the ridiculous, involves a radioactive sample, a vial of poison, cats in boxes and a Geiger counter.

This mystery cat was designed as a parody to highlight the odd duality, multiple-states and counter-intuitive nature of quantum mechanics, as well as to make those involved in this revolutionary field at the time question their observations, theories and collective wisdom. To make them go back to first principles. This group included the likes of Albert Einstein (1879-1955), Boris Yakovlevich Podolsky (1896-1966) and Nathan Rosen (1909-1995). The theory in question was the Copenhagen Interpretation, one of the oldest and most important explanations of quantum mechanics, proposed by Niels Bohr (1885-1962) and Werner Heisenberg (1901-1976).

This all took place when quantum mechanics was a new and evolving discipline. A time when many were trying to figure out what this new science actually meant and what its implications were for the modern scientific community. Schrödinger's hypothetical cat is an aloof motif still used today to illustrate the strangeness of quantum logic, the act and consequences of close observation and measurement at tiny scales, as well as the confused ambiguity of the observer changing the observed.

The Cynic's Paw

Soseki's cat, another paradigm-shifting cat, which in fact made its debut twenty years earlier, was a different type of construct, a pure literary one. It launched the career of Soseki Natsume (1867-1916), now considered by many as modern Japan's greatest novelist, after his return to Japan from an unhappy period of study in Britain.

His cat, an alley cat named Chibi, 'little one', caused a similar paradigm-shifting sensation on publication within the fields of Japanese literature and creative writing. Chibi was also created to mock, to observe the observer and cynically challenge the collective wisdom of the Meiji era (1868-1912), Japan's revolutionary period when, just like modern physics, the nation was rapidly modernising, evolving and confronting another type of peculiar duality: how to square the nation's traditions with those of a modern Westernised nation.

It wasn't just Japan and physics, however, that were changing. Many nations were also embracing much significant change. New international standards were appearing for the first time for the length and definition of a day, the number of days in a week, as well as for weights and measures, for instance, and even the standardisation of time itself. All of which impacted on Japan, as well making its adaptations complicated. Japan adopted a seven-day week in 1873 and then standardised time in 1886 in the wake of the International Meridian Conference in 1884. This led to the birth of the *Toki no machi*, the Town of Time, Akashi, a city on the Seto Island Sea in Hyogo Prefecture through which the 135th meridian east line passes and therefore where Japan Standard Time (JST) is set. Before this, time was noticeably distinct across nations, and within them, with towns keeping time differently depending on where its observer and measurer was located.

Leaping Eras: Born in Edo, Dying in Tokyo

In the Meiji era many were trying to figure out what Japan's rapid new development meant and how to engage with the newly imported ways of thinking and the terminologies and precisions required to measure things. In much the same way as in the field of physics, an uninvited fictional cat slinked challengingly onto the scene.

Natsume, the youngest of eight children, was born in Shinjuku in 1867 the last year of Japan's Edo period (1603-1868), a long and mostly peaceful period (that preceded the Meiji era) during which Japan was shut off from most of the world and Edo, where Shinjuku is located, was Japan's capital city. The city of Edo, one of the world's largest at that time, was renamed Tokyo in 1868 when the shogun was overthrown, and the Meiji Emperor (1852-1912) moved his official residence to the renamed Tokyo.

Like an unwanted kitten from a large litter, Natsume, the future author, was put out for adoption and lived with two different households, only returning to his parental home at the age of nine following the separation of the couple at the second household he shared. In spite of this lonely and unsettled early existence, Natsume went on to become an excellent student, which culminated with him being sent by the Japanese government to study in Britain at the age of 33. He had to leave his pregnant wife and child behind in Japan. He didn't actually enjoy his time overseas but it was a rare experience that, as with other prominent Japanese people of the time, propelled his career forwards.

Along the way he picked up the pen name Soseki, which is written using two *kanji* characters, 'gargle' and 'stone', which apparently means stubborn. It is a term based around a torturous Chinese tale about being true to your nature and arguing one's case even when you are wrong, stubbornly refusing to admit defeat, and was chosen during a period when Japan's literati all knew Chinese literature and enjoyed toying with it. Natsume's actual name was Kinnosuke Natsume. Today many Japanese authors look to American and Russian writers for inspiration but Natsume and other authors of his era, including the likes of Ryunosuke Akutagawa (1892-1927) a major admirer of Natsume, were fascinated with Chinese literature. In fact, this keen interested is one of the factors behind Akutagawa agreeing to go to China in 1921 for several months as a special correspondent for a major Japanese newspaper. What this tells us about Natsume and why he chose that name is anyone's guess, according to Meredith McKinney, one of his translators and of course a cat-lover herself. "Stubbornly wrong-headed?" she asks, adding, "Anyway, it was meant to be a lightly humorous self-parody in the style of the day."

After his return to Tokyo and a series of unwanted and initially rejected visits, a stray cat took up residence in Natsume's home, becoming his purring muse and inspiring him to write his debut work, a short story written from the perspective of a cat, *Wagahai wa neko de aru* (*I Am a Cat*). The published title of the work coming from its first line. After it was initially read out with the title *Nekoden* (*Cat Story*), at a weekly gathering of writers, students and scholars at Natsume's home it was published in the literary journal *Hototogisu*, the title of which in English means lessor cuckoo, in January 1905 to great acclaim. Due to the huge popular reaction it elicited, more than ten further instalments were published, creating a serial and then a novel. It was illustrated by Fusetsu Nakamura (1866-1943), an artist who, like Natsume, had studied abroad, in his case in France. The book put Natsume firmly on Japan's literary map.

The sardonic cat's caustic observations of its neighbourhood and the household of its 'master' Professor Sneeze and his pretentious scholarly associates are fragmented and only tied together by the cat which wanders independently through the life of a Meiji period household and its neighbourhood without a formal, traditional or linear storyline. Poking fun en route at everyone encountered and observed, including Professor Sneeze who no doubt is Natsume's alter ego, is the order of the day. Natsume, through his cat, tickles the whiskers of Meiji's hypocritical elite who often mimicked everything Western, like copycats, sometimes to the point of absurd parody:

My master's face is pockmarked. I am told that pockmarks were common enough before… but these days… a face this scarred feels a bit behind the times… How singularly unfortunate for him!

… though he is normally to be found asleep in front of it, he does actually spend much of his time with some difficult book propped up before his nose. One must accordingly regard him as a person of at least the scholarly type.

Though they adopt a nonchalant attitude, keeping themselves aloof from the crowd, segregated like so many snake-gourds swayed lightly by the wind, in reality they, too, are shaken by just the same greed and worldly ambition as their fellow men.

The urge to compete and their anxiety to win are revealed flickeringly in their everyday conversations, and only a hair's breadth separates them from the Philistines who they spend their idle days denouncing.

This tale of an incommodious animal roaming the streets of a major metropolis cynically surveying, mostly unnoticed, at a distance all around it, some have argued, reflects Natsume's "non-human" sojourn in the United Kingdom, reportedly the unhappiest years of his life and not just the author's views on Tokyo's educated elite.[120] After the publication of *I Am a Cat*, Natsume's writing career took off, allowing him eventually to become a full-time author. Still popular today and seen as a quintessential must-read author for Japanese students, Natsume is known for his skilful fusion of Edo sensibilities and Meiji modernity, a pivotal period that shaped modern-day Japan. Among works such as *Kokoro*, *Botchan* and *Sanshiro*, which was one of film director Akira Kurosawa's (1910-1998) favourite books, Natsume wrote 15 novels, which are full of fascinating and idiosyncratic characters with depth, and often a touch of loneliness. Books that still resonate with readers today.

Freethinking and Individualism: Another Modern Paradox?

Individualism and personality were important themes for Natsume, who was something of an outsider and like his cat enjoyed observing society, objectively scratching away at it judgmentally. He developed a wide and close circle of disciples, which included the likes of a young Akutagawa whom he encouraged and mentored along with other 'students' at weekly meetings at his home.

This said, Natsume, with his stubbornness undimmed, avoided or kept a distance from his actual peers. He wrote and spoke about the importance of personal freedom and nurturing individuality, which he considered a moral duty. Natsume argued that individuality should be pursued, and everyone had the right to think and act freely as an individual. Nonetheless, he also understood the complexities and competing forces of the rights of the individual and collective group rights and needs, as well as the need for occasional obeisance and for personal freedom and tolerance to be subjected for peace. However, this should not mean individuals should not have aspirations and individual dreams.

Natsume argued that the stability of the collective was a prerequisite for individualism to flourish. For some these social properties seem correlated and can't be described or managed independently. Academics today would probably refer to this as the 'paradox of liberalism' the idea that societies can't prioritise individual liberty above all other political goods without undermining the foundations of individual liberty itself. It is a modern term coined in the 1970s by the Indian economist and Nobel laureate Amartya Kumar Sen. The theme of the place of the individual in society is also, of course, one that Confucius devoted his life to explaining, becoming an inspiration for centuries for many in China, Japan and beyond.

After all, even an independent and intolerant cat needs a reliable and peaceful household in which to flourish and find a safe bed, creating a valuable if slightly odd co-dependence. Natsume thought that individualism wasn't about being self-centred or egotistical but about developing one's own approach while at the same time respecting the personalities of others and fulfilling one's duties and responsibilities. A balance that many groups and individuals still struggle to achieve today, in and outside Japan. In reality, society and the individual should not be antagonistic, even if forcing it into this dynamic is beneficial to some, culture should provide the inputs from which an individual lives their life allowing them to flourish. This somewhat eternal theme of the individual in relation to the collective community, society and other individuals, is one that Japanese authors including the likes of Kobo Abe (1924-1993) and contemporary authors such as Fuminori Nakamura (b. 1977) struggle with and is reflected within their works. In Nakamura's case, in his 2018 collection of essays, *Jiyushiko* (*Freethinking*).

That said, Natsume's actual cat outlived his fictional cat, which dies in the final instalment of the story. The real cat lived with the author in Tokyo and died in 1908 several years before the author's own death at age 49. So in an odd way, Natsume's cat, like Schrödinger's, was alive and dead at the same time depending on by whom and how it was observed.

From Obscurity to Cultural Icon

Unlike Natsume's cat, which caused an immediate sensation in Japan, Schrödinger's cat had little impact in his lifetime, only subsequently shifting from obscurity to the celebrity status it now enjoys in the scientific community and beyond, many years later.

It is still a much-discussed feline and research papers continue to be written about it. These span many fields including quantum jumps that can be reversed, loops; transitions, parallel universes, the fine-structure constant, reality splits and the Many–Worlds theory. In the canon of scientific literature, it seems to have taken on multiple new lives of its own.

These two cats conjured up by the furtive imaginations of trailblazing founders of modern physics and modern Japanese literature respectively, are now cultural icons. Both have spawned impressive publishing responses. It is, however, unlikely that either of them knew about each other's paradigm-shifting cat.

Natsume was interested in science and notably shared rooms in London with Kikunae Ikeda (1864-1936) a Japanese chemist who later discovered the *Fifth Basic Taste*, which he named *umami*, and subsequently developed for use as a condiment generally known as MSG.[121] According to John Nathan's fascinating biography *Soseki: Modern Japan's Greatest Novelist*, Ikeda and Natsume debated some of the big issues of the time including education, religion and science in their London lodgings, something that probably led to Natsume taking a more scientific and objective approach to literature. In 2002 the world caught up with Ikeda when dedicated glutamate receptors were identified by researchers in human mouths, finally confirming scientifically *umami* as a primary taste.

Max Planck (1858-1947), another Nobel laureate, suggested in 1900 around the time Natsume and Ikeda were both in London that energy was emitted in discreet packets, quanta, and not continuously. The theory later gave birth to quantum mechanics, but this was long before Schrödinger's cat came on the scene. That came after Natsume's death, and before cats from Japan or Japan itself gained cultural infamy and clout.

Not a Dead Cat Bounce: A Purr Across Time

One of the charms of *I Am a Cat* is that it can be reinterpreted no matter what language it is being read or rendered in. For each and every reader or translator there is a different cat that thinks and behaves outside the box of society's norms, allowing Natsume's narrative to continue to flourish and delight in the same way as so many quirky cats do on the internet these days.

I Am a Cat has been translated into many languages including English, French, German, Spanish and Chinese, where there are said to be around 20 different versions of this single tale. It has also created a narrative structure that others now exploit inside and outside Japan. The British author Nick Bradley's 2020 debut novel *The Cat and The City*, for example, cleverly uses the now familiar plot device of binding a collection of fragmented stories together through a wandering Tokyo cat. It's another example of the breadth and longevity of the trend, as well as the numerous cats that Natsume has seeded.

Interestingly, *neko*, the Japanese word for cat, is written with a single *kanji* character made up of two underlying component parts, another subtle type of duality in form. These component parts are known as roots or radicals. *Neko*'s roots—sub-letter particles—consist of 'beast' on the left side and 'seeding' on the right creating the special singular *kanji* character used to write the noun cat in Japanese.

Cool for Cats

These feline frameworks of modernity developed some twenty years apart, exploiting the power of fragmented observation and fictional cats as a lens to view the world through, give voice to the timeless adage that whether a *Felis silvestris*—a wild, or quantum cat —or a *Felis bungaku*—a literary cat—it's cool to be a cat in the spheres of physics or literature, in Europe, Japan or far beyond.

Still, it might be surprising that the cat population of Japan surpassed dogs in October 2015 reaching nine million, a critical transitional stage. The number of cats in Japan is now more than half the number of children under the age of 15, which is probably enough to make demographers have kittens. Cats and dogs combined outnumber children.

Japan's cats receive wide coverage from international journalists writing about Japan's cat islands (where cats outnumber people eight to one), cat cafes in Tokyo and the depiction of the feline in Japanese woodblock prints, folklore and art, as well as cats in pop-culture. But these days Japanese cats aren't just big in Japan: some

Japanese cats are now international superstars. Today, the most famous Japanese cats are probably *maneki-neko*, Hello Kitty and Doraemon, none of which are real.

Many people mistakenly think that the beckoning-cat, *maneki-neko*, often displayed in restaurants and shops to bring luck, is Chinese. It isn't. She is a Japanese original, a Japanese bobtail with an upright welcoming paw that is thought to have originated in Edo in 1852. She is said to have been the inspiration for Hello Kitty another Japanese bobtail launched into the world in 1974. Hello Kitty, technically a Japanese-British hybrid, was named after a cat (also called Kitty) that Alice plays with in Lewis Carroll's (1832-1898) *Through the Looking-Glass*. Though Sanrio, the owner of her valuable intellectual property, states that she isn't a cat but a cartoon girl, a twin born in a suburb of London under the Scorpio star sign.[122]

There are several theories about the Edo origins of the *maneki-neko*, one, according to the Gotokuji temple, the 'Lucky Cat Temple', in Tokyo, is of a cat living at their temple beckoning a feudal lord and his samurai retainers inside with its paw miraculously saving them from a life-threatening lightning strike. Another often cited origin tale is of a poverty-stricken woman whose cat appears in a dream telling the destitute lady that the solution to her woes is to make cat figures out of clay and sell them, something she does alongside promoting the tale of her visionary pussycat. As sales increased and she became rich, the legend of the transforming power of lucky cat figures spread in a type of virtuous circle that has now spiralled out internationally.

The international popularity of *Doraemon*, one of the other superstar Japanese cats, a blue time traveling robot cat from the late sixties, who in fact pre-dates Hello Kitty, is a much more recent creation. *Doraemon* has become hugely popular in many countries across Asia, including India for instance. Its newfound popularity is, however, having some unexpected consequences.[123] A worried politician in Pakistan, for example, launched a legal petition to have the number of hours the country's children are exposed to this unusual cat with its special gadgets that are used—sometimes disastrously—to help the hapless boy in the story, Nobita Nobi, get out of trouble and make more of a success of his life. Apparently, this fictional cat from the future is having a "negative impact on the educational and physical well-being of children." This is, of course, not the intention or what Nobita's descendant, Sewashi Nobi, had in mind when he sent this multi-functioning flying robot cat into the past with the hope of transforming his lazy, book-loathing, bullied, and somewhat uncoordinated great-grandfather into something more respectable, with the ardent aim of improving their family's lot for generations to come.

In short, stealthy, cool Japanese cats have been slinking their way out of Japan for some time, now entertaining the international community in myriad forms and formats. They are now part of so-called Japanese Soft Power. But cats have populated the pages of Japanese literature for centuries since they first arrived in Japan, a thousand years ago, initially to guard temples from mice.

Even so, cats have helped others like Natsume establish their literary reputations, for example, the free-style poet Sakutaro Hagiwara (1886-1942). His importance was cemented, two decades after Natsume's cat first appeared in print, within Japanese literary circles with his poem and anthology of poems *Ao neko* (*The Blue Cat*) in 1923. They depict the procrastination, despondence and the sad suffering of the human race. This was followed by a novella in 1937, *Neko machi* (*The Town of Cats*). Junichiro Tanizaki (1886-1965) who is held in similar regard to Natsume as one of Japan's greatest writers, wrote the novella *Neko to shozo to futari no onna* (*A Cat, A Man and Two Women*) in 1936. This story is about a rivalry for attention from three female characters: a cat named Lily, a spurned ex-wife and a new younger second wife.

Analysis shows that the number of books in Japan with the word cat in their titles has increased steadily, surpassing dog books in 2008, and may now have started to accelerate, increasing this gap further, another quantum leap of sorts. The narrative motifs of the cat, unlike cats themselves who require a huge amount of sleep, never seem to tire or become exhausted. Teasing apart these connections has confounded many for decades. There are now so many examples that PhDs on the figure of the cat in Japanese literature and creative writing are being written.

Alongside the books, Japan's cat population is forecast to grow at a rate of four percent a year, while the number of dogs on the other hand is expected to decline, as is the population of humans in Japan. Cats cost half as much to look after as dogs and Japan's urbanised aging and shrinking population is a factor behind these figures. However, it's not just cats and books about them that are on the rise. The cat food market is now worth a staggering two billion dollars annually.

Japan's ubiquitous cats are generating an array of new business opportunities especially for creative individuals. It isn't just the publishing world that has identified this as a targeted growth market. Mars, better known for its treats for humans, has built up the largest market share for cat food in Japan with more than 10 percent of the market.[124] One of its leading brands is Kal Kan, originally delivered from the Stirling Packing Company, has been enjoyed by cats since 1936, the year Tanizaki penned his famous timeless tale about the battle for custody of Lily the cat.

Despite their popularity predatory cats and their many promoters have not yet hunted dogs and their tales, like cats have done for dozens of different species, into extinction. That said, cats and cat memes are abundant on the internet in Japan like elsewhere. Even though the medium is relatively new this isn't really a new phenomenon. In the early 1980s, for example, there was the *nameneko* craze triggered by a photo published in 1979 of cats dressed up like a Japanese motorcycle gang with the caption "All Japan Fast Feline Federation – You Won't Lick US!"

There have been all sorts of catty commercial nonsense and business opportunities, images, anime, manga and spin-offs including *Nontan*, for example. This is a children's book series by Sachiko Kiyono (1947-2008) about a naughty playful kitten, which was first published in the late seventies just before the *nameneko* craze took off, and has since expanded into 40 volumes selling millions of copies in Japan, France and China. Japan even has a crime-solving cat, also launched at a similar time, that helps a reluctant and delicate detective solve his curious cases in the multi-volume multi-million selling series *Mikeneko Homuzu (Calico Cat Holmes)* by the absurdly prolific Naoki Prizewinning mystery writer Jiro Akagawa (b. 1948). Like other similar publishing successes this reasoning cat has turned into a valuable media franchise with its own television series and more.

Brilliantly creative compelling cat literature is not a fad, but a long-term established trend. Japanese authors continue to observe, write about and use cats as a metaphor for Japan's changing society and family dynamics. *Neko no kyaku (The Guest Cat)*, published in English in 2014, is an internationally acclaimed recent example of this genre. This *New York Times* bestseller written by the poet Takashi Hiraide (b. 1950) initially gained attention outside Japan in France, before being published in America and subsequently around the world in more than 15 countries. In fact, the award-winning *The Guest Cat*, from a recognised and acclaimed Japanese poet, with its meandering laconic narrative flow and another cat named Chibi, is the type of cat work that Natsume might have actually enjoyed reading and understood as a flattering homage. However, other variant tales written since his day would probably be harder for him to digest and some contemporary narratives and their large number might overwhelm him, inducing an allergic reaction from his literary sensibilities.

There is, however, nothing quite like a cat from Japan it would seem. Cats are now a conventional part of Japanese literary fiction and contemporary Japanese fiction is littered with them. Japanese books featuring cats are often selected, some say too often, for publication in English translation. Books like Hiraide's *The Guest Cat*, *Tabi neko ripoto (The Travelling Cat Chronicles)* by Hiro Arikawa (b. 1972), and *Hon o mamorotosuru neko no hanashi (The Cat Who Saved Books)* by Sosuke Natsukawa (b. 1978), for instance. Cats also feature prominently in several of Haruki Murakami's (b. 1949) novels, some with their own special mixed literary pedigrees for the well-read to speculate about. Murakami has written about alternative cat worlds such as his *Neko machi (Town of Cats)* included in *1Q84*, published in 2011.

Interestingly, this Murakami work was ranked as the 'best work of fiction' published during Japan's Heisei era (1989-2019), when Emperor Akihito (b.1933) reigned, according to a survey of experts who had contributed book reviews to the *Asahi Shimbun*, one of Japan's most prestigious national daily newspapers. The results of the survey were published on the cusp of the changing eras, as the new imperial era Reiwa was about to commence, probably far too early to determine the 'best' or most 'influential' novel from an era just coming to an end. Nevertheless, journalists, academics and filmmakers from outside Japan, as well as inside, often look to Japanese authors and their works, especially Murakami's, in order to explain and explore contemporary Japan and frame its Heisei era in particular.

While the future for dogs in Japan looks precarious, unless perhaps if you're an in-style diminutive toy poodle or chihuahua, it is still completely cool to be a cat. The feline form will continue to inspire, play a major role and flourish in books to come as Japan's cat-loving audience of readers keeps moving onwards and upwards. Dogs it would appear have only a cat in hell's chance of reversing these now-established trends.

Different Strokes

Perhaps none of this, including this super position that cats appear to occupy, should really surprise us as cats and humans have been living connected lives for almost 10,000 years since cats were first domesticated. Evidently, cats have historically helped generate many milestone-like leaps in the canons of numerous different types of literature. *Beware of the Cat* by William Baldwin (1518-1563) written in 1561, is yet another notable example of this and many others exist.

Despite being written hundreds of years after the first Japanese, and some believe the world's, first novel, *Genji monogatari* (*The Tale of Genji*), *Beware of the Cat* is believed by some to be "the first novel published in the English language."[125] This work, sometimes known as *Gulielmus Baldwin*, also distorts reality, is satirical with its ire thought to be focused on Catholicism, and involves the language of cats, as well as the often awkward-states that cats can unbeknownst to us, and perhaps also sometimes themselves, bear witness to. It is also the origin of another narrative dimension: the British construct that cats are blessed with nine lives.

Japan of course also has its own pre-Natsume pedigree with a very rich and well-documented long history and linage of legendary tales about supernatural and fear-inducing cats, as well as storytelling about unusual realms with abnormal states with their own quantum-like distortions.[126] These types of tales flourished during

Japan's Edo period when publishing took off alongside reading and population growth. At this time, many homes were lit with fish oil lamps attracting cats, strays and pets, often generating impressively large and shapely shadows, and seeding night-time tales of mystery phantom disturbances, including tales of elusive *bakeneko*, shape-shifting supernatural cats, as well as their monstrous two-tailed purring peers the *nekomata*.

In addition to this multitude of cats, Japan also has much classical narrative prose and poetry that avoid chronological or progressive timelines, that can appear stylistically fragmented and playful with our typical concepts of time. But the arrival of Natsume's sardonic cat, Chibi, in 1905 is considered to have bred a brand-new back-alley linked to past masterful catty portrayals, that many subsequent Japanese writers have wandered down with brilliant creative aplomb. Few would disagree with the conjecture that Natsume's mocking tale of a tiny furry cat shifted Japanese literature in a wonderful new direction.

The best scientists delight in drawing connections and finding them where others don't look. They are often the connections that create paradigm shifts, which change how we see the world, as both Natsume and Schrödinger have shown. These are the types of explanatory links that bring important quantum-like new insights, seeding new branches in all forms of literature. The key to finding them is often keen-eyed observation and going back to first principles or as this is often described in Zen Buddhism, the beginner's mind: *shoshin*.

Within these entangled existences, the latest cognitive behaviour research actually seems to indicate that cats, with their keen powers of observation, olfaction and acute hearing, and own special timekeeping, are better at decoding human expressions and behaviour than humans are at reading theirs. Perhaps this is what we really need to be watchful of.[127]

The great Winston Churchill (1874-1965), another Nobel laureate, in his case in Literature not Physics like Schrödinger, was in his own way aware of this and reportedly preferred pigs, who apparently treat humans as equals, as opposed to cats that look down on all of us. No wonder cats' eyes, when creatively assumed, can shift tastes and publishing paradigms so successfully. Japanese 'Cat-Lit', seeded by brilliant creative momentum, is for many the crème de la crème.

From Body Art to Literature: Zen and the Art of the Tattoo

Everyone seems to want a tattoo these days. The numbers are staggering: more than a third of people between the ages of 18 and 30 in the United States and Britain now have tattoos, and the number is expected to keep on growing. It is not just the young, celebrities, sportsmen and women, but also society's 'civilised elite' that are adorning, decorating and branding their bodies with tattoos.

Tattoos are everywhere: on the arms of royalty, on television, on the ankles of politicians' spouses, on the internet and book covers. No serious crime fiction fan could have missed the international bestselling book *The Girl With the Dragon Tattoo*, for instance. However, the king with the Japanese dragon tattoo and the impact the craft and Japan's artisans have had around the world and on Japanese literature, are much less known.

The word tattoo is a loanword, which quickly entered the English language in the 18th century when Captain Cook (1728-1779) returned to Britain after his epic Pacific voyages on *HMS Endeavour*. The term comes from *ta-tau* (to strike or mark) in Polynesian languages. Its use spread with the publication of Cook's adventures in 1769, which included detailed observations and records of the 'tattooed savages' that the adventurer and his team encountered. However, the practice is, in fact, far older in Europe and elsewhere. The world's oldest known tattoos are said to be the sixty that were discovered on the mummified body of Iceman Otzi, found in an Italian glacier in 1991.[128] Otzi apparently died around 3250 BCE. Tattoos have been also found on mummies in China, Chile, Egypt, and the Philippines.

The practice is also very old in Japan, with a similarly long pedigree and illustrious past. It was common amongst the Ainu, the indigenous people of northern Japan, a community that attracted so much excited international interest outside Japan at the turn of the 20th century as Japan was opening up to Western travellers and explorers. Visiting and writing about the 'noble savages' with their tattooed moustachioed women-folk lead to headlines in newspapers such as "The Quaintest Subjects of the Mikado" (*The St. Louis Republic*, 1904), "A Nation in Which Women and Men Wear Moustaches" (*The San Francisco Call*, 1897), "Strangest People in the

World" (*Daily Press, Newport News*, 1908), and "The Religious Ceremony of Getting Drunk: A Visit to the Ainus, the Strange Japanese Aborigines on the Island of Yezo" (*The San Francisco Call*, 1912). Early photo-mechanical images, the precursors to cinematic documentaries and modern cinema, such as *Les Aïnos à Yeso* (1897), also contributed to this fascination. Helping propagate a myth that the Ainu were descended from ancient Europeans lost in the Far East.

The juxtaposition of first contact with an ancient inaccessible people depicted by these early Western visitors, as hairy Caucasian 'aborigines' living within the previously inapproachable territory of the Japanese archipelago was alluring.[129] Japan was, unlike the islands of Lilliput and Blefuscu, the only real nation featured in Jonathan Swift's (1667-1745) fictional travelogue *Gulliver's Travels,* and the 'discovery' of the Ainu no doubt was therefore destined to generate sensational coverage, as well as false and easy to exploit connections, commentary and headlines about the bizarre nation of Japan.[130] Journalists, writers and opinion leaders can at times behave like yahoos, metaphorically and literally, and this fascination with the Ainu and the journalistic responses induced were the kind of articulation rooted in prejudice which forget that the process of 'discovery' is actually multi-faceted and multi-directional.

The fact that the Ainu, despite only being officially recognised as indigenous people of Japan by the Japanese government in 2008, had their own oral literary canon, with delicate poetry and the sacred epic magic sword narrative, *Kutsune Shirka,* for instance, were glossed over or totally ignored. These are narratives that manga and anime storytellers have now picked up on with tales such as *Goruden kamui (Golden Kamuy)*. The oral canon of course didn't fit the 'aboriginal' narrative of the era of first discovery or echo the period's sensational headlines in the English language press.

Japanese language storytelling about the Ainu is, however, not just a contemporary graphic phenomenon. In 1936, for instance, the judging panel of the Akutagawa Prize, in only its second year, unanimously selected as its winner *Koshamain-ki (The Chronicles of Koshamain)* by Tomoya Tsuruta (1902-1988), a subversive tale set in the early Edo period (1603-1868) of a third generation Ainu chieftain battling against duplicitous Japanese individuals trying to topple and ingest the northern territories.

This short story published the year before the Second Sino-Japanese War (1937-1945) has been described as a surprisingly overt attack on Japan's imperial ambitions and the means Japan used to achieve those ambitions. *The Chronicles of Koshamain*'s reception and the public debate spawned about its merits, show how masterfully crafted narratives with layered commentaries and subtle messaging are read is often very much in the eye of the beholder.[131] It also shows that the judges of Japanese literary awards have for a very long time been, as they continue to be, progressively open to different perspectives and voices, even dissenting ones on the margins of society.

In fact, the practice of tattooing was also common amongst the inhabitants of Okinawa in the south, *hajichi*, hand tattoos, in their case associated with rites of passage. The practice goes back further to Palaeolithic times and is even mentioned in some of Japan's earliest books such as the *Nihon shoki* (*The Chronicles of Japan*). Nevertheless, *irezumi*, Japan's traditional and now internationally renowned style of tattoos, really took off in Japan's Edo period when the nation was wrapped up in its own internal affairs.

Tattoo art grew in parallel with the development and popularity of Japanese woodblock printing (*ukiyo-e*). Similar techniques and motifs were used as well as Nara ink, a black soot-based ink that turns greenish blue after being inserted under the skin. Japan was isolated from the West during this period for more than two hundred years when the unique colourful decorative designs of *irezumi*, and its sophisticated techniques developed independently, Galapagos-like, without any material outside influence creating the full-body tattoos, as well as the complex and unusual images that Japanese tattoos are now world famous for.

During this period, rough confident men who worked semi-naked in loincloths, such as firemen and carpenters, proudly wore tattoos as a style of decorative permanent attire. Like many other iconic Japanese cultural exports, including woodblock printing, this craft later received more respect and acknowledgement as an art form outside Japan than from inside the country once Japan had reopened to the world elsewhere. In 1881, the future British monarch Prince George (1865-1936), visited Japan while serving in the British Navy and like many others before him (to his mother's great disapproval) got a Japanese tattoo. The blue and red dragon on his forearm was never seen in public, but he did reportedly show it to the Meiji Emperor (1852-1912).

Celebrity Endorsements

Endorsements can come in many forms: conscious and deliberate, paid and placed, and serendipitous. Just like celebrity endorsements such as Elizabeth Taylor (1932-2011) touting Colgate-Palmolive shampoo or the Japanese author Shusaku Endo (1923-1996) plugging Nescafé Gold Blend on Japanese television or a Royal Warrant of today, high profile individuals with tattoos have also helped increased awareness and the prestige of Japanese tattoos massively outside Japan. Despite this, they were still technically illegal in Japan, having been prohibited in 1872, when the sixteen-year-old prince got inked. The decision to prohibit them reflected a Japan that was desperately trying to clean up its act so it could take its place in the world amongst the ranks of leading 'civilised' nations.

Ukiyo-e, manga, anime and karaoke all had mass-market appeal and were very popular in Japan before foreign appreciation and recognition led the country's intellectuals, elite and government to embrace them as something that the nation should be proud of and promote abroad. This isn't the case with *irezumi, horimono* (another Japanese word used to describe tattoos), and *tatou*, a loanword that is used to describe Western-style tattoos in Japanese.

The nation still hasn't come to accept tattoos quite as readily as many other countries have. Government officials have tried to ban workers from having them; gyms, spas, and swimming pools prohibit people with them or insist on them being concealed; and the Japanese Tourist Agency is struggling with policy and rules related to the growing number of tattooed tourists visiting the country. Japan is not, however, unique in regards to this distaste. Judaism, for example, officially prohibits Jews from getting a tattoo, and this community has indelible dark memories of tattoo history, due to the involuntary ones from the Holocaust. This aversion to engraving the skin, which rabbis consider as hubris and an unlawful manipulation, is so strong that many worry that having a marked body will stop them from being buried later in an orthodox Jewish cemetery. The evolution of the art of the tattoo in Japan is not straightforward either and is now, like many Japanese sub-culture phenomena, a topic of academic study.

Their association with penal establishments, prohibition, gangsters, antisocial behaviour, criminality, the underclass, and certain lower-class professions, has meant that ever since the Edo period, tattoos have mostly been hidden from public view. They have been treated like invisible kimono underwear and only revealed when it is appropriate and to create maximum impact.

Impulse-driven casual tattooing is still unusual in Japan, as is marking one's body to commemorate, often when drunk, shared social events. Appointments are required and a proper traditional Japanese tattoo will be seen as a major endeavour, as well as a time consuming and significant financial investment. One that is carried out with serious intent, and rarely on a whim. A full-body tattoo can take years and cost tens of thousands of pounds. They can be life changing either intentionally or unintentionally.

A Narrative Device

Tat-lit doesn't exist yet as an international recognised publishing genre, but the popularity and fascination with tattoos is not new. Even Winston Churchill

(1874-1965) had one. Tattoos have, of course, featured prominently in many book genres; spanning adventure, crime, science fiction and mystery. Some of the world's leading international authors and most famous books have used tattoos, or tattooed individuals as important narrative devices.

These include *Moby-Dick* (1851) by Herman Melville (1819-1891), *Treasure Island* (1883) by Robert Louis Stevenson (1850-1894), *The Red-Headed League* (1891) by Arthur Conan Doyle (1859-1930), *The Illustrated Man* (1951) by Ray Bradbury (1920-2012), *Skin* (1953) by Roald Dahl (1916-1990), and *Papillon* (1969) by Henri Charriere (1906-1973) to name just a few. This huge canvas of storytelling, all expertly drawn, reflect the motifs versatility.

Roald Dahl's short story is a brilliant example. Set in Paris, a man has a picture of a beautiful woman painted on his back by a famous artist and then tattooed for preservation. Many years later it is auctioned off in an art gallery for a significant sum with much debate on how the 'human canvas' can be managed and exhibited. The story's plot twists and black humour are even more macabre when you consider that there are actually museums in Japan with collections of persevered human tattooed skins.[132]

These days the 'Human Work of Art' is an established cultural category.[133] Museums outside Japan are also now recognising traditional Japanese tattoos for their artistic value and are arranging installations and exhibitions, albeit rather differently. The travelling international exhibition *Perseverance: Japanese Tattoo Tradition in a Modern World* is one such show.[134] Specialist websites where tattoo ideas and templates can be accessed, photo-sharing apps and reality television programmes such as *Miami Ink*, *LA Ink*, *Ink Master*, *America's Worst Tattoos* and Britain's *Tattoo Fixers*, have exposed the world of tattooing to a mass-market helping to amplify interest and demand.

The morphing of Japanese anime and manga imagery with traditional Japanese tattoo techniques and designs has broadened appeal and created new terms such as *otattoos* (otaku-tattoos/geek-tatts). Specialist tattoo travel firms now arrange trips to Japan for individuals that wish to copy Prince George and decorate their bodies with Japanese art either modern or traditional.

Japanese authors and publishers can't ignore them either, especially as Junichiro Tanizaki (1886-1965), one of Japan's best and most highly respected modern authors came to fame with a debut novella titled *The Tattooer* (1910)—also known as *Shisei*—which he wrote at the age of 24 In the story, set in the 1840s, a master tattoo artist, Seikichi, obsessed with finding the perfect women to tattoo, drugs a young woman and tattoos a black spider onto her back.

"To give you beauty I have emptied my whole soul into this tattoo," he mumbled. "From now, there is not a single woman in Japan that will rival you! Never again shall you know fear. All men, all men shall be your victims…"

The decorative spider appears to come to life, subsequently transforming the female protagonist into a demonic femme fatale. It ploughs the now often-trod furrow of men being consumed by awakened female passion, a trope which perhaps reflects the perpetual social anxiety such desires continue to instil in some. Like much of Japan's best creative writing, Tanizaki's novella has been successfully adapted for film.

Anthropologists, socialists and Japanologists have different views on why people get tattoos. Social branding, shared peer-experiences, and fashion are widely thought to be behind most people's decisions. The *Guinness Book of World Records* lists the oldest man getting his first tattoo as a 104-year-old British man who had his nickname and date of birth tattooed—Jake 6.4.1912—on his birthday to raise money for charity with his grandson. It would no doubt have been a special form of bonding and experience sharing. Nevertheless, tattoos as simple fashion statements or designer accessories to be displayed, are a relatively new concept in Japan.

Talismanic Induction

Traditionally, in Japan, tattoos have generally been done as some form of initiation and induction, for communal membership, for protection, as a talisman or to affect transformation. The bestselling American author Dan Brown understands the narrative and consequences tattoos can have when he writes in *The Lost Symbol*, "the act of tattooing one's skin was a transformative declaration of power, an announcement to the world: *I am in control of my own flesh*." Nevertheless, everyone has his or her own particular reason. The American actor, Johnny Depp is on record as saying, "My body is my journal, and my tattoos are my story."

Despite Japan's ambivalent attitude towards tattoos, Japanese authors are conscious of how the motif has been used successfully in the past. Some decorate their stories and narratives with them. They are used as plot devices to help solve crimes, to develop and describe marginalised characters and depict changing power dynamics in relationships. They are seen as a microcosm from which to view and describe Japan and its social ills as well as to depict different types of characters through their individual choice of tattoo, be it *irezumi*, *tatou*, full-body or any other.

Two Japanese novels that follow the tattoo crime fiction tradition that Conan Doyle helped establish are *Kurotokage* (*The Black Lizard and the Beast in the Shadows*), published in 1934, by Edogawa Ranpo (1894-1965), an important pioneer of crime fiction in Japan and *Shisei satsujin jiken* (*The Tattoo Murder Case*) by Akimitsu Takagi (1920-1995) published in 1948. Interestingly, one of Japan's best known authors and still one of Japan's most controversial, Yukio Mishima (1925-1970), had a cameo role in the 1968 film adaptation of *The Black Lizard*, a dark, perverse film with a few echoes of Dahl that features a master thief with a lizard tattoo on her shoulder who is a collector of jewels and bodies.

The Tattoo Murder Case, Takagi's debut novel, a locked-room mystery with severed body parts and a missing beautiful full-body tattooed torso, introduces the reader to the post-Second World War world of Japanese tattoo art, including the Edo Tattoo Society, within the context of a gripping, unfathomable murder mystery.

> LET'S CELEBRATE The Japanese art tattoo! read the crudely mimeographed flyer, under a blurry photograph of a glowering, muscular man covered from shaven head to foot with tattoos of exotic sea creatures in a matrix of stylized Hokusai-style waves. The fine print gave the date and time for the first post-war meeting of the Edo Tattoo Society, and solicited entrants for a tattoo contest. Akimitsu Takagi, *Shisei satsujin jiken* (*The Tattoo Murder Case*).

If one were curiously inclined and have sufficient time, an internet search for *tattoo* and *Mishima* will not only bring up images of permanent and temporary tattoos that pay homage to this notorious author and images of his face but, if you look long enough, you may find a forearm with an uncredited English translation of Mishima's so-called death poem carved into it: "A small night storm blows / Saying 'falling is the essence of a flower' / Preceding those who hesitate." It is adorned with a few pink cherry blossoms to provide a decorative background to the black ink.

Seishi Yokomizo (1902-1981) another highly successful author of detective novels and historical fiction, who like Edogawa, has a literary prize named after him, also uses tattoos as a narrative device in his books. Contemporary examples of Japanese tat-lit include Shu Fujisawa's (b. 1959) novel *Shisei* (*The Tattooer*), which interestingly has the same title as Tanikazi's novel and shares some themes. However, in Fujisawa's novel the act of being tattooed is initiated by the female recipient in a deliberate conscious decision that she hopes will be both transformational and protective.

Akame shijuyataki shinju misui (*The Paradise Bird Tattoo (or, Attempted Double-Suicide)*) by Chokitsu Kurumatani (1945-2015) is another example. It depicts the polarised extremes of boredom and the grittiness of life on the margins of Japanese society in 1970s Osaka. A more recent, award-winning, example is Hitomi Kanehara's (b. 1983) bestselling debut novel *Hebi ni piasu* (*Snakes and Earrings*), which describes a possessive murderous relationship with a tattoo artist. It would thus seem that for some scribes in Japan wanting to generate their own permanent personal story as an author, embedding a tattoo in the narrative of their debut work is a rather good place to start.

Non-Japanese authors, combining Asiatic themes with tattoos, have also picked up on the possibilities creating a curious circularity of literary influences. *The Concubine's Tattoo* by Laura Joh Rowland, published in 1998, and the Booker Prize short-listed title: *The Garden of Evening Mist* by Twan Eng, published in 2012, being just two examples. The latter manages to combine a serene Japanese garden in Malaysia, a traditional Japanese tattoo, failing memory, looted treasure and a Japanese wartime internment camp in one book.

Nick Bradley is yet another recent interesting example. In his case he even manages to blend in an extra powerful Japanese literary motif, the cat, in his debut work *The Cat and The City*. His novel of 15 seemingly disparate narrative threads woven together into a vivid picture representing contemporary Tokyo commences with a chapter titled "Tattoo". This sets the structure for this fragmented tale, with a high-school girl getting a map (based on one copied from Alphabet's consumer application Google Maps) of the Japanese capital, with a small cat within it, tattooed on her back creating an illustrated contemporary study of the Japanese metropolis through candescent contrasts.

The influence of Japanese Zen Buddhism is, of course, widely acknowledged, and as with other pursuits and Japanese crafts some like to draw parallels between Zen and tattoos. There is no doubt Zen's influence can appear in strange and diverse places. Apple's Steve Jobs (1955-2011), for example, was a fan and is said to have been impressed with Zen's simplicity, clarity and impact on Japanese design. Echoes of this interest can be observed not just in Apple's products but also in its approach to marketing and events and, of course, in Apple Stores, designed with similar objectives to traditional rooms for Japanese tea ceremonies, part of Zen ritual, to increase desire, with stripped back architecture, clever use of light, controlled turning and touching of fine products, and the unboxing of consumables and collectables. Zen insights and Zen as a way of life that can be blended with a love of nature have penetrated much of Japanese culture and arts. But does this extend to tattoo parlours? Despite the parallels that many often feel compelled to sketch, perhaps contrasting, as opposed to linking or directly associating, Zen and tattoos might actually be the better avenue of discovery and study, even if conducted incompletely.

The power of incompleteness, the idea that truth can only be reached through the comprehension of opposites, contrasts or rival concepts, good and evil, black or white, sweet and sour, for instance, are critical Zen concepts. Good workmanship spanning the art of selecting and understanding utensils and materials, be they inks, metals, types or paper, urns for tea, needles or machine tools, in addition to immense care and precision, and the importance of the clever reveal, are also all-important elements of Zen and its patterns for life.

Satori, awakening, as opposed to enlightenment, *nirvana*, thought to be found through practice, and especially meditation, is Zen's main quest. It stills the mind and produces a state of serenity and peace for both body and mind. Simplicity, however, always trumps the decorative. These and other such Zen-features, unlike tattoos, can easily be detected on stage at Apple product launches, even if Apple does not prohibit its staff from having tattoos. They can also be found of course in traditional Japanese tea ceremonies, where one would expect to find them, which also take place in specially constructed locales and involve a lot of anticipation and waiting.

Traditional Japanese tattoos often include images of animals, mystical creatures, demons and Buddhist deities, but unlike Japan's famous serene Zen gardens and temples, they do not typically exude simple tranquil and stripped back understated beauty. Some wearers of tattoos do, however, leave them hidden, exploiting the art of concealing beauty so powerful that one dare not reveal it. Instead they allow them to be discovered with the type of smile of philosophy that a master of a Japanese tea ceremony would surely understand. But gaudy vulgarity and fast fashion, not delicate beauty, seem more the order of the day, with most wearing their tattoos as visible badges of skin-deep painted prestige.

That said, modern Japanese tattoos still have their own form of sophistication, fascinating pedigree and also have global reach and impact. In the case of full-body tattoos they can also remain incomplete for long periods until their needlework is concluded. They often also boost artificially confidence, enhancing a certain type of self-expression. For many, nonetheless, they seem to share little in an aesthetic or philosophical sense with Zen.

Nevertheless, some are still determined to make the link and compare *horishi*, Japanese tattooers, and their craft to that of Zen masters. They argue that getting a tattoo in Japan is a Zen-like transformational experience that encompasses dedication, pain management, repetition, ritual, routine, silence, controlled breathing and concentration on nothingness, followed by an awakening of sorts. In sharp contrast, outside Japan having the Japanese character depicting the word Zen or the *enso* symbol associated with it (an incomplete circle) tattooed onto one's body is considered trendy. It can be done quickly on the spur of the moment, but probably brings only fleeting enlightenment.

> For thirty minutes Kenzo watched in fascination, hardly daring to take a breath. Kinue went through this same process, he thought, and his breathing quickened as he pictured his lover squirming in agony under the invasive needles. Kenzo couldn't help thinking that it was wasteful to expend so much effort on decorating one's mortal skin, but at the same time he felt there was something sublime and even awe-inspiring about a woman who would voluntarily endure so much pain. Akimitsu Takagi, *Shisei satsujin jiken (The Tattoo Murder Case)*.

The book, *Zen and the Art of Archery* (1948), by the German philosopher Eugene Herrigel (1884-1955), is often said to have introduced the concept of Zen into continental Europe's zeitgeist. There were, however, books before it such as *Zen in English Literature and Oriental Classics* by R.H. Blyth (1898-1964), a British Japanologist and poet, published in 1942. Nonetheless, its publication triggered hundreds of books with similar titles including the 1970s classic *Zen and the Art of Motorcycle Maintenance*. In California, where Jobs grew up and set up Apple in 1977 with Steve Wozniak in his parents' garage, it was a Zen Temple initially established in an old Synagogue near the Golden Gate Bridge that encouraged the propagation of Zen Buddhism for his generation in sixties and seventies California. This was built on interest in Zen generated by the Beat Generation, with its famous haiku writing poets such as Gary Synder (b. 1930) who hails from San Francisco, that predates this.

The teachings of Shunryu Suzuki (1905-1971), the temple's Soto Zen monk published in a book *Zen Mind, Beginner's Mind* in 1970, has also played a major role in increasing interest in Zen Buddhism to trend-setting Californians and its mighty entrepreneurs, in addition to other influential monks who have followed in Suzuki's wake. Their age was one with a growing fascination in Japan and pioneering individuals in California developing what one might call a brand-new creative operating language: a new alphabet, not a typical slick American sans-serif font used for packaging and branding, but an exciting original script beginning with the letter *a*, for Apple, and ending with the letter *z*, for Zen. A blended set of approaches that imprinted a new vibe on business and culture on the cutting-edge. Japanese culture has played an important contributory role in this.

Simplicity, and the power of clear thinking, is very hard to achieve in a society overflowing with noise; opinions; and hyperactive, opinionated self-promoting individuals but when it can be achieved its effects and influence can be hugely significant. Jobs we known attended Suzuki's lectures and was mentored by one of his team, Kobun Otogawa (1938-2002), who presided over Jobs's marriage ceremony. Emptying your cup of speculation and opinion, letting go of your mind is, often said to be, one of the first steps in Zen. According to the monk Suzuki, the real secret of the arts is "always be a beginner." The so-called beginner's mindset, *shoshin*.

Observing reality, considering the facts before expressing opinions, recalling why you started and thinking from first principles, can be very powerful and enlightening approaches, but elusive ones. When society expects and educates everyone to express a confident opinion, project an identity of self, look sophisticated and sound articulate, while promoting and selling themselves alongside their ideas. Overconfident underachievers, one might say, and noisy opining, as opposed to quiet civility and observant modest under confident overachieving are the qualities of our age. Opinions rarely peacefully follow observations and the facts, or words and deeds, as they should.

Factors that make it even more perplexing, when one tries to consider the facts surrounding how an incomplete circle, the sacred *enso* symbol or the Japanese lettering for Zen became a must-have tattoo and a sign of sophistication for some. It does look like a low risk, low cost, quick beginner's tattoo. It is very easy to be drawn into the world of tattoos and perhaps the *enso* symbol is simply a non-threatening slightly easier to remove or conceal appetiser, a single nervous first bite into the fruits of tattoos. Tattoos can be fascinating, compelling and highly addictive as well as wonderful plot motifs. They most certainly tell stories. Unfortunately, many people end up regretting getting tattooed on an impulse. They are much harder to discard than a stale or hackneyed California Roll. So before going down the path of getting one, careful consideration is recommended.

One may, in the first instance, prefer to pick up one of the many brilliant Japanese novels where tattoos are featured. Even if it is a short tale that only features a tattoo in passing to conceal and function as a clever incomplete metaphor, such as the one designed to cover a bald spot in Ryunosuke Akutagawa's (1892-1927) short story "Hina" ("The Dolls"). It is certainly a low-risk way to get under the skin of Japan and most readers won't have any regrets.

Christian Stories of Japan

The Holy Grail, the cup of Christ, is a motif that features in the lore of King Arthur, Hollywood movies and bestselling novels. The word grail comes from the Old French word *graal* and Old Catalan and means: "a cup or bowl made of earth, wood or metal". Lord Tennyson (1809-1892), Dan Brown and many others have written stories about the quest to find this mythical goblet. The Grail features in at least one opera by Wagner, as well as cropping up regularly in the visual arts, including the cinema. *Indiana Jones and the Last Crusade* and *Monty Python and The Holy Grail* being just two memorable examples.

There can be little doubt that Christ and the narrative of Christianity have had a direct and indirect impact on Japanese literature and culture, as well as most Western creative arts and societies. But have authors and all the famous fictional heroes been searching in the wrong country for the Holy Grail? Might the Holy Grail actually look much more like a traditional Japanese bowl, such as the *donburi*, a deep and thick set bowl larger than a typical rice bowl, than the one depicted in films? Might it, in fact, be located somewhere in Japan?

In 2015, the British Press excitedly reported that the Nanteos Cup, believed by some to be Christ's chalice, made from wood from the True Cross, had been found and returned to its rightful owner after a robbery.[135] The cup, which is said to have healing powers, had apparently been stolen while loaned to a sick women to aid her recovery. This cup, though wooden, looks remarkably like a *donburi*. Nevertheless, it would still seem extremely unlikely that Christ's *donburi*, whatever that in fact might be, could have found its way to Japan.

Since medieval times, the cup used at the Last Supper is considered by many to reside at the Spanish Cathedral of Valencia. Nonetheless, the answer to what may seem like an odd question really depends on whether you take a literal or metaphorical interpretation of the meaning and function of the Holy Grail. Religious motifs, narratives and symbols can move in rather mysterious ways.

After all, according to some scholars, Japan had a Christian century between 1549-1650.[136] This century started with the arrival of Jesuit missionaries in Japan, hundreds of years after the Crusades (1095-1291), the foreign narrative generating adventures designed to 'recover' Jerusalem and its surrounding areas from Islamic Rule.

Japan's Christian century came much later and was closer in time to the end of the *Reconquista* in the Iberia Peninsula, another long dramatic period in its case of nationalistic restoration cantered on Christianity that stretched into the 1490s, and the Spanish Inquisition (1478-1834), which led to Muslims and Jews being required to convert to Catholicism. These determined travelling Jesuits, from this part of the world, didn't just carry new ideas and religious doctrines with them on their challenging quest to bring the gospel to Japan.

The Hidden Faithful

One of the first encounters with a Jesuit priest was described as follows in an early 17th century Japanese book:

> Although man-shaped, the Padre is undistinguishable from demons and monsters. The nose is so big it looks like a smothered conch shell glued to the centre of the face... He shaves the top of his head so that the scalp is exposed as much as could be covered by a small cup. His words are like nothing ever heard, and his voice resembles an owl's hooting. Everyone says his appearance was stranger than that of a mountain spirit.[137]

Being Christian in Japan was from the start by no means an easy existence in the Christian century or the centuries that followed.

Ryunosuke Akutagawa (1892-1927), the prolific master of short stories, describes a proselytising priest in action in his incomplete tale "Jashumon" ("Heresy"), written in 1918, as follows:

> At this time a grotesque priest—the like of whom had never before been seen—appeared in the Capital preaching the Mary Religion. As he was much talked about, there will be some of you who did come to hear him. He was compared with the *tengu* which are depicted in books and come from the land of Shintan (China), or with the devil that haunted the palace of one of the royal princesses.

Japanese Christians were often tortured and persecuted for their faith in much the same way as the Marrano Jews of the Iberian Peninsula were during and after the

Reconquista. Like these Jews, these Christians often for long periods were forced to practise their religion in secret leading to them being given the moniker *Kakure Kirishitan, Hidden Christians*. They often used disguised ritual objects and symbols to practise their imported religion secretly without drawing attention to themselves. Something that, like the Holy Grail, has given them a mysterious aura and encouraged some rather fascinating Japanese storytelling. Fictional adventure stories about these periods, in which Christians in Japan are described as the Hidden, feature, for example, in an international best-selling young adult book series, *The Tales of the Otori*, by the British author Lian Hearn, the first of which has the title: *Across the Nightingale Floor*, as well as, of course, many monumental works by numerous Japanese storytellers.

The depiction in *Japan and The Japanese Illustrated* in 1874 of the tragic plight of many Christians, alongside an illustration, demonstrates how harsh conditions really were at times. The illustration in the publication presents two people watching over an individual lying motionless on a mat with a pile of wood beneath them, one crouching fanning flames and other holding wood looking down towards the prostrate person on the mat who is being cremated, with the following caption:

> The Christians… "are assigned a miserable crowded quarter" in the city, "like the ghetto of the… Jews" in the "Middle Ages"… "is virtually a prison." "The police keep watch over them until they have drawn their last breath, and it is their business to remove the corpses, and dispose of them somehow,—no one knows where or how; but so that the name of"… "crucified one shall not be pronounced over their ashes."

Over a six-decade period after the Jesuits arrived in 1549 an estimated 300,000 people were converted to Christianity and an estimated 4,000 died due to their imported un-Japanese beliefs.[138] Many suffered terribly—men, women, children, often from poorer backgrounds—from the result of the aggressive "attempt by the Christian Church to spread the Gospel in the Orient" and the Church's "determination" to proceed with this policy despite its tragic humanitarian costs.[139] That said, initially the exotic Portuguese and Spaniards and their religious beliefs, sparked curiosity and excitement amongst Japanese of all classes.

According to the Japanese Agency for Culture, during this period, "Christianity's foreignness became one of its greatest assets. People turned to Christianity precisely because it represented something new."[140] Often those who accepted the religion as opposed to simply toying with it mostly, but not exclusively, came to this new religion as marginalised social outsiders and remained thus, at the bottom of society's hierarchical heap. Seeking alternatives in life through switching to a new religion, albeit a foreign one, reflects something about the spiritually adventurous individuals making the choice, as well as the religion itself. This is still very much the case in modern day Japan where many are religiously apathetic, and an increasing number of people are attracted to new modern alterative spiritual options.

The proselytising priests brought many things with them to Japan, not just biblical tales. These included, for instance, Western-style striking mechanical clocks and a printing press. This press was the first in Japan to use movable type, which was brought from Rome to Amakusa in Japan.[141] Unlike Japan's first generation of commercial publishers, who focused on demand and existing, often somewhat racy, Japanese interests, the priests operated their press, the use of which preceded domestic commercial publishing, to print religious texts locally that they hoped would create new spiritual perspectives, as opposed to simply meet existing primal tastes.

Following the arrival of the Jesuit missionary Francis Xavier (1506-1552) in July 1549 in Kagoshima, for a few decades from the early 1590s until their religion was banned, these priests generally printed books to assist them in helping the spread of Christianity in Japan. Books with an equal entitlement, they believed, to speak for all classes of men, high and low, showing that all are equal, even within Japan's seemingly immutable inherited human hierarchies with the Warlords and Emperors at their pinnacles. However, like any sensible publisher building a list of publications, they also published some secular works and dictionaries, including *Aesop's Fables* and an abridged edition of the important Japanese classic *Tales of Heike, Heike monogatari*.

Xavier himself stayed in Japan for just over two years, a shorter period than the five years that the fictional Portuguese traveller who recounted Sir Thomas More's (1478-1535) tale of *Utopia* spent in that mysterious island nation, or the length of time that some of Japan's most famous modern writers, such as Ogai Mori (1862-1922), spent studying overseas. Nevertheless, it was still a significant proportion of Xavier's life span, and the impact was considerable.

New Types of Publishing History

Despite the press growing into one of the largest of its kind worldwide, many of the books produced by the Jesuit Mission Press, known as *Kirishitan-ban*, were subsequently burnt or destroyed. These were acts of cultural destruction that, as the German-Jewish poet, a distant relative and friend of Karl Marx (1818-1883),

Heinrich Heine (1797-1856) famously wrote, are sadly so often a precursor to the burning and murdering of people. Remarkably, Heine, considered a degenerate by the Nazis, issued this warning in a play he set in 1492 in Muslim Granada, during the *Reconquista* and Granada's final year as Western Europe's last independent Muslim state. In this case it was the Christians doing the book burning, destroying the Koran, as opposed to having their own carefully printed books incinerated. The Nazis also famously made bonfires out of books they didn't approve of before subsequently incinerating millions of people. Sadly, the banning and burning of books continues unabated. What Marx himself, famous for his own dictum and observation that religion is "the opium of the people" alongside his political philosophy, that has inspired much revolutionary change and so-called collectivism, would have made of all this is a fascinating question to ponder.

Oddly, in Meiji Japan (1868-1912), centuries later, when Japan was opening up fully to the West and jettisoning some of its traditional approaches and attitudes, and Christianity was allowed to enter Japan again Marxism arrived alongside it, becoming reasonably popular. This was in reaction to the moral blankness and spiritual emptiness that modernisation caused for some. At the time, Marxism, mostly amongst the educated elite class, became a practical social framework that in 1900s filled the void that these abrupt changes brought. Some of the educated elite embraced Marxism like a religion with the zeal of a new convert. This, like Christianity before, which ended up getting banned, was considered dangerous by the authorities at the time.

After the 17th century edict against Christianity in Japan, however, there were some books that survived. A copy of one of these now rare *Kirishitan-ban* books, the romanised Latin-script Japanese language *Santos no gosagyo no uchi nukigaki (a Compendium of the Acts of the Saints)*, luckily survives in Oxford University's Bodleian Japanese Library. Interestingly, this book arrived at the library in 1659 as part of the English polymath and scholar of amongst many things Jewish law, John Selden's (1584-1654) collection. It is amazing that this 1591 book was actually printed in Japan using moveable type two years before the very first Japanese book was printed from moveable type, making it not just a significant milestone in religious publishing, but also in Japan's publishing history, as well as a very useful source for cross-cultural studies.

For those interested, a digital copy can be accessed online through the library's website. The library describes its digital copy as "published by the Jesuit mission at the Kazusa Seminary in Shimabara-shi. The text of the Acts of the Saints is taken from an abridgment of the Flos sanctorum and other sources, and translated by two Japanese Jesuits, Brother Paulo Yoho and his son, Brother Vincent Hoin."

Originally this was thought to be the only existing copy but recently a second copy has been found in the Marciana Library in Venice.

The first Japanese, as opposed to translated book, printed in Japan using movable type, in 1593, was also a religious text: the *Kobun kokyo (Classic of Filial Piety)*.[142] At the time of its printing, Japan already had a long history of publishing but moveable type printing was not yet part of this particular Japanese narrative. Japan's oldest book is believed to have been published in 615, and the nation's oldest surviving book that includes a publication date, owned by the Ishiyama-dera a temple in Shiga Prefecture, is inscribed with the date 1052 in red ink. Intriguingly, this is the very same temple where allegedly under moonlight the opening few pages of the world's first novel, *Genji monogatari (The Tale of Genji)*, were written with the refined but racy brush strokes of an aristocratic Japanese lady-in-waiting, Shikibu Murasaki (circa 978-1014).

Nevertheless, following the Japanese invasion of Korea (1592-1598) by the warlord Hideyoshi Toyotomi (1537-1598), a copper movable type printing press was brought back to Japan from Korea and presented to the emperor. Toyotomi unified a feuding nation and preceded Ieyasu Tokugawa (1543-1616), the first shogun of the Tokugawa Shogunate and instigator of Japan's long and isolated Edo period (1603-1868). After unification, Toyotomi had run out of domains in Japan to conquer and probably good advisors too, and like many authoritarian leaders with limited options who fall into the trap of hubris when their power grows more concentrated, he looked abroad, in his case to Korea, launching a military campaign that in hindsight looks reckless and illogical. This is how this looted technology came to Japan.

Wars have a tendency not to trace the chosen path by those who launch them and in this regards this foreign adventure was no exception. Toyotomi overextended himself, with long supply lines, leading to a reversal after initial military success and a subsequent stalemate in Korea. This was mostly due to China's assistance through the provision of canons, a type of artillery that the Japanese invaders lacked, and highly motivated local resistance. This unnecessary futile war left Japan and Toyotomi's clan depleted and discredited. An estimated 60,000 to 100,000 Japanese perished in this foreign war and thousands of Koreans. This helped Tokugawa. Following Toyotomi's death age 62 from natural causes and the subsequent battle at Sekigahara in 1600, Tokugawa was able to establish a brand-new feudal regime and system of governance led by him and his clan, and not Toyotomi's anointed successor his young son, Hideyori Toyotomi (1593-1615). Bad decision-making can create sudden turns in history that can allow society to rearrange in a different order, components that one might have previously considered destined never to change.

Before the decisive Sekigahara battle Japanese forces in Korea were ordered home in 1598 on Toyotomi's death by the Council of Five Elders, a group of powerful Japanese warlords, which included Tokugawa, a type of advisory national security committee that was set up shortly before Toyotomi's death. This was the culmination of events that subsequently facilitated the end of Japan's long brutal Warring States period (1467-1615), an end to all similar foreign adventures, as well as the expulsion of Catholics, or as Akutagawa called it the 'Mary Religion', from Japan in 1614. It ushered in an armed but peaceful new order of local cultural formalisation and consolidation that lasted for centuries.

Sadly, the Japanese invaders didn't just bring back a printing press from Korea: they brought back around 38,000 severed noses from the Korean soldiers they killed instead of the usual heads used as the required proof for payment. These noses are still enshrined in a monument in Kyoto. Toyotomi's warriors also brought back with them skilled potters and other craftsmen, as well as scholars of Confucianism and its associated systems of governance. All of which played an important role in Japan's subsequent development. The Emperor ordered that copies of the Confucian treatise on obedience, a text very distinct from the type of saintly martyrdom depicted in the *Santos no gosagyo no uchi nukigaki*, be printed using the looted machine.[143]

About four years later in 1597, a Japanese version of the machine was developed using wooden as opposed to metal type. This Japanese version of the Korean machine was used to produce a new print edition of the *Nihon shoki (The Chronicles of Japan)* Japan's second oldest history book written in around 720. These chronicles contain within its 30 volumes mythical accounts and ancient stories including origin tales of how Japan was created, not in seven days by a single deity but by primal gods that created Japan, and fixed her in its rightful place, from a floating bridge of heaven. Following its printing, hundreds of other books were printed using the new machine.

The arrival of this new printing technology became one of the catalysts, alongside encouragement from the newly formed Tokugawa leadership, for the development of commercial publishing in Japan a decade or so later. Its arrival helped book production evolve and transform, whether it be the transcription of religious and historical texts or the publication of commercial storytelling. Interestingly, most commercial publishers actually reverted to traditional block printing methods and did not use the new movable type technologies as the local publishing market developed and expanded.

Japanese publishers from around this time have fared much better than their Jesuit Mission Press colleagues, despite their earlier use of movable type. Hozokan, a Kyoto based Buddhist publisher can trace its roots back to 1602 and is considered to be Japan's oldest publisher. It publishes books on Buddhism, targeting both specialists and general readers. To put this in historical context, Johannes Gutenberg (1400-1468) invented his metal movable type press in 1450 almost 150 years before the first movable type technology arrived in Japan. While Cambridge University Press, which claims to be the oldest university press in the world, was founded in 1543 after King Henry VIII granted letters patent. More's *Utopia*, describing an ideal island state, was published in Latin in England in 1516. Korea and China, however, both had this type of printing technology long before Europe or Japan.

Japan's Christian century ended abruptly with the last Christian uprising before this foreign religion was officially prohibited in 1614. Catholicism was considered a major risk to the new social and military order, which lead to the last phase of the Christian century being a clandestine one. The Dutch and Chinese, who unlike the Portuguese and Spanish were considered non-religious people, were, however, allowed to trade with the government and its agents in a limited, managed way. This turned Christians into society's chief bogeymen, as some countries today seem to be doing with Muslims. But some believers, who had to choose between martyrdom, obedience, *filial piety* or concealment, have continued the rituals, chants and prayers from those early days, handed down orally in secret, right up to the present day often blending their beliefs with local Buddhist and Shinto practices.

Rituals create a reality, which would be nothing without them, with or without mythical goblets, grails and bowls. These Hidden Christians often used traditional folklore substitutes to replace, for example, statues of the Virgin Mary cradling baby Jesus. Some used a traditional Japanese *Yama-Uba*, a special type of mountain crone, holding and nurturing *Kintaro*, the legendary Japanese folk hero—the Golden Boy with super-human strength—in place of the *Mother of God*, as well as encoded pictographs, and symbolic terminology that combined Latin, Portuguese and Japanese. This was done in a not a totally dissimilar manner to how some Jewish communities, originally from the Iberian Peninsula, in London, combine Spanish, Portuguese, Ladino, English and Hebrew in prayers and the terminology used for officiating over their community practices.

Mixing, fusing and segmenting spiritual and ritual practices are a trend that continues in Japan. This is probably something easier to achieve and justify in a nation not culturally grounded in monotheism, where no faith has managed to achieve a monopoly on religious beliefs. Like a modern democratic nation believers are free to select their leaders in a type of coalition, in their case divine ones, and don't live in a spiritual dictatorship. Newcomers to Japan are often perplexed by the symbiotic relationships some religions seem to have in Japan and the pick-and-mix attitudes of many Japanese people in terms of their practices, something that is often unimaginable in the nations they have arrived from. Some contemporary economists might even judge this as a healthy competitive spiritual marketplace, with clever behavioural and benefit-associated segmentations of offerings.

Nevertheless, despite the nation having around 150,000 temples and shrines, many with small connected spiritual landscapes and gardens, which people visit regularly, surveys show that religion doesn't play a significant role in people's lives. However, polls and how they frame questions can often be misleading, and as we all know organised religion and seasonal spiritual ritual are distinct for many, as are tourist visits to notable places of religious architectural importance. Much of this is an amalgamation of myth and celebration, and many have an aversion to any form of state-sponsored religiosity.

In many villages and small towns Shinto shrines are located on the same street, on the opposite side of the road, from a Buddhist temple, ruling out the common strategy of simply going after a type of monopolistic geographical segmentation or at the very least making it an inefficient approach to increasing congregant market share. If you ask a *kannushi*, a Shinto priest, about this you are likely to be told, with a kindly grin, that it works rather well: we bless the newly born, the newly wed, and new vehicles celebrating the seasons and happy milestones of life while our Buddhist friends across the street look after death and future lives through the cycles of reincarnation. It is a non-exclusive practical service segmentation with one developing a specialism for enhancing our current lives and the other the afterlife, encouraging many, mainly the superstitious as opposed to the devout, to be born Shinto and die Buddhist, or those seeking or requiring a completely different type of salvation to die Christian.

> Our practice is for everyone. Usually when someone believes in a particular religion, his attitude becomes more and more a sharp angle pointing away from himself. But our way is not like this. In our way the point of the sharp angle is always towards ourselves, not away from ourselves. So there is no need to worry about the difference between Buddhism and the religion you may believe in. Shunryu Suzuki (1904-1971), *Zen Mind, Beginner's Mind.*

In Japan, a nation many international journalists today describe as secular, believing in God or converting isn't generally something to be ashamed of, something to hide. Individuals with belief aren't treated with scepticism, disdain or as unusual, no matter their profession. These days some might even argue that this open-minded connected but incomplete approach to spirituality, can lead to sharpened peripheral vision, one that eventually creates a full circle of awareness. What, however, is indisputable is that this has all helped generate some brilliant and extremely powerful books and storytelling.

Japan's Doors to the World

The hidden faithful, these clandestine Christians, were first miraculously 'discovered' in the 1865 around the time of the *Japan and The Japanese Illustrated* article, when Japan had reopened to the world and foreigners and foreign religions. First contact was made by Father Bernard Petitjean (1829-1884) of the Societe des Missions Éstrangèr de Paris. Initially, US Protestant missionaries were allowed entry and safe-passage within Japan after *The Japan-US Treaty of Amity and Commerce* was signed in 1860, following the arrival of Commodore Perry (1794-1858) from America which pushed Japan's markets open again, eventually bringing Japan's Edo-long shogun-run period to an end. Others followed. This was Christianity's second wave in Japan; the first was Catholicism in the 16th century, and the second was mainly Protestantism.

That said, some frame Protestantism and Catholicism as two wholly distinct religions, each with a long, prestigious and complex history in Japan while others simply see both as an imported Western religion. There are nuances regarding this. The distinctions and segmentations are all in the eye of the beholder one might say. It has even been argued that America, the dynamic, entrepreneurial restless nation with its famous frontier spirit we know it as today, was founded on dissent, mostly by Protestant emigrants from Europe seeking religious freedom in the continent's vast open prairies and the endless opportunities they provided for pioneers and the adventurous. While in contrast Japan, a narrow, stretched archipelago riddled with mountains, many volcanic, is a land built on forced consent, obligation and long-standing hierarchies. Like all such hypothesises, many of which are superficially attractive and often overdone, there is often a grain of truth to them, and the arrival of Americans and a second wave of Christianity certainly unleashed a cultural earthquake.

> To a Christian admiral knocking from outside, there responded a brave upright general, a 'reverer of Heaven and lover of mankind' from within. Yet we their biographers do know that despite all the differences on their outward garments, the souls that dwelt in both were of a kindred stuff. Unwittingly they worked in concert, one executing what the other intended. So does the World-Spirit weave his garment of Destiny, underneath the vision of purblind mortals, yet wonderment to the eye of the thoughtful historian.

So writes Kanzo Uchimura (1861-1930), the influential Christian intellectual leader and writer, in his book *Representative Men of Japan (Daihyouteki Nihonjin)*.[144] He continues:

> Thus we see that the Japanese Revolution of 1868, like all healthful and permanent revolutions, has its origin in the righteousness of the God-made necessity. The land that had been obstinately closed against greed, opened itself freely toward justice and equality. Self-sacrifice of the rarest kind, based on a voice, from the uttermost depth of the soul, did fling open its doors to the world.

That all said, Uchimura, alongside many others, actually often struggled to meld Christianity with Japanese history and principles. In his case he called his fusion, an indigenous pacifist Christian movement, *Myukyokaishugi*, the Non-Church Movement.

From the moment of birth, the customs of the place and time into which we are born seem destined to forge our experiences and behaviour. Some manage to break free from these bonds of birth, but it is hardly ever a smooth or easy escape. Some have gone as far as describing this European religion's fit—European in the sense that it arrived on European vessels—with Japan, as like that of a 'badly fitting suit'. Such individuals believe that the warp and the weft of Japanese history, language and culture are too distinct for easy mass assimilation of most foreign religions.

It was during this period when Japan was exposed to more and more Western influences, including new hairstyle, forms of attire, as well as dinners and banquets arranged by non-Japanese families now celebrating Christmas in Japan, that Santa Claus finally made his first documented appearances in the Land of the Rising Sun. His very first appearance in Japan may well have been in the book, *Santa Kuro*, published by Nobuyoshi Shindo (1878-1951) in 1900. A black and white drawing of a familiar, but slim-looking Santa Claus appears on *Santa Kuro's* inside cover.

This early image of the legendary bearer of gifts, as well as the book itself, can be viewed online at the National Diet Library of Japan. The tale of *Santa Kuro* is set in Nagano, Japan, and tells the story of a poor Christian farming family who save a farmer from a distant village. This unknown farmer subsequently saves their Christmas when they fall on hard times by bringing gifts for the family's son and a message of thanks for their belief in God and for their kind act of saving an unknown stranger.

Another later example is a magazine published in 1914, *Kodomo no tomo* (*The Children's Friend*), which includes a more traditional looking Santa Claus, wearing a stretched red and white coat and a red and white hat, is also cited as an early Japanese Santa Claus book. By this time regular sightings of Santa Claus were taking place in Japan. In 1912, for example, a familiar looking Santa Claus, rendered by the pioneering Japanese graphic designer Hisui Sugiura (1876-1965) was even featured in *Mitsukoshi* magazine, the famous department store's in-house magazine.

Kodomo no tomo is, however, often included in pictorial histories of Santa Claus and analysis of the curious evolution and history of Santa Claus and his varied depictions around the world in different cultures. *Kodomo no tomo*'s rendering of Santa Claus is much more Western, with a much less slim Santa, and less Japanese looking than when he first appeared in Japan a decade or more earlier, as a rather svelte-looking *Santa Kuro*.

Today, Santa Claus has iconic status in Japan and the Hidden Christian Sites in the Nagasaki region are registered as a **UNESCO** World Heritage site. If you visit them you will notice symbols including small crucifixes in the guttering of some of the homes in the hamlets where members of the community lived and where some still live today. The region also boasts in a beautiful ocean-view setting a museum dedicated to Shusaku Endo (1923-1996) a subtle but eloquent satirist, who is probably Japan's most famous Catholic author.

Sadly, the aging community of Hidden Christians after so many centuries of endurance in splendid but persecuted isolation is now diminishing and threatened with cultural extinction from the forces of modernity, religious freedom and urbanisation. Nonetheless, tales about them and their descendants continue to be featured in the narratives of some of Japan's best contemporary authors keeping their stories vividly alive. The Bible itself, the ultimate international narrative text with its many scriptured idioms, similes and poetry, both the Old and New Testaments, also continues to provide its own special inspiration. If you open one of these Japanese books you will encounter a glorious and gripping written universe.

An excellent example of this is *Tobosha (The Fugitive)*, by Fuminori Nakamura (b. 1977), a multi-award-winning writer known for his fast-paced narratives that somehow manage to hypnotically combine psychological suspense with literary fiction. The protagonist in Nakamura's 500-page work is a descendent of one of Japan's Hidden Christians. In this well-researched mesmerising tale of faith, war and love, which was initially serialised in several leading newspapers including the *Tokyo Shimbun*, and the *Hokkaido Shimbun* before coming out in book format in 2020, Nakamura takes the reader on a gripping journey. One that spans the periods when Japanese Christians lived in hiding in fear for their lives, through to the Second World War and the present day. Nakamura visited Nagasaki, the Endo Shusaku Literary Museum—located in Sotome where some of Endo's works are set—and other famous Japanese Christian sites to research *The Fugitive*, which his Japanese publisher proudly describes as the "definitive Fuminori Nakamura" novel.

That said, Nakamura has also written about alternatives, cults, as well as Hidden Christians, in his blockbuster novel *Kyodan X* (*Cult X*), for example. When pressed with what the difference is between a religion and a cult, he explains that it is not a simple question of old or new, or one being better than the other, but about whether an individual is treated with respect and their dignity protected. Cults destroy the lives of their believers and adopt control techniques that span verbal abuse to corporal punishment. However, burning books isn't right either and the approach and attitudes of the Crusaders wasn't right. "I don't think God wants war," he explains. In terms of his own religious beliefs, he says he is constantly thinking about whether "God exists or not, and if so, what kind of existence God has. The Old Testament, the New Testament, the Koran, Buddhist scriptures, of course, I am impressed as I read them. And after I have, I keep pondering that question."

Pagan-like Popular Culture

Despite these continuing narratives, social rules are often said to regulate and govern mainstream behaviour in Japan rather than a single monotheistic religion with an associated abstract, or what some locally might even term an arbitrary, arrangement of morals and sins. That is perhaps why modern democratic Japan is still sometimes described as a secular collectivist nation, especially in comparison to America with its deep-seated culture of individualism or what some cynical viewers from afar term as its extreme forms of ego-gratification. Collectivist is a moniker that even the likes of Wang Huning, a highly influential senior Communist Chinese advisor, the so-called advisor-in-chief to several Presidents of China, and a member of China's important Politburo Standing Committee, has used to describe Japan.[145]

This is perhaps an unexpected observation from one of the thought leaders of the world's largest Communist nations, especially when you consider that Communism is defined as "a philosophical, social, political, and economic ideology and movement whose goal is the establishment of a Communist society, namely a socioeconomic order structured upon the ideas of common or social ownership of all property and the absence of social classes, money, and the state." That said, China has been endlessly Sinicising and moulding the meaning of the term Marxism, a good example of this is the 2023 five-part propaganda television series *When Marx Met Confucius* where a Chinese robe-wearing Marx and Confucius dressed in a suit discuss the choices and challenges contemporary China faces. Nonetheless, apparently China still officially plans to fulfil the long-term Marxist vision of developing into a society with no private property, after an initial stage of socialist modernisation.

This collectivist observation arguably is probably relevant even within some of the small marginalised Hidden Christian communities, who needed to work together as clandestine collectives to survive while keeping their beliefs. Nonetheless, the creative communities in Japan, whether utilitarian, collectivist, universalist or not, have long held a fascination with marginalised individuals or groups of all forms that don't seem to play by the same rules be that at the level of the individual or collectively, as they are thought to be freer from the claustrophobic norms of mainstream society and its hierarchies of class.

Today such minority groups include Christians who make up less than one percent of the population, a similar proportion to the Jewish population in the United Kingdom, for example. Despite the contribution that many fabulously talented Christian Japanese writers have made to the literary canon of Japanese storytelling and the powerful inspiration that biblical narratives and the plight of a Christian existence in Japan has provided others, Christianity itself, though performing an important role in the development of modern education in Japan, has in fact played a relatively marginal role in the overall course of Japanese history.

Some believe that guns, initially the smoothbore musket, which arrived in Japan on a Portuguese ship from Macao some six years before the first Jesuits, have played a much larger role in the course of Japanese history. When it comes to heavenly tastes that embody what the nation has truly taken to its heart, a sponge cake, the *kasutera*, Castella Cake, that these sailors also brought, has probably smuggled in, alongside new ingredients, such as sugar, and recipes, one of the most long-lasting and widest influences.

Ever since Japan's very first close encounters with the Christian West in all its manifestations, Dutch, English, Spanish, Portuguese, German, and American, there has, of course, been an impact. Repercussions from this have flowed and continue to flow through the ether of Japanese and world history. This has allowed Japanese popular culture to exploit religious imagery and festivals in a creative pagan-like mass-market manner. This is probably the case for almost all religions with significant presences in Japan perhaps with the one exception of Buddhism (also a foreign faith), which was first adopted in Japan by its aristocrats and leadership during the Heian period (794-1185), and today reflects the more refined sophisticated side of Japan. Alongside this longevity, Buddhism has also had one additional historic advantage that has helped protect its proprietors: regular income derived from funeral fees, memorial rites and tomb management maintenance.

One example of how Japan has subjugated religious ritual and imagery is what Japan has done with Christmas. Ordering a delivery of Kentucky Fried Chicken (KFC) for Christmas dinner is not uncommon and far more popular than people outside Japan might sensibly expect;[146] at some point Colonel Sanders and Santa Claus overlapped into the same character. In addition, Christmas has recently become much more like our Valentine's Day and is Japan's major date night when young people stress about not having a partner. Instead, New Year is the special spiritual time for many families. Birthday rituals, of course, differ significantly by individual, family and country. So it is not really that unexpected that Japan celebrates Jesus's birthday in myriad ways spanning the devout to the commercial and from the superficially trivial to the not at all. Even though it is not an official holiday in Japan, for many Christmas's iconic international status still marks an annual optimistic seasonal turning point.

Many outside Japan might associate the word 'greasy' with KFC when asked, but your author has fond and enjoyable memories of this chicken being served at a series of spring cherry blossom viewing parties attended by many Japanese politicians, journalists and civil servants, arranged by the prime minister's office, during the 1990s, proving that even the familiar and unsavoury can morph into something better when it travels. It is impossible, however, to imagine KFC being similarly served at one of the three annual summer garden parties hosted, for example, during the reign of Queen Elizabeth II (1926-2022) at Buckingham Palace, a similar British equivalent to such gatherings, alongside the tubs of ice cream with their royal warrants and more traditional fare. Ordering a special fluffy sponge cake, the type British people might eat in the summer, decorated with fresh strawberries, which are associated with prosperity in Japan, and fried chicken on Christmas Eve is now a seasonal event looked forward to by many across Japan. Ritual and good, carefully selected unusual foods seem to fit like a hand in a glove, creating lasting traditions of both religious and secular varieties.

That said, the emperor and empress do actually also hold a regular garden party, *En'yukai*, held twice a year in spring and autumn, and reports of KFC being served to their guests have, unlike past events with the prime minister, unsurprisingly, been impossible to identify, and neither have one of the several types of possible *Goyotachi* marks, imperial warrants, been spotted on KFC's multi-sized sharing buckets.

Despite all this, the search for Christianity and associated religious relics are actually drawing people to Japan. Travellers from South Korea (where there is a large Christian community), often as part of a cruise, are being taken on tours of the Christian sites in Nagasaki such as those related to the Twenty-Six Martyrs of Japan killed by order of Toyotomi.

Mercenaries and Missionaries

Endo's masterpiece, *Chinmoku* (*Silence*), is based on their stories. It is a somewhat rare narrative by a Japanese author with a non-Japanese lead character: Father Sebastian Rodriques, based on an actual Italian, who is confronted with the harsh fact there is no glory in martyrdom if the saviour remains conspicuously silent. This 1966 work of historical fiction has now been adapted for film by Martin Scorsese, starring Andrew Garfield, Liam Neeson and Tadanobu Asano, bringing the tale to world attention.

Endo described the work in a 1989 introduction to an English-language translation of another of his books *Foreign Studies* (*Ryugaku*) as follows:

> One of the main themes of *Silence* concerns the question of whether Christianity, a religion that developed largely out of European ways of thinking, can ever take root in Japan. In that novel, one of the characters tells the missionary, Rodriques, 'Japan is a mudswamp.' This is a reflection of my own doubts formed during my stay in France as to whether Western culture (not civilization) can ever truly take root when planted in Japan.

The mudswamp is an often-exploited motif used by Endo to depict Japan's inability to fully entertain Christianity.

Courageous contemporary Japanese authors who have picked up the challenge and have tried to follow Endo's example, writing works or including sections within their books with non-Japanese protagonists or embedded alternative foreign narrative perspectives, regularly find these sections edited out by their Japanese publishing houses. Not just on the grounds of length but because they argue these unorthodox viewpoints and imported non-indigenous perspectives will distract narrative flow, jar and confuse and potentially put off Japanese readers. The mudswamp of contemporary Japanese fiction publishing one might say.

Endo, who is probably still one of Japan's best-known authors, also wrote the brilliant and thought-provoking novel *Fukai kawa* (*Deep River*) about a diverse group of Japanese tourists, each of whom has a religious or spiritual experience while visiting India. This work also delicately depicts the struggle for many in marrying Japanese worldviews, sensibilities and history with Christian ones—the so-called translatability of Christianity—while in addition cleverly framing these contradictions within its narrative dialogue, and also managing to touch on the spiritual commonalities between religions and the torment many experience when finding one's individuality. It is also fascinating for eloquently framing multiple passages to India, not from a British or Western perspective, but one from another Asian nation.

The award-winning Kittitian British author and playwright of *Crossing the River*, Caryl Phillips, a big Endo fan, says that before he commences a new writing project he always picks up and reads *Silence*.[147] Interestingly, Endo did the same with Graham Greene's (1904-1991) books, showing yet again the many unexpected and somewhat mysterious horizontal chains that link the creative process, be they religiously themed, unorthodox perspectives, or not, can have and, of course, the importance of reading outside of one's home territory.

Akutagawa, probably best known outside Japan for his first published short story "Yabu no Naka" ("In a Grove"), which was made into the award-winning film *Rashomon* by Akira Kurosawa, also wrote many short stories with Christian themes. "Hokyonin no Shi" ("The Death of a Christian") (1918), "Kokuiseibo" ("Black Robed Maria") (1919) and "Kirishitohoro Shoninden" ("The Life of a Holy Fool") (1919) are good examples of some of these short stories.

More surprisingly, Junichiro Tanizaki (1886-1965), who like Endo came very close to winning the Nobel Prize in Literature, also had a connection to the church. His grandfather, who he was particularly close to, was a member of the Eastern Orthodox Church. Tanizaki is not known for religious narratives but for his stories about sexual obsession, such as *Shisei* (*The Tattooer*), and the type of narratives included in this novella *Yume no ukihashi* (*Floating Bridge of Dreams*), in which the narrator searches for his lost mother, a lost traditional Japan and his lost childhood through a bizarre, complex relationship with his stepmother. But by his own admission, the influence of seeing his grandfather praying to the Virgin Mary and Christianity were important.

Without it he claimed he wouldn't have become a feminist.[148] This, of course, reflects his own particular definition and form of mother-worship and in parallel his adoration of sexualised females and their polar opposite mothers that he is famed for. Tellingly, revealing that for some, including probably many of Tanizaki's readers who find his novels transfixing, no matter the approach adopted, truth can only be reached and fully understood through a Zen-like worship of the relativity of nature's elements, by appreciating polar-opposites, with their sometimes-competing roles and functions.

Japan's inbound tourists, who are generally interested in hot springs, art islands like the one in Seto, sushi, and also the nation's perceived paradoxical topsy-turvy elements, have not yet started searching for the Holy Grail in Japan and have certainly not yet discovered The Tomb of Christ, in Aomori Prefecture. According to a local legend, Christ didn't die on the Cross, but escaped to Japan where he became a rice farmer—no doubt with his own special *donburi*—and lived until the age of 106. The legend began in 1933 with the discovery of a Hebrew text in Japan about the life and death of Jesus.

The existence of the alleged last resting place of Jesus in Japan might perplex, confuse and annoy many but Japanese monasteries are already on some travel agendas alongside temples, shrines and sushi. One such destination is Japan's first convent established in 1898 in Hokkaido where, unlike Belgium's beer brewing monks, Trappistine candy butter is made and sold by the 80 or so nuns that live and work there. The nuns face direct competition for their snacks, which support their "self-sufficient" way of life not from Shinto priests or Buddhists but from monks at the Trappist Monastery nearby who make butter, jam and cookies.

Channelling the Bible

As we have seen, a meaningful number of leading Japanese authors have been influenced by Christianity. They have often expressed a fascination with the lives of missionaries in Japan, Japan's so-called Christian century and also the search for meaning in the harsh aftermath immediately after the Second World War. Despite being few in number these books and authors, not all who have actually been Christians themselves, have made a lasting and oversized impact on Japanese literature and the arts. The Bible—both Old and New Testaments—has also been widely read in Japan for many reasons: out of curiosity, as a source for inspiration and by many who are not members of churches or religious groups or professional writers.

These books and their narrative themes reflect that following Perry's dramatic arrival in Japanese waters, during Japan's subsequent Meiji era while the nation's oligarchs and samurai focused most of their efforts on modernising Japanese industry and tools of production, Christians in Japan often focused on a different type of modernisation. Theirs spanned human capital that incorporated education, the arts, publishing, and social work, planting the seeds for the Japanese socialist movement, for instance, and creating new networks of influential intellectuals. Arguably, they were the moral warriors of their age.

Ayako Sono (b. 1931), the sometimes-controversial conservative columnist and author, is an interesting example. A devout Catholic, she was one of the first female writers to gain prominence after the Second World War with her short story "Enrai no kyakutachi" ("Guests From Afar"), about the occupation. She also wrote "Kyo-o Herode" ("Herod the Mad"); as well as the highly regarded short story "Nagai kurai fuyu" ("Long, Dark, Winter").

Other notable authors with similar influences include Shiina Rinzo (1911-1973), Toshio Shimao (1917-1986), Ayako Miura (1922-1999), Sawako Ariyoshi (1931-1984) and Hisashi Inoue (1934-2010) and, of course, Uchimura, albeit from an earlier generation, whose eloquent English prose still resonates today. They wrote about managing guilt while searching for love after surviving the atomic bomb, mental illness, sacrifice, abortion, domestic violence, Christian values in a Japanese context and aging, the common literary denominators being author faith and the aspiration for a better and fairer social fabric across Japan. Many of their works were dramatised for television and film. Three examples are *Shi no toge* (*The Sting of Death*), *Chichi to kuraseba* (*The Face of Jizo*) and *Hyoten* (*Freezing Point*).

Unsurprisingly, biblical themes and stories associated with Christianity continue to be popular amongst both contemporary readers and writers, helping spawn an ever-growing plethora of bestselling and highly influential novels. In the summer of 2020 the *Yomiuri Shimbun*, one of Japan largest national newspapers started publishing daily instalments that ran for almost a full year of a novel by Mitsuyo Kakuta (b. 1967), *Taranto* (*The Talents*), in its morning edition. The type of literary serialisation the newspaper often champions that ensures a new work will be read by millions and become a major success when subsequently released in book format. At the time of its publication in the newspaper *The Talents* was the first major new work from Kakuta, one of Japan's most read contemporary female authors, for five years.

Her tale was inspired by *The Parable of The Talents*, a biblical parable from the New Testament where a master divides his property among three servants before going away, despite the fact that Kakuta, a very prolific writer, herself is not a Christian. The parable famously states that "To everyone who has will more be given." Kakuta's narrative revolves around a woman called Minori, the war memories of her 90-year-old grandfather, Paralympic athletes, and Minori's school-aged nephew. Minori's family run an udon restaurant in Kagawa, an area in Japan located in the Seto Island Sea, where Japan's now famous art island is located, well known for its udon restaurants.

The lessons of the parable are multi-fold but are said to show that success is the product of hard work, that we are not all created equal, that we need to make the most of the talents we have and ultimately, that we will all be held accountable. It is the genesis of the so-called Matthew Effect, as the parable is found in the Gospel of Matthew. This is the label for the phenomenon of accumulated advantage, gains that span fame, status, economic capital and perhaps also authorship of fiction and non-fiction. Values that even the likes of Toyotomi and Tokugawa might have understood, and ones that established shrines and temples with excellent locations might too, but ones that Marx would, no doubt, recoil against.

The narratives that each post-war generation of writers have grappled with of course mirror the times and social turns they have lived in and their values, concerns and tastes. One Japanese manga artist, Hikaru Nakamura (b. 1984), has even created a multi-million selling tale, *Seinto oniisan* (*The Saint Young Men*), featuring a young Jesus Christ and Gautama Buddha on a holiday break sharing a small flat in a Tokyo suburb. A travel break through which, these two international icons, both hope to understand modern Japan and its idiosyncrasies. Her quirky comic tale includes many extremely funny episodes with these giants of world religion staying in character as they confront modern day evils such as the Yakuza, as well as a scene where Jesus Christ experiences his own birthday in Japan, the so-called season to be jolly and of goodwill. It is an experience that evokes in him a stunned despondency and jealously towards Santa Claus.

Many of the issues we face today, however, are often not that dissimilar from the past, but of course they also include the new, such as novel forms of income inequality, globalisation and the increasingly complex rise of Asia, living with ubiquitous technology in our digital age, the unstoppable race to create a god-like AI, secular materialism, and rapidly ageing populations.

It has been said that Japan, an island nation exposed to the global winds of change, where monotheism never really put down broad roots, a nation that developed and modernised in its own peculiar kaleidoscopic manner, is the perfect location from which to observe and reflect on our rapidly changing world. The nation's history and periods of aggressive expansion, resilience and regression may even include lessons for some world leaders today. From this vantage point and juxtaposition, a new generation of brilliant Japanese authors, like Kakuta and Nakamura, are writing the narratives of today's Japan, our times, and their lives. Perhaps this is the Holy Grail to be found in Japan.

Part Five

Booze, Books and Bonking

The tiny incidents of daily routine are as much a commentary of radical ideals as the highest flight of philosophy or poetry. *Cha no hon* (*The Book of Tea*), Tenshin Okakura (1862-1913).

Literary Elixir: Bars, Cocktails and the Literati

Oscar Wilde (1854-1900) had a thing for them, though how many 'green fairies' he actually managed to devour is anyone's guess. With its exotic translucent green appearance, absinthe has had many devotees. It was in mid-19th century Paris that this popular tipple picked up its moniker, when it was a favourite of creatives such as the surrealist poet Arthur Rimbaund (1854-1891). James Joyce (1882-1941), Ernest Hemingway (1899-1961), were also known to have favoured this mysterious green drink with its reportedly hallucinogenic properties. Of course, this fashionable anise-flavoured wormwood-based Swiss concoction also made its way circuitously from Europe and the French city of light to Japan. Unlike in Paris, absinthe, *abusan*, was never truly in mode, becoming the in-crowd's drink of choice, but neither did absinthe's arrival on Japanese shores go unnoticed by the curious, those thirsty for adventure, or the literati.

Over time the green fairy or as at least one Japanese author dubbed it the 'devil's drink', generated local creative ripples with Japanese characteristics. The highly potent absinthe features in a short story by Ryunosuke Akutagawa (1892-1927), *Kappa*, and in Osamu Dazai's (1909-1948) seminal novel *Ningen shikkaku* (*No Longer Human*). Works by two of Japan's most important authors, both strong drinkers who died young.

Absinthe, despite its legendary strength, which can range from 40 percent proof to 80 percent and the alleged psychedelic properties of some of its ingredients, has never been banned in Japan, as it has in some other nations. Varieties are still available today some with local twists that include botanicals such as butterfly pea extract. An enhancement that turns drinks into an alluring almost transparent blue shade, when mixed correctly. The price of this imported liquor, which Dazai uses in his tale as a metaphor for loss, put this exotic and destructive potion out of reach for most in Japan. Creatives in Japan looking for stimulation and cheap intoxicated escape tended to down local mixes, not imported green ones. Top of the list was a local engineered refreshment, golden-brown in colour, called *Denki Bran*: electric brandy.

Denki Bran was the invention of Denbei Kamiya (1856-1922) and is still served at what became his eponymous bar in the heart of Asakusa, a working-class downtown area in Tokyo. The bar is located close to one of the capital's major and oldest Buddhist temples, Sensoji, with its famous Kaminarimon, lightning gate, the red image of which adorns the covers of many guidebooks. Kamiya Bar quickly became an after-work magnet for people working in this lively area and for the adventurous from beyond including many from the Japanese world of letters. Kamiya learnt his trade from a French drinks merchant in Yokohama before he set up a bottle shop in the area in 1880. Like absinthe, Kamiya's *Denki Bran* is somewhat of an enigma and very much a rare taste.

Japanese pubs and taverns are generally known as *izakaya*, a word made of up of parts *iru*, to stay, and *sakaya*, sake shop. In Japan, informal seated areas, tasting rooms within or next to bottle shops, that allowed customers to taste a merchant's range of offerings and enjoy a decent snack at the same time evolved into *izakaya*. These ever-popular informal drinking establishments are now internationally famous and loved by tourists.

Kamiya's shop, initially named Mikawaya Meishuten, also followed this well-trod developmental path. Its proprietor, however, decided to be more adventurous. He expanded opening what is now considered Tokyo's first and oldest surviving Western-style bar, a now legendary establishment, which was remodelled and renamed, becoming Kamiya Bar in 1912.

Outside Tokyo, including in trendy Shoreditch, London, as well as across Japan, you can find *kaku-uchi*, small tasting areas within liquor stores, the precursors to *izakaya*, where you can stand and drink the proprietor's sake stock by the glass or cup. Outside London, it is their low prices that are their main attraction. This was also one of Kamiya Bar's main selling points alongside the pull of its original inventive blend *Denki Bran*.

Denki Bran was described by the 'bad boy author' Dazai in *No Longer Human* as the fastest guaranteed route to drunkenness. This all helped ensure that the Asakusa bar was destined to become the favoured watering hole of many of Japan's literary greats. *Denki Bran*, a secret recipe, thought to be a brandy-based mixture of gin, vermouth and fortified wine served in a shot glass, was electric as it was new, totally intoxicating and excitingly modern. Much like electricity, *denki*, which was arriving in Japan around the time of the concoction's genesis. In fact, the drink was launched in 1882 with a slightly different name utilising the full word brandy, making Kamiya's beverage sound more like a real brandy than it really was.

In parallel, Japan's first electric streetlight appeared in Ginza in 1882, the same year Kamiya started purveying his inappropriately branded drink. Within a few years of their launches, in 1886 Tokyo Electric Lighting, a private company, started operating as the nation's first electric power company. It began supplying electricity to the public the following year and by 1896 Japan had 33 such companies. In many ways Kamiya Bar, born in these fermenting transformational times when the country was being electrified, a survivor of the Great Kanto Earthquake of 1923 that killed more than 100,000 people and the devastating city-destroying Tokyo firebombs of the Second World War has followed the twisting arc of Japanese history and the nation's modernisation.

The bar is also something of a legend among publishers and bookworms because so many of Japan's most famous modern authors are said to have drunk there at least once, not just Dazai, who himself has inspired many to take up writing and encouraged in others a taste for demon drink. Among those drinkers were Yasunari Kawabata (1899-1972), Junichiro Tanizaki (1886-1965), and Kafu Nagai (1879-1959) an eccentric and somewhat of a rogue that enjoyed the company of women of the stripping, dancing and entertaining kind, who also had what some consider an unhealthy fixation with the vanishing colourful cultural elements of past eras, a world he yearned for that for him seemed to be disappearing far too rapidly. On occasion the now internationally infamous writer Yukio Mishima (1925-1970) also frequented the bar. The zeitgeist, with its bright cultural currents, has moved on, but Kamiya Bar and *Denki Bran* remains.

Due to *Denki Bran*'s unusual flavour and strength, connoisseurs recommend drinking it with a beer chaser. It was originally 45 percent proof and priced for consumption at a cost lower than a glass of beer. Today, Kamiya Bar is also famous for its retro cafeteria-like feel, a design based on a German beer hall. Its everyman atmosphere is somewhat reminiscent of a British working men's club. It has a welcoming, friendly vibe and these days it offers *Denki Bran* at two different strengths 40 percent proof or 30 percent proof. Customers buy tickets from a vending machine for its offerings of food and drink and of course its signature cocktail, which can now be bought by the bottle at stores across Japan, not just at its downtown Tokyo birthplace.

Kamiya Bar stocks two types of gin on its often-overlooked bar shelves: Nikka Wilkinson Gin, a local gin, and the British Plymouth Gin, a Navy strength strong gin, with its own long history reaching back to 1793. In an unusual twist for the literary inclined, Plymouth Gin is the favoured gin of the bar staff for the ever-popular gin and tonics served at a bar in another capital city location with an equally illustrious history, the Athenaeum, a gentleman's club in Pall Mall, London.

This club, now open to female as well as male membership, has a significantly different atmosphere to Kamiya Bar despite having its own literary and impressive connections with past members and patrons such as Sir Noel Coward (1899-1973), Sir Winston Churchill (1874-1965), Charles Dickens (1812-1870), Charles Darwin (1809-1882) and Henry James (1843-1916). The shared tastes in gin and linkages to fine writing, alongside its mature patrons, is probably all these two locals have in common. Kamiya Bar has an open, communal feel. With now somewhat ageing regulars that often include kimono-clad comedians and others working in local traditional entertainment establishments, alongside retired and off-shift local merchants, as well as the odd tourist and publisher. It is another world indeed.

Kamiya Bar is also a firm favourite of the British, Yorkshire born, author David Peace, a former long-term resident of Japan, known for his books *The Dammed United*, *Patient X: the Case-Book of Ryunosuke Akutagawa* and the *Tokyo Trilogy*. It is no doubt a drinking hole, unlike a stuffy London Pall Mall club, he feels comfortable within. Probably, not just because it doesn't require him to wear a jacket and tie. It is located in an edgy working-class neighbourhood, as opposed to near St. James's Palace and The Mall, the grand processional road leading up to Buckingham Palace. He may also like it for its *nikomi*, Japanese stews, *agedashi* tofu and the deep-fried sweet shrimp, as well as its welcoming, unpretentious canteen style.

Kamiya Bar wasn't just electrifying for modern Japan's literary greats and their publishing agents, helping light up their conversations, allowing them to spark off ideas on each other and inspiring scenes in new works. It also generated a small fortune for its entrepreneurial owner, whose family still owns the business. When Kamiya, who imported vines from France, started a vineyard and was also involved commercially with the railways, died, he was known as Japan's 'King of Wine'.

The Tokyo National Museum in Ueno is a lucky beneficiary of Kamiya's enterprise and liquid tastes, following a donation of 668 items he owned, mostly ornamental ceramics and other small artifacts from the Qing Dynasty (17th–20th century China). Kamiya's collection housed at the museum includes unusual and striking items. Many that can be held in one hand almost like a glass of his famous *Denki Bran*. A delightful small incense burner carved from white stone is one lovely example, and a beautiful carved red pomegranate made from a single piece of agate designed to look as if the gemstone has been partially ripped open and is bursting with fertile seeds is another. The Tokyo National Museum also boasts amongst its large collection some blue Korean-style plates and other items once owned by one of Kamiya Bar's clients, the author Kawabata. Though very different in style from the type of functional plates used to serve the dishes that accompany the drinks at Kamiya Bar.

Like absinthe, which has its own rich legacy spanning art, fiction and a cocktail based on it invented by Hemingway, *Death in the Afternoon*, also the title of one of Hemingway's books, *Denki Bran* seems to pop up in fascinating and diverse places.

Not just next to glasses of Asahi beer on tables at Kamiya Bar. These include, for example, new works of fiction by contemporary Japanese authors such as *Yoru wa mijikashi arukeyo otome* (*The Night is Short, Walk on Girl*) by Tomohiko Morimi (b. 1979), a bizarre fantasy set in Kyoto, which like Tokyo boasts many drinking spots, that unfolds as a college student spends a night out unwittingly attracting the attention of a range of men, including a long-time admirer of hers.

This particular sparky Japanese golden-brown concoction, even if it is somewhat of an acquired taste and a drink that many only wish to try once, has a natural momentum seemingly giving it legs of its own, allowing it to walk on from each generation to the next. It does not require the help from the type of over eager promoters currently trying to catalyse a renaissance in the consumption of Wilde's beloved mind-stretching green fairy and other exotic international snifters and artisanal spirits.

Lupin, founded in 1928, is another of Tokyo's famous literary watering holes, establishments often referred to in Japanese by publishing insiders as a *bundan baa*, where a more conventional cocktail, the Moscow Mule, is the recommended beverage. It is served in a copper mug. Located in Ginza, a famous upmarket shopping district, down a flight of stairs in a back street, Lupin, with its black-and-white image and red logo of the famous French gentleman thief with his top hat and monocle, is close to the former office of an important Japanese publisher. It is said to have been another popular location for Dazai, and his pals, as well as authors like Ango Sakaguchi (1906-1955) and Sakunosuke Oda (1913-1947), part of the so-called *Burai-ha*, a group of dissolute, decadent but super-talented writers, as well as artists and individuals, for instance, working in the theatre. In its early days, uniformed waitresses served drinks at Lupin cafe style.

One can still sit perched at the small L-shaped bar, made of *yachidamo* (ash tree) installed in 1935, and drink a whisky from the same cloudy shot glasses that were used to serve Dazai at the bar last century. At that time ice and imported liquor were expensive and drinks were often cut with water. One can enjoy drinks while looking up at framed black-and-white photographs of the famous *Burai-ha* authors displayed in one corner. The boom in mineral and soda water and their use as a mixer of choice and the love of ice-packed highballs was very much a phenomenon of the future, not of these memorable decadents. According to Lupin's menu Ango favoured an egg, gin, lemon and soda drink called the Golden Fizz, but the barman when asked, cheerfully explains, Ango only drank Golden Fizzes on one occasion when he was feeling under the weather.

The bar had a difficult period during the war and its immediate aftermath. Lupin was forced to drop its foreign name during the war years and used the name *Pan-tei*,

Mansion Bread instead. After the war when booze was in short supply, and much was counterfeit, bootlegged or both. The bar proudly procured "reliable" liquor on the black market, which it claims encouraged its clientele to return. These days, Lupin is no longer an important literati, *bundan*, meeting spot, but you may find a poet or lyricist propping up the bar looking for inspiration and conversation, amongst the tourists. If you strain your eyes, you may spot some magazines, newspaper clippings and manga behind the bar, which feature Lupin and its clientele within their pages, including *Bungo sutorei doggusu* (*Bungo Stray Dogs*), a massively successful manga about an armed detective agency in Yokohama that features characters with supernatural powers named after important authors, including of course Dazai, as well as Fyodor Dostoevsky (1821-1881) and Akutagawa, who grapple with cases far too dangerous for the police, in its action-packed graphic pages.

Bungo Stray Dogs's creator, a notorious introvert, visited Lupin with confidence-boosting staff from the series' publisher Kadokawa as part of his research. Reportedly he sheepishly staked out the bar with their help, not having the courage to go in alone, before it featured as a bar located in Yokohama, not Tokyo, in the manga, a city where the manga's protagonists battle the Japanese mafia. A creative decision that has helped put Lupin on the international tourist map for a new generation of readers. The manga has become a media franchise spanning anime and light novels, and not just in Japan. As a result of the Korean language adaptation, many Korean fans include Lupin on their must-visit lists of Japanese destinations. This even includes female fans and tourists, who unlike *Bungo Stray Dogs's* creator seem to have the gumption to be able to visit and drink alone at the windowless basement bar's counter. Taking in its atmosphere while enjoying the same bevvies as their heroes. The bar's retained gaslights of old, now converted to be powered by electricity, create a dimply-lit space where drinkers and tourists can, if they wish, drink alone ignoring others and let their imaginations run riot.

Several other Tokyo bars are often mentioned in the same breath by Japan's drinking literati. These include a discreet cosy alcove-like one at the Hill Top Hotel, a small hotel popular amongst publishers and authors located near Meiji University, as well as the Imperial Hotel and its bar, which still retains a few leftovers of Frank Lloyd Wright's (1867-1959) famous design on one of its walls. None, however, serve electric brandy. The Hill Top Hotel is legendary in a similar manner to the Algonquin Hotel and its Blue Bar in New York in its heyday. The Hill Top, *Yamanoue*, Hotel has, however, until very recently been very much part of this era's publishing circuit. Authors are put up there by publishers as deadlines approach—'canned', *kanzume*: isolated from outside distractions—and publishers and editors hold events and meetings at the hotel. The hotel itself has inspired a few books by writers such as Shinpei Tokiwa (1931-2013) and Shotaro Ikenami (1923-1990). That said, at the time of writing it is closed for renovations, something that will also happen to the Imperial Hotel in the very near future.

Tokyo has many restaurants, hotels and bars with rich literary connections. This is probably not surprising in a capital with a long history that has often included the Japanese metropolis being one of the largest and most literate cities in the world. Near the Ueno museum where Kamiya's booze-derived artifacts are preserved, within walking distance, is one such establishment, *Seiyoken*. It has a 150-year history and an important literary pedigree alongside the role it has played in terms of introducing Western cuisine to Japan. Authors such as Kawabata and Nagai frequented it and enjoyed its quaint views of the Shinobazu Pond a vista cherished by artists. It is where many, but not Nagai, who had lived abroad, tasted beef, the eating of which was taboo in Japan, and French food for the very first time.

Nagai, from an elite background with a father in shipping, had spent time in Shanghai, France and the United States. He is remembered for amongst other things his snooty superior comments about the authenticity of the uniformed attire, their scrappy nature, and the poor manners and attitudes of the Japanese serving staff at these supposedly modern Western-style establishments in Japan, such as *Seiyoken* and Japan's first Western hotels.

He would pointedly, compare them to what he, a man of the world in all its meanings, had experienced on his international travels. How times have changed in terms of the quality of French restaurants in Japan, a number which now boast Michelin stars and service levels. Nagai is best known for *Ude kurabe (Geisha in Rivalry)*, a work published in 1918, that captures the changing times and his fondness for Tokyo's Shimbashi entertainment quarter. His attitude to life and his activities including his role at Keio University's influential literary magazine, *Mita Bungaku*, have spawned much publishing folklore.

> It wasn't only boardinghouses that Yamai cheated. When he received advances from publishers for books that he had not yet written, he either left the books unwritten or, if he did write one and get it published, in the meantime he took the manuscript to another publisher and sold it all over again. From time to time, in order to add to the length of a manuscript that he was selling, he even inserted pages from the writings of his friends and then disposed of the whole manuscript as his own. This misuse of friendship was naturally made without a single word of apology. He cheated foreign-style restaurants; he cheated tobacco shops; he cheated tailors. Kafu Nagai, *Ude kurabe (Geisha in Rivalry)*.

Twisted Cocktails and Sacred Spirits

Japanese publishing folklore is replete with amusing tales set in Western-style locations including one about the author Kyoka Izumi (1873-1939) at the Imperial Hotel, Japan's first Western-style hotel founded in the 1880s. Izumi who despite being male is deliberately used as the name for one of the lead female characters in the manga *Bungo Stray Dogs*. In this fictional world, a defector from a criminal gang with a doll-like personality with a special ability known as 'Demon Snow'.

In the real world away from the pages of this literature-inspired manga, Izumi also had a reputation for being an eccentric as well as writing about the grotesque and the fantastic. When an American publisher invited him to the Imperial Hotel to discuss a translated edition of one of his works he was somewhat taken aback. The Izumi of this world, considered one of the supreme stylists in modern Japanese literature, had limited interest in Western food and almost no international experience. As more and more Western dishes started to adorn their table at the Imperial and the American editor eagerly said through her interpreter how much she loved his work, which obviously she had and could not read, and how she ever so much wanted to publish him in English translation, he was reportedly totally bemused. An astute waiter seeing his discomfort and the unfolding situation brought him unsolicited a *tamagoyaki*, a Japanese-style rolled omelette, and a glass of hot sake. This apparently appeared to help the conversational flow but didn't lead to an English edition. The opportunity, like the food ordered at the Imperial, had no obvious appeal to him.[149] Izumi's works have subsequently been published in English translation and his plays such as *Yasha ga ike* (*Demon Lake*), are still performed in Japan.

Authors and publishers can still be spotted at the Imperial's *Rendez-Vous* lounge situated near its entrance and propping up the long and elegant counter at its famous bar. Sadly some international editors and publishers also still continue to misread, misunderstand and talk at unresponsive Japanese authors and publishers through interpreters, causing much mirth from those on the receiving end, sometimes eliciting the unheard comment from those in the know and wishing to signal their superiority that nothing has changed since Izumi's cup of sake with that American at the Imperial.

In those days long before the boom in bottled and mineral water, for some alcohol, mostly sake, was considered a substitute for water. In the 1930s around 80 percent of alcohol consumption in Japan was sake. Today, trendsetters outside Japan are finally discovering the delights and range of sake available at a time when beer is now actually Japan's most popular alcoholic beverage and has overtaken sake in terms of market share, according to Kirin Holdings, a brewer of beer. Beer has an estimated 30 percent share, while sake these days only represents about seven percent of Japanese alcohol consumption.

Nevertheless, it still is culturally important. Rice, water and salt have traditionally been components of spiritual and ritual practise in Japan and sake, a combination of two of these, rice and water, has a special place. Barrels of sake are donated and displayed at shrines and the New Year is often welcomed with a wooden cup of sake drawn from a barrel. The New Year can be considered a great purification with sake playing an important role within this annual rite to rid lives of the impurities, unhealthy peculiarities, and defilements of the year passed with the pure replacing the impure. Sake also plays a role at births, weddings, funerals and other rituals commemorating lost loved ones. The word sake is very old indeed and can be found within the *Nihon shoki, The Chronicles of Japan*, the nation's second oldest written record of Japanese history. As is the word for hot spring, *onsen*, linking hot spring bathing and sake to the creation of the Japanese nation itself. Despite, the major changes in the nation's drinking habits, sake is, of course, still drunk for the pure pleasure of it. Many names for trendy Japanese ways of doing things that appear within the titles of books published internationally on Japan and words often associated with the Land of the Rising Sun and its culture, unlike the word sake, are in fact relatively new and can't be traced back to the historical core of Japan's early evolution as a society.

Ninja, for instance, only came into wide use in the 1950s. It has been argued that the word, ninja, was coined by the author Futaro Yamada (1922-2001) who penned mysteries and tales of ninja. The 1985 Hollywood film *American Ninja* and subsequently the series *Teenage Mutant Ninja Turtles* also known as TMNT, certainly helped the term on its way internationally. The precursor to this word, *shinobi*, apparently harder for English speakers to pronounce, which uses the same *kanji* characters used to render ninja in written Japanese, is thought to have first appeared in print in a book by the printmaker Yoshitoshi Kinoshita (1839-1892) titled *Buyo benryaku* (*Military Strategy*), published in 1856. That said, the word *shinobi*, written using different lettering, *kanji*, appears in the *Taiheiki* (*Chronicle of Great Peace*), an epic set between 1319 and 1367. This etymological phenomenon is by no means limited to booze-soaked vocabulary, prose and martial spirits but similarly, the words samurai, the military caste, and *bushido*, martial spirit, are said to have come into use in the Muromachi period (1336-1573) and the Meiji era (1868-1912) respectively. Surprisingly, samurai, a word everyone now immediately associates with Japan, is thought to have initially been pronounced *saburai*[150] with samurai only much later becoming the common pronunciation in the middle of the Edo period (1603-1868) during Japan's long peaceful era. At that time the role of the sword-carrying *saburai* warrior was changing, due to the lack of major internal and external wars, leading to quite a few members of this military caste becoming writers and poets, as well as in a few cases drunks.

Fascinatingly, the much more ancient word sake, only became termed *nihonshu*, Japanese alcohol drink, later in the late 19th century, as a translation of the English term for sake, Japanese rice wine. Many in Japan initially ignored the new nationalistic term, but these days both sake and *nihonshu* are widely used. Shochu, a drink that has been growing in popularity, which is distilled, as opposed to brewed like sake, and often dubbed Japanese-style vodka, is these days drunk in higher quantities than *nihonshu*, with around a 10 percent market share. Both, however, are far behind beer in terms of the volumes drunk, but ahead of wine and whisky. These are amazing figures when you consider that in the 1930s in Dazai's day *nihonshu* represented around 80 percent of alcohol consumed.

Shochu is, of course, technically a type of sake, in the broadest sense of the word and is distilled from various ingredients, including sake dregs. This white liquor can also be made from potatoes, wheat and *soba*.[151] The letters used to write *shochu* consist of two characters burn, and alcohol, but the second character, alcohol, is a more complex symbol, with its own narrative history, than the one used typically today for sake. It can be loosely deciphered as fortified alcohol. Thus *shochu* can be translated directly as burned fortified alcohol, not the most appetising of descriptions in English. Nonetheless, it is still the favoured beverage of some well-known contemporary authors especially when served as a lemon sour, a mix of *shochu*, soda water and lemon. Though author tastes and drinking choices these days mirror the rich diversity of what Japan now has to offer, ranging from beer, champagne the preference of one up-and-coming award-winning female poet, sake, highballs, ginger ale and on very rare occasions these days a shot of *Denki Bran*.

Message in a Bottle

Epistemology and etymology, just like drinks, cocktails and the beverage industry, as well as contemporary Japanese wordsmiths and publishers, have interesting, interconnected stories to tell when successfully and creatively uncorked. The age-old vintages of the words sake and *onsen* may to a degree help explain Japan's bar and bathing culture and the ongoing success of its traditional inns, *ryokan*, that combine both within their hospitality packages. One doesn't need to be a serial imbiber to know that some things in life are far better for being consumed or experienced directly. Nevertheless, these connections a worth exploring.

Invitations to a *ryokan* or other types of Japanese inns, palaces of pleasure and relaxation, and seasonal parties can often shake things up, triggering serendipitous moments, helping reduce inhibitions that subtly or abruptly change the course of things. Kawabata's seminal novel *Yukiguni (Snow Country)*, cited by the Nobel committee when he became the first Japanese author to win the prize in 1968, a tale of a trip to a *ryokan* at an *onsen* in Yuzawa, is a classical example of this. There is no doubt that Kawabata's trip to Yuzawa and the inn where he wrote parts of the novel, the first part of which was published in 1935, fortified the course of his writing career, providing it with momentum.

> It was not usual for him to get drunk on so little; but perhaps he was chilled from the walk. He began to feel sick. His head was whirling, and he could almost see himself going pale. He closed his eyes and fell back on the quilt. Komako put her arms around him in alarm. A childlike feeling of security came to him from the warmth of her body. Yasunari Kawabata, *Yukiguni (Snow Country)*.

Today, *Snow Country* is used as a tool to promote tourism. Despite its narrative of extra-marital affairs, a dilettante and geisha, which might be considered somewhat racy in today's cultural climate, it has been featured in junior high school textbooks, as an important classic of Japanese literature. The room Kawabata stayed in at the *ryokan* is now preserved as a museum and there is even an award-winning vodka-based cocktail called the yukiguni, invented in Japan and mixed around the world.

This type of serendipity is something that Tanizaki, who almost won the Nobel Prize in Literature a few years earlier in 1964 after making the short list, the year before his death, experienced when he was 27. After the publication of his debut 1910 novella *Shisei (The Tattooer)*, a tale of obsession, a giant spider tattoo and a beautiful young woman, Tanizaki was invited to a get-together near Kiyomizu-dera, the Pure Water Monastery, in eastern Kyoto. Geisha who had read and enjoyed *The Tattooer* were invited and by all accounts a jolly good time was had by all. Among his hosts was Shotaro Kaga (1888-1954), a young man from a wealthy Osaka merchant family, a city located in the same Kansai region as Kyoto. Even though quixotic drinks were not served, the event apparently left a strong mark on the young up-and-coming author, who was also from a well-to-do merchant-class family, though in his case a Tokyo-based one.

Kaga, who was younger than Tanizaki, and others discussed Europe, leaving a sophisticated and erudite impression of internationalism and good taste, surrounded by beautiful women, all expressed in a memorable regional Japanese dialect. There is no doubt that this circle of drinking friends and acquaintances in its own beneficial manner helped change the course of Tanizaki's life. He wrote about it in his novel,

Seishun monogatari, (*Tales of Youth*), serialised in the magazine *Chuo Koron* between September 1932 and March 1933. A decade or so after the youthful Kyoto shindig, following the destruction of Tanizaki's home in Yokohama during the 1923 Great Kanto Earthquake, Tanizaki took the major decision to move to the Kansai region of Japan, taking up residence in Kyoto, a decision that refreshed him, changed his perspective and also his profile as a writer. His status as an author grew immensely after the move with his most successful novels coming after what might be termed as doing a geographical following a disaster.

One of his seminal works *Chijin no ai* (*Naomi*) was published the year after the move. In the 1940s he published *Sasameyuki* (*The Makioka Sisters*), a tale set between 1936 and 1941 of a wealthy Osaka merchant family, reminiscent of Kaga's, and their search for a suitable husband for one sister. This title when directly translated means *lightly falling snow* and the work is considered one of Tanizaki's best. Following its publication Tanizaki won several important literary and cultural awards in Japan. Perhaps unsurprisingly, one of the characters in *Bungo Stray Dogs* is named after Tanizaki, an assassin with orange hair who hates earthquakes and has a superpower called Light Snow. This character from the pages of the graphic world of manga lives alone with his sister, Naomi.

Kaga, a collector and businessman stockbroker with a love of all things refined, had other literary friends in addition to Tanizaki such as Soseki Natsume (1867-1916), another of Japan's literary greats, and yet another name of a character in *Bungo Stray Dogs*. Kaga collected orchids and published an important orchid book, *Rankafu*, built an impressive villa, and helped cultivate businesses, as well as ferment publishing relationships. He also played a very significant role in the development of the Japanese whisky industry. He backed Masataka Taketsuru (1894-1979) the founder of the Nikka Whisky Distilling Company, with financing, becoming the company's first chairman.

Taketsuru acquired proper whisky making skills in Scotland, very different from the chemistry-like techniques that exploited manufactured colourings and flavourings often deployed at the time to make local brandies and whiskies. Having returned to Japan with a Scottish wife, Rita Cowan (1896-1961), Taketsuru needed backing, after a career switch, for a new independent drinks business, which he founded in 1934.[152] It was initially called Dai Nippon Kaju, Great Japanese Juice Company, before becoming Nikka. The firm remained independent for a significant period but in the 1950s the Asahi drinks group, founded in Osaka in 1889 as the Osaka Beer Company, brewer of the beer found in Kamiya Bar served as a complement to *Denki Bran*, gained majority control. The Kaga family owned shares up until the early 1990s as did the Taketsurus' adopted son, Takeshi. All played important roles, including Kaga, in the business and the development of the Nikka brand and the love of quality whisky making and drinking in Japan. Nikka whisky is now internationally famous, and just like Kaga's literary friend Tanizaki, award-winning and appreciated by sophisticated connoisseurs across the globe. In 2023 Taketsuru Pure Malt, named after the founder, was crowned the World's Best Blended Malt. This would no doubt delight him, Tanizaki, Kaga and Taketsuru's long-suffering but super dedicated wife, Rita.

Kaga's impressive villa and his compound in Kyoto Prefecture has become the Asahi Group Oyamazaki Villa Museum. Amongst its art collection are works by Claude Monet (1840-1926) including *Water Lilies* (1907) and other oil paintings with images of Monet's beloved Giverny Gardens in the outskirts of Paris, as well as ceramics and works of sculpture by Henry Moore (1898-1986) and Alberto Giacometti (1901-1966) who, like some of the ingredients of absinthe, hails from Switzerland. The first chairman of Asahi, Tamesaburo Yamamoto (1893-1966) was another friend of Kaga's. The museum boasts about its links to Kaga and Tanizaki as well as Natsume, and contains two annex structures called the Dream Box and the Underground Jewelry Box, built in 2012 and 1996 respectively and both designed by architect Tadao Ando (b. 1941). In the latter, three Monet paintings are on permanent display in a cylindrical gallery. Being a member of this type of blend of people, within a given social circle of *bunjin*, men of culture, combined with a set of businessmen and intellectuals, was an important badge of pride for some and an aspirational dream for many others. There are many marks and fuzzy creative links if you keep looking. This impressive and transformational beverages company, whose name Asahi can be translated into English as 'sunrise', has many shared cultural connections and not only with famous Japanese authors. It was a picture by Monet titled *Impression, Sunrise* that coined the name of the movement, Impressionism. This 1872 painting, unlike *Japanese Bridge* and *Morning in Étretat* is not, however, owned by Asahi; it resides in Paris.

Within the Nikka division at Asahi, nestled alongside its famous whiskies is another important brand with its own impressive narrative pedigree, Wilkinson, the brand of the gin that sits alongside Plymouth Gin on Kamiya Bar's shelves. This drinks business started as a carbonated water business, *tansan*, designed for export, not local consumption like *Denki Bran* or *Nikka*. It was founded by an enterprising Englishman John Clifford Wilkinson (1852-1923), originally from Yorkshire, who exported *tansan* across the region.

According to its official, no doubt somewhat embellished foundation story, the chance discovery of a naturally carbonated spring in the mountains of Takarazuka while Wilkinson was out riding led to him setting up a bottling company. The city, where the source of the spring is located, is now also famous for the extremely popular all-female theatrical musical performance company, the Takarazuka Review, a company founded in 1913, that amongst others owns a large, tall theatre complex with a heliport on its roof next to the Imperial Hotel in central Tokyo, as well as its first theatre near the source of Wilkinson's bubbly water and a hot spring in what is now the city of Takarazuka.

Today, Wilkinson Tansan is Japan's mixer of choice and found in many of the highballs served in bars across Japan, and as bottled water at important international conferences held in Japan. Some compare this natural bottled sparkling water, Japan's most popular and probably its first, to Perrier, though its functional transparent bottles could not look more different than Perrier's stylish highly distinct bulbous translucent green ones. Wilkinson also produces one of the world's most drinkable ginger ales, sold in a smart ribbed green bottle.

The narratives of each of these enterprising drinks pioneers, with their direct and indirect links to some of Japan's greatest writers, like cocktails, each with their own amazing histories and flavours, are for those so inclined well worth exploring further. Be warned though, you may find yourself pouring a rabbit hole of a history lesson, if you take up the challenge and try to bring this heady brew of entrepreneurial men to a narrative boil.

Under the Influence

As we all know, the alleged creative benefits and delights of liquor and stimulants are not confined to Japan and its community or writers and publishers. This wagon is certainly not an example of so-called Japanese exceptionalism. Famous authors in many different countries have experimented with the green fairy, cocaine, opium, magic mushrooms and mescaline, for example. Some less adventurous authors swear by the simple benefits of a given number of sugars in a mug of tea before they write, or copious cups of green tea or coffee to keep them alert and focused when writing. There may actually be some scientific facts behind some of these lesser habits. Access to sugar and coffee, both stimulants, are reported by historians who study the economy and its longitudinal trends to have contributed to increases in worker productivity in Britain in the 1800s, for instance, encouraging individuals to work longer and more intelligently.

In 1950s California, before being banned, liberating psychedelics and stimulants, such as LSD and Benzedrine, were embraced by intellectuals and beatniks looking for a range of things spanning mind-boggling alternative perspectives, mystical enlightenment, as well as devices to help deal with deadlines, stress, the weariness of life or loss, and the fear and ignobility of failure. International publishing folklore is a glass full of stories of festooned authors addicted to drink or drugs or both, as well as mythical hard to verify statements about enhanced routes to publishing success, by writing high, such as "write drunk, edit sober," that are said to have helped given writers marshal their spirits to write another day.

Many famous writers, not just the celebrated American ones of past ages like Hemingway, Edgar Allan Poe (1809-1894) F. Scott Fitzgerald (1896-1940) and John Steinbeck (1902-1968) have fallen under the spell of this dangerous mythical creature, the Cocktail Fairy. Some drinks are golden and fizz, a few turn blue and others can turn you green if you are not careful, while some allegedly are a magical tonic, a creative elixir that fires up the imagination, transforming you into a writer with significant international success, when, of course, shaken and not stirred. This has decanted credibility onto the myth that alcohol and other stimulants are the handmaid of literary success, the essential tools of the trade. This old-school mythical genie that allegedly can magic away writer's block and conjure up brilliant plot devices, is it seems impossible for some to put back into the bottle once uncorked.

It is, however, often a complex blend of factors that liberates and unleashes the creative spirit encouraging inspired individuals to seize the day and pound their keyboard or pick up a pen or writing brush to express themselves with legendary effect. Drinking with friends or colleagues and taking drugs within a group certainly, according to many who indulge in such activities, induces new experiences and reduces inhibitions allowing some to flap their wings unabashed, but there is still limited evidence that it increases the rate of creative productivity, even if it makes many under the influence feel more intelligent, social or creative. Motivation, and quality of effort and output are not synonymous.

Some of Japan's most successful creatives alongside the nation's celebrated authors, have been colossuses when it comes to drinking. The Russian film director Andrei Konchalovsky (b. 1937), for example, after a rancorous visit to the home of probably Japan's most famous film director, Akira Kurosawa (1910-1998), where Kurosawa personally prepared the sashimi they enjoyed, commented after an epic amount of vodka had been drunk: "he really knew how to drink." Moderation was not Kursoawa's favoured cut.

> My greatest pleasure each week came on Thursday nights when I would drink and eat with my friend, the scholar of English literature Yoshida Kenichi, and his friends, including the critic Kawakami Tetsutaro and the novelist Ishikawa Jun. The three men, though very different personalities, all qualified as bunjin (dilettante man of culture) of the pre-war variety, and the first requisite of a bunjin was that he was fond of liquor. Donald Keene, *On Familiar Terms: To Japan and Back, A Lifetime Across Cultures.*

Red, White and Bubbly

Historically, many have probably drunk more and more frequently than they have written, and some members of the literary set have consciously used liquor and its strategic withholding or opportune deployment for memorable effect, and not just within written-form narrative fiction. One now long-retired British chief executive of a large international publishing house, for instance, made a habit of inviting senior employees based overseas, and some not, including individuals from Japan, when visiting London, to parties at his flat in a white stucco building in Notting Hill. There, to lubricate the small talk, he would serve strong Bloody Marys and chicken liver pate on Melba toast to his guests in a similar manner as the author Ian Fleming (1908-1964), of James Bond fame, apparently was accustomed to do.

This captain of industry would discreetly make select guests aware that Fleming was an old acquaintance of his and like himself a product of the British Navy, even though their paths never actually crossed in the Royal Navy. Thus creating myths that these impressionable young executives would take back to their markets and share with colleagues and booksellers about the upright dynamic strong-willed gentleman who led their international organisation.

While, in contrast, George Weidenfield (1919-2016), the charismatic and super-connected co-founder of the publisher Weidenfield and Nicolson, for instance, from a slightly older generation, who was active during the golden age of long publisher lunches and book launch parties took a distinct but equally impression-inducing tact. His preferred tipple of repute being milk. Drinks and cocktails are sometimes said to be analogues of life, place or people, analogues that generally reflect those describing them more than those enjoying them and perhaps also even those serving them. Drinks can be bracing, cool, dry, dangerous, fortified, sweet and forgettable, concentrated, pressing, punchy, mellow, lethal, pretentious, as well as being spiced-up and bloody-minded. What you offer your guests or drink in front of them also as we have seen sends a message that can become an engineered memorable narrative of its own.

Agatha Christie (1890-1976), a teetotaller and a British author that has outsold most if not all, is famed for gulping down glasses of cream in lieu of champagne, at her generously hosted parties. She had a preference for Devonshire cream, apparently. If this helped her write or promote her works, or milk her guests for ideas, information or good reviews is hard to ascertain, but sometimes abstention is the reverse side of addiction. In Japan invitations to the homes of authors, editors or publishers and film directors are rare. One is much more likely to be invited to a party in a hotel, a restaurant or bar, if the relationship is developing in a positive direction. Their rarity increases the impact and influence of invitations to someone's home when they do occur whether in Tokyo, Kyoto, Osaka or London.

Nonetheless, seasonal publishing-related get-to-togethers are common in Japan just like in other capital cities. One Tokyo-based editor, for example, likes to gather a group of Akutagawa Prizewinners together on the banks of Tokyo's Kanda River in close walking distance to his apartment, when possible, during the cherry blossom season. It is very much a bring-your-own type of bash, mostly *nihonshu* and beer alongside exotic cans of new Japanese liquid concoctions and your own favoured nibbles. In spring you will invariably find yourself crouched on a blue tarp, mingling, grasping drink glasses facing others in similar postures, who are probably feeling less physical discomfort.

Despite being informal and unsophisticated, there is something very special about communing with a small group of authors with a cup of sake beneath cherry trees, close to a capital city's famous river. It is a visual experience reminiscent of the type of Japanese woodblock prints that some impressionist painters famously admired, as opposed to the ones they painted, as well as scenes captured in writing by ancient Japanese poets. If one is lucky enough to be at the right publishing picnic at the right time, you may get a sense of the winds, and writing trends, blowing through the newly blooming branches of Japanese publishing, as well as the cherry trees above, with their magical fleeting blossoms, you are sat beneath.

A contrasting but also noteworthy British example of publishing posture and networking through the deployment of booze alongside the exploitation of idiosyncratic location is Jeffrey Archer (b. 1940), an author who has incidentally been very popular in Japan, and whose life is as dramatic as his many bestsellers. Archer is known for throwing parties that have been the talk of the town in his London penthouse flat that looks out down onto another capital city river, the Thames. At his annual party, which was a must-attend event in publishing circles when he was at his height as an author and a political influencer as a friend of Margaret Thatcher (1925-2013), Krug Champagne and shepherd's pie was served, showing off his contrasting tastes for both the luxurious and traditional simplicity.

It was certainly not a student-like bring-a-bottle event. Archer's hosting choices make seeing who is there and being seen a complex juggling act, especially for international guests less familiar with London's cocktail party etiquette and traditional British comfort food. Alongside holding a glass of expensive superior bubbly in one's hands and stabbing through mash potato to get to the meat below, guests also coolly admire the views and try to make selective small talk.

Many a publisher, local or from further afield, has returned to their office to boast about attending, not revealing how many others did alongside them or who they actually met, stating with pride that what really impressed them most was not the people, or the cultural mash up, but the fact that Archer owned art by Monet, depicting the same magnificent view of the Thames that his select group of guests were privileged to see from the windows of his penthouse apartment. No matter what they thought of Archer personally or the quality of his writing, or if the paintings were copies or not, most can't seem to restrain themselves from sharing this factoid and a few other easy to spread Archer anecdotes, amplifying his name in publishing circles, and generating persistent demand for invitations to his events, and perhaps to a lesser degree his manuscripts.

Nestled between two telescopes not far from Chofu, a city on the west side of Tokyo, in the grounds of the National Astronomical Observatory of Japan is a cherry blossom tree with a stout trunk that Naoki Prize winning authors are said to have congregated around each year in spring to drink and chat under the tree's flowering blossoms. This exclusive literary *hanami*, cherry blossom-viewing party, is somewhat differently contrived and probably actually more exclusive than an Archer party. Though sharing not so dissimilar networking objectives. It, however, has one additional advantage that attendees, if they still have the urge for stargazing after their drinks have been depleted, can pop into the observatory on their way home to experience distinctive heavenly views of a very different scientific nature through telescopic mirrors, as opposed to dirty London windows. Also if their eyes and minds are still functioning sufficiently they can learn about the so-called samurai astronomer, and master *Go* player, Harumi Shibukawa (1639-1715) the creator of Japan's first terrestrial and celestial globes and other famous calculating Japanese starwatchers of yesteryear.

Distilled Creativity

Today, publisher liquid lunches and booze-filled book launches are much less common. The hardcore drinking of the pre-war literary set may be mostly a thing of the past, but booze-ups do still take place. Dotted around the 23 wards of Tokyo in walking distance of each other, down in basements and tucked away making them easily missed without an introduction are a few very hard to find literary, *bundan*, bars.

The distances between these small inconspicuous bars, reminiscent of private member clubs, at least the ones this author knows of, allow you to leave to try another one, without your host or hostess becoming aware, if on a given night the atmosphere is not to your inclination. They are all within walking distance of a lively *izakaya*, favoured by the industry, full of atmosphere and good food, where prodigious drinkers and old-fashioned publishers who want to eat something substantial and have a pre-drink to get their creative juices flowing, before entering the Tokyo literary bar scene, can prepare themselves, physically and mentally.

Behind the counter in one of these bars are bottle after bottle of Kaku Suntory whisky marked with the handwritten names of the authors and editors and others they belong to awaiting their return. On the counter you may see recently published books by the bar's clientele. In another, as you sit chatting with writers, photographers and publishers someone who has won a literature or culture prize that day may suddenly appear out of nowhere to be greeted with flowers from bar staff, witnessing and marking their success in shaded semi-private comfort, surrounded by an appropriate set of people. Special occasions such as these may be acknowledged or ignored by others seated at the bar, depending on the conversational flow and other social factors.

At least one of these bars is used by industry figures, with budgets, to host Christmas parties and other such seasonal jamborees. Authors and editors come seeking recognition, encouragement, debate, friendship, creative stimulation, and to relax after a major deadline. According to staff at established bars with long intertwined histories and literary links that go back decades, many come to see the staff behind the bar at pivotal career moments. The connections to authors, professors, editors and critics from certain gilded universities such as Waseda with reputations for producing Japan's literary elite, can sometimes stretch far back to student days or to when a writer made their writing debut, and in some cases even over multiple generations.

Some individuals standing or seated behind counters have witnessed much of a writer's career: the lows, the highs, slumps and the drunken excitement of new titles and important positive reviews. Everyone at given moments needs a witness or a friendly smile of encouragement. Bars with continuity and a genuine interest in writing and writers can provide that alongside liquid escape from the melancholy of life as a writer in a mega city like Tokyo. "Writers and editors come, not baseball players or builders. I don't know why! Does that make us a literary bar?" one owner says with a grin. They come when they need to, alone or with colleagues. Some want to talk, others just want to drink and think."

One, now long retired, London-based Japanese journalist working for a large international wire service liked to advise young impressionable journalists before moving to Tokyo that the secret to a successful relocation to Japan, and the key to understanding contemporary Japan, was to locate a small bar and then finding the courage to go there as often as possible, every night if practical, for at least a month after moving. Social learning has many classrooms and many instigators and the results, according to this advice, would be transformational. He also included amongst this sage advice that after a few months, a different frequency of visitation was probably advisable to insure career longevity.

> Nonetheless, he did not feel he could jauntily push open the door of an establishment he had never seen before. He felt a sense of strangeness. He had heard this was an area that had its share of dangerous bars. The door of a bar he was looking at that very moment opened. A young man wearing wooden sandals with straw insoles came through the doorway, followed by a young woman with a fair complexion. Her skin was clear and she wore essentially no makeup; her physique was still that of a young woman. Junnosuke Yoshiyuki (1924-1994) 'Tejinashi' ('The Illusionist').

This author put the journalist's advice into practice, more or less, leading to a host of new diverse non-expatriate friendships, as well as a broad range, even if a somewhat self-selected array, of new perspectives of the Japanese capital and the lives of the people living within it. These spanned a very wide base of professions and ages. Oddly, the tinnier the bar, the bigger the impact it often seems to have. Chance meetings at their counters can help change lives. Some streets are like warrens filled with bars that once entered mix up and breed new narratives of the tiny incidents of the everyday that collapse time and provide escape from the suffocating collective and the stereotypical. They can even offer at times a state-of-the-nation or city tableau, often in hugely unexpected ways.

If one looks up as one exits or enters almost any commuter station in Greater Tokyo, you will probably see a dental clinic above and a smattering of small bars often highlighted by neon lighting, grabbing your attention like exclamation marks. Close to the station you will also, no doubt, find a convenience store stocked with cans of exotic mixes in what the industry terms as their ready-to-drink (RTD) format for those who wish to drink alone or at home. Much less so these days you may also find a bookstore. Tokyo has many more dental clinics than bookshops, and the number of bars is a magnitude greater than both.

Most bars offer a reasonable range of food by Japanese standards and an excellent one when compared to most British pub food, even though both are still relatively underrated. Agglomeration effects have probably boosted devotional drinking and the clusters of drinkers near places of work or bars closer to home can induce diverse, comforting and important network effects. Particularly in dense cities that can often feel oppressive and lonely, while at the same time displaying exhausting but intoxicating magical effects, which have drawn people to them in the first place.

One contemporary prizewinning novel that beautifully captures the atmosphere, social dynamics and need for small bars is *Sensei no kaban* (*The Briefcase*) by Hiromi Kawakami (b. 1958). It is not a tale of editors, publishers and authors in literary bars, but of a student who meets her former mathematics teacher at the counter of a little bar and the unconventional relationship that subsequently evolves from a random bar-bound sporadic association of two lonely individuals to a relationship that is quirky and meaningful. The relationship between the two oddballs, who enjoy a drink and the comforting altered reality that their bar allows them to escape into, over time expands into extra-bar realms, after bar staff suddenly arrange a trip to the mountains to hunt for and enjoy exotic mushrooms. Something that Japan is blessed with a huge variety of including some odd ones such as *maitake*, which literally translates as dance mushroom. The book's delicate narrative sensitively shows that support and social comfort in Japan can be spawned in many different ways, and at all ages, and can even emerge from the stools at the counters of little oasis-like bars within the metropolis.

> It wasn't as though I had returned to my high school days, but neither did it feel like I was actually in the present – all I could say was that I had caught the fleeting moment at the counter of Bar Maeda. It seemed like we had ended up within a time that didn't exist anywhere. Hiromi Kawakami, *Sensei no kaban* (*The Briefcase*).

Reading Between the Bars

Inevitably, this cuts many ways. Individuals who have owned and run clubs and bars have sometimes crossed the counter, becoming award-winning writers. The purveying of drinks and publishing of books is certainly not a one-way street. It is well known that Haruki Murakami (b. 1949) ran a jazz bar called Peter Cat with his wife, Yoko, in Kokubunji west Tokyo, before making his debut as a writer. Bars, jazz clubs and music; he worked in a record shop when he was a student are all aspects that feature in his works.

Masako Togawa (1931-2016), a Japanese chanson singer-songwriter and author who is better known for being a television personality and for her afro-like permed hair, is a classic example. In the 1960s she converted a coffee shop into a nightclub

Aoi Heya, Blue Room, creating a chanson club popular amongst celebrities with an infamous legend-making VIP section. What is much lessor known is that backstage and while waiting for clients she wrote detective fiction, mystery novels and short stories, some rather good ones. Togawa won an important award for the genre, the Edogawa Rampo Prize and was also nominated for the Naoki Prize, for commercial fiction.

> He walked in and ordered the stew that was the speciality there and a glass of cheap whisky cut with hot water. He was drinking more these days and was aware that it was a bad sign. Masako Togawa, *Hi no seppun* (*A Kiss of Fire*).

Togawa was a pioneer in other regards too. Hiring mostly individuals from the LGBT community to work in her club. Her novels, especially the scenes set in bars and clubs, and the characters that inhabit them, have an authentic resonance and contain the small details that only someone with her experience could have written. They provide an interesting snapshot into the heady nightlife and TV world, as well as other bizarre underworlds and subcultures, of Japan's relentless go-go growth years in the decades leading up to the end of the Showa era (1926-1989). A colourful time that many now look back to with affection when anything seemed possible and Japan was changing rapidly and becoming outwardly confident. Nowadays, people pine for the nostalgia generating covered kitsch shopping arcades and station buildings of their youth that are increasingly being knocked down and redeveloped, and retro coffee shops, as well as the era's bars and clubs, like Blue Room, with their old-style furnishings and warming vibes. This is the case even if this dynamic can-do past was tough and unpleasant for many and present-day Japan is actually safer, richer, more inclusive and significantly less polluted.

Togawa's plotted twists and dramatic turns, like a small glass of Denki Bran, are not for all. The spirit of Hemingway it is not. It is probably more fun for curious readers to decide for themselves which have aged better and whose creations are the more unnaturally engineered. This is not, however, a suggestion to try them in combination. Allegedly, the VIP room at the Blue Room club was rather lively with games of strip poker, for instance, being played and all sorts of fascinating individuals popping in and out, including writers, translators, editors, and celebrities. Togawa's English-language translator, Simon Grove, a former investment banker and before that an official at the British Embassy in Tokyo, according to rumour, enjoyed his visits to see his author *in situ* and oddly, or perhaps luckily for the others attending, never seemed to lose a single item of clothing when he was invited to join a game of strip poker at the Blue Room.

Literary Elixir: Bars, Cocktails and the Literati 299

Some bar staff write, as do some drinkers at bars, but behind each bar owner there is often a fascinating narrative if you have time to listen, and if they have the time to recount their own tale, of their journeys up to the point of pouring your drink. There are many impressive and odd reasons why individuals open bars in Japan. There are those who like Murakami on graduation don't wish to enter the corporate world, those who leave the corporate world behind looking for something completely different, as well as bar staff working at famous Japanese hotels who discover they can earn more and gain more control if they set up their own bar. Some inherit them. It is not unheard of for a patron or sponsor to set up some owners with a bar. While one British publishing chief executive, the one with a fondness for Bloody Marys, claimed to have won the deeds to a bar in a late-night poker game in Tokyo, after hitting the town once a budget meeting at a group subsidiary had been completed, an evening match which must have had much higher stakes than a translator's items of clothing, no matter how smart or well-tailored, and higher spirits.

The 80-year-old proprietor of one literary bar, where she has worked for four decades, for instance, fell into her role after her partner bought a bar on a whim. Others go to bartending school or learn their trade at famous bars such as Bar Radio, a bar that also has a similar forty-year trading history. This bar has ventured into publishing, helping broadcast its presence and brand widely, with the release of a popular cocktail book that some like to call, in a somewhat exaggerated manner, Japan's *Savoy Cocktail Book*, a manual-like book that is seminal in the real sense of the word written by Harry Craddock (1876-1963) a barman who worked at the Savoy Hotel. Craddock's book was first published in the 1930s when most people in Japan were mostly drinking sake. It is still in print and lists more than 700 cocktails. *Ba rajio no kakuteru bukku* (*Bar Radio Cocktail Book*), is much newer, first published in 1982, but is still considered a classic in Japan. A copy of it can often be located, if one asks a bartender of a certain age what books they have behind their counter. Younger bartenders, however, these days prefer the internet when looking for cocktail advice.

There is more to Bar Radio's book than its recipes. It contains essays by authors, illustrators and editors, as well as by the bar's legendary founder Koji Okazaki (1944-2021), with titles such as *The Masterpiece: The Izakaya, On Sake, Bars That House Spirits*, and *Our Base*. Some of these writer/aficionados have experimented and written about the devil's drink, *abusa*, the green fairy, like Japanese authors of old, but in their own manner reflecting their times and particular tastes. These days, Japanese bartenders, spurred on by their knowledgeable and demanding clientele, like Japanese whisky, regularly win international competitions.

Mix It Up

Times have certainly changed immensely since Dazai drank with his pals in Ginza and Asakusa, and when booze was mostly only available on the black market after the war ended, and mixers such as Wilkinson *tansan* were unknown and out of reach to most in Japan. However, as we have seen some drinks, books, bars and spirited individuals have played an oversized role in the development of Japan's interconnected bar and publishing cultures. Bar staff of a certain age often cite *Yoshu tenkoku (Foreign Liquor Heaven)*, a magazine launched in April 1956, as an important cultural catalyst at the root of much of this cultural evolution.

The magazine was launched by Suntory, now a major Japanese drinks company with global operations feted for its canny promotional skills, which in those early days was still called Kotobukiya. The magazine's launch came about one year after the *Guinness Book of World Records* was launched in August 1955, another publication linked to a drinks company. The differences between their geneses is stark. The *Guinness Book of World Records* was launched, following a row about which game bird is the fastest flyer in Europe, as a source book for pub quizzes and trivia. Today, it has an impressive online presence and is generally referred to as *Guinness World Records* not wanting to be defined by its book format, but is still in print, while *Foreign Liquor Heaven*, also sometimes translated as *Western Liquor Heaven*, a very different type of beast, is no longer published. It was launched, not to settle arguments or for other fact-based trivial pursuits, but to encourage Japanese salarymen to try the new types of liquor Suntory was selling.

Takeshi Kaiko (1930-1989), who went on to win the Akutagawa Prize in 1958 for his work *Hadaka no osama (The Naked King)*, and subsequently quit Suntory on winning, was working in the company's public relations and advertising department when he proposed the idea for a magazine to the company's managing director. *Foreign Liquor Heaven* was launched as a controlled circulation magazine, with the title chosen by the managing director, for customers at the company's branded bars known as Tory's Bars, where Suntory's whisky was sold with an initial circulation of 20,000. The magazine won an advertising award the year Kaiko won his literary prize and at its peak had a circulation of 200,000. Several well-known writers, artists and illustrators were involved with the publication including the artist Ryohei Yanagihara (1931-2015) and the novelist Hitomi Yamaguchi (1923-1995).

The magazine, with its sophisticated style and content, had a beautiful modern layout. It was impressively illustrated and was only lightly advertised, with the odd exotic but relatively tasteful nude sprinkled within its pages. The target audience was, of course, men, but the readership was wider. Its typical pagination was about

40 pages with content ranging from bar etiquette, essays, profiles of drinks and illustrated articles on cocktails to try, the history and culture of drinking, and short stories, originals and translations. It even featured international travel and drink. *Foreign Liquor Heaven* was published monthly until 1963.

One issue features an internationally famous Swiss festival, Fête des Vignerons, the winegrowers' festival, that only takes place every few decades in Vevey on the shores of Lake Geneva, another vocabulary and phrase cards designed as mini English lessons to be cut out and stored behind the bar or perhaps for use when traveling with amusing English language prompts, such as *Good morning, Ladies are fond of dogs, The wind is blowing, What is the matter with you? What shall I do?* and *Good night*, with Japanese transliterations below. No doubt included mostly in case a non-Japanese speaking individual suddenly appeared at the counter of a bar run by one of Suntory's many clients.

A good example of the type of short story choices made by its editorial team, very much with *Foreign Liquor Heaven*'s target audience in mind, is one with the Japanese title: *Eggu-kun no hana* (*Master Egg's Nose*). A short vintage crime tale by the British crime writer and poet Dorothy L. Sayers (1893-1957) published in translation. It features her sleuth Montague Egg, a travelling English liquor sales representative of Plumment & Rose, Wines and Spirits, Piccadilly, who alongside being a super salesman is an accomplished amateur detective.

In this particular tale, Mr. Egg's keen powers of observation and smell allow him to deduce, whodunnit style, who murdered a retired judge, Lord Borrodale, a customer of his firm's vintage port, whose dead body is found locked in a study, in a short story originally titled "The Poisoned Dow '08". A sniff at a decanter discloses nicotine poisoning, a discovery that eventually leads to the grand reveal that the butler did it. The ever-alert Montague Egg, of course, suspected the butler was involved from the start, as he greeted Monty, as the protagonist is also known as, on his arrival addressing him as "sir". Something that a butler would never normally do and also by not demanding that Monty enter Lord Borrodale's impressive dwellings through the tradesman's entrance, allowing him to enter unchallenged for the first time through the front door. Egg, in addition to solving crimes in Sayers's stories, frequently quotes maxims from *The Salesman's Handbook*, which include commercial pearls of wisdom such as "The salesman with the open eye sees commissions mount up high."

Incidentally, Asahi, Suntory's major competitor and the owner of the Nikka brand is said by many in the trade to be the better and more skilful crafter of drinks, while Suntory, they say wins hands down when it comes to sales, marketing, clever promotion and knowing its customers. Trying to differentiate these two major firms and their array of products is not, however, a simple choice between the industrial and the artisanal. Today, there is much more to both firms and their products.

Spirited Away

Most bars in Japan, not just the ones writers and editors go to, are comparatively safe. Few have bouncers standing outside and hired security. But arguments can still flare up. The history of world literature is full of skirmishes for primacy but most don't generally take place in tiny bars run by old Japanese women, with an uncanny ability to force drunk peacocking male authors on benders to take their quarrels outside.

According to this proprietor, fights don't happen as often now days and when they do it is mostly pompous grandstanding from individuals wanting everyone to notice their presence. Once things are outside, where nobody can observe them it normally calms down quickly. "They do what they are told when I order them out," she says, "and if not other customers provide a hand."

Outside this proprietor's bar, if one bothers to look up, you will see the bar's first and only now dimly lit and slightly grubby obtuse street sign. One observant open-eyed Suntory salesmen paid for it to be installed years ago after decades of the bar buying Suntory's distinctive bottled whisky. Of course, Suntory's logo is included below the bar's name on the sign and the bar only stocks its whisky.

The proprietor, like most others, goes out of her way to protect her clients' privacy but is still a fountain of knowledge with many amusing anecdotes about the evolution of Japan's drinking culture, the nation's wordcraft, and the persistent links despite changing tastes between Japan's literarti, bars, cocktails and liquor. After a healthy discussion about whether books and magazines and bar staff have made a difference, and are the elixir for publishing success, and more than a few drinks, Mitsuyo Kakuta (b. 1967), one of a small cluster of individuals drinking at the bar that night, and probably one of Japan's most widely read contemporary female writers, looks up at the proprietor standing behind the bar serving, who has just recounted the many twists of fate that have brought her to this moment in time, including the fact that she doesn't drink, and turns and states, "What you should be asking is not why Japan is like this, but why nowhere else is. Why can't women outside Japan come to a bar alone and drink, and leave safely taking the train home, and why shouldn't a widowed octogenarian single-handedly run a tiny bar in a metropolis into the night, if she wishes to. What is odd about that? That's the real question," she says, with a tipsy smile, as she puts on her coat, leaving. She exits into a poorly lit door well facing a small deserted dark side street, not enlightened by Suntory's worse-for-wear illuminated sign hanging in the bar's entrance, to take the last train home alone. A sobering thought indeed.

How to Read a Film: Kurosawa and His Books

"Is it necessary, really, to learn how to read a film?" asks the seminal book on film studies, *How To Read a Film*, in the first line of its preface. James Monaco, who wrote this quintessential book in 1977, which has since been updated many times and now stands at 736 pages, obviously thinks so. As do many lecturers, who recommended the book as an introductory text for students studying or interested in film, and of course his publisher, Oxford University Press (OUP). But what would Japan's most highly regarded film director, who put Japanese filmmaking on the international map, Akira Kurosawa (1910-1998) have thought?

Kurosawa didn't go to film school. In fact, he didn't attend any institutes of higher education, finishing formal education at the age of seventeen. He did, however, read an awful lot of books and often recommended aspiring students of film and directors to follow his example, and read, as well as write, and direct. Kurosawa read major works that many claim to have read, but often actually haven't, such as the epic chronicle of the 1812 Napoleonic invasion of Russia *War and Peace*, by Leo Tolstoy (1828-1910), a 1,296-page book he said he had read at least thirty times.

When he was growing up Kurosawa reportedly read everything he could get his hands on without discrimination: both the classics and contemporary fiction. It's something that Japan's most notorious author Yukio Mishima (1925-1970), born Kimitake Hiraoka who took his pen name at age 16 to spare his father, a civil servant, any potential embarrassment, also claims. It's probably true to say that books influenced Kurosawa's cinematic storytelling more than anything else. However, it seems highly unlikely that *How To Read a Film* was on Kurosawa's reading list alongside works by the authors he is known to have read and admired such as William Shakespeare (1564-1616), Fyodor Dostoevsky (1821-1881), Soseki Natsume (1867-1916) and Maxim Gorky (1868-1936).

Kurosawa made his directorial debut in 1943, 34 years before Monaco's text was published and before students started formally being taught how to read, analyse, appraise, deconstruct and critique films. By the time of its publication Kurosawa had already directed 25 of the 30 films he made during his career. Nonetheless and unsurprisingly, as he is considered a visionary and one the world's greatest directors, Kurosawa does get a mention, even in the early editions, of this book, which became an instant classic when it was initially published in the 1970s.

According to Monaco, filmmakers outside Japan were unaware of the long history of Japanese filmmaking, including "the more interesting styles of silent films in which 'Reciters' were used to describe and explain action – a device borrowed from Kabuki theatre, until the unexpected success of Kurosawa's *Rashomon* at the Venice Film Festival of 1951," where it won the Golden Lion. Interestingly, one of Kurosawa's older brothers, Heigo, was a well-regarded 'reciter', *benshi*, at a cinema in Kanda, an area in Tokyo famous for its large number of second-hand bookshops. Nevertheless, as motion pictures with synchronised sound, took off in the 1930s the role of the *benshi* became an anachronism and slowly became obsolete even in Japan.

Tragically, Heigo killed himself in 1933. Three years later Kurosawa got his first job in the film industry as a trainee assistant director. This didn't stop him from reading or change the types of books he read. Kurosawa still read pulp fiction, contemporary Japanese literature and the great Russian authors, but his approach became more analytical. He started reading more carefully, asking himself as he read about the author's objectives and how each author went about expressing these in words and within narrative prose. He also started making notes and, importantly, he also started writing screenplays.

Unsurprisingly, the first film Kurosawa directed, a decade after the death of his brother, whom he idolised, *Sanshiro Sugata (Judo Saga)*, was an adaptation of a newly published novel by the judo master and Naoki Prizewinning author Tsuneo Tomita (1904-1967). The action film was set in the 1880s when judo was founded by Jigoro Kano (1860-1938) out of the traditional Japanese martial art *Jujutsu* with the help of Tomita's father—one of the Four Guardians of Kodokan Judo—and other similar exceptionally proficient fighters. Tomita's father was Kano's sparring partner.

The film established Kurosawa's reputation in Japan as an exciting and important newcomer and the experience helped shape how Kurosawa portrayed fighting and fighters in his films going forward. Kano, like Kurosawa himself, had a major lasting impact on how the world saw Japan as a nation as well as his chosen profession. He was the first Asian member of the International Olympic Committee (IOC). Kano helped shape many things besides his sport, which would many years later become a popular international and Olympic sport. He'd influence the Olympic movement in Japan and the nation's so-called Olympic literature. He also indirectly influenced Kurosawa's career through his sparring partner's son's novel published the year before Kurosawa's first film went on general release. In turn, Kurosawa's film played an important role in the subsequent revival of judo as a sport in Japan after a period of prohibition of it and all other Japanese martial arts during Japan's post-war occupation.

The Art of Storytelling

It was another Japanese author, though, Ryunosuke Akutagawa (1892-1927), that brought Kurosawa and Japanese filmmaking international attention and recognition. Akutagawa is best known internationally for his debut short story "In a Grove", which brilliantly employs multiple narrative perspectives in the form of witness statements of a rape. Readers of "In a Grove" are left wondering about the reality of the crime and its 'truths' in this intriguing kaleidoscopic but compact tale; an authentic reflection perhaps of the real world, where the true nature of things cannot always be readily determined. Akutagawa's short stories, of which he wrote many, followed and developed the long and continuing tradition of masterful short story writing by Japan's leading authors of each generation.

Kurosawa's award-winning film *Rashomon*, his 11th film, sensationally used the title of another Akutagawa short story that the director and his team cleverly combined with "In a Grove" creating a unique film format that introduced the non-linear literary technique, now sometimes dubbed 'the Rashomon effect', to the world of cinematic storytelling. In 1951, it became the first post-war Japanese film to be submitted to an international film festival. The Venice Film Festival, where it won the Grand Prix. It also won the Academy Award for best foreign-language film. As a result, it exposed Japanese filmmaking to a truly international audience.

Rashomon became an instant classic. It not only triggered a brand-new approach, it also influenced many leading directors outside Japan including the likes of Steven Spielberg, who at the time of writing is currently working on a television adaptation of the film. This has all helped embed the role of the short story in Japan as an excellent source and important creative format. Masters of the modern Japanese short story, writers like the Akutagawa-nominated author Kanji Hanawa (1936-2020) who specialises in the genre, have found their stories, sometimes with and sometimes without their consent, being used at Japanese film schools to teach scriptwriting.

Most of Kurosawa's films were literary adaptations and he constantly argued that reading and writing were the critical components to cinematic success. He believed that memory is the source of creativity and that reading and writing creates memories, alongside living an interesting life, without which the creative process does not function. Some academics argue that 'reading like an author' can have measurable cognitive benefits improving, for example, brain connectivity, as well as having more general health benefits.¹⁵³ This is something that Kurosawa seems to have understood instinctively.

Kurosawa also knew that the secret of creative invention was curiosity, at times excessive behaviour, determined grit, and a sprinkle of independent and obsessive stubbornness. In order to gain more artistic freedom, Kurosawa, with the support of Toho Co. Ltd, decided to open his own production company, the Kurosawa Production Company. It was set up in 1959, a vanguard and pivotal year for many in Japan, not just Kurosawa. The year had an important imperial wedding between the Crown Prince, and future Emperor Akihito (b.1933), and Michiko Shoda (b. 1934). This wedding was the first to be broadcast live in Japan, helping usher in a new audio-visual age, powered by television, as opposed to film. This new age brought many books to big and small screens across Japan, but also made life harder for directors of the likes of Kurosawa that required costly production budgets and targeted cinema audiences. It was also the year the deadly Isewan Typhoon hit Japan.

Despite these challenges, Kurosawa's new production company made some classics including *Red Beard*, a film released in 1965, adored by many. It is a literary adaption based on a short story by Shugoro Yamamoto (1903-1967), about an arrogant young clinician trained in a Dutch medical school in Nagasaki who is assigned to work under a rural doctor nicknamed Akahige (Red Beard). The film a clever literary mix also incorporates elements of Dostoevsky's 1861 novel *The Humiliated and Insulated*. Kurosawa's newly formed production company, founded the year Yamamoto's story was published, went on to make the highly influential *Yojinbo*, a film that has inspired films outside Japan, such as a *Fist Full of Dollars* (*Koya no yojinbo*) and some other terrific films. Yamamoto's short story was published in *Bungeishunju*, a literary magazine that today still plays an important role, founded by another legacy-making influential creative, the author Kan Kikuchi (1888-1948).

By some measures Kurosawa is the most successful and important film director outside the English-speaking world. In 2018, the BBC conducted a survey of 209 international film critics to come up with a ranking in *The 100 greatest foreign-language films*.¹⁵⁴ Two of the top five ranked films were made by Kurosawa and he is the only director to have two films in the top five: *Shichinin no samurai* (*Seven Samurai*) is ranked number one, and *Rashomon* is number four. Kurosawa has a total of four films included in the list ranking him, in terms of the number of films, alongside directors such as Federico Fellini (1920-1993), Andrei Tarkovsky (1932-1986) and Ingmar Bergman (1918-2007).

Following Kurosawa's advice on storytelling is probably, therefore, a very good place to start. He argued that it is only through writing scripts that you learn the specifics about the structure of film and what cinema is, and all you need to do that is paper and a pencil. It is often argued that writing helps process ideas and memories, as well as develop clarity of thought. Many experts and fans have commented on Kurosawa being a champion of this and that he drew and painted how he wanted scenes in his films to look, a technique dubbed 'Every Frame a Picture'. One talented admirer has even created a cartoon strip, tilted *Kurosawa The Note Taker* portraying the importance he placed on reading and writing. This is how Kurosawa honed his craft. He wrote many scenes and scripts for the films he directed. Films like his debut film as a director, and films he didn't direct, like *Sengoku burai (Sword for Hire)*, which is based on a novel by the Akutagawa Prizewinning author Yasushi Inoue (1907-1991), another author known for the quality of his novella and short stories.

Kurosawa's approach to storytelling was to write and rewrite, drawing on his experiences as well as his emotional memories, including his literary memories from the vast number of books he had read. All of which contributed to the formation of his humanistic worldview. Sometimes he'd loosely adapt classic works of European literature or contemporary Japanese fiction for the screen and sometimes he'd combine and blend well-known narratives to great effect. When asked if his works had a common thread, he reportedly said they all posed a common question: "Why can't people be happier together?"

How to Read like Kurosawa

Some individuals, not just aspiring directors, want to read like Kurosawa with the aim of mimicking or capturing his creativity. Others just want to do so to understand him and his films better, and others simply want to read about him. There are many websites and online resources to help budding aficionados, including reading lists from book recommendation sites such as *Book Riot* with articles and headlines like "What to Read If You Love Akira Kurosawa."

That said, Kurosawa actually talked publicly about his favourite books on national television in Japan. They included *War and Peace* by Leo Tolstoy, *Sanshiro* by Natsume, *The Idiot* by Fyodor Dostoevsky and *Heike monogatari (The Tale of Heike)*, a Japanese medieval classic, which has been referred to as Japan's *Iliad*. A list of Kurosawa's top one hundred films exists thanks to a memoir, which was published posthumously, but sadly unlike David Bowie (1947-2016), another creative genius who believed strongly in the power of reading and was a great lover of all things Japanese, Kurosawa did not publish a list of his favourite 100 books.[155] Interestingly, none of the books that are known Kurosawa favourites, or books that have clearly influenced the films he made, appear on Bowie's 100 must-read books reading list.

Bowie's inclusion of one Japanese literary author, Yukio Mishima (1925-1970) and his book *Gogo no eiko* (*The Sailor Who Fell from Grace from the Sea*), might have raised a comment from Kurosawa as Mishima was famously at times dismissive of Kurosawa's films, despite or perhaps because of his own interest in appearing in films and having his works adapted for film. Some renowned Japanese directors also criticised Kurosawa's films as not being 'Japanese' but made for foreigners in a similar manner to how the works of Haruki Murakami (b. 1949) are dismissed today by some Japanese literary critics. That said, Bowie's exclusion of anything written by Dostoevsky, Tolstoy or Shakespeare might have also surprised Kurosawa, but he would probably have approved of Bowie's inclusion of the *Iliad* in his list of must-read books.

Inspired and Inspiring

Brilliant wordsmiths and their narratives inspired Kurosawa probably more than anything, and he in turn has inspired multiple new generations of individuals working in film, television and other mediums. Many notable films and television dramas are adaptions of or have been inspired by his films including *The Virgin Spring* (Ingmar Bergman), *Star Wars* (George Lucas), *Breaking Bad* (Vince Gilligan), *She's Gotta Have It* (Spike Lee), *The Magnificent Seven* (Antoine Fuqua), *A Fist Full of Dollars* (Sergio Leone), *The Outrage* (Martin Rift), *A Bug's Life* (John Lasseter), to list just a few.

Impressively, when Kurosawa won his final Oscar, on his birthday in 1990, two delighted super-fans presented his award to him: George Lucas and Spielberg. Despite this form of praise Kurosawa didn't welcome the comparison some make between the warriors in his films and the cowboy films he inspired. He dismissed cowboys as gangsters, refusing to acknowledge that they could have moral equity with the samurai portrayed in his films.

There have been countless books written about the Emperor, *Tenno*, of Japanese Film, as he was known, making Kurosawa's publishing legacy an impressive one. Books and Kurosawa, in life and death, are a powerful combination. He wrote about his life in *Gama no abura jiden no yunamono* (*Something Like An Autobiography*), which he penned in Japanese in 1981. Reviewers, scholars, collaborators and fans have contributed biographies, memoirs and scholarly works including, for instance, *Kurosawa Akira vs Hariuddo—Tora Tora Tora!—sono nazo no subete* (*All The Emperor's Men – Kurosawa's Pearl Harbor* and *Akira Kurosawa and Intertextual Cinema*), to the canon of film studies. Added to this, documentaries have also been made.

One recent book by Peter Tasker that exploits a Japanese literary format known as *zuihitsu*, which means literally 'at will and pen', presents a fragmented multi-narrative kaleidoscopic viewpoint of Kurosawa and his films in a Rashomon-like manner that would both delight and fascinate him. *Zuihitsu* often leave imprints through subtle implication, building a story through the contribution of fragmented pieces in a not too dissimilar manner to an impressionist painting, a technique also often skilfully exploited in classical Japanese poetry and modern Japanese short stories. Kurosawa would also approve of the production values of Tasker's stylish *On Kurosawa: A Tribute to the Master Director*, another book that, will no doubt, end up on the must-read lists of aspiring filmmakers and Kurosawa admirers.

In a fascinating twist, Japanese publishing executives these days often actually recommend that ambitious young manga editors and storytelling creatives, keen to learn and master their craft, of all varieties, watch his films. Films, alongside other storytelling channels like literature, manga and poetry, can generate fabulous lenses through which to scrutinise Japanese society spanning the prosaic and pesky to the sublime and sophisticated. Nonetheless, Kurosawa would probably still encourage such aspiring originators to focus their research on reading fiction that explores humankind in all its many forms, rather than non-fiction or film literature even if it is about him. A good place to start is probably with Japanese short stories and novellas, the formats that helped propel his career to a global level.

Books by contemporary Japanese authors, including Fuminori Nakamura (b. 1977) who has had around seven adapted for film in Japan and Mitsuyo Kakuta (b. 1967) whose books have ended up as unmissable television dramas and films, are still a rich creative reservoir that are regularly exploited locally. Digital technologies and streaming are generating new demand and opportunities for diverse creative storytelling in traditional as well as new formats. Who knows what future undiscovered creative cuts and blends lie in store?

New technologies are also changing the genesis of storytelling in positive ways but at the same time also instilling fear amongst contemporary writers that their craft may become commoditised. Following Kurosawa's example of reading, mixing, merging and repurposing Japanese fiction (no matter where you or your audience is based) seems to be the perfect starting point for filmmakers. Not just to learn how to 'read a film' but as frontrunners reading the market and its opportunities in novel ways that will surprise and inspire a new generation of film buffs, storytellers and international audiences.

Changing Nations: The Japanese Girl With a Book

A picture or a single look is said to be worth a thousand words and a good work of art or a sketch, according to Napoleon Bonaparte (1769-1821), better than a long speech. To bring some portraits or works of art to life for modern audiences context is required and a history that sparks curiosity often needs to be conjured up. Sometimes, however, a backstory can be as vivid and extraordinary as the image captured in oil itself. One such person is Toshiko Soma (1898-1925) rendered in 1914 age 15 in *Shojo* (*Girl*), the last of several portraits of her by the Japanese artist, Tsune Nakamura (1887-1924).

It was painted the year when Japan declared war on Germany, on 23 August, in this instance on the side of the Allied Powers of the First World War (1914-1918). This act that led to Japan taking over German-leased territories in China and German controlled islands in the North Pacific Ocean such as the Marshall Islands, which are now an associated state of the United States. This war left most nations and empires depleted and impoverished, with probably two notable exceptions: the United States and Japan. Highlighting Japan's shift from recent geopolitical debutantes to one of the so-called Great Powers.

In Nakamura's painting, an intelligent healthy-looking girl, mature for her age, is depicted gazing out in the direction of the artist, not directly at the viewer, with a quizzical expression. We get a sense that she may be challenging the artist as to the purpose of this sitting, and wondering how their futures might unfold once the painting was complete. Her oversized forearms and long fingers rest on a closed yellow-covered book to highlight her education and openness to ideas, but perhaps also indicate a chapter in her life is about to end or start. A reproduction of the portrait is on the artist's Wikipedia entry and on various other websites.

Nakamura, an artist from the Hakubakai Yoga school of Westernised artists, as opposed to practitioners of traditional Japanese art, was an associate of Rokuzan Ogiwara (1879-1910) a recognised Japanese sculptor of some repute who studied painting and sculpture in New York and in Paris with Auguste Rodin (1840-1917). His international study was partly paid for by the patrons that these two Japanese artists shared: Toshiko Soma's parents.

Nakamura hadn't actually wanted to be an artist. He would have preferred a career in the military but contracting tuberculosis when he was 17 closed off that route for him. Tuberculosis was considered a romantic and artistic condition in Japan at that time and during his initial recuperation Nakamura decided that he wanted to become an artist, which eventually led to him in 1911 living and working at Toshiko's parents' studio in Tokyo. Shortly after moving in, he started coughing up blood as his condition worsened.

Toshiko became his preferred model and muse. The sculptor Ogiwara had left the Shinjuku studio by then and had tragically died. Nakamura painted several portraits of Toshiko including images of her reading and also scandalously half-naked. The same year as this final portrait by Nakamura, who was in his late 20s and living off the support of Toshiko's culture-loving parents, Nakamura painted another portrait of Toshiko, still a young teenage girl and a student at Joshi Seigakuin, a Christian school for girls: *Shojo Razo (Girl Nude)*.

This portrait, which shows a shy-looking Toshiko with Renoir-like flushed cheeks sitting on a Western-style sofa, naked with a yellow cloth on her lap looking gently at the artist, was displayed publicly at an exhibition in Tokyo. The two, the artist and his young muse, living in close proximity were apparently falling in love. Nevertheless, Toshiko's parents perhaps unsurprisingly received a complaint from her school after the picture's public display questioning their approach to parenting, as well as their good Christian values.

Subsequently, in August 1915 Nakamura did the right thing and asked Toshiko's parents for their daughter's hand in marriage. The proposal was turned down by Toshiko's mother, Kokko, leading to Nakamura drifting away from the Soma's circle, and subsequently setting up his own studio in Shinjuku, Tokyo. He died almost a decade later, aged 37, on Christmas Eve 1924. It is unclear if his proposal was public knowledge, but the teenage Toshiko's future marriage prospects and reputation would not have been enhanced by the half-naked portrait and this particularly exuberant episode.

Tastemaker Parents

The Somas, Aizo and Kokko, weren't your typical early 20th century Japanese parents. They were both Christians and met because of their faith. Kokko was a pen name taken on at school, coined by a teacher, due to Toshiko's mother's early literary ambitions. The name had an embedded message of caution, as it was written using two seemingly contradictory *kanji* characters, letters, 'dim' and 'shining'.

Only moderate success and prominence would be considered acceptable for most women with cultural ambitions in Japanese society during its Meiji era (1868-1912), when the nation was frantically modernising and trying to catch up with the West after more than two hundred years of self-imposed isolation. Therefore, to assure success a strategy of not allowing one's natural talent and ambition to shine too brightly was optimum.

Her wealthy husband, Aizo, didn't share those views. He believed not only in romantic love, but partnerships based on equality, as well as temperance. He encouraged his wife to embrace modernity and they worked together in myriad ways while also having nine children, including their oldest Toshiko. Neither of them were born in Tokyo, but in 1901, three years after they married and a few years after the birth of their first child Toshiko, they bought a bakery in the Japanese capital outside Tokyo University, Nakamuraya. (There is no connection to the artist Nakamura.) This kicked off their careers as entrepreneurial trendsetting bakers, a dynamic and radical couple active within Tokyo's expanding cultural scene. In 1909 they moved their growing business to Shinjuku, an up-and-coming part of Tokyo where a station had been opened in 1885. The station developed rapidly as more and more lines were added, and it eventually became what is now described as 'the world's busiest station' by the *Guinness Book of World Records*.

Baking Faith: Righteousness and Hope

Changing one's location, doing a geographical within a city or moving to a new country or town to reinvent oneself or one's career or simply to escape an awkward past, is something many have tried and still do today, sometimes with remarkable results especially if the timing is right. The decision by Aizo and Kokko to make this move away from their surroundings of the nation's most important seat of higher learning was made just before Japan entered a new democratising and more prosperous and open period, the Taisho era (1912-1926). The name Taisho when translated directly into English means 'the era of great righteousness'. Though a frenetic era of upheaval, it was a period of hope and increasing international openness, what might today be termed globalisation.

Aizo and Kokko were aged 31 and 25 respectively when they started their careers in the baking and confectionary business and despite her young age, Kokko was already showing a real flare for spotting new trends, canny promotion, and opportunistic cultural networking. She and her husband built a studio behind their shop in Shinjuku for Ogiwara for him to use on his return to Japan.[156] Ogiwara lived at the studio in close proximity with the Soma family. This positioned them at the intersection of business, art and culture in this expanding and soon to become vibrant part of Tokyo, a location with a very different profile to the area enclosing Tokyo University.

Their circle included activists, poets and university professors as well as artists—locals, returnees and non-Japanese alike—generating a creative milieu that led to the creation of new products and business ideas. This included their *kurimu-pan*, a type of cream bun still popular today, which they invented and launched in 1904, as well as new ways of packaging and selling snacks, such as the crispy bite-sized snack *karinto*, and much more besides. Talented up-and-coming artists who subsequently became famous, designed their all-important shop front sign and logos, including another Nakamura, Fusetsu Nakamura (1886-1943). He had also studied in Paris and had some of his work exhibited there at the 1900 Exposition Universelle where he even won a minor prize. He is also remembered for his delightful illustrations of Soseki Natsume's (1867-1916) breakthrough work, *Wagahai wa neko de aru* (*I am a Cat*) that generated its own type of cultural quantum leap.

The Somas also became involved in the Pan-Asian Movement, which might today be called the Indo-Pacific Alliance. They were also part of the compact network of so-called Japanese Christian intelligentsia. The business flourished and they added a cafe and restaurant and the studio expanded from an atelier into a cultural salon attracting Japan's literati, as well as intellectuals and artists including Nakamura, their daughter's portrait painter.

Bread of Affliction: Buns and Longing

It wasn't just their daughter, Toshiko, who inspired an artist. Kokko also had a magical effect on others, especially on Ogiwara, who is sometimes referred to today in Japan as the 'Rodin of the East'. Ogiwara reportedly fell in love with a Soma woman, just like Nakamura was destined to do a few years later. Ogiwara, also a Christian, struggled with his conflicted feeling for his patron, Kokko, who personified beauty unrequited love, and Ogiwara is often quoted as having said, "Love is art, struggle is beauty." Ogiwara's final work *Woman*, which he completed in the Nakamuraya studio, is considered an important Japanese masterpiece. It was the first modern sculpture to be designated an Important Cultural Property by the Japanese government. Twenty days after completing his final masterpiece, in 1910, Ogiwara abruptly left the Nakamuraya studio and tragically died shortly afterwards that year, in April, at the age of 30.

A 2007 television drama, *Rokuzan's Love*, tells his story focusing on his 'forbidden love' for Kokko, the artist's muse and, according to the television drama, the model for *Woman*. The actual model, however, for what is probably his most sensual work, was officially a different unnamed woman. This wasn't, however, the first or only television drama to feature Nakamuraya and their tale. The first was *Buns and Longing*, broadcast nationally in Japan also by TBS in 1969.

Following the artist's death when *Woman* was exhibited at the Nakamuraya atelier for the first time, which had by then been transferred to the second floor of the Soma's Shinjuku bakery and opened to the public, Kokko's children, including an 11-year-old Toshiko, reportedly knew immediately upon seeing it, who the real inspiration behind *Woman* was. "That's *Okasan* (mum)," they declared on seeing it for the very first time. Ogiwara's official cause of death was tuberculosis, but some speculate that he actually killed himself, using poison, having perfected his greatest work depicting the perfect woman, the woman he loved, Kokko, Toshiko's mother.

Whatever the truth behind the rumours surrounding both Kokko and Toshiko and their relationships with these troubled, pioneering urbane artistic Japanese men, who both lived embedded lives amongst the Soma family, neither of these two dynamic Soma women—mother nor daughter—developed a long-term sustainable partnership with a Japanese artist, even if they are both now imprinted on modern Japanese art and its somewhat bohemian narrative history. There was also much more to each of these unusual women and their lives than that of simply artists' muses and objects of desire.

Changing Places: Tomorrow's Women

Toshiko and her mother, Kokko, were living in an exciting period in Japanese history, especially for young residents in and around Tokyo. The nation was urbanising and changing fast. The First World War had created a mini-economic boom for Japan and Tokyo was becoming an exciting metropolis with a population of more than two million with money to spend.

Japan attended the Paris Peace Conference in 1919, as a military and newly industrialised power and one of the five major nations taking charge of a new world order. Japan found itself sitting on the side of the table with the rule-makers not the rule-takers. Before the exuberant Taisho period commenced in 1912, Japan had already opened up to the West and adopted many Western ways, through fashion, cuisine and changed its outlook and view of the nation's place in the wider world.

Wearing Western clothes; clutching Western-style books in portraits as Toshiko had done or carrying books as fashion accessories, were seen as acts of modernity and intelligent erudite sophistication.

Things were very different in the decades that proceeded. In 1890, for example, only 31 percent of girls completed primary level education. This subsequently rose to 72 percent in 1900, and a decade or so later in Taisho Japan, women had started entering the workforce as waitresses, nurses, bus conductors, and typists, often wearing Western-styled uniforms. This helped spawn new fashions, and individuals known as *mobo* and *moga*, modern-boys and modern-girls.

Even Freudian psychoanalysis had arrived in Japan in translation, as had Lewis Carroll's (1832-1898) *Alice's Adventures in Wonderland,* Arthur Conan Doyle's (1859-1930) Sherlock Holmes, and Charles Darwin's (1809-1882) *On the Origin of Species*. In the 1920's Tokyo, alongside Calcutta, were the first Asian hubs for psychoanalysis, where this new discipline influenced by local languages, religion, folklore and philosophy, including Buddhism and Confucian values, developed. Western cookbooks and style guides were also being published in Japanese for Japan's increasingly newly literate population who had an insatiable appetite for reading and all things Western. Trendy European style cafes were opening up catering for this new generation who felt and acted very differently from their parents and grandparents. Entrepreneurs began launching new business ventures often targeting this new class of urban-dwelling consumers.

Edo Japan (1603-1868), when the nation was mostly cut off from the world and ruled by shoguns, was now a distant memory, an alien world. This new generation, with its open and experimental attitudes, and the 'New Japan', would have seemed as perplexing and incomprehensible to earlier generations, as early Edo would now have seemed to Taisho youth. New treats such as Nakamuraya's newly invented *kurimu-pan* were being launched and bell-bottom trousers were being worn and hair shorn short.

Attitudes towards sexuality became less Victorian and were again much more open. They could even at times be fluid and new style romance writers like Nobuko Yoshiya (1896-1973) with her independent and adventurous spirit started romancing Japan's reading public helping create a new genre of increasingly popular and commercially successful books, the modern romance. She was so prolific and successful that she earned enough royalties to support her chosen lifestyle, which included being the first woman in Japan to own a car and adopt her partner in an early form of same-sex marriage. While same-sex marriage is very slowly becoming legal across Japanese municipalities, for a long time adoption was a useful legal loophole. Being adopted allows same-sex couples to share a single family name and confers legal rights on their partnership, mirroring those of a child and a parent, including, for example, rights such as inheritance.

Tokyo Calling

When economic prosperity, increasing openness and political and emerging societal freedom converge, a city can feel as if it is the epicentre of the world. Taisho Tokyo was just that for some, a hugely exciting and enjoyable time full of strangeness and opportunity up until the 1923 devastating Great Kanto Earthquake, which tragically destroyed much of Tokyo and changed the nation's trajectory.

Some anti-liberal demagogues, of course, denounced this copycat Westernisation and laissez-faire liberalism as a betrayal of the nation and its traditions. Nonetheless, Tokyo was becoming a little like Japan would in the heady 1980s when, according to people like the musician Ryuichi Sakamoto (1952-2023), Tokyo was the most interesting city in the world,[157] sucking in the talented and curious, such as Sakamoto's friend and collaborator David Bowie (1947-2016). Bowie was a great fan of Japan and was fascinated by Japanese authors like Yukio Mishima (1925-1970), as well as designers and musicians. Sakamoto, the composer, singer and songwriter, had a major influence on his work. Bowie spoke publicly about his love of the country and even considered moving to Japan permanently in the 1980s. He already had his own private residence in Kyoto. He acquired the property with the proceeds of doing a TV commercial for the food and drinks company Takara Shuzo. At Bowie's request, the advert was filmed at the Zen temple Shodenji, in the northern outskirts of Kyoto; in a city of over 2,000 Buddhist temples and Shinto shrines, this was Bowie's favourite. Sadly, Bowie eventually settled on New York as his base.

Back in the Taisho era, Tokyo was also becoming a metropolis for political Pan-Asianism with Vietnamese nationalists and Chinese republicans, as well as Indian revolutionaries, interacting with Japanese students and intellectuals. By the dawn of the 20th century, the West had become increasingly aware of Japan and its attractions. The Nobel Prize committee recognised the insights of Rudyard Kipling's (1865-1936) writing on the manners and customs of the Japanese when they awarded him his Nobel Prize in 1907, the year the Somas started planning their move to Shinjuku. Kipling made two well-documented trips to Japan, the first when he was still an unknown Indian-born man traveling through Japan en route to the United States in his 20s. In fact, by the early 1900s so many books had been published 'Explaining Japan' that some authors even felt compelled to write books that both summarised and refuted them. Japan, or at least Tokyo, was becoming the land of the rising hipster, and started to attract the attention of adventurous individuals from outside Japan, in the same way as it would in the 1980s.

Taisho Era Talent Management

One such man was a blind violin-playing Esperanto-speaking Russian poet called Vasili Eroshenko (1890-1952). He moved to Japan in 1914 to study massage at the school for the blind in Tokyo, the year Toshiko's final portrait by Nakamura was painted. Learning Esperanto, the first so-called International Language invented in 1887, was de rigueur in Japan at the time and some trendy Japanese clubs and associations encouraged their members to speak this artificially created easy-to-learn universal language, the name of which means 'one who hopes'.

Eroshenko stayed for about two years, learning to speak Japanese and even started publishing children's books in Japanese, before returning again in 1919 through Shanghai from India. He became a major celebrity travelling across Japan drawing large crowds. Being blind and blond made him an object of fascination. The fact that he was blind and could therefore not judge the Japanese by their skin colour, added to his charismatic allure. He gave talks alongside Japanese authors including Mimei Ogawa (1882-1961), famed for his short stories, fairy tales and children's books. Many writers became regular visitors to the Nakamuraya cultural salon. The salon rapidly became a night-time campus for Tokyo radicals, intellectuals and artists, as well as a place to learn about art, and study the Russian language as well as discuss exciting new forms of literature. All of this fascinated Kokko; in 1913 she started taking Russian lessons from a professor at Waseda University.

Eroshenko was probably one of the best-known foreigners living in Japan at that time. He would be known today in Japan as a *gaitare*, a foreign celebrity or media personality. He, like many other talented Taisho individuals, fell into Kokko's orbit and ended up living with the Somas in Shinjuku, something that the Somas weren't afraid to make widely known. The Somas liked to hire and consult foreign residents when it came to developing new condiments, breads and products. They also benefited from the halo effect of the constant presence of individuals like Eroshenko around their Shinjuku shop.

Nakamura, their daughter's portrait painter, painted a famous portrait of Eroshenko wearing a *rubashka*, a type of tunic worn by Russian peasants, which they proudly exhibited. In many ways, Eroshenko became an early Bowie-like figure in the way he assumed the role of brand ambassador and product promoter for the Somas and Nakamuraya. There were, however, unfortunate side effects to Eroshenko's growing status and influence. The Japanese authorities reportedly considered him a potential Bolshevik and, despite or perhaps because he was a poet and free spirit, the most dangerous foreigner living in Japan. He was abruptly deported in 1921, a controversial decision that made headline news. The same fate, of course, would not befall Bowie, that other famous experimentalist and rebel.

In a savvy business response to Eroshenko's deportation, Kokko managed to keep his visibility, and what might today be called brand equity, alive by adopting Russian style uniforms for their employees the year of his deportation in honour and memory of him. She also hired a Russian baker, launched a range of Russian-type bread, and cleverly added a 'Russian' soup, borscht (it is actually apparently Ukrainian) to their restaurant's menu, a sensible selection in a soup-loving nation like Japan where most meals are served with a broth of some type.

Rising Prose

In addition to artisan bakers and trendsetting cafes, Taisho Japan also had its own trendsetting 'it' magazine for the young literary in-crowd, *Shirakaba* (*White Birch*), a monthly publication which ran from 1910-1923. There was increasing interest in Russian and international literature, a trend that Nakamuraya and its owners embraced and stoked brilliantly.

The presentation in 1913 of the first Nobel Prize in literature to an Asian author and the first non-European to win the prize, Rabindranath Tagore (1861-1941), a Bengali polymath, provided yet more momentum to these trends. Naturally, it delighted the Japanese literati, and inspired many Japanese authors writing in the Japanese language into thinking that international success was a possibility. Yasunari Kawabata (1899-1972) Japan's first Nobel literature laureate who won the prize in 1968 would have been a teenager at the time.

Tagore's influence is not limited to just aspiring and notable Japanese creatives. It is very broad. Paul McCartney, for instance, who with the help of the Beatles and their pivotal concerts at the Budokan in 1966—concerts attended by some of Japan's literary elite such as Yukio Mishima (1925-1970), Shusaku Endo (1913-1996), Hiroshi Akutagawa (1920-1981) the son of Ryunosuke Akutagawa (1892-1927)—changed Japan's cultural flows from haircuts to songwriting, cited Tagore in his book *The Lyrics* (2021) as a major influence on his songwriting. The winds of change be they social, celebrity, lyrical or political can blow and create unpredictable kaleidoscopic patterns, things great and small mosaicked together forming a new patchwork cultural tapestry. Of course, his influence has not just been international. One of Tagore's compositions, "Dispenser of Indian Destiny", became the National Anthem of India in 1950, "Jana Gana Mana".

In 1915, two years after Tagore won his Nobel Prize another Bengali used Tagore's literary success to escape India and gain safe passage to Japan, later joining Eroshenko at Nakamuraya. It was a decision that changed the Somas and Toshiko's lives dramatically. His name was Rash Bihari Bose (1886-1945). He was aged 29 but with a dark past, and was on the run, having tried unsuccessfully to assassinate Lord Hardinge (1858-1944), the Viceroy and Governor General of India in Delhi on 23 December 1912. Hardinge who was with his wife riding an elephant at the time was wounded in the shoulder. His wife was unharmed. The incident, an act of insurgence designed to spark a revolution, even led to questioning of the Under-Secretary of State for India in the Houses of Commons in London about the conspiracy and the arrest of the perpetrators. Bose used an alias, Priyanath Tagore, pretending to be a relative of the Nobel laureate, to escape to Japan.

From Glamour Model to Sari-Wearing Mother

Initially on Bose's arrival, various Pan-Asian groups in Japan's underground networks of radicals, activists, progressives and revolutionaries who wanted Asians to unite against European imperialism, develop an Asian voice and system of values—some as a form of liberalism and others as nationalists—hid and looked after Bose.[158]

His first visit to the Somas at Nakamuraya was in the spring of 1916, the year after Nakamura the artist had moved out. It was here that he would occasionally stay overnight in hiding. In their attempt to track him down and have him deported back to India, the British authorities hired private detectives. But like others, Bose eventually ended up living at the cultural salon on the second floor of Nakamuraya in Shinjuku unbeknownst to the British spies looking for him.[159]

Interestingly, in 1916, the Indian Nobel laureate who had indirectly helped Bose escape to Japan did actually visit the country, and the Somas would undoubtedly have been involved with his visit and associated events. The trip, which lasted several months, caused considerable excitement drawing crowds and was covered in Japanese newspaper such as the *Asahi Shimbun*. This was partly due to three short poems Tagore had written on Japan's victory over Russia in 1905. Tagore gave several notable speeches, including one on India and Japan, arguing against jingoistic nationalism, even though he was a staunch patriot and believed in the value of the East and independence.

For some, Japan, an island nation with a large, prioritised Navy and a growing empire, was believed to be slowly becoming the Britain of the East. In an eloquent speech just before leaving Japan on the first of his five visits, titled *The Spirit of Japan*, he warned the nation against "imitation of the outward aspects of the West" and about "the hounding wolves of the modern era." Despite this, the place of nature in Japanese literature and culture and the so-called Japanese aesthetic is said to have had a deep impact on him, as did he on many in Japan. He described this temperament towards nature as "the genius of Japan." But during later visits after the Taisho era had ended, Japan's increasing militarism and jingoism, which seemed to be replacing dynamism and openness, is said to have troubled him.[160] The era ended on Christmas Day 1926, with the death of the emperor, ushering in the Showa era (1926-1989), corresponding to the reign of Emperor Hirohito (1901-1989), which as its two *kanji* characters depict many hoped would be one of enlightened peace. But the aspirations of rising nations in a hurry, can be blindsided by success, ambition and bloody narrow-mindedness with tragic consequences.

Even after Bose's deportation order was finally rescinded, following several months in the Nakamuraya cultural salon's guesthouse, Bose's status in Japan remained extremely precarious. That is when a solution was proposed by a leader and controversial figure in the Pan-Asian Movement, Mitsuru Toyama (1855-1944), a shadowy and elusive figure sometimes referred to as the Shadow Shogun who was also the founder of the Black Dragon Society (Kokuryukai), a paramilitary nationalist group. He proposed that the Soma's eldest daughter, Toshiko, should marry Bose, as both were still unmarried, and a marriage would allow Bose to apply for Japanese citizenship.

Toshiko's parents were initially taken aback by this suggestion and not apparently delighted by the prospect of their daughter marrying an Indian revolutionary, but they decided to ask their daughter directly if she was interested in becoming Bose's human shield and marrying him. They were already familiar as Toshiko had been helping look after Bose and translate for him, but she was only 19, and despite the heady times, international marriages were still very rare in Japan.

It took several weeks for Toshiko to make her mind up, but she eventually decided to go ahead with the proposed plan, and they were married in July 1918 in a secret private ceremony. About a year later Toshiko gave birth to a son and a daughter followed shortly afterwards. But life was a constant worry and they moved multiple times, wary of surveillance, kidnap or assassination. Toshiko learnt some Bengali and even occasionally wore a sari. Her new life on the run with a fugitive that the British considered a terrorist would have been totally unimaginable when she had originally sat for those portraits in her early teens for the artist Nakamura, who had unsuccessfully asked her parents for her hand in marriage.

How Strong is the Shield?

By all accounts Toshiko was dedicated and devoted to her husband. The couple bonded and apparently fell in love. Toshiko had morphed in the space of just a few years from a career-defining artist's muse to the life-saving wife of an Indian anti-colonialist revolutionary and a mother of two. In July 1923, a few months before much of Tokyo was destroyed by the Great Kanto Earthquake that killed more than 100,000 people, Bose was naturalised, becoming a Japanese citizen finally allowing the couple to move into their own home in Sendagaya. Sadly, their home was destroyed shortly afterwards in the earthquake of 1 September and, like many others, a secure and simple family life would continue to elude Toshiko and her family.

Tragically, despite her husband's newly found security in Japan, Toshiko's health began to fail. Less than two years later, in March 1925, the year of Mishima's birth, she died from a respiratory illness, probably tuberculosis. Her death was one year after the death of Nakamura, her portrait painter, and tragically a few years after the first use in humans of the anti-tuberculosis BCG vaccine in 1921. It was a period when the spectre of death hung over Tokyo. Despite watching over her husband and keeping him from danger, fate caught up with them.

Toshiko was only 26 years old, but in her short intense life, and especially the period since her semi-naked portrait was exhibited, her life had been a feverish whirlwind of events reflecting both the opportunities and extremes of Taisho Japan. A period that came to an end one year later in 1926 with the death of Emperor Yoshihito (1879-1926) when the Showa Emperor, Hirohito (1901-1989), took over from his father and the Showa era began. Sometimes individual acts can change nations and history. Toshiko's husband had tried to instigate such a change in India before his arrival in Japan. But unpredictable seismic events like pandemics or the huge 1923 earthquake, can trigger dramatic change too. Such events stop nations or individuals from exploiting golden new opportunities and alter the natural course of things. In this regard, Japan and its Taisho era are no exception.

Bose continued to fight for Indian independence: campaigning, writing, lobbying and organising, and even launched a bilingual English-Japanese journal titled *The New Asia*. He chaired the Indian Independence Conference in Bangkok in 1942, which helped found the Indian National Army (INA) and the Free India movement.

The task of bringing up his children was left to Toshiko's parents after her death. Despite this, Bose never remarried nor wished to, and he was buried together with

Toshiko after his own death, also from a respiratory illness, in 1945. It was sadly before India gained its independence in 1947, leaving a potential symbolic intersection with a historic milestone unfulfilled. Bose and Toshiko's son was killed in action during the Second World War while fighting Allied Forces in Okinawa, but their daughter married a Japanese man and gave birth to her own daughter. But this was not the final twist in this unpredictable Indo-Japanese narrative.

Revolutionary Indian Curry

In 1872 Robun Kanagaki (1829-1894), a well-known author and journalist published a book containing the first recipe in Japanese for making curry. It was based on a British Royal Navy recipe and wasn't authentic Indian-style curry. Despite this, curry, or as it is generally known in Japan curry-rice, quickly became a very popular Japanese dish. It has not just found its way into the pages of the National Diet Library's collection of around 10 million books thanks to Kanagaki's book but also appears as Library Curry, the signature dish of the sixth-floor cafeteria of the library, Japan's national deposit library in Tokyo. This in itself highlights the extent of curry's popularity.

In another spiced-up anti-colonial act in defiance of British culinary rule and British curry's occupation of Japanese palates, Bose, following the death of his wife, approached his father-in-law, Aizo, about selling and serving authentic Indian curry at Nakamuraya. Subsequently, a plan was cooked up and an India room set up in 1927 at their cafe allowing the Somas to start serving Indian-style curry for the first time in Japan, which soon became known as *Indo-Karii*. Bose chose the ingredients for the dish that quickly become one of their signature dishes, chicken curry with rice and pickles. It is still served today in Japan, proving that transformative legacies can come in many flavours.

Amazingly, there is actually another newer Indian curry restaurant, Nair's Indian Restaurant in East Ginza, founded in 1949, linked to another India revolutionary, the freedom fighter A.M. Nair (1905-1990), a second front in the battle to occupy Japanese palates and taste buds. Nair, who studied engineering at Kyoto University, supported Bose in some of his activities and published a book in 1982 titled *An Indian Freedom Fighter in Japan: Memoirs of A.M. Nair*. Copies, with its red cover containing his black-and-white photograph, are displayed prominently in the restaurant, which serves a good and reasonably priced lunch. If you visit, then a table upstairs and the signature dish, Murugi Lunch, a chicken dish, are recommended.

Pioneering Artisan Bakers: A Flavour of Things to Come?

The Somas and Nakamuraya continued to curry favour with Japanese consumers by supporting and feeding people after the devastation of the Great Kanto Earthquake and launching eye-catching new products. In 1929 they started selling branded chocolate and in 1940 they launched curry buns. All of this helped them navigate their business through the ups and downs of Japan's Showa era and the Second World War, right up to the present day. Unlike their brave-hearted daughter, Toshiko's parents lived long lives, dying one year apart, her father in his 80s in 1954 and her mother in her late seventies in 1955. Kokko who always appeared to know her own mind, died the day after she was moved into a retirement home having fulfilled her youthful writing ambitions and more. She published several books in March 1944, and February 1953, thus, ensuring that her light and narrative would never dim.

Trendsetting innovation continued and in the 1970s Nakamuraya decided to draw on its own heritage by teaming up once more with an artist. This time to help develop a new, improved product line of traditional Japanese sweets known as *yokan*, one of Japan's most popular delicacies that are often given as gifts. Nakamuraya asked Shiko Munakata (1903-1975), an international award-winning woodblock printer, to create new package designs for their range. He drew on India for inspiration and created three different types of wrapping paper designs using motifs of an Indian deity. Instead of covering the entire container, the wrapper was designed to be tied over the box housing the *yokan* and be removable. This was a first in Japan, which turned Nakamuraya's *yokan* into affordable and exotic works of art that could be displayed, as well as delicious snacks. Some observers have pointed out that the semi-naked black-haired deity, providing the protective wrapping for these perishable delicacies, bears more than a fleeting resemblance to Toshiko.

A restaurant and cafe, called Manna, in the basement of the Nakamuraya building in Shinjuku where the Nakamuraya Salon—now a museum—is located on the third floor, still sells Bose's popular curry dish. For almost twenty years ready-to-eat packages, also based on Bose's original recipe, have been sold across Japan at convenience stores extending Indian curry lineage deep into the heart of culinary Japan. The momentum of Toshiko's narrative shows that the products of embracing uncertainty and the strange with open-minded creative flare can be lasting, unexpected, and incredible.

Unsung Women from History and the Future of Japan

If you find yourself in Shinjuku, pop into Kinokuniya, one Japan's best bookshops, located on the opposite side of the road from the Nakamuraya building, and pick up a novel in Japanese or in translation by one of Japan's current cohort of brilliant female writers or perhaps even one of the indomitable Kokko Soma's books. Then cross the road taking a look at Toshiko's portrait and some of the works on display in the Nakamuraya Salon before heading to the building's basement to enjoy a curry. It is the perfect way to pay homage to Toshiko, the progressive unyielding human shield, as well as other early Japanese pioneers and their narratives, while also savouring unusual narratives of the present, and possibly Japan's future.

You will also be sharing a culinary experience with some characters that feature in at least one Haruki Murakami (b. 1949) novel, *1Q84*, and perhaps also an experience the author, like many others, has enjoyed himself. If a visit to Tokyo isn't an option, please at least visit the Nakamuraya Salon Museum of Art (Tokyo) website where you will be able to see images of some of the works of art mentioned here.

Much has been written about Bose, sometimes simply depicting him as a Bengali firebrand, a rebel against the Raj, a Japanese patsy, or as a figurehead of Bengali regional pride, as well as the artists that frequented the Nakamuraya salon and the Somas.[161] However, the story of the 'Japanese girl with a book', Toshiko, who was at the apex of this network of individuals trying to change nations, has rightly also been impossible to erase from history, but is sadly often forgotten or passed over. Toshiko is just one of many unsung women from Japan's rich history, and unsurprisingly it has taken more than a thousand words to try to tell her tale.

Bonkbusters and The Land of the Rising Sun

When we hear the term bonkbuster we immediately think of the 1980s and books with titles like *Lace, The Bitch, Savages, The Stud, Hollywood Wives*, and *Once is Not Enough*. The so-called queens of the genre are the American and British writers Jilly Cooper, Shirley Conran, Jackie Collins, Danielle Steel and Jacqueline Susann. It was, however, in fact Sue Limb, a British writer and broadcaster, who actually coined the term in 1989. It is a portmanteau of blockbuster and bonk, a British expression meaning sexual intercourse.

Dictionaries define the word as "a type of popular novel characterised by frequent explicit sexual encounters between the characters" or "a novel characterised by graphic descriptions of the heroine's frequent sexual encounters." We may not necessarily associate such titles with Japanese literature but under these definitions Japan has its fair share of the genre and has experienced several bonkbuster booms with bestselling books written by women for women frequently on the bestseller lists. Perhaps, this shouldn't be as surprising as it sounds. Japanese women have often been pioneers within literature and have used narrative fiction especially autofiction as a means to gain respect and independence, as well as to be subversive or comment on the ills and delights of Japanese society.

This type of literary subversiveness is, subtly and sometimes not so subtly, reflected in the narrative undercurrents of many talented Japanese writers in a similar manner to that of some internationally famous and notable authors in other genres of fiction outside the world of the bonkbuster, such as Agatha Christie (1890-1976). Writers who are known for their masked commentaries on those in authority and society. Literary subversion is said to have helped redefine the rules governing gender roles, social class and much else. Many works, as in Christie's case with whodunnits, have also been commercially extremely successful. In Japan sex has generally been an important part of the story; Japan may have its old, seemingly immutable traditions and lingering social and gender hierarchies, but it is by no means a nation of prudes. It is a country with rather permissive views on sex and sexuality.

"The fabric twisted into a rope. Okabe's fingers passed quickly over the soft part of me he had now exposed and sank inside. No matter when it happened, my body was always ready the moment he touched me," writes the Noma Prizewinning author Mari Akasaka (b. 1964) in *Baibureta* (*Vibrator*), a tale about a troubled bulimic journalist confronting her personal demons and discovering her sexuality, which is perhaps one of many possible recent good examples of this phenomenon. It is not a new phenomenon, however, and has actually been part of Japanese literature from the first golden age of female writers in Japan's Heian period (794-1185) when aristocratic ladies wrote for other noblewomen, often in chapter instalments which were handed out to the ladies at court.

Stories such as *Genji monogatari* (*The Tale of Genji*) that describes the shinning prince Genji's latest promiscuous liaisons, lovers and troubles and the tale of *Koshoku ichidai onna* (*The Life of an Amorous Woman*), a 17th century story of a fallen lady, an ageing beauty living in a grass hut. In the of case *The Life of an Amorous Woman* written by a male author Saikaku Ihara (1642-1693), the inventor of the so-called genre of 'floating world', *ukiyo-zoshi*, prose. Male authorship may for some technically put this particular work out of scope, even though Saikaku was the leading author of his age. Initially a poet, his breakthrough work published in 1662 titled *Koshoku ichidai otoko* (*The Life of an Amorous Man*) was consciously organised in 54 chapters, making it structurally reminiscent of *The Tale of Genji*, with its 54 scrolls. It helped turn Saikaku into one of Japan's most popular and consequential authors. Courtship methods and the manner of how sexual acts and their nature are depicted in prose have, of course, changed significantly since these early tales of women and men "who loved love" were written, but in their own classical and stylistic manner some of these titles still probably fall within the broad scope of being classic bonkbusters.

Going back even further to the creation myths of Japan, the nation's early legends include strong female deities like its sun goddess Amaterasu (in contrast to the male equivalents in most other cultures such as Apollo or Helios). In the Land of the Rising Sun, Amaterasu is the all-important goddess of the sun and the universe, as well as the ancestor of the Japanese imperial family. Stories about her are not distant, sexless or prudish, rather they are on occasion racy and riotous.

In one story, after a row with her uncontrollable brother, Susanoo, she hides in a cave in anger and the world is plunged into darkness. She is only coaxed out, bringing sunlight and prosperity back to the world, by a wild striptease and the raucous laughter of the other gods and goddesses watching eagerly. The wild interplay between the sun goddess, Amaterasu, and the storm god, Susanoo, are more than a reflection of ancient gender dynamics, they are said to be the personification of nature itself. Just as Arthurian legends have a difficult to define role and important place in the heritage of Britain, Japan's ancient legends still have a place in the hearts of many Japanese, and probably even more so in the hearts of the nation's talented storytellers.

The narratives of bonkbusters in the English-speaking world include very different types of goddesses. But the common thread is that the protagonists are usually determined women striving for independence, a little like the authors themselves who often researched and knew their markets well and wrote large numbers of titles designed to sell. All the queens of the genre have been published at least once in translation in Japan. Jacqueline Susann's novel, *Once is Not Enough*, which reached the number one spot in the *New York Times* bestsellers list and was made into a film with the same title starring Kirk Douglas, for instance, was published in 1988 by Shinchosha. Despite, their success and the plots being full of glamour, twists, skulduggery, sex, optimism and sometimes even happy endings, these narratives often now feel dated and most of these titles are currently out of print in Japan.

Historically, there was a popular Japanese slogan: *Risshin-Shusse* (to rise, success in life, advance yourself socially). This 'American Dream' type of upwardly mobile sentiment is one that bonkbuster heroines and authors would certainly aspire to. It is said to have been triggered by the British author Samuel Smiles's (1812-1904) book *Self-Help* (1859) becoming available in Japan in translation in the Meiji era (1868-1912). At that time, improving one's status, as opposed to coping with or accepting one's existing inherited 'proper' position in society, was a new phenomenon. As access to education and literary rates increased, these changes extended to the roles available to women and male-female dynamics and expectations. Intellectual energy was unleashed, not just through these new types of books becoming available in Japanese translation, but also new locally authored books and magazines.

In contrast, the bonkbuster genre took off in the 1980s during the Reagan-Thatcher period of deregulation, globalisation, and economic expansion that came after a decade of austerity. A decade which followed the sexual liberalisation of the Swinging Sixties when the repeal of restrictions restraining publication of 'erotic' fiction subsequently had a major impact on reading habits. The tipping point was the publication in 1965 of *Memoirs of a Woman of Pleasure* (commonly known as *Fanny Hill*), John Cleland's (1709-1789) novel written in 1748 from prison.

In the 1980s regimes were collapsing, creating a sense of opportunity for all. Women won equal pay rights and had more authority and control in the workplace. New technology including video recorders, cassettes and mobile phones had arrived on the scene, along with the first personal computers, changing how media was consumed along with popular tastes. This was the age of MTV, thrusting ambition and conspicuous spending. Large bonkbusters written for the mass-market were very much part of the eighties phenomenon and helped 'educate' a generation of young women and girls.

During Japan's Meiji era, the new printing technologies and universal education for women were a catalyst for change. Literacy rates doubled to nearly 80 percent—higher than most countries—and virtually all children remained in the education system up to the upper secondary level. Comparatively, it was only in the 1940s that humankind as a whole passed a literacy rate of 50 percent. Unlike in the past when noblewomen wrote for other aristocrats, it provided exceptional and opportunistic Japanese women with a creative outlet and an accessible emerging mass market of voracious readers. It had a profound and far-reaching impact. These new mass-market media formats were ripe for exploitation by first movers and fast followers. In a similar manner to how some have pounced on new social media platforms, such as Instagram and TikTok, transforming their profiles and prospects. Growing cultural confidence created many new publishing opportunities in Meiji Japan.

It was a time when women's magazines and periodicals were being founded, books translated, and new approaches tried. Charlotte Brontë's (1816-1855) *Jane Eyre* was published in translation during this period in 1896 in a magazine serial format. The serialisation was cancelled after four issues. Apparently, Japanese readers weren't ready for an "indomitable heroine." By the 1930s, the market had matured with some of the publications targeting female readerships reaching circulations of hundreds of thousands.

Like a fictional heroine, Ichiyo Higuchi (1872-1896) had seen a classmate Kaho Miyake (1869-1943), author of *Yabu no uguisu* (*The Warbler in the Grove*), getting published in a literary magazine, and decided to follow in her footsteps and become a novelist to help support her family, who had hit very hard times after the death of her father from tuberculosis. At one stage she lived in Yoshiwara, Tokyo's red-light entertainment district, an experience that fed into her stories as her writing career developed. Her novel, *Nigorie* (*Troubled Waters*), for example, is the story of a popular tavern and its star 'geisha', whose name Oriki, is written using letters meaning Powerful One. It describes life on the margins, struggles and relationships, including a tragic one with a futon salesman.

Higuchi died when she was only 24, having written 21 short stories, novellas and other works, but in her short life she had a major impact and is considered to be a pioneer and the first important female Japanese writer of modern Japan. Many women followed her example. Fumiko Hayashi (1903-1951), for instance, who moved to Tokyo with her lover before she had turned 20 wrote *Horoki* (*The Diary of a Vagabond*), which sold in the hundreds of thousands in instalments. She wrote mostly about spirited independent women and difficult relationships.

Another was Chiyo Uno (1897-1996) who having found success as a writer and after winning a prize for short stories, left her first husband to follow her dream of living life as an independent modern woman in charge of her own destiny. She published books including *Irozange (Confessions of Love)*, started her own fashion magazine, *Style*, and also worked as a kimono designer. The *New York Times* even ran an obituary of her under the title "Chiyo Uno, 98, Writer Whose Loves Shocked Japan" that mentioned her four divorces and that the emperor awarded her the distinction of being a 'Person of Cultural Merit'. The nation's conspicuous success internationally, inspired many to try to rise alongside the country.

They and other such working women including the commercially successful romance writer, Nobuko Yoshiya (1896-1973), who lived openly as a lesbian and wrote a novel titled *Yaneura no nishojyo (Two Virgins in the Attic)*, in 1919. All followed in the wake of Higuchi. Yoshiya loved golf and just like any aspiring heroine in an American bonkbuster owned a racehorse, as well as her own automobile. Interestingly, since 2004 Higuchi has featured on Japan's five-thousand-yen banknote. It's hard to image Jackie Collins, or any other bonkbuster author, replacing Winston Churchill (1874-1965) and joining Queen Elizabeth II (1926-2022) or King Charles III on England's five-pound notes. Smuggling radical ideas into romance novels or other genres is a tool that many talented, pioneering female writers have used internationally and in Japan, this has and continues to encourage readers to forge their own particular routes into society's unchartered territories.

Foreign literature still has a major impact on Japanese writers and readers. According to industry experts and academics, the three most important books in Japanese publishing history written by non-Japanese women are *Wuthering Heights* by Emily Brontë (1818-1848), *Anne of Green Gables* by L. M. Montgomery (1874-1942) and J. K. Rowling's (b. 1965) Harry Potter series. After the false start in the Meiji era with *Jane Eyre,* by Emily's sister Charlotte, all the works by the Brontë sisters including *Wuthering Heights* were published in translation in the 1930s in Japan. *Anne of Green Gables*, as *Anne of Red Hair*, was published in Japanese after the Second World War. Anne's literary ambitions, strong-willed personality, and optimism struck a chord, as did the fact that, like many in post-war Japan, she was an orphan.

These books have led to Japanese spin-offs, adaptations, manga and anime. As has been the case outside Japan, they have inspired new generations of authors and creative writers. For example, Taeko Kono (1926-2015), who won almost all of Japan's major literature prizes and Yuko Tsushima (1947-2016), author of *Kitsune wo haramu (Pregnant with a Fox)*, were both influenced by Emily and her sisters.

The Canadian novelist Margaret Atwood (b. 1939) is a fan of *Anne of Green Gables* and wrote on the 100th anniversary of its publication about the importance of the book, its impact on Japan and how the bestselling manga *Bishojo senshi sera mun* (*Sailor Moon*), mentioned in regards to its links with curiosities such as the kaleidoscope in this book's preface, is its descendant.[162] It is, however, still far too early to know how J. K. Rowling, Hermione Granger and her friends will inspire the next generation of female writers in Japan. No doubt storytelling by and for Japanese women in all their diverse forms and formats will increasingly start to have a major impact on writers and readers outside Japan, in a type of perpetual virtuous circle.

Nevertheless, some critics dismiss the Brontë sisters as up-market romantic pulp fiction, like Mills & Boon. This is a debate for critics, scholars and so-called experts, but the Brontës and Mills & Boon, founded in 1908, do have one important thing in common. They are all big, or more accurately huge, in Japan. Mills & Boon established its presence in Japan in 1988 under the name Harlequin just as the bonkbuster revolution was taking place in the English-speaking world. The Japanese office takes its name from the North American distributor, based in Canada, that bought the British publisher in 1971 and was subsequently bought itself by News Corp's HarperCollins division in 2014. Japan is now one of Harlequin's largest overseas markets.

It has been truly innovative with the way it localises content, promotes its books and designs its covers. Harlequin Japan has published and sold adapted international titles as manga, published for cell phones, championed e-books, subscriptions and direct purchasing. Its major relationship (product) categories in Japan are arranged marriages, offices, and sheikhs. Arranged marriages in Japan, which are more like formal introductions, are on the increase and account for about 40 percent of marriages today. Surveys show that 20 percent of Japanese infidelity occurs at work. Sheikh titles such as: *The Sheikh's Innocent Bride*, and *The Desert Sheikh's Captive Bride* are popular in all Harlequin markets and not just Japan.

'Light novels' (*raito noberu*), which generally target high-school students with short attention spans, are now an established trend in fiction, creating new outlets and formats for Japan's growing number of highly creative writers to exploit. Kazuki Sakuraba (b. 1971), for example, started her career writing light novels and has now gone on to publish award-winning novels. She won the prestigious Naoki Prize for commercial fiction in 2009 for her book *Watashi no otoko* (*My Man*), which has been made into a film—described as Lolita-style love in a post-disaster landscape by *The Japan Times*—directed by Kazuyoshi Kumakiri (b. 1974).[163] There are already more than twenty different light novel imprints in Japan targeting young women with this format with names like *Arian Rose*, *Angelica*, *Fairy Kiss*, and *Juliet Bunko*, as well as, of course, the genre knows as Boys Love (BL), manga and light novels about idealised romantic or sexual relationships between male characters generally written by women for women. The power of love is a force, including the non-conformist varieties, which can have transformational consequences, both personally and commercially.

In 2023 two female authors, Michi Ichiho (b. 1978) and Yu Nagira (b. 1973), who both have emerged out of the BL publishing genre, were nominated for the Naoki Prize for commercial fiction. One of the nominated titles, however, was a 'sisterhood' narrative about the relationship between two girls and not a traditional male-male BL-style tale. According to senior Japanese publishing executives, the nominations may mark a turning point and an emerging new trend, with the industry trying to discover and manufacture BL crossover stars alongside light novel authors who will attract young readers in the new Reiwa era that has followed the Heisei era (1989-2019).

In Reiwa, and in the wake of the #MeToo phenomenon, at least in the era's initial stage, many youthful potential book-buying women apparently want to keep a healthy distance from problematic men. Japanese society, alongside others in the region, has for some time become increasingly less male-dominated and for some marriage and traditional relationships and gender roles are deemed anachronistic. What is indisputable is the data surrounding the fall in the perceived desirability of marriage, the number of individuals having children out of wedlock and the birth-rates amongst those who are married.

New titles targeting this new generation now seem to have a lightness to their content, with gawky naivety in their plots, as opposed to being hearty tales of romps, bonks and intense ravishings. Apparently, the hope is that by initially encouraging, through fictional escape into quirky award-winning fantasies, framed with less traditional gender role narratives, these potential lifelong readers will develop regular book-buying habits. This time neither title won the prize, but Nagira's book *Nanji, hoshi no gotoku* (*Thou, art like a Star*), also went on to be nominated for the Honya Taisho, the influential Japan Booksellers' Award, the winner of which is selected by staff working at bookshops not a panel of judges. This has helped generate significant publicity for both shortlisted authors and their particular style of narrative fiction.

Some senior Japanese editors are concerned about this emerging trend and urge caution. They worry that if this continues and develops momentum turning into a mainstream channel with a new literary linage, it could lead to a renewed Galapagosisation of the Japanese novel. It could, they fear, put writers back into a lonely distant metaphorical cave just as interest outside Japan in the current crop of Japan-based contemporary female writers and their powerful wordcraft is on the rise, generating attention that is helping Japanese fiction find its place in the sun. Conversely, others from younger generations believe it is an exciting new trend that will continue to create new demand.

It is, however, far too early to be able to judge whether this will happen, and if it were to, if this would be beneficial or detrimental in the longer term or is just a short-term storm in a teacup for creative writing. Though the reality is that many inside and outside the world of publishing do worry about the current new era's reportedly sterile, geeky, detached and emotionless feel, and the growing cultural domination of the video game, manga and anime sectors that BL authors are often said to be part of.

Nonetheless, tastes and reading patterns experience cycles and are ever evolving and changing. In 2020, for instance, the first non-Japanese Asian writer, a South Korean national, Won-pyung Sohn (b. 1979) won the Japan Booksellers' Award. Many translated editions have achieved this status in the past but not works originally penned in Korean, Chinese or in fact in any other Asian language. Sohn, who writes about the traumas of modern existence in South Korea and the nation's suffocating social pressures, went on to win the award for a second time in 2022, for her novel about a working-class woman *Counterattack at Thirty*. Another interesting example is Kotomi Li (b. 1989), a writer born in Taiwan that now lives in Japan and writes in Japanese, who won the Akutagawa Prize in 2021 for her speculative novel *Higanbana ga saku shima* (*An Island Where Red Spider Lilies Bloom*). A fully-fledged content triangle linking Greater China, Japan and South Korea has not yet emerged—it is probably more of an Asian paginated-mosaic—but publishing executives and readers across the region are increasingly aware of books, authors and narratives garnering attention and acclaim in each national market, even if this network of literary influence can still appear highly asymmetrical at times.

There is so much more to women's fiction in Japan than romantic escapist teenage fantasies. There are important award-winning female authors writing bestsellers with enough bonking for them to be technically classified as bonkbusters. Their titles are extremely well written, often less optimistic than a typical bonkbuster of yesteryear, with more marginalised and deviant characters that are also nevertheless striving for independence as well as discovering their sexuality but often in a very Japanese and unusual manner. Romance is not dead, but unlike Harlequin romances, happy endings are rare. *Myuzu* (*Muse*) by Mari Akasaka (b. 1964), *Hebi ni piasu* (*Snakes and Earrings*) by Hitomi Kanehara (b. 1983), *Beddo taimu aizu* (*Bedtime Eyes*) by Amy Yamada (b. 1959) and *Hana yori kekkon kibidango* (*Proposal, Not Flowers*) by Mariko Hayashi (b. 1954) are a few interesting examples.

The desire to be wanted by a man. The desire to get a man. Most females go into hysterics if either of these can't be fulfilled or the fulfilment of these two desires is unbalanced. Their pussies get all irritable, restless. What is hysteria, after all? It's a disease of the pussy. Hitomi Kanehara, *Oto fikushon (Auto Fiction)*.

Some of these writers have scandalised Japan with their narratives about multiple parallel male partners of out wedlock, fierce sexual longing and tales of wombs consumed or unconsumed by the flames of desire. Gender, sex, race, genre, language or place of birth, for instance, or the nature of a marriage or relationship category—same sex, asexual, orthodox, clean, highly sexualised—shouldn't in fact define you or restrict your ambitions, nor should body parts, as the bonkbuster queens and other diverse skilful writers have impressively shown. It is who you are, not what others think of you that matters.

Nevertheless, a determined subversive female gaze from the Japanese archipelago, an Asian nation stretched geographically, with competing fragmented demographic groups, exposed to change and a multitude of extreme local risks, is probably one of the perfect locations from which to observe and reflect on our adjusting world. Japanese women are incredibly well-educated, literate and rather international, making them a well-read and well-travelled population. Though the importance of their role has often been underestimated in terms of the nation's development, they are increasingly shaping Japan's future and this time not quietly in the shadows. Many are coming out dissident-like from behind the scenes wanting recognition, responsibility, praise and visibility, and this is not limited to the nation's ambitious and highly talented wordsmiths.

Perhaps one of Japan's brilliant current cohorts of creative writers will author a new title in the years to come, one fit to help carry off the Nobel Prize. Becoming the third Japanese individual to win a Nobel Prize in Literature, and the first Japanese woman to join the nation's many men, such as Leo Esaki (Physics) and Ryoji Noyori (Chemistry), whose talents have been recognised internationally and have won Nobel prizes in their different fields. These contemporary scribes and storytellers don't yet outsell their male colleagues outside Japan, but more titles by Japanese women are now being translated and are often winning well-deserved acclaim and international prizes. It may thus just be a matter of time.

Now, that would be an exciting and important new first even if it turns out to be recognition and acclaim for narratives of gawky naivety or individuals who 'love life more than love itself', bullies and the bullied, or something brand new that blindsides the critics and readers. Creating a precedent, one might say, with its own distinct style and linage that can be traced back to the many impressive pioneering female wordsmiths that have come before. Prizewinning narratives will probably reflect far more than a million love songs of bygone ages, and will, no doubt, establish a truly memorable legacy.

Today and in the future, to win or standout, tales written by winning authors may not actually need to be replete with old-fashioned bonking, traditional surrenders to waves of ecstasy or even the more modern kaleidoscopic types of frequent explicit sexual encounters of our times. An instinct for controversy often helps, but the best storytelling, verse and lyrics are generally those that are empathetic, bend imagined genre boundaries, and open up new horizons.

As we continue to confront the daily extremes and increasing desolation of our topsy-turvy world, this author, and many others too, one would assume, will be delighted to take such an outcome, as a happy ending to the brilliant and twisting tale of the irrepressible rise of the Japanese bonkbuster.

It was like a twining plant, made of a mixture of desire and worry and misery and love and splendid smiles and abundance and everything else in our collective unconscious. Even if the vine was severed with a hatchet, or burned to the ground, nothing would take away the landscape inside people's hearts or the time that lived on inside them. *Moshi moshi Shimokitazawa* (*Moshi-Moshi*), Banana Yoshimoto.

A Rich and Never-ending Story

To oversimplify a little, literature, somewhat like gravity, is a powerful additive force. It has a compounding effect that acts as a vector for propagating ideas and narratives that constantly surround us. Some elicit empathy controlling trajectories, for better or worse, ranging from those about the lightness of being to the acute heaviness of human existence. The number of books published also continues to expand relentlessly, adding constantly to the universe of the world's letters. Literature, like gravity, *juryoku* weight-power in Japanese, also comes in waves and exerts a mysterious pull.

All languages, not just Japanese, can generate remarkable shapes and bodies. Some weighty, that change and define how we see, navigate, chronicle and feel our way to finding our places in the world. Since ancient times, some languages, including Japanese, and some words, have even been said to have magical elements to their etymologies, *kotodama*, that bring things into being or banish them through their use or a timely utterance, giving words transformative power, as well as spiritual importance. Storytelling, mirroring how gravity binds the universe together, also functions as a port in a storm, providing solidarity in suffering, that fuses societies together. Books, including countless ones from Japan, still often cast spells on readers.

Today ideas, attitudes and cultural concepts that spread and replicate through repetition and imitation are known as memes. Some philosophers and anthropologists argue that words are memes that can be pronounced and that memes generate and influence behavioural systems and their trajectories. Even if the most prominent ones are these days built on binary code and not traditional lettering.

It should therefore not really be surprising that in the 1940s when America was grappling with what some described as "the most alien enemy the United States had ever fought," the nation's Office of War Information and Foreign Morale Analysis Division should turn to cultural anthropologists to try to understand the enemy: its words, and the cultural forces which powered and held together Japan's behaviours. There were a multitude of questions that needed answering to facilitate the decision-making and complex judgements required to win the war expediently, following Japan's surprise attack on Pearl Harbor in December 1941. Determining whether Japan, the nation and its leaders, were really inscrutable or were in fact readable was of paramount importance.

Field trips were of course out of the question. Many went to libraries to read up on the nation. Some studied the development of the written and spoken word of Japanese propaganda and others looked to Japanese storytelling and to individuals of Japanese descent living in America, many in internment camps, to discover the rules, attitudes and values that governed Japanese culture. Others watched Japanese films.

According to Ruth Benedict (1887-1948), a respected American anthropologist and folklorist, in her book *The Chrysanthemum and the Sword*, published in 1946 and based on her Office of War Information assignment, she was greatly aided by the nation's literature:

> Unlike many Oriental people they have a great impulse to write themselves out. They wrote about the trivia of their lives as well as about their programs of world expansion. They were amazingly frank. Of course, they did not present the whole picture. No people does.[164]

Listening directly to the voices of the people you are interested in and reading what they write and say about themselves, as opposed to those who ventriloquise on their behalf or who are paid professional interpreters of their behavioural etiquettes for cross-cultural audiences, is a very worthy and often fascinating approach, as hopefully this book has also shown in its own small way.

Nonetheless, no matter how good the intentions, starting with the premise that one is studying an alien or enemy nation, even if events sadly make that a necessity, may unfortunately warp your perspective and the hypotheses one generates. As one becomes more accustomed with people and places one often starts seeing the similarities, the forces that bring people together, and their degrees of calibration, as opposed to raw differences and polarising contrasts.

Much has been said and written about Japan and Japanese literature before then and since. The tedium of existence and the depiction of boredom and the mundane in Japanese novels is something that has been compared to Russian literature, for example, and contrasted with great American novels and storytelling. Apparently, Americans like winners more than tales of the lonely complicated every day, preferring solutions, gravity-defying heroes who control their outcomes, and narratives with clear conclusions and happy endings.

Tragic conclusions, failing heroes and heroines, individuals unable to escape gravity-like invisible cultural pressures, and awful turns and twists of fate leading to untimely deaths, alongside the very precariousness of existence itself, are often said to be the preference in Japan. There is even a Japanese term, *hoganbiiki* that describes the genre of Japanese storytelling that depicts these types of individuals, and tales that resonate with the love and admiration of tragic and failing underdogs who refuse to comply and try unsuccessfully to buck the system. These sentiments may or may not be un-American or un-Hollywood, but they are actually reasonably common themes in other nations too and not just in the storytelling of Japan. Of course, Japanese books and writing are also broader than this and more diverse than what is readily available in translation in most languages.

The viewpoints of each nation's preferences no doubt also very much depend on where the observer is based or educated and their exposure to different types of storytelling, as well as the genre and forms of storytelling, which are or are not included in each nation's so-called national narrative. Comparison between countries is healthy, but there are many benchmarks, not just American ones. These days, no matter where you live, the generation of an analogy to America and its terminology and jargon has seemingly become an unstoppable force. Nevertheless, it is important that the prism of America and the gravitational pull of its dynamic culture and ever popular internet memes, which often spawns a desire in others to ape American cultural semantics and debates, does not end up distorting and defining how we see the Japanese archipelago, or in fact how Japan sees itself in an international context. Viewing Japan, however, through a global lens, not a bilateral one, especially from the outside, even when familiar beacons of the past present fine resolution allowing new features to emerge, can also be a fraught encounter. Other options on how to read Japan, that place the nation in the sun shedding fresh light on it do in fact exist.

Sadly, for many, however, opinion still trumps empathy, research or facts, leading to the unreliable, superficial and the misinterpreted being mirrored, perpetuating stereotypes. Japanese intellectuals will often counter saying that commentators, scholars, opinion leaders and most missionaries (who in somewhat more traditional ways) visit Japan to impart, not to truly observe. They base their views on existing or scripted observations about the old, changing or new Japan, the scant translations of Japan's immense literature they have stumbled across, and unreliable anecdotes of passing travellers, based on a juxtaposition that reflects only a patchwork of understanding of the world outside their home nations. Thereby polluting Japan and international perceptions with unreliable prose and comment.

They often have a case. The nobility of failure, for instance, making up for lack of success with purity of purpose and doing things the sincere and proper way, have helped, for example, turn British tennis players who never quite win Wimbledon, into national icons. They stand alongside other sportsmen and women, such as the Olympic ski-jumper Eddie the Eagle, as well as other celebrated figures, such as the explorer Ernest Shackleton (1874-1922) whose ship *Endurance* sank off the coast of Antarctica in 1915. Perhaps, less so today, but in 20th century Britain, honour and recognition were bestowed, just like in Japan, on many heroic authentic failures.

Much has and continues to be written about Japan's exceptionalism, its outlier status and the nation's unique peculiarities. Its lack of phobias related to robots and a Frankenstein complex, for example, as well as this absence of the element of victory and success within its most celebrated tales of heroes. Some international commentators have even argued the cultural background of this embrace of brilliant failures, and implicitly defeat and losers, remains "a bedrock underlying the modern Japanese psyche and shapes the Japanese as individuals and a society even today." This type of convenient easy-to-repeat rhetoric and other such well-trod tropes encourage those who opine for the case of Japanese exceptionalism, and too often is accepted unchallenged without a good look at the evidence.

Shackleton allegedly recruited his ice-cap team of polar adventurers with the following famous advertisement in a newspaper: "Men wanted for hazardous journey. Small wages, bitter cold, long months of complete darkness, constant danger, safe return doubtful. Honour and recognition in case of success." On many measures he and his team weren't successful, but Shackleton and his expedition still left a lasting iconic legacy. Shackleton's exploits, for instance, are used today to teach leadership skills in a similar manner to how tales about prominent samurai and Japanese warlords and the poetry they wrote, including some about stubborn birds that refuse to sing, are in Japan. Shackleton's storied tale has no doubt been enhanced through the extreme imagery, that evoke the pioneering spirit of a bygone age, recorded and frozen in time by the innovative Australian photographer Frank Hurley (1885-1962), the expedition's official photographer, and also the saga's persistent often exaggerated retelling.

It is nonetheless the type of rhetoric one can imagine that Takamori Saigo (1828-1877), one of the chief architects and rebel leaders behind the overthrow of Japan's last shogun, before he subsequently himself became a defeated failed insurgent, might have exploited. As he put it:

> A man of true sincerity will be an example to the world even after his death… When an insincere man is spoken well of, he has, so to speak, got a windfall, but a man of deep sincerity will, even if he is unknown in his lifetime, have a lasting reward: the esteem of posterity… He who cares neither about his

life, not about his fame, nor about rank or money – such a man is hard to deal with. Yet it is only such a man who will undergo every hardship with his companions in order to carry out great work for his country.[165]

Heroes don't necessarily need to be morally right or even make the right decisions, or be victorious, they do, however, need to be selfless. There are many tales in many nations about such individuals, saintly or not, sacrificing themselves for the sins or traditions of others. Japan is not the only country that understands this or tells tales about these types of rare individuals.

Yet despite many such quintessential celebrated Japanese individuals, traditional Japanese arts are still frequently praised for their unique placing of nature and not humans, nor ego, at their creative cores. Conversely, just like the wheels of history, Japanese literature and arts change and evolve composing patterns that reflect new ideas, concepts and many previously unimaginable personality types—spanning the authentic to the highly contrived and self-indulgent—even if the skeletons of the past regularly pop-up in unusual creative ways and locations. Literary and storytelling trends in Japan, just like elsewhere, ebb and flow with tales that confront difficult realities to those that imagine new possibilities, from the absurd to the utopian, and everything in-between. Japan is, of course, not an observable sovereign singularity, which is why this book is titled *Kaleidoscope Japan*.

Japan can and should be read in so many different ways and it is a real blessing that the nation has and has had so many talented writers and that it writes itself out. That is why reading still matters today in all its forms even tales about the tiny mundane incidents of common everyday existence. The 'trivia' of lives lived and the epic every day, as well as tales of grand and tragic heroes. Why we should all try to find even more time for it. A regular literary fix, especially of the Japanese variety, can contribute to a healthy constitution, an open mind and as all bookworms know, we are shaped by what we read.

As we have seen, literary influences can come from many places and seemingly often at pivotal times. Along this long literary linage clusters of knots reflecting different forms of extreme individual expression and periods of intense change can suddenly appear clustered together. These literary knots when untied or read in sequence can function as fascinating time machines that scramble time, linking readers directly to the thoughts of expressive individuals living through dynamic, complex and uncomfortable change.

A good illustrative example of this is the emergence of a new Japanese literary genre, the *i-novel*, in the early years of the 20th century, to name one of many such possible examples, and also one not discussed already. The genre appeared initially undefined within a flurry of publications, just as a new word, 'psychoanalysis' arrived in Japan with the translation of *Dream of an Unmarried Woman* by Sigmund Freud (1856-1939), alongside Freud's terms such as ego and super-ego, forces that embed cultural rules within human psyches. Sometimes revolutions seem to come in clusters.

The new lexicon describing it emerged later. This new Japanese literary genre with authors at its narrative heart was subsequently given the moniker the *i-novel* (also known as *shi-shosetsu*), a type of confessional autobiographical Japanese novel generally written from a first-person perspective.[166]

Today the *i-novel* genre, which is often celebrated as something unique and indigenous to Japan—somewhat like the nation's narrative scroll art—is known outside Japan in its broadest sense as autofiction, the transmuting of personal experience into published stories. In its own perspective-bending manner, the *i-novel* facilitated the chronicling of life in Japan, which was changing precipitously, through new literary lenses and the relative viewpoints of each observing writer. Oddly, however, most of the significant things in lives, especially when it comes to this author, tend to happen with our absence, not in our presence, but for these Japanese authors the experience, what actually happened to them, was the only conclusive reality. This created magnifying mirrors, often used to present an alternative model for modernity and existence. Their works are very much a reflection of their time, even if the format they gave birth to and pioneered, before it gained its label, remains popular.

This new type of revelatory Japanese fiction was born when Albert Einstein (1879-1055) was publishing his papers on the Special Theory of General Relativity with its own revolutionary concept: space-time and the prediction of light bent by gravitation. Einstein's ideas ripped apart the traditional understanding of physical reality that many held. New theories, like his and Freud's, can often have broad cultural impact becoming the dominant paradigms of a generation. Not only changing perspectives, artistic imagery and storytelling, but as in Einstein's extreme case redefining how we perceive the boundaries and structure of the universe, and the nature of time itself.

Exciting new theories can also on occasion generate a cocktail of cultural headwinds, and in some very extreme cases produce a confused cultural disorder, including unhinged mental states, as well as weird dysfunctions in the less-scrutinised corners of society, even those located far away from where the theories were initially generated. This was a new age, incrementalism and absolutism were out, replaced by relativism. Heaviness and weighty objects, as Einstein explained, distort space-time, and these novels were heavy and deeply reflective: spanning the confessional, dark deeds, and bizarre mental attitudes, and were designed to distort norms.

Another rather extreme, but equally fascinating example, is a highly unusual group of post-war Japanese authors, active during another paradigm-shifting period of profound socioeconomic change for Japan. Soon after the Second World War ended, many people were infused with reactionary angst, fears of cultural degeneration, disaffection and widespread collective anxiety about anxiety itself, creating what might be termed an anxious generation and what Freud would no doubt label as the obsessive tensions between civilisation and its discontents. Some commentators have sensationally described these times and the shift from militarism to modern democracy as the environment that the political and martial castration of a defeated Japan spawned. Dubbed the 'Decadents', these authors established a publishing genre centred on basic bodily needs and innate indulgences (spanning desires from the sexual to the gluttonous), which was given the moniker 'flesh literature', *nikutai bungaku*, by Japan's commentariat.

Both of these self-observing genres have a very different interplay with nature, the observed and the environment to many renowned types of classical Japanese poetry, for example. Nonetheless, both of these schools of writing can still be brilliantly creative, even if their altered-states and unusual and at times grotesque individualised perspectives, are of a new sort when compared to the more typical ones beautifully portrayed in much of Japan's more storied and traditional creative writing. The displacement of the human individual as the centre of the universe is not, however, part of the narrative worlds these two genres tend to conjure up. Literary currents run at all speeds. Today, in some of the very best Japanese fiction and storytelling, as in life, absence, the unseen, information and facts that are strategically withheld, mirroring the traditional aesthetic of incompleteness championed by other Japanese art forms, is often embraced with powerful affect.

With each generation new genres and protagonist-types continue to emerge. The timing of their arrivals and narratives are as this book has tried to show also often intriguingly indicative. Contemporary works, such as Tomohiko Morimi's (b. 1979) *Yojohan shinwa taikei* (*The Tatami Galaxy*), published in 2018, can, for instance, transport today's adventurous readers looking for an out of body experience into the messy undernourished mind of a Kyoto-dwelling, nutrient and sexually starved, millennium-age Japanese university student, and his circle of misfit associates.

If you want a journey to a very different Japan, off the beaten track, behind the stereotypical haze or want to experience a new-fangled "stellar assemblage" there are many contemporary writers like Morimi that can provide you with a literary vehicle to young adult parallel worlds and unusual social sets and amalgamations. Literary treats and what your brain actually craves, however, generally reflect your identity, experience and education, as well as age. Typically, for many readers, Japanese literature at its most beguiling reflects the cultural superstructure that most nations typically build around adolescence and coming of age, courtship and marriage, death and funerals, and the spiritual world, as well as the occasional oversized importance of the maverick outsider, be they a local or one from afar, one who wins or one who fails. All of which when well written can make space-time flex, convulse and ring.

These sorts of tales leave imprints of acts, fleeting instants of achievements and cultural phenomenon, giving them permanence, that reflect both the faces people and society consciously present to the outside world, *tatemae*, and also those that might have otherwise remained within concealed and hidden from inquisitive observers, *honne*, true feelings and desires: such as the crazed-appetites and fears that many cunningly cloak or disguise from others. For long periods culture supports the balances and complex trade-offs that communities require, keeping society's paved order and this peculiar dichotomy that many think is particularly strong in Japan, going. Many only reveal sensitive details and important information if they can find an excellent reason to do so that compels them, typically opting initially for gilt-edged silence as the default. This is in contrast to being transparently chatty, holding one's heart on one's sleeve, when most information is only held back on the rare occasion when there is an exceedingly good reason not to divulge it. That is why literature, with the rare and momentary glimpses it can provide, is such a meaningful observational tool. In Japan's case this chronicling of existence is often conducted through suggestion with a lightness of touch that provides fragmented shard-like glances into what is hidden under things, spanning the full spectrum of society's every day, life as we find it, rather than an intense and grand gaze upon the nation itself.

As opposed to being simply hidden in plain sight, non-literary secret invisible worlds do, however, actually exit, which specialist viewing devices are needed to observe. Some of the colours of the natural world and the building-blocks of life or its anomalies, for example, are invisible and go unnoticed to the untrained or unenhanced human eye. They require polarised light, for instance, in vertical form (like traditional Japanese text) or horizontal form, for us to observe nature and life in its full panoramic and technicolour glory. Rendering the invisible visible, opening up new vistas of discovery that allow previously inaccessible realms and shadow lands to be explored and interrogated, and then finally captured in the arts.

Japan's sympathy with and understanding of the secrets of the natural world have been labelled by some as the genius and spirit of Japan. What we consider and directly observe, our perceptual activity, of the present, due to the structure of the biological apparatus we have inherited, is actually the very recent past. Not all individuals see colours in the same way. Some medical conditions can lead to distorted vision, fracturing light, creating so-called kaleidoscope eyes. Nature uses some colours to trick and deceive or to attract and as camouflage while many animals; fish, cats and insects, perceive the world very differently to us.

Society and civilisation is bound together by much that is invisible or hidden and, like gravity itself, mysterious in origin, including emotional forces such as solidarity, hope, purpose, uncertain fate, dignity, joy, risk, creative ingenuity, love and determined toil. It is not simply the polished branded products and materialism that we are relentlessly presented with that creates community. Fittingly, despite not by any means being considered a chaotic nation, displaying the hidden colours of Japan, and its myriad natural forms and its social bonds may actually require active optical intervention; and a metaphorical *mangekyo*, the ten thousand flowering mirrors that make up the etymology of this Japanese word for kaleidoscope.

The manager of a specialist kaleidoscope shop in Tokyo describes these optical devices as "philosophy tubes that surprise their users with perspectives that take their imagination to unexpected higher levels." Today, astronomers use giant mirrors floating in space to capture and manipulate light in order to see the faint and far-off objects that allow them to look back through time, to the origins of the physical universe, identifying the naked fragmented details, the hidden concealed secrets of the cosmos and the source of its power.

That said, you don't need to be a cosmic hunter with massively expensive equipment to find your centre of gravity or place in the universe. With the right literary exposure, the ribbons of colour, even the counter-shaded variety, that stream through Japan and life in Japan, for example, in all their mesmerising diverse hues, are instantly presentable in an accessible readable format, right before your eyes. In ways that can be sophisticated, luminescent and revealing. All you need to do is pick up or download a book or short story.

Jakucho Setouchi (1922-2021), the wild child turned Buddhist nun, superstar writer and modernising translator of *Genji monogatari* (*The Tale of Genji*), who, of course, loved playing with cardboard kaleidoscopes as a child, knew this as have many other Japanese authors and their loyal readers. Setouchi's *Inochi mangekyo* (*Life Kaleidoscope*), a collection of essays from more than 25 Japanese writers examining the human condition of life in Japan, grouped across three sections headed "Living In The Present", "Living With Nature", and "Life and Death", published in 1990, clearly shows that this concept, the *mangekyo* analogue, difference at every turn, and an appreciation of what is meant by the title of this book *Kaleidoscope Japan* is understood by many, even if each of these individual authors has a different pattern of perspective.

This applies to readers as well as authors. Narrative fiction, like colours, evoke different emotions and sensory responses in individuals especially when penned by a particularly watchful author or cluster of writers, who make sure their own perspective, personality and ego enhances, and does not obfuscate, the worlds they conjure up in literary form. Novels, with their textual seas of magical words and sentences, can cast spells in a manner that probably no other form of entertainment quite matches, creating avenues for marvellous escapes. Most books don't provide all the answers or claim to be able to explain away the complexities of life, but the good ones provide a refuge, as well as alternative and sometimes heightened perspective.

Numerous quirky parallels and rhetorical analogies reflecting these types of phenomena exist, including, intriguingly, some, which can even be found within the latest medical research, for instance. Research that appears to show that the perspective and consciousness altering psychoactive compound found in magic mushrooms, psilocybin, can help treat anxiety, depression, eating disorders and post-traumatic stress disorder, for instance, through the blurring and eradicating of boundaries and the governing order between nature and self. By bending the rigid rules that we are all trained and educated to use to navigate and delineate our lives, rules that encourage us to interact with others with so-called cultivated social success. Providing relief, deflection and escape, be it stress induced by human-created catastrophes or natural disasters, chronic pain, bloody savage battles and wars, vengeful rivalry, depression, dementia, or someone's sudden change in status or a tragic bereavement.[167]

This medicinal causal ingredient, research shows, has palliative pharmacological effects that encourage consciousness of the real world with its physical realities and multitude of interfering brutal faults to slip away momentarily, opening up lasting new and heightened perspectives. It expands the frontiers of the mind, apparently acts as a gateway to self-understanding, generates breakthrough-like senses of connection, as well as therapeutic cures for psychological disorders.

In a similar manner to these newly emerging psychedelic drugs, which are often based on synthetic editions of the naturally occurring active compound psilocybin found in mushrooms with its magical sensory ingredient, Japanese fiction and verse, with its crowd of perspective-shifting genres including, for instance, its famed magical-realism, have helped generations of Japanese individuals deal with the altered-states and anxieties that a swiftly shifting society can force on people, be they a samurai warrior, a farmer or labourer, a monk, or even a member of the Japanese imperial family. This is not to suggest that Japanese literature and successful authorship is mushroom-derived.

The risks and side effects of a book that doesn't agree with you are minimal when compared to a bad trip from psilocybin with side effects that can include dizziness, nausea, headaches and suicidal ideation. Narrative fiction, of course, has its own unreliable narrators, hallucinogenic properties, and warped and compressed timelines, as well as the disorientating and the unreal. But the best type of literature even if it is of the do-it-yourself (DIY) variety has the power to help process extreme emotions and can often provide anti-anxiety escapism, as well as be in its own particular manner mind-bending and gloriously intoxicating.

Reading and then learning to write may be the prime objective of most educational systems worldwide, alongside learning to count, but it is the act of writing, a highly potent means of expression, that really brings the type of clarity of thought and understanding that can alter destinies and societies. Once the product of pen or ink brush strokes are widely shared and broadly read. Luckily, Japan has been one of the most literate nations on the planet for a very long time. With the right reading list, you probably don't need the revelations of ten thousand shimmering Japanese literary mirrors, or be an insatiable book-devouring reader, to reach this heightened state of emotional escape and consciousness, but you do need to become a regular reader.

All the same, as many keen-eyed observers have correctly pointed out, the mirror is actually a very important cultural symbol in Japan, with a role that stretches far beyond the tilted refracting mirrored surfaces found at the core of kaleidoscopes. Mirrors, for example, stand at the heart of Shinto shrines, as they are believed to represent and manifest the soul of the celestial sun goddess Amaterasu. Among the precious Imperial Regalia of Japan is the *Yata no kagami*, a mirror. It represents wisdom and is one of three legendary sacred treasures, alongside a necklace and a sword, said to have been brought to Earth by the grandson, *Ninigi no mikoto*, of the sun goddess herself, an ancestor of the Japanese imperial line.

Mirrors are believed to draw out the divine reflecting eternal purity. According to Benedict: "Japanese feelings about the mirror are derived from the time before the 'observing self' was inculcated in the child… It does not foster vanity nor reflect the 'interfering self.' It reflects the depths of the soul." In these mirrors one should try to see, reflected in the looking-glass, not shame, not ego, nor vanity, not desire, not parody, nor the conspicuous elements of one's past or present, pride or prejudices, or one's home nation but reality undistorted by the illusion of self.

In this way, Japanese mirrors function as a door, a polished vector, to a different form of consciousness, a heightened one with clarity and their own special cultural flow. If you don't see yourself reflected back in the mirror, then you are said to be at the point where you have reached enlightenment or are in the presence of or connected with the divine; a never-ending task for most of us flawed, self-centred myopic mortals. It requires eyes unclouded by the cataracts of over education, current convention, groupthink, stereotypes and the noisy echo chambers of contemporary life and its prejudices, and also a profound appreciation of the importance of the natural world. "If you want to appreciate something fully, you should forget yourself. You should accept it like lightning flashing in the utter darkness of the sky," the Zen Soto Buddhist monk Shunryu Suzuki (1904-1971) advises.

Perhaps in a similar manner if you can read a novel by a Japanese author without pre-conceptions, without seeing yourself and your experiences reflected back at you in its narrative structure, and are able to engage with and enjoy its characters and themes for what they are, with an open empathetic mind, without being acutely conscious of the author's gender, age, ethnicity or nationality, for example, then perhaps you have the ability to see Japan's soul and the nation's glorious kaleidoscopic elements, turns, voices and patterns.

Like most things in our world there are no absolutes. It is probably relative, a matter of tuning and where you point and how you handle your kaleidoscope. The more you read, the wider you read, the more intense and unusual your reading trips, and the more you listen to the voices of authors and the narratives of the characters inhabiting their works, blurring the boundaries between you, the reader and the synthetic narrative terrain, the closer you are on the route to understanding Japan, whatever that might actually mean for you personally.

In this sense the gateway to Japan and the critical lens for its contemplation are the books and verse written by its skilful wordsmiths, a hypothesis that is much easier to understand and is better expressed in the eloquent words of the gentleman master of Japanese aesthetics Kenko Yoshida (circa 1283-1350): "It is a most wonderful comfort to sit alone beneath a lamp, book spread before you, and commune with someone from the past whom you have never met."[168] Like a twining complex plant that is always adding new shoots, even if some tendrils are severed, pruned or eventually edited out, or if these shoots seem at first glance impossible to transplant outside their native terrain, there is a never-ending, growing rich literary landscape to be relished in Japan, that reflects people's hearts, a multitude of memories and times lived.

If Japan, the nation, is built on wood and concrete, hard graft, crisis, technology, robotics, engineering and failing heroes or *bungaku*, Japanese literature, a term which can be translated directly as 'the study of things written', and creative storytelling, is for you to determine. Nonetheless, I hope this book has at the very least shown some of what the nation's bookish psychedelics have to offer and their wondrous scope as well as why the lens of literature is a useful and engaging one. Whatever you might conclude this will not, however, be the final word for Japanese literature.

Appendix

Cited Japanese Works of Fiction Available in
English Language Translation At Time of Writing
(Deduplicated in order of appearance) *

Title: English/Japanese	Author/Translator
A Cup of Sake Beneath the Cherry Trees/selection taken from *Essays in Idleness*/ *Tsurezuregusa*	Kenko Yoshida/Meredith McKinney
The Devotion of Suspect X/ *Yogisha ekkusu no kenshin*	Keigo Higashino/Alexander O. Smith
The Tattooer/Shisei	Junichiro Tanizaki/Howard Hibbett
The Makioka Sisters/Sasameyuki	Junichiro Tanizaki/ Edward Seidensticker
A Cat, A Man, Two Women/ Neko to shozo to futari no onna	Junichiro Tanizaki/ Paul McCathy
In Praise of Shadows/ Inei raisan	Junichiro Tanizaki/Edward Seidensticker & Thomas Harper
Snow Country/Yukiguni	Yasunari Kawabata/ Edward Seidensticker
The House of the Sleeping Beauties/ Nemureru bijo	Yasunari Kawabata/ Edward Seidensticker
The Dancing Girl of Izu/Izu no odoriko	Yasunari Kawabata/ Edward Seidensticker
Kitchen/Kitchin	Banana Yoshimoto/Megan Backus
Moshi-Moshi/ Moshi moshi Shimokitazawa	Banana Yoshimoto/Asa Yoneda
The Tale of Genji/Genji monogatari	Shikibu Murasaki/ Edward Seidensticker
Madame de Sade/Sado koshaku kujin	Yukio Mishima/Donald Keene
Confessions of a Mask/Kamen no kokuhaku	Yukio Mishima/Meredith Weatherby

The Sea of Fertility/Hojo no umi (tetralogy)	Yukio Mishima/ Michael Gallagher, E. Dale Saunders, Cecilia Segawa Seigle, Edward Seidensticker
No Longer Human/Ningen shikkaku	Osamu Dazai/Donald Keene
The Gun/Jyu	Fuminori Nakamura/ Allison Markin Powell
Be With You/Ima aini yukimasu	Takuji Ichikawa/Sai Kawashima
The Cape/Misaki	Kenji Nakagami/Eve Zimmerman
The Great Passage/Fune wo amu	Shion Miura/Juliet Winters Carpenter
The Pillow Book/Makura no soshi	Shonagon Sei/Meredith McKinney
Shame in the Blood/Shinobu kawa	Tetsuo Miura/Andrew Driver
In a Grove/Yabu no naka	Ryunosuke Akutagawa/ Takashi Kojima
The Hell Screen/Jigokuhen	Ryunosuke Akutagawa/Jay Rubin
Kappa/Kappa	Ryunosuke Akutagawa/ Takashi Kojima
The Life of a Stupid Man/Aru aho no issho	Ryunosuke Akutagawa/Jay Rubin
Miss Bokko/Bokko-chan	Shinichi Hoshi/Marina Hoshi Whyte
The Handkerchief/Hankachi	Ryunosuke Akutagawa/ Glenn W. Shaw
The Dancing Girl/Maihime	Ogai Mori/Richard Bowring
The River Ki/ Kinokawa	Sawako Ariyoshi/Mildred Tahara
Absorbed in Letters/Gesaku zanmai	Ryunosuke Akutagawa/Takashi Kojima and John McVittie
Norwegian Wood/Noruwei no mori	Haruki Murakami/Jay Rubin
Heaven/ Hebun	Mieko Kawakami/Sam Bett & David Boyd
Convenience Store Woman/ Konbini ningen	Sayaka Murata/Ginny Tapley Takemori

Amrita/Amurita	Banana Yoshimoto/Russel F. Wasden
Kokoro/Kokoro	Soseki Natsume/Meredith McKinney
Yellow Man/Kiiroi hito	Shusaku Endo/Teruyo Shimizu
Beautiful Star/Utsukushii hoshi	Yukio Mishima/Stephen Dodd
Salvation of A Saint/Seijyo no kyusai	Keigo Higashino/Alexander O. Smith with Elye Alexander
*The Chronicles of Lord Asunaro/ Asunaroko funtoki***	Kanji Hanawa/Meredith Mckinney
*Backlight/Gyakosen ***	Kanji Hanawa/Richard Nathan
Japan Sinks/Nippon chinbotsu	Sakyo Komatsu/Michael Gallager
*The Refugee's Daughter/ Nanmin no musume ***	Takuji Ichikawa/Emily Balistrieri
Muddy River/Doro no kawa	Teru Miyamoto/Ralph McCarthy
Naomi/Chijin no ai	Junichiro Tanizaki/ Anthony Chambers
After the quake/Kami no kodomo-tachi wa mina oduru	Haruki Murakami/Jay Rubin
Horses, Horses, in the End the Light Remains Pure/Umatachi yo, soredemo hikari wa mukude	Hideo Furukawa/Doug Slaymaker & Akiko Takenaka
Tokyo Ueno Station/JR Ueno-Eki Koenguchi	Miri Yu/Morgan Giles
Cult X/Kyodan X	Fuminori Nakamura/Kalau Almony
The Eighth Day/Yokame no semi	Mitsuyo Kakuta/Margaret Mitsutani
Somersault/Chugaeri	Kenzaburo Oe/Philip Gabriel
1Q84	Haruki Murakami/Jay Rubin
Vibrator/Vaibureta	Mari Akasaka/Michael Emmerich
Innocent World/ Insento warudo	Ami Sakurai/Steve Clark

Snakes and Earrings/Hebi ni piasu	Hitomi Kanehara/ David James Kawashima
Black Rain/Kuroi ame	Masuji Ibuse/ John Bester
Hiroshima Notes/Hiroshima noto	Kenzaburo Oe/David L. Swain & Toshi Yonezawa
The Crazy Iris and Other Stories/ Kakitsubata	Kenzaburo Oe, Masuji Ibuse, Tamiki Hara, Katsuo Oda/David Swain, Ivan Morris, George Saito, John Bester
Two Little Girls Called Iida/Futari no Iida	Miyoko Matsutani/Pauline Bush
One Love Chigusa/Won rabu Chigusa **	Soji Shimada/David Warren
Hydrangeas/Ajisai	Junnosuke Yoshiyuki/ Lawrence Rogers
Places/Basho	Jakucho Setouchi/Liza Dalby
The Housekeeper and the Professor/ Hakase no ai shita sushiki	Yoko Ogawa/Stephen Synder
Pregnancy Diary/Ninshin karenda	Yoko Ogawa/Stephen Synder
Monkey Brain Sushi: New Tastes in Japanese Fiction/Yamada-san nikki	Masato Takeno/Alfred Birnbaum
The Sailor Who Fell From Grace With The Sea/Gogo no eiko	Yukio Mishima/John Nathan
Sherlock Holmes: A Scandal in Japan/ Shaarokku homuzu tai Ito Hirobumi	Keisuke Matsuoka/James Baker
The Tatami Galaxy/Yojohan shinwa taikei	Tomohiko Morimi/Emily Balistrieri
Some Prefer Nettles/Tade ku mushi	Junichiro Tanizaki/ Edward Seidensticker
Beauty and Sadness/ Utsukushisa to kanashimi to	Yasunari Kawabata/Howard Hibbett
The Dolls/Hina	Ryunosuke Akutagawa/Takashi Kojima and John McVittie
Last Winter, We Parted/Kyonen no fuyu, kimi to wakare	Fuminori Nakamura/ Allison Markin Powell

The Temple of Wild Geese and Bamboo Dolls/Gan notera & Echizen takeningyo	Tsutomu Minakami/ Dennis C. Washburn
Doll Love/Ningyo ai	Takako Takahashi/Mona Nagai & Yukiko Tanaka
The Lady Killer/Ryojin nikki	Masako Togawa/Simon Grove
A Kiss of Fire/Hi no seppu	Masako Togawa/Simon Grove
Something Unexpected/Fuino dekigoto	Junnosuke Yoshiyuki / Lawrence Rogers
Inspector Imanishi Investigates/ Suna no utsuwa	Seicho Matsumoto/Beth Cary
The Tokyo Zodiac Murders/ Senseijyutsu satsujin jiken	Soji Shimada/Shika MacKenzie & Ross MacKenzie
Stand-in Companion/Daitai hanryo **	Kazufumi Shiraishi/Raj Mahtani
The Doctor's Wife/Hanaoka seishu no tsuma	Sawako Ariyoshi/Wakako Hironaka & Ann Siller Kostant
I am a Cat/Wagahai wa neko dearu	Soseki Natsume/Aiko Ito & Graeme Wilson
Botchan/Botchan	Soseki Natsume/Joel Cohn
Inter Ice Age 4/Daiyon kanhyoki	Kobo Abe/E. Dale Saunders
The Woman in the Dunes/Suna no onna	Kobo Abe/E. Dale Saunders & Machi Abe
Narcissism/Narushishizumu	Yasutaka Tsutsui/Andrew Driver
Sadism/Sadizumu	Yasutaka Tsutsui/Andrew Driver
Woman Running in the Mountains/ Yama wo hashiru onna	Yuko Tsushima/Geraldine Harcourt
Running Man/Hashiru otoko	Yasutaka Tsutsui/Andrew Driver
Men Without Women/ Onna no inai otokotachi	Haruki Murakami/Philip Gabriel & Ted Goossen
Shank's Mare/ Tokaidochu hizakurige	Ikku Jippensha/Thomas Satchell

Night on the Milky Way Train/ Ginga tetsudo no yoru	Kenji Miyazawa/Roger Pulvers
The Scarlet Gang of Asakusa/ Asakusa kurenaidan	Yasunari Kawabata/Alisa Freedman
*Monkey Man/Monki Man***	Takuji Ichikawa/Lisa Lilley & Daniel Lilley
The Town of Cats/Excerpt from 1Q84	Haruki Murakami/Jay Rubin
Points and Lines/Ten to sen	Seicho Matsumoto/Makiko Yamamoto & Paul C. Blum
Maria Beetle/Mariabitoru	Kotaro Isaka/Sam Malissa
Sanshiro/Sanshiro	Soseki Natsume/Jay Rubin
The Guest Cat/Neko no kyaku	Takashi Hiraide/Eric Selland
The Travelling Cat Chronicles/ Tabineko ripouto	Hiro Arikawa/Philip Gabriel
The Cat Who Saved Books/Hon omamoroto suru neko no hanashi	Sosuke Natsukawa/ Louise Heal Kawai
The Black Lizard and the Beast in the Shadows/Kurotokage & inju	Ranpo Edogawa/Ian Hughes
The Tattoo Murder Case/ Shisei satsujin jiken	Akimitsu Takagi/Deborah Boehm
The Paradise Bird Tattoo (or, Attempted Double-Suicide)/ Akame shijuyataki shinju misui	Chokitsu Kurumatani/ Kenneth J. Bryson
Heresy/Jashumon	Ryunosuke Akutagawa/Takashi Kojima and John McVittie
Foreign Studies/ Ryugaku	Shusaku Endo/Mark Williams
Deep River/Fukai kawa	Shusaku Endo/Van C. Gessel
Silence/Chinmoku	Shusaku Endo/William Johnstone
The Night is Short, Walk on Girl/ Yoruha mijikashi arukeyo otome	Tomihiko Morimi/Emily Balistrieri

Appendix

Geisha in Rivalry Tale/Ude kurabe	Kafu Nagai/Kurt Meissner & Ralph Friedrich
The Illusionist/Tejinashi	Junnosuke Yoshiyuki/ Lawrence Rogers
The Briefcase/Sensei no kaban	Hiromi Kawakami/ Allison Markin Powell
Troubled Waters/Nigorie	Ichiyo Higuchi/Robert Lyons Danly
The Diary of a Vagabond/Horoki	Fumiko Hayashi/Joan E. Ericson
Confessions of Love/Iro zange	Chiyo Uno/Phyllis Birnbaum
Bedtime Eyes/Beddotaimu aizu	Amy Yamada/Yumi Gunji & Marc Jardine
Auto Fiction/Oto fikushon	Hitomi Kanehara/David James Kawashima

*Excludes manga, anime and most other such formats.

** Provisional Japanese title

Notes

All Japan-related books, and books of this nature, draw on books, newspaper and magazine articles and research from earlier generations, as well as contemporary specialists.

I owe a debt of gratitude to many but I would like to acknowledge in particular Ian Buruma's *A Japanese Mirror: Heroes and Villains of Japanese Culture*. This book alongside Harel van Wolferen's *The Enigma of Japanese Power* and Richard Storry's *A History of Modern Japan*, all of which I read in the late 1980s during my first sojourn in Japan, had a major impact on me and how I saw Japan as a young man. These well-researched books opened my eyes not just to many new ideas, facts and concepts but inspired me to read and learn more about Japan, and read a few years later my first short story in Japanese (*Bokko-chan* by Shinichi Hoshi) and first novel in Japanese (*Norwegian Wood* by Haruki Murakami).

Since those days, I have sort out and hungrily devoured Japan-related information in publications I have read regularly including, for example: *The Economist*, *The Financial Times*, and *Nature*. This book and the essays within it draw on decades of reading and a considerable amount of research at the library at The International House of Japan. It also utilises information published in the *Red Circle Factbook*, an open access online compendium of facts about Japanese literature and publishing. Readers can find more information on many of the facts included in this book within this online compendium, and through the embedded hypertext links to source materials that many of the *Red Circle Factbook's* articles include.

Additionally, this book includes information based on discussions and interviews with the Japanese authors who are members of Red Circle's curated group of award-winning writers; and interviews with people working in the Japanese book trade as editors, journalists, reviewers, translators, booksellers, printers, writers and publishers, as well as colleagues in the international community of publishing, and industry websites.

The notes below list many of this book's sources, primary and secondary, Japanese and English, but is by no means exhaustive. I apologise for any important ones I have missed and would again like to thank everyone who has contributed information and ideas to this publication directly or indirectly, knowingly or unknowingly, and everyone who has supported and continues to support Red Circle Authors and our effort to promote Japanese writing and writers internationally.

I would also like to thank all those diligent and helpful Wikipedians, book bloggers and translators out there in locales unknown who share so much and with such care, as well as, of course, all the amazing authors whose works I have cited, quoted and enjoyed reading to such an extent that I decided to research, write and publish this book.

Preface
1. *The Kaleidoscope, Its History, Theory and Construction with Its Application And Useful Arts* by Sir David Brewster, John Murray, 1858.
2. Information from publications from the Brewster Kaleidoscope Society (BKS), an international society founded in 1986 for kaleidoscope enthusiasts.
3. Global music tastes: Singing in tongues, *The Economist*, 29 January 2022.

4   *Representative Men of Japan* by Kanzo Uchimura, 1908, Keiseisha, Tokyo.
5   Marcel Proust, *Within a Budding Grove*, 1917.

Part One: Japanese Literature, Writers and Ruin
Scoping The Terrain
6   Topsy-turvy 1585: A Translation and Explication of Luis Frois S.J.'s Tratado (treatise) Listing 611 Ways Europeans & Japanese are Contrary, Robin D. Gill.
7   *China Daily*, 19 December 2017.
8   Peter Mayer, Publisher of the Incendiary 'Satanic Verses,' Dies at 82, *The New York Times*, Neil Genzlinger, 11 May 2018.
9   What would Google Do? Reverse-Engineering the Fastest Growing Company in the History of the World, Jeff Jarvis, Harper Business, 2009.
10 *Perversion and Modern Japan: Psychoanalysis, Literature, Culture*. Edited by Nina Cornyetz and J. Keith Vincent. London and New York: Routledge.
11 From Beneath the Wheel to Zen: Hermann Hesse and Japan – Exhibition at Museum Hermann Hesse, Montagnola, Switzerland, March 2018.
12 *The Tale of Genji*, translation Arthur Waley, Houghton Mifflin Company, 1935.
13 Murakami Haruki and the literary sources of ancient Japan, Diego Cucinelli, May 2014, *Ades International Symposium on Asian Languages and Literature*.
14 Budo Shoshin Shu, Shigesuke Daidoji.
15 *Leadership*, Henry Kissinger, Penguin, 2022.
16 *Shukan Shincho*, 2 April, 2009.
17 Princess Aiko's Yearbook Essay: "Praying for Peace in the World", *Sankei Shimbun*, 24 March 2017.
18 The New Year's Poetry Party at the Imperial Court: Two Decades in Postwar Years: 1960-1979. Edited by Marie Philomene, The Hokuseido Press.
19 *The Edo Inheritance* by Tokugawa Tsunenari (translated by Tokugawa Ichiro), International House of Japan, 2009.
20 Review of Reviews, John Barrett, December 1902.
21 Muchu ni naru! Edo no sugaku, Susumu Sakurai, Shueisha Inc 2012.
22 *The Marketing of Urban Human Waste in the Early Modern Edo/Tokyo Metropolitan Area*, Kayo Tajima.
23 Bunkyosha, publisher website for Unko Sensei workbook series.
24 Purity and Danger: An analysis of concepts of pollution and taboo, Mary Douglas, 1966.
25 *Inflation un öffentliche Meinung*, Else Kanin, Königsberg Pr. 1929 (German)/Inflation and Public Opinion.
26 Darwin, C. R. 'Galapagos. Otaheite Lima' (1835). *Beagle* field notebook.

Short Story Writing
27 Poems that Decode Japan's Intellectual DNA: The Ambassador's choice by Lars Vargo, *The Circle*, 23 January 2020.
28 *Under the Overcoat* by Alex de Jonge, *The New York Review*, 18 April 1974.
29 The long, steady decline of literary reading, Christopher Ingrahm, *The Washington Post*, 7 September 2016.
30 MacDonogh, Giles (2003), *The Last Kaiser*, New York: St Martin's Press.

Rubble Rising Prose
31 Mishima Yukio, Kyoko no ie soko de watashi ga kaita mono.
32 Mishima Yukio, Osuka Wairudo ron, 1950.

33 Teixeira, Pedro M., *The Portrayal of Suicide in Postmodern Japanese Literature and Popular Culture Media* (2014). UVM Honors College Senior Theses. 15.
34 Suicides among Japanese children at record high during pandemic, *Reuters*, 14 October 2021.
35 Foreword to Encyclopedia of Science Fiction (1978), ed. Robert Holdstock by Isaac Asimov.
36 *Representative Men of Japan* by Kanzo Uchimura, 1908, Keiseisha, Tokyo.
37 *The Chrysanthemum and the Sword*, Ruth Benedict, Houghton Mifflin Company, 1946.
38 *The Nobility of Failure: Tragic Heroes in the History of Japan*, Ivan Morris, 1975.
39 Catfish Are Off the Hook After Tokyo Ends 16-Year Earthquake Prediction Study, David Thurber, *Associated Press*, 26 April 1992.
40 *A History of Modern Japan*, Richard Storry, Penguin, 1960.

Grim Tales: Primeval Trolls and Eating Disorders
41 *Hebonsha Encyclopedia*, 1984 (Japanese).
42 *Japanese Demon Law: Oni from Ancient Times to the Present*, Noriko T. Reider, Utah State University Press, 2010.
43 *The Tale of the Juniper Tree* by the Brothers Grimm, translated by Joyce Crick, *The Guardian* 29 September 2009.
44 A translation of this tale by Roger Pulvers is included in the award-winning illustrated collection of classic Japanese fairy tales.
45 Yamauba: Representation of the Japanese mountain witch in the Muromachi and Edo periods by Noriko T. Reider, *International Journal of Asian Studies*, July 2005.
46 Man admits abandoning disabled sister in forest by Julian Ryall, *The Telegraph*, 20 November 2015.
47 Jikka, the fairy tale dwarf home for Japan's seniors, Andrea Lo, Melissa Hassett, CNN Style, 10 December 2018.
48 'Dendera': Yuya Sato on his fable about old women battling a bear, by Nolene Clark, *Los Angeles Times*, 25 February 2015.
49 An Ethereal Forest Where Japanese Commit Suicide by Alexa Keefe, *National Geographic*, 23 February 2017.
50 Ukemochi no Kami, *Britannica*.
51 Anorexia: it's Not A New Disease, by Carol Lawson, *The New York Times*, 8 December 1985.
52 The Rise of Eating Disorders in Japan: Issues of Culture and Limitations of the Model of "Westernization" by Kathleen M. Pike MD, PhD & Amy Borovoy PhD *Culture, Medicine and Psychiatry*.
53 Naomi Wolf, *The Beauty Myth*.

Literary Fallout: The Legacies of Hiroshima and Nagasaki
54 *Writing Ground Zero: Japanese Literature and the Atomic Bomb*, by John Whittier Treat, The University of Chicago Press.
55 How We Retain the Memory of Japan's Atomic Bombings: Books, Yoko Ogawa. *The New York Times Magazine*, 6 August 2020.

Part Two: Influencers, Dolls and Devices
The Chick-Lit of Ancient Japan
56 *On Familiar Terms: To Japan and Back, A Lifetime Across Cultures*, Donald Keene, Kodansha International, 1996.
57 *Envisioning The Tale of Genji: Media, Gender, and Cultural Production*, Edited by Haruo Shirane, Columbia University Press.

58 The Sensualist, What makes "The Tale of Genji' so seductive by Ian Buruma, *The New Yorker*, 13 July 2015.
59 Cultural Adaptation to Psychoanalysis in Japan, 1912-52, Yasuhiko Taketomo, Vol 57, No. 4, *Reception of Psychoanalysis* (WINTER 1990).
60 *The New York Times*, 9 April 2006.
61 *Bridget Jones's Femininity Constructed by Language: A comparison between the Japanese translation of Bridget Jones's Diary, and the Japanese subtitles of the film*. Furukawa, Hiroko (2009), Online Proceedings of the Annual Conference of the Poetics and Linguistics Association (PALA).

Ultra-Influencers: Fictional Victorians that Changed Japan
62 Japan Sherlock Holmes Club is the sole nationwide Sherlockian society in Japan, established in 1977. See: http://www.holmesjapan.jp/english/.
63 Discovering Holmes: Mizuki Tsujimura in conversation with (Taidan) Masamichi Higurashi.
64 *The Sign of the Four*, ch. 6 (1890) Sherlock Holmes in *The Sign of the Four* (Doubleday p. 111).
65 *Beatrix Potter's Americans:* selected letters (ed. 1982).

Doll Women and Their Literature
66 *The Life and Thought of Japan*, J.M. Dent/E.P. Dutton, 1913.
67 *Ningyo ai no seishinbunseki (Doll-Love Pschoanalysis)* Hiroshi Fujita, Adosha, Tokyo, 2006.
68 Cross-Cultural Reading of Doll-Love Novels In Japan and The West, Akiyoshi Suzuki, *Journal of East-West Thought*.
69 Cult of the Living Doll in Tokyo, Kaori Shoji, 8 February 2010, *The New York Times*.
70 Queer Dress and Biased Eyes: The Japanese Doll on the Western Toyshelf, *Journal of Popular Culture* 43.1 (2010).

Whodunnit: Detective Fiction's Sudden Death
71 *Unbeaten Tracks in Japan: An account of Travels on Horseback in the interior including visits to the aborigines of Yezo and the Shrines of Nikko and Ise* by Isabella Bird, John Murray, 1880 & 1885.
72 Andrew Gordon (2003). *A modern history of Japan: From Tokugawa times to the present*. New York: Oxford University Press.
73 *Narrative of Expedition of the American Squadron to the Chinese Seas and Japan*, Commondore Perry.
74 Pandemic practice: Horror fans and morbidly curious individuals are more psychologically resilient during the COVID-19 pandemic, Personality and individual differences. 2021;168:110397.
75 *Detective Fiction and the Rise of the Japanese Novel, 1880–1930*, Satoru Saito.
76 *Writer's Digest* (10:27-29, February 1930), Hugo Gernsback.
77 *The Haunted Tower—Perfect Popular Culture*, special exhibition at the Ghibli Museum, Mitaka.
78 *Japanese Science Fiction: A View of a Changing Society* by Robert, Matthew, (Nissan Institute/Routledge Japanese Studies).
79 *A History of Modern Japan*, Richard Storry, Penguin, 1960.
80 Japanese Democratization and the Little House Books: The Relation between General Head Quarters and The Long Winter in Japan after World War II, Noriko Suzuki, January 2006, *Children's Literature Association Quarterly* 31(1): 65-86.
81 *MacArthur and the American Century: A Reader*. Edited by William M. Leary.
82 *Orphans by Design: 'Mixed-blood' Children, Child Welfare, and Racial Nationalism in Postwar Japan*, Kristin Roebuck, *Japanese Studies*, 36:2, 191-212.
83 *The Art of Censorship in Postwar Japan*, Kirsten Cather Fischer, 2012.

84 Japanese manga ruled obscene, BBC News, 13 January, 2004.
85 *Encyclopedia Heibonsha*, 1984.
86 *Poison Woman: Figuring Female Transgression in Modern Japanese Culture*, Christine L. Marran, Minesota Press, 2007.
87 *Tetsudo misuteri no keifu, The Genealogy of Railway Mysteries*, Takayuki Haraguchi, Kotsu Shimbunsha, 2016 (Japanese).

Portable Devices Loved by Japan's Literati
88 Kyosendo, Kyoto Folding Fans Since 1832.
89 Mokkan. Wooden Documents from the Nara Period, Joan R. Piggott, *Monumenta Nipponica* Vol. 45, No. 4 (Winter, 1990), pp. 449-470.
90 Recent Archaeological Excavations at the Todai-ji, *Japanese Journal of Religious Studies* Vol. 19, No. 2/3, Archaeological Approaches to Ritual and Religion in Japan (Jun- Sep., 1992).
91 The Fan Circle International.
92 *The Nobility of Failure: Tragic Heroes in the History of Japan*, Ivan Morris, 1975.
93 History of Fans, The Fan Museum, Greenwich, London.
94 Japonism, The Art Story.
95 The Decay of Lying, Oscar Wilde.
96 Fanology: The "Secret" Language of Hand Fans, *Owlcation*, 16 November 2016.
97 *In the Country of Fans, Japan*, November 28, 2018 to January 20, 2019. Exhibition at Suntory Museum of Art.

Part Three: Robots, Runners and Riders
Tales from the Robot Nation
98 Towards a monopolization of research in artificial intelligence, Natural Sciences Sector, Unseco, 20 July 2018, *UNESCO Science Report: towards 2030*.
99 *New Robot Strategy*, Japan's Robot Strategy – Vision, Strategy, Action Plan, The Headquarters for Japan's Economic Revitalization, 10 February 2015.
100 *Shinpeki sanpo* (Mathematical problems Suspended from the Temple) Fujita Sadasuke and Fujita Kagen et. al. 1790, and subsequent volume titled *Zoku Shinpeki sanpo*, 1806.
101 *Rethinking Identity in Modern Japan: Nationalism as Aesthetics*, Yumiko Iida.
102 *Ningyo ai no seishinbunseki (Doll-Love Pschoanalysis)*, Hiroshi Fujita, Adosha, Tokyo, 2006.
103 Miri Nakamura (2007), Marking bodily differences: mechanized bodies in Hirabayashi Hatsunosuke's 'Robot' and early Showa robot literature, Japan Forum, 19:2, 169-190.
104 *Shrinking Population Economics: Lessons from Japan*, Matsutani Akihiko (translated by Brain Miller), 2006.
105 *Runaround*, Isaac Asimov, 1942.
106 *The Economist*, July 16, 2022.
107 *The Toho Studios Story: A History and Complete Filmography*, Stuart Galbraith IV.
108 *Literary umami*, Eri Hotta, *TLS*, August 10, 2018.

Literary Racers
109 *Shoe Dog: A Memoir* by the Creator of Nike, Phil Knight, 2016.
110 Why Japan Is the Most Running-Obsessed Culture in the World, Tyghe Trimble, *Men's Journal*.
111 The Running Novelist, Learning How to Go The Distance, Haruki Murakami, *The New Yorker*, 2 June 2008.
112 Yusai Sakai, *The Telegraph*, 17 October 2013.

113 Haruki Murakami, *The New York Times*, 2 June 2008.
114 Kino, Haruki Murakami, *The New Yorker*, 16 February 2015.

Narratives from Off and On the Tracks
115 Growth of Independent Technology, Eiichi Aoki, Japan Railway & Transport Review, October 1994.
116 *Early Japanese Railways 1853-1914: Engineering Triumphs That Transformed Meiji-era Japan*, Dan Free, 2017.
117 *Narrative of the Expedition of an American Squadron to the China Seas and Japan*, Francis L. Hawks, Lambert Lilly, 1923.
118 Railroad Expansion and Industrialization: Evidence from Meiji Japan, John P. Tang, *The Journal of Economic History* Vol. 74, No. 3 (September 2014).
119 Town of Cats, Haruki Murakami, *The New Yorker*, 29 August 2011.

Part Four: Cats, Tatts and Christians
Soseki's Cat: A Quantum Leap
120 Fülöp, Márta. Natsume Soseki: Culture Shock and the Birth of the Modern Japanese Novel, *Exploring Transculturalism* (2010): 63-80. Web.
121 Umami the Fifth Basic Taste: History of Studies on Receptor Mechanisms and Role as a Food Flavor, Kenzo Kurihara, *BioMed Research International*, 2015(6): 189402.
122 Hello Kitty is not a cat, plus more reveals before her L.A. tour, Carolina A Miranda, *Los Angeles Times*, 26 August 2014.
123 PTI wants Japanese cartoon series 'Doraemon' banned, *Dawn*, 3 August 2016.
124 Pet Cat Food Market 2017 Global Trends, Market Share, Industry Size, Growth, Opportunities and Forecast to 2021, *PUNE*, INDIA, January 20, 2017.
125 Beware the Cat and the Beginnings of English Fiction, William A. Ringler, Jr. NOVEL: *A Forum on Fiction*, Vol. 12, No. 2 (Winter, 1979).
126 *Kaibyo: The Supernatural Cats of Japan*, Zack Davidson, Chin Music Press, 2017.
127 Emotion Recognition in Cats, Angelo Quaranta, Serenella d'Ingeo, Rosaria Amoruso, Marcello Siniscalchi, *Animals*, 2020, 10(7), 1107.

From Body Art to Literature: Zen and the Art of the Tattoo
128 Oldest tattoo ever found: Marks on 'Iceman Otzi' proved to be first known body art, Andrew Griffin Thursday 17 December 2015, *Independent*.
129 *Unbeaten Tracks in Japan: An account of Travels on Horseback in the interior including visits to the aborigines of Yezo and the Shrines of Nikko and Ise* by Isabella Bird, John Murray 1880 & 1885.
130 Ainu Fever: Indigenous Representation in a Transnational Visual Economy, 1868–1933, Christina M. Spiker, 2015.
131 *Manufacturing Modern Japanese Literature*, Edward Mack, Duke University Press, 2010.
132 Dead Skin, Living Art... The Museum Of Tattooed Skin, Sean Reveron, August 5, 2020, *CVLT Nation*.
133 *A Japanese Mirror: Heroes and Villains of Japanese Culture*, Ian Buruma, 1984, Jonathan Cape.
134 Middlebury College Museum of Art, June 10–August 7, 2016, Middlebury, Vermont, USA.

Christian Stories of Japan
135 Burglars stole priceless medieval chalice thought to be the Holy Grail after the elderly lady who protected it for 25 years left the house overnight for the first time, Wills Robinson & Gemma Mullin, *Daily Mail*, 16 July 2014.

136 *The Christian Century in Japan 1549-1650*, Charles Ralf Boxer, Ishi Press International.
137 *The Edo Inheritance by Tokugawa Tsunenari* (translated by Tokugawa Ichiro), International House of Japan, 2009.
138 *In Search of Japan's Hidden Christians*, John Dougill, Society of Promoting Christian Knowledge.
139 Shusaku Endo, *Foreign Studies*, Ryugaku, introduction to English language translation edition 1989.
140 Japanese Religion: A Survey by the Agency for Cultural Affairs, Kodansha International, 1972.
141 Research on the 1593 Jesuit Mission Press Edition of Esop's Fables, Richard L. Spear, *Monumenta Nipponica*, Vol. 19, No. 3/4 (1964).
142 *World Within Walls: Japanese Literature of the Pre-Modern Era, 1600-1867* Donald Keene, New York: Holt, Rinehart and Winston.
143 *The Samurai Invasion of Korea 1592-98*, Stephen Turnbull, Osprey Publishing.
144 Kanzo Uchimura Founder of the Non-Church Movement, William H. H. Norman, *Contemporary Religions in Japan*, Vol. 5, No. 4 (Dec., 1964).
145 Thinker-in-Chief, *The Economist*, February 12th 2022.
146 Christmas in Japan: Hundreds queue outside of KFC branches in Tokyo for Japanese Christmas tradition, Megan Townsend, *The Independent*, 24 December 2015.
147 Confessions of a true believer, Caryl Phillips, *The Guardian*, 4 January 2004.
148 *A Japanese Mirror: Heroes and Villains of Japanese Culture*, Ian Buruma, 1984.

Part Five: Booze, Books, and Bonking
Literary Elixir: Bars, Cocktails and the Literati
149 Bunjin Akujiki, Bizarre Eating and The Literati, Kozaburo Arashiyama, Shinchobunko, 1997 (Japanese).
150 Nihon kokugo daijiten.
151 Deconstructing 'Kokushu' The Promotion of Sake as Japan's National Alcoholic Drink in Times of Crisis in the Sake Industry, Dick Stegewerns, University of Oslo, 2017, *Feeding Japan*.
152 *Japanese Whisky, Scotch Blend: The Story of Masataka Taetsuru, His Scottish Wife, and the Japanese Whisky Industry* by Olive Checkland.

How to Read a Film: Kurosawa and His Books
153 8 Science-Backed Reasons to Read a (Real) Book, *Real Simple*, Abigail Wise, 5 September 2019.
154 The 100 greatest foreign-language films, *BBC Culture* (https://www.bbc.com/culture/article/20181029-the-100-greatest-foreign-language-films).
155 David Bowie's top 100 must-read books, *The Guardian*, Liz Bury, 1 October 2013.
156 Nakamuraya Salon Museum of Art, Kaikan Kinentokubetsuten (Special Anniversary Exhibition), 29 October 2014.
157 Ryuichi Sakamoto: 'To create something is a strange thing to do', Leo Lewis, *The Financial Times*, 3 July 2020.
158 Rash Behari Bose And His Japanese Supporters: An Insight into Anti-Colonial Nationalism and Pan-Asianism, Eri Hotta, *International Journal of Postcolonial Studies*, Volume 8, 2006.
159 *Underground Asia: Global Revolutionaries and the Assault on Empire*, Tim Harper, Belknap Press.
160 Tagore's Critique of Nationalism in Japan 1916, Yoshihiro Ohsawa, Hikaku Bungaku *Journal of Comparative Literature*, 1981 Volume 24 Pages 97-108.
161 *Rebels Against The Raj*, Ramachandra Guha, Knopf.

Bonkbusters and The Land of the Rising Sun
162 Nobody ever did want me, Margaret Atwood, *The Guardian*, 29 March 2008.
163 Watashi no Otoko (My Man), Mark Shilling, *The Japan Times*, 19 June 2014.

A Rich and Never-ending Story
164 *The Chrysanthemum and the Sword: Patterns of Japanese Culture*, Ruth Benedict, Houghton Mifflin Company, 1946.
165 *The Nobility of Failure: Tragic Heroes in the History of Japan*, Ivan Morris, 1975.
166   *The Structure of Scientific Revolutions*, Thomas S. Kuhn, 1962.
167 How ecstasy and psilocybin are shaking up psychiatry, *Nature,* 27 January 2021.
168 *A Cup of Sake Beneath the Cherry Trees*, Yoshida Kenko, translated by Meredith McKinney, Penguin Classics.

Index

A

Abe, Kobo 8, 47, 196, 197, 198, 199, 235
Akagawa, Jiro 240
Akahata Shimbun 208
Akasaka, Mari 101, 327, 333
Akihito, Emperor 71, 241, 307
Akutagawa, Hiroshi 319
Akutagawa Prize 29, 30, 38, 48, 72, 73, 90, 91, 222, 244, 293, 300, 308, 333
Akutagawa, Ryunosuke 9, 43, 50, 51, 53, 55, 72, 87, 88, 92, 123, 125, 137, 233, 235, 253, 255, 260, 270, 277, 280, 282, 306, 319
Ando, Mikie 222
Aoi, Yu 225
Arikawa, Hiro 240
Ariyoshi, Sawako 70, 71, 179, 272
Asahi Bunko 161
Asahi Shimbun 241, 320
Asami, Mitsuhiko 66
Asano, Atsuko 208
Asano, Naganori 23
Asimov, Isaac 77, 186, 187, 192, 200, 201
Atwood, Margaret 99, 331

B

Bartolini, Luigi 10
Basho, Matsuo 217
BBC 125, 129, 307
Bird, Isabella 4, 140, 143, 153
Booker Prize 250
Brewster, David xi, 180

bundan 281, 282, 294
Bungeishunju 307
Bungo Stray Dogs 43, 282, 284, 288
bunjin 289, 291
Burai-ha 281

C

Carroll, Lewis 7, 122, 123, 238, 316
censorship 25, 37, 48, 150, 154
Chikamatsu, Monzaemon 75
Chiossone, Edoardo 141
Christie, Agatha 57, 224, 225, 292, 326
Chuo Koron 48, 53, 288
Churchill, Winston 242, 246, 280, 330
Cold War 78, 142, 155, 196
Conan Doyle, Arthur 58, 122, 125, 147, 180, 247, 249, 316
constitution 50, 56, 57, 145, 149, 150, 343

D

Dazai, Osamu 9, 43, 74, 146, 277, 278, 279, 281, 282, 286, 300
De Sica, Vittorio 10
Dostoevsky, Fyodor 13, 43, 52, 282, 304, 307, 308, 309
dystopia 35

E

Edogawa Rampo Prize 298
Edogawa, Ranpo 134, 137, 147, 154, 180, 185, 249
Einstein, Albert 168, 231, 344

Elizabeth I xi, 166, 169
Enchi, Fumiko 118
Endo, Shusaku 8, 61, 75, 152, 245, 265, 269, 270, 319
Eroshenko, Vasili 318, 319, 320

F

First Sino-Japanese War 122, 128
First World War 311, 315
Foreign Correspondents' Club of Japan 7, 52
Frank O'Connor International Short Story Award 45
Freud, Sigmund 8, 116, 344, 345
Fujin Sekai 118
Fujita, Toko 83
Fujiwara, Kaneie 115
Fukazawa, Shichiro 97
Furukawa, Hideo 89, 90

G

Genji 8, 14, 15, 16, 21, 47, 113, 114, 116, 117, 118, 119, 120, 132, 164, 241, 259, 327, 347
Gernsback, Hugo 146, 147, 181
Ghibli 44, 146
Glover, Thomas B. 216
Guinness Book of World Records 37, 60, 124, 206, 215, 225, 248, 300, 313

H

Hagiwara, Sakutaro 239
Hamaguchi, Osachi 224
Hanawa, Kanji xxi, 39, 65, 66, 78, 79, 80, 89, 138, 229, 306
Hara, Tamiki 103, 224
Hayakawa 77, 78
Hayashi, Fumiko 329
Hayashi, Mariko 113, 333
Heike 16, 17, 66, 164, 257, 308
Heine, Heinrich 258
Hesse, Hermann xv, 12, 13, 39
Hesse, Johannes xv
Higashino, Keigo 4, 16, 76, 210

Higuchi, Ichiyo 329, 330
Hino, Ashihei 29, 30, 48, 49
Hirabayashi, Hatsunosuke 182, 184
hiragana 36, 157
Hiraide, Takashi 240
Hirai, Taro 147, 180
Hirohito, Emperor 22, 46, 181, 321, 322
Hoganbiiki 203, 341
Hojoki 88
Honda, Tetsuya 10, 161
Hori, Tatsuo 73
Hoshi Awards 60, 61
Hoshi, Shinichi 51, 58, 198, 358
Hototogisu 233
Hozokan 260
Hugo Awards 146

I

Ibuse, Masuji 103
Ichiho, Michi 332
Ichikawa, Takuji xxi, 11, 66, 209, 220
Igarashi, Hitoshi 7
Ihara, Saikaku 327
Iijima, Tadashi 134
Ikeda, Kikunae 236
Ikeido, Jun 213
Ikenami, Shotaro 283
Inoue, Hisashi 272
Inoue, Yasushi 308
Isaka, Kotaro 225
Isewan Typhoon 65, 66, 68, 71, 72, 76, 78, 90, 307
Ishida, Ira 135, 222
Ishigaki, Rin 44
Ishikawa, Takuboku 219
Ishikawa, Tatsuzo 48, 53
Izumi, Kyoka 284

J

Japan and The Japanese Illustrated 256, 263
Japan Booksellers' Award 207, 208, 332, 333
Japanese Agency for Culture 256
Japanese Language Council 154

Japonisme 69, 168, 169, 170, 171
Jesuit Mission Press 257, 260
Jippensha, Ikku 32, 217

K

Kadokawa 282
Kafka, Franz 13
Kaga, Mariko 135
Kaga, Shotaro 287, 288, 289
Kaiko, Takeshi 300
Kakuta, Mitsuyo xxi, 11, 16, 45, 66, 92, 117, 118, 120, 209, 272, 273, 302, 310
kaleidoscope xi, xii, xix, 150, 179, 180, 331, 347, 350
Kamono, Chomei 88
Kanagaki, Robun 156, 323
Kanehara, Hitomi 16, 101, 250, 333, 334
kanji 3, 16, 28, 36, 41, 148, 154, 155, 156, 157, 158, 159, 233, 237, 285, 312, 321
Kasai, Kiyoshi 10
katakana 157, 159
Kawabata, Yasunari 5, 7, 9, 10, 46, 47, 48, 49, 50, 52, 73, 88, 134, 135, 219, 220, 279, 280, 283, 287, 319
Kawakami, Hiromi 16, 88, 297
Kawakami, Mieko 16, 73
Keene, Donald 53, 115, 291
Kikuchi, Kan 307
Kinokuniya 28, 215, 325
Kinoshita, Yoshitoshi 285
Kipling, Rudyard 39, 217, 317
Kirihara Shoten 26, 166
Kishimi, Ichiro 183
Kitagawa, Utamaro 82
Kiyono, Sachiko 240
Kobayashi, Hideo 48, 49
Kodansha 89
Kodomo no tomo 264, 265
Koga, Fumitake 183
Kogawa, Joy 104
Kojiki 40
Kojima, Nobuo 49, 50, 57
Kokumin no tomo 56

Kono, Taeko 330
Kosumoporitan-sha 148
Kurahashi, Yumiko 199
Kuroiwa, Ruiko 145, 146, 147
Kurosawa, Akira 51, 61, 87, 88, 91, 234, 270, 291, 304, 305, 306, 307, 308, 309, 310
Kuroyanagi, Tetsuko 149
Kurumatani, Chokitsu 249
Kusama, Yayoi 129

L

Li, Kotomi 333

M

MacArthur, Gen. Douglas 50, 57, 148, 149, 157
Machida, Shinya 60, 89
Mainichi Daily News, The 218
Makino, Count Nobuaki 126
Makino, Teruya 161
Manyoshu 14, 42, 45, 163
Maruyama, Eikan 123, 127
Marx, Karl 257, 258, 266, 272
Matsumoto, Seicho 157, 159, 160, 225
Matsuoka, Keisuke 130
Matsuo, Kiyotaka 29
Matsutani, Miyoko 104
McKinney, Meredith 18, 59, 114, 233
Meyer, Peter 7
Miike, Takashi 61
Minakami, Tsutomu 138
Minamoto, Yoshitsune 17, 164
Mishima, Yukio 7, 8, 9, 10, 39, 47, 48, 52, 53, 55, 68, 69, 70, 71, 73, 77, 78, 123, 135, 221, 249, 279, 304, 309, 317, 319, 322
Mita Bungaku 283
Mitsukoshi 265
Miura, Ayako 272
Miura, Shion 43, 207, 208
Miura, Testsuo 46
Miyake, Isseu 109
Miyake, Kaho 329
Miyamoto, Teru 19, 82

Miyazaki, Hayao 100, 146, 147, 218
Miyazawa, Kenji 217, 218
Mizoguchi, Kenji 32
Montgomery, L. M. 132, 330
Morimi, Tomohiko 132, 281, 345
Mori, Ogai 56, 57, 58, 224, 257
Murakami, Haruki 3, 6, 10, 16, 17, 39, 45, 74, 88, 91, 92, 93, 206, 209, 213, 221, 224, 240, 241, 297, 299, 309, 325, 358
Murasaki, Shikibu 113, 118, 119, 259
Murata, Sayaka 11, 16, 73
Museum of Modern Japanese Literature 89

N

Nagai, Kafu 47, 279, 283
Nagira, Yu 332
Naigai Shuppan Kyokai 123
Nakagami, Kenji 10, 38
Nakamura, Fuminori xxi, 9, 11, 92, 111, 137, 138, 139, 235, 265, 266, 310
Nakamura, Hikaru 273
Nakamura, Koichi 159
Nakano, Hitori 190, 225
Nakazawa, Keiji 103
Naoki Prize 11, 61, 91, 125, 182, 195, 213, 240, 294, 298, 305, 331, 332
Naoki, Sanjugo 182, 195
Naruhito, Emperor 14
Nathan, John 47, 236
National Book Award for Translated Literature 91
National Diet Library 123, 264, 323
Natsukawa, Sosuke 240
Natsume, Soseki 27, 47, 74, 180, 191, 219, 232, 233, 234, 235, 236, 237, 239, 240, 241, 242, 288, 289, 304, 308, 314
New Asia, The 322
NHK 147, 215, 221
Nihon shoki 245, 260, 285
Nikkei 61
nikutai bungaku 345
Ninomiya, Sontoku 95
Nishimura, Kyotaro 225

Nitobe, Inazo 53, 54, 55
Nobel Prize xiii, xv, 5, 7, 9, 10, 30, 39, 64, 87, 98, 152, 212, 219, 270, 287, 317, 319, 320, 334
Nobuhara, Ken 123
Noma, Seiji 89

O

Oda, Katsuzo 104
Oda, Sakunosuke 281
Oe, Kenzaburo 9, 12, 46, 47, 49, 50, 57, 60, 92, 103, 104, 152
Ogawa, Mimei 318
Ogawa, Yoko 16, 109, 119
Ogura, Hiroshi 184
Okakura, Tenshin 121, 131, 275
Olympic Games 5, 71, 80, 181, 210
Ono, Ikko 44, 90
Ooka, Shohei 152
Opium Wars 85
Orientalism 69
Oyama Publishing 151

P

Pacific War 114
Penguin 7, 62, 153
Perry, Commodore Matthew C. 83, 85, 86, 140, 144, 147, 167, 216, 263, 271
Pillow Book, The 45, 59, 114, 117
Poe, Edgar Allan 51, 147, 179, 180, 291
Proust, Marcel xix
Pulvers, Roger xxi, 218, 219

R

Ran, Ikujiro 220
Red Circle xvi, xxi, 358, 372
Red Circle Minis xvi, 372
Reischauer, Edwin O. 47
Rinzo, Shiina 272
romaji 157
Rowling, J. K. 4, 330, 331
Rushdie, Salman 7
Russo-Japanese War 54, 55, 128, 181

S

Saigo, Takamori 79, 83, 84, 342
Sailor Moon xii, 331
Saito, Satoshi 26, 166
Sakaguchi, Ango 146, 281
Sakurai, Ami 101
Sato, Atsushi 90
Sato Takako 208
Sayers, Dorothy L. 301
Second Sino-Japanese War 244
Second World War 8, 10, 35, 38, 46, 58, 103, 116, 137, 140, 142, 148, 155, 156, 159, 175, 184, 188, 196, 224, 249, 265, 271, 279, 323, 324, 330, 345
Seidensticker, Edward G. 47
Sei, Shonagon 45, 114, 119, 151
Seki, Takakazu 26, 27
Setouchi, Jakucho 108, 118, 224, 347
S-F Magazine 77, 78
Shakespeare, William 25, 75, 124, 304, 309
Shibusawa, Eiichi 152
Shibusawa, Tatsuhiko 152
Shimada, Masahiko 10
Shimada, Soji xxi, 10, 39, 105, 124, 159, 160, 195, 223, 225
Shimao, Toshio 272
Shimazaki, Toson 219
Shinchosha 58, 328
Shindo, Nobuyoshi 264
Shinjinsha 187
Shinseinen 146
Shiraishi, Kazufumi xxi, 10, 11, 12, 45, 91, 125, 173, 195
Shiro, Masamune 196
Shoda, Kenjiro 26
Shoda, Michiko 71, 307
Societe des Missions Éstrangèr de Paris 263
Sohn, Won-pyung 333
Soma, Toshiko 311, 312, 314, 315, 317, 318, 320, 321
Sono, Ayako 271
Suzuki, Shunryu 252, 253, 262, 350
Swift, Jonathan 40, 244

T

Tagore, Rabindranath 5, 64, 319, 320
Taguchi, Randy xxi, 13, 93, 224
Taiheiki 285
Takagi, Akimitsu 150, 249, 252
Takahashi, Genichiro 10
Takahashi, Takako 138
Takayama, Chogyu 37
Takeno, Masato 119
Takeuchi, Naoko xii
Tanaka, Hidemitsu 211
Tanizaki, Junichiro 5, 10, 47, 87, 118, 125, 134, 219, 239, 247, 248, 270, 279, 287, 288, 289
Tezuka, Osamu 67, 71, 180, 184, 185, 195
Togawa, Masako 152, 297, 298
Tokiwa, Shinpei 283
Tokuda, Shusei 219
Tokugawa xi, 21, 24, 25, 28, 79, 259, 260
Tokugawa, Ieyasu 21, 25, 259, 272
Tokugawa, Mitsukuni 21
Tokyo National Museum 280
Tolstoy, Leo 52, 304, 308, 309
Tomita, Tsuneo 305
Toyoda, Sakichi 177, 178
Toyotomi, Hideyoshi 259, 260, 268, 272
Tsuhara, Yasumi 45
Tsuji, Hitonari 72, 73, 91
Tsujimura, Mizuki 125, 126
Tsuruta, Tomoya 244
Tsushima, Yuko 208, 330
Tsutaya, Juzaburo 82, 84, 86, 87
Tsutsui, Yasutaka 45, 200, 201, 202, 211, 212

U

Uchida, Yasuo 66
Uchimura, Kanzo xv, 13, 24, 39, 140, 144, 264, 272
Ueda, Akinari 31, 32
Uno, Chiyo 330
utopia 33, 34, 35, 36, 39, 55, 98, 185, 257, 261

V

Vargo, Lars 42, 43, 44

W

Wago, Ryoichi 90
Waley, Arthur 118, 119
wasan 25, 27, 177
Wells, H. G. 55, 145
White Birch 319
Wilde, Oscar 57, 68, 69, 70, 168, 277, 281

Y

Yamada, Amy 333
Yamada, Futaro 285
Yamaguchi, Hitomi 300
Yamaguchi, Momoe 73
Yamamoto, Shugoro 61, 289, 307
Yamashita, Hiroka 138
Yamazaki, Mari 197
Yasunari, Sadao 125
Yokomizo, Seishi 249
Yomiuri Prize 37, 43
Yomiuri Shimbun 37, 53, 60, 89, 207, 272
Yosa, Buson 133
Yosano, Akiko 118
Yoshida, Kenko xii, 1, 64, 350
Yoshida, Mitsuyoshi 25, 177
Yoshimoto, Banana 4, 6, 16, 39, 74, 337
Yoshino, Hiroshi 43
Yoshiya, Nobuko 316, 330
Yoshiyuki, Junnosuke 108, 153, 296
Yoshizawa, Hisako 116
Yoshu tenkoku 300
Yu, Miri 90, 91, 222

⭕ Circle Editions

Circle Editions, an imprint of Red Circle Authors, publishes books about, on, and from Japan, spanning Japanese literature, publishing and culture.

Book cover design by Aiko Ishida alongside the graphic design within the book including, for example, the page depicting multiple renderings of the word kaleidoscope in Japanese. Illustrations by Kayoko Akiyama. All photographs contributed by the book's author.

⭕ Red Circle

Red Circle Authors is a London based boutique publishing company that publishes the Circle Editions imprint and the series *Red Circle Minis* with the aim of showcasing Japan through the lens of storytelling and fine writing.

Red Circle Minis, which launched the company's publishing programme, is a series of newly commissioned works of fiction from a carefully selected and curated group of leading contemporary Japanese authors, each book in the series is a first edition published in English first, while Circle Editions publishes a broader selection of writers and content.

For more information about Red Circle, our books, our authors, and Japanese literature and storytelling please visit:

www.redcircleauthors.com

www.ingramcontent.com/pod-product-compliance
Lightning Source LLC
Chambersburg PA
CBHW030047100526
44590CB00011B/353